Rodeo in America

Wranglers, Roughstock, & Paydirt

Rodeo

University Press of Kansas

n America

Wayne S. Wooden & Gavin Ehringer

Vincennes University
Shake Learning Resources Center
Vincennes, Indiana 47591-9986

Published by the University Press of Kansas (Lawrence, Kansas 66049), which was organized by the Kansas Board of Regents and is operated and funded by Emporia State University, Fort Hays State University, Kansas State University, Pittsburg State University, the University of Kansas, and Wichita State University

Library of Congress Cataloging-in-Publication Data

Wooden, Wayne S.

   Rodeo in America / Wayne S. Wooden and Gavin Ehringer.

     p. cm.

   Includes bibliographical references and index.

   ISBN 0-7006-0813-3 (alk. paper)

   1. Rodeos—United States—History. 2. Cowboys—United States—Biography. I. Ehringer, Gavin. II. Title.

GV1834.5.W66 1996

791.8′4′0973—dc20   96-16328

British Library Cataloguing in Publication Data is available.

Printed in the United States of America

10 9 8 7 6 5 4 3 2 1

The paper used in this publication meets the minimum requirements of the American National Standard for Permanence of Paper for Printed Library Materials z39.48-1984.

List of Illustrations *vii*

Acknowledgments *ix*

1 ⋆ Introduction and Brief History of Rodeo *1*

2 ⋆ Rodeo Events & Judging *17*

3 ⋆ Growing Up Cowboy *33*

4 ⋆ Going Down the Road *49*

5 ⋆ Rodeo Cowboys or Professional Athletes? *70*

6 ⋆ Support Programs & Health Issues *84*

7 ⋆ Stock Contractors & Animal Welfare *108*

8 ⋆ Contract Personnel, Clowns, & Bullfighters *157*

9 ⋆ Rodeo Committees & Special Programs *172*

10 ⋆ Women and Rodeo *186*

11 ⋆ The Many Faces of Rodeo *201*

12 ⋆ Rodeo Cowboys, Hollywood Style *221*

13 ⋆ Economic Concerns & Marketing Strategies *234*

14 ⋆ Professional Rodeo at the Crossroads *252*

Notes *265*

Appendix *273*

Index *281*

Contents

Illustrations

Rodeo pageantry on parade 135

Contestants line up during the grand entry 135

Ty Murray welcomes rodeo fans 136

A bull rider wearing a comical cowboy shirt 137

A competitor prepares for his next ride 138

Ty Murray prior to one of his rides 139

A rider waits his turn 139

Bull rider Aaron Semas 140

Bareback rider Roger Lecasse 140

A saddle bronc rider gets ready 141

A bull rider straps on his spurs 142

A saddle bronc rider breaks from the bucking chute 143

Robert Etbauer 144

A bareback bronc rider 145

Adam Carrillo 145

Rodeo's danger is most apparent in the bull riding 146

Rooster Reynolds 147

Joe Beaver 147

Barrel racers Sherry Potter-Cervi and Charmayne (James) Rodman 148

Performer Gerardo "Jerry" Diaz 149

A Native American drummer 149

Rodeo clown Charlie "Too Tall" West 150

A rodeo fan's innovative effort to obtain tickets 150

One of the many vendors at contemporary rodeos 151

Rodeo queens Wendi Lund and Jennifer Douglas 152

8 Seconds, the story of bull rider Lane Frost 153

Lyle Etbauer with his three sons 153

A young cowboy practices roping 154

A hat vendor steams a crease into a hat 155

Tools of the trade 156

Acknowledgments

WAYNE S. WOODEN

Several people assisted with the rodeo project, and I wish to first thank my parents, Wes and Kay Wooden, who introduced me and my two sisters to the sport of rodeo when we were youngsters. My father had been an amateur bronc and bull rider in his youth in the 1930s in Humboldt County, California, and as an adult was a registered Corriedale sheep breeder. As a youngster I would help him show sheep during the summer fair circuit in Northern California, and we would watch the professional and amateur rodeos that accompanied the various county fairs and exhibits.

Several PRCA cowboys offered suggestions, including Clayton Price and Richard Bucher, and I wish to acknowledge several of my undergraduate students who helped in assembling the book, especially Sean Hiscox, Aaron Betancourt, and Randal Beasley. Appreciation is also in order for the assistance provided by Richard M. Leonard, Cori Spencer, and the Department of Behavioral Sciences at California State Polytechnic University, Pomona.

I am grateful that Lewis A. Cryer, commissioner of the Professional Rodeo Cowboys Association, was able to address my senior-level sociology class, "Rodeo Cowboys and Contemporary Society," and for the special assistance that PRCA staff members Kay Bleakly and Steve Fleming provided in the distribution of my survey to the rodeo cowboys in the beginning stage of my research.

Early on in the project, I discussed my plans with Michael Briggs, now editor in chief at the University Press of Kansas. Mike was enthusiastic from the start and patient with me as I worked on conducting the research, gathering the material, and assembling the book. His constructive suggestions and unwavering support are indeed appreciated.

I am particularly grateful for the collaboration of Gavin Ehringer. Having been a follower of Gavin's informative "Rodeo Arena" column in *Western Horseman* magazine, I was pleased that he agreed to assist me in completing this book. His unique style as a journalist blended with my more academic sociological approach, and it is to be hoped that the result of our combined efforts will be of interest to a wide range of readers and will help to educate both the beginning rodeo fan and the seasoned veteran about this exciting sport.

Several rodeo committees welcomed me as I traveled across North America gathering material for this book. I am indebted to the rodeo families of Industry Hills, Lake Elsinore, Norco, Jurapa, Salinas, the Cow Palace, Santa Maria, Reno, Las Vegas, Odgen, Cheyenne, Calgary, Dodge City, Oakdale, Prescott, and several other localities for their courtesies and support.

A special thanks also to stock contractors Cotton Rosser and John Growney who went out of their way to make me feel welcome behind the chutes at their rodeos. I also wish to thank *Western Horseman* for allowing us to reprint portions of several pieces from Gavin's column that first appeared in that magazine.

GAVIN EHRINGER

I also wish to acknowledge several individuals, including *Western Horseman* publishers Randy Witte and the late Dick Spencer, both of whom encouraged me to write and gave me the opportunity to author articles in their highly regarded publication. I'd also like to thank the magazine's editorial staff members—Pat Close, Gary Vorhes, Brenda Goodwin, Kathy Kadash, Rick Swan, Dwayne Brech, and Fran Smith—as well as the marketing director, Butch Morgan, who seems to know everyone in professional rodeo and has helped me with many story ideas over the years.

This book would not have been possible without the help of the Professional Rodeo Cowboys Association, and I am especially indebted to Sherry Compton, Kendra Santos, and Steve Fleming of the PRCA media department for their help over the years. Thanks also go to the International Professional Rodeo Association, the National High School Rodeo Association, the National Intercollegiate Rodeo Association, and the National Little Britches Rodeo Association.

Many cowboys and barrel racers have given of their time in interviews and in conversations. These people gave me a better understanding of the cowboy sport, and I thank them all. In particular, I wish to thank Billy, Robert, and Dan Etbauer, Ty Murray, Tuff Hedeman, Butch Small and his family, Roy Cooper, Kristi and Chuck Peterson, Bryan McDonald, Jade Robinson, Craig Latham, Mark and Marvin Garrett, Fred Whitfield, and Adriano Moraes. I also acknowledge former competitors and stock contractors Pat Beard, Cotton Rosser, Cindy Moreno, John Growney, Jim Shoulders, Bruce Ford, June and Buster Ivory, Cecil Jones, Gerald Roberts, Don Gay, and Mack Altizer.

In my travels, many rodeo committees have extended their friendship, and special thanks go to the rodeo committees of the Calgary Stampede, Cheyenne Frontier Days, Dodge National Circuit Finals Rodeo, Pikes Peak or

Bust Rodeo, Park Rapids Rodeo, Chief Joseph Days Rodeo, National Western Stock Show & Rodeo, Rowell Ranch Rodeo, and the National Finals Rodeo.

I'd also like to thank former NLBRA President Jim Chamley, Bull Riders Only President Shaw Sullivan, photographers Dan Hubbell and Ken Opprann, and *Quarter Horse Journal* editor Lesli Groves. Thanks also to the great reporters who cover the sport on a weekly basis: Ed Knocke of the *Dallas Morning News*, Brian Painter of the *Daily Oklahoman*, Dwayne Erickson of the *Calgary Sun*, and Brett Hoffman of the *Fort Worth Star-Telegram*.

Finally, I'd like to acknowledge my family: Alison and Jarvis Owens, Bill and Martha Ehringer, Edith and Leslie Noller, and my sister, Wendy. Thanks for all the love and support over the years.

1

INTRODUCTION

AND BRIEF HISTORY

OF RODEO

here's an irony to the fact that bull rider Brent Thurman and country singer Willie Nelson both lived in the same town, Austin, Texas. For in real life, as in Nelson's song "My Heroes Have Always Been Cowboys," Thurman grew up dreaming of being a cowboy.

Unlike many of his fellow cowboys, Thurman didn't come from a rodeo or ranching background. He'd taken an interest in rodeo as a boy, progressing through the ranks of junior and high school competition. Eventually, he rose to the top of his sport, joining the Professional Rodeo Cowboys Association in 1988.

At the age of twenty-five, Thurman was living his dream. A professional bull rider, he was competing in his second National Finals Rodeo (NFR), an event sportswriters often refer to as rodeo's Super Bowl. It was the last day of the ten-round competition, and Thurman was getting ready to take his final ride. After saying a quick prayer, he slid a gloved hand into the leather handle of his plaited rope. Another cowboy leaned over the chute, pulling the rope tight around the chest of Thurman's bull, Red Wolf. As more than 17,000 ticket holders and several hundred thousand television viewers looked on, Thurman nodded his head, and the gate swung open.

Seconds later, Thurman lost his balance on the spinning bull, leaning precariously toward the inside of the spin—into the area the cowboys refer to as "the well." Thurman spun atop the whirling bull and, for a moment, seemed to stop as in a freeze-frame. Everyone in the arena gasped or grew silent. Thurman fell to the ground, and the huge bull continued on its spinning course. At that moment, a photographer snapped a picture, capturing the 1,800-pound brindle bull suspended in air except for one huge hoof balanced on the cowboy's skull.

Medics rushed toward the fallen cowboy. Minutes passed, and the audience remained quiet. Unconscious, blood streaming from his nose and mouth, Thurman was taken from the arena on a stretcher. As the paramedics pushed the stretcher down the clean white hallway that led to the elevator, blood poured from Thurman's mouth, leaving a trail of bright red spots along the freshly waxed gray tiles. Less than a week later, Brent Thurman died.

In a haze that bordered on nausea, another cowboy made ready to ride his final bull. Like Thurman, Adriano Moraes had dreamed of competing at the National Finals Rodeo. A native of São Paulo, Brazil, Moraes had taken up the sport in his mid-teens, progressing to the Brazilian national bull riding title. Only two years after moving to Texas, Moraes had qualified for the National Finals, the first South American of any nationality to do so.

As he successfully rode each bull at the rodeo, Moraes moved steadily toward a second goal: to make qualified eight-second rides on ten consecutive bulls at the NFR, something that had been done only twice before in the rodeo's thirty-five-year history—and never by a first-time NFR qualifier. But in light of his friend's accident, many wondered if Moraes would even go on, much less rise to greatness. With no time to collect his thoughts, Moraes eased down onto the bull's back and nodded his head. As the animal leapt from the chute, Moraes matched the beast move for move. His ride lacked the usual crispness and precision that characterizes a great bull ride, and Moraes began to get off balance. But just as Moraes was about to fall, the bull stepped sideways, seemingly positioning himself underneath the cowboy and helping him regain his tenuous position on top. The horn sounded, signaling the end of the ride. Moraes swung his leg over the bull's back, landed on his feet, then scrambled away.

Moraes grabbed his black cowboy hat and sailed it skyward. He then punched the air with both fists like a victorious prize fighter. Finally, he kneeled on the arena floor and prayed. When he arose to the cheers of the crowd, he *walked over toward the arena announcer and in his halting English said, "I dedicate that ride to Brent Thurman."*

RODEO: AN INTRODUCTION

Moraes's selfless words capture an essential ideal of sports, and of rodeo. In his most triumphant moment, he shared his glory with a fallen competitor. One can consider what happened at the 1994 National Finals Rodeo and conclude that the sport of rodeo is a brutal, brutish, violent activity. Or one can look at the events from another perspective and see that the sport has its moments of utmost humanity. Neither perspective is wholly right or wholly wrong.

Certainly rodeo is about violent competition. But it is also about honor and camaraderie. World champion all-around cowboy Ty Murray, trying to put Brent Thurman's death into perspective, said: "It's a dangerous sport, there's no denying that. But that's part of why Brent did it. It's just like race car driving or downhill skiing. It's about overcoming unbeatable odds and excitement and thrills."

People are drawn to danger, and rodeo provides plenty of that. In pitting man against beast, rodeo presents an especially stark expression of human frailty. It is truly a life-or-death challenge, one that most people are content to experience vicariously. As sixteen-time world champion roughstock rider Jim Shoulders once said, "People don't want to see a rodeo cowboy die, but they want to be there when he does."

Many come to see the spectacle of the cowboy cheating death, and that is all they understand about rodeo. But for the rodeo aficionado, the appeal is more complex. To truly understand the sport, one needs to see it as a celebration of life, and of a lifestyle that has all but passed away. Rodeo is a reaffirmation of the Old West and of countless people who knew death on intimate terms and who struggled, like Brent Thurman, to cheat it.

Rodeo carries traditions unique to the Americas and is a mixture of both Latin- and Anglo-American cultures. To the casual spectator, rodeo can seem like a secret fraternity, one with its own rules, lingo, dress, and conduct. And it is true that underneath the cowboy hats are individuals that have somehow remained apart from society as a whole. They have their own culture, their own distinct customs, and their own morality, which enables them to create a world that is, in many ways, separate. It is not an alien culture, simply one that many people have lost touch with. Our agrarian forefathers certainly would not feel disoriented around a rodeo arena, since animals played an integral parts in their lives and the mastery of animals was simply a part of daily farm and ranch work. But most North Americans today are two or more generations removed from the land, and even many of today's farmers use machinery to perform tasks once assigned to livestock.

Rodeo, with its intimate association between man and animal, puts us in touch with our history and reminds us of small-town celebrations, Fourth of July gatherings, patriotism, and a kind of agrarian life that seems remote to most Americans in the late twentieth century. Although some academics would dismiss that statement as embracing "the cowboy myth," our contact with the sport leads us to argue that cowboy mythology remains a guiding force in the lives of the men and women who compete in the sport, and in many of the communities they come from. Certainly, it may be an idealized view of America's past, but it is an ideal that still influences the actions and activities of the small segment of society that participates in this most American of sports.

Although rodeo's inherent danger certainly appeals to our baser instincts, it also can serve to elevate us to greater levels of compassion. It may seem quaint or contrived to say that many people in rodeo adhere to a high moral code, often referred to as "the cowboy code," but time and again, the athletes and the people who help to stage rodeo competitions go beyond the norm in their efforts to help people, both within the sport and in the larger community.

Most rodeos are not-for-profit endeavors. Proceeds from the sale of tickets and concessions are usually directed toward charities, either local or national. And along with the institutional charity built into the foundation of the rodeo system are frequent examples of spontaneous charity by rodeo competitors and rodeo committees alike. For example, in the wake of the 1995 bombing of the Alfred P. Murrah Federal Building in Oklahoma City, members of the International Professional Rodeo Association (IPRA) initiated a donation program to aid in victim relief. Professional Rodeo Cowboys Association (PRCA) steer wrestling champion Ote Berry of Checotah, Oklahoma, dedicated $12,000 in prize earnings from a Guthrie, Oklahoma, contest to a similar victims' fund.

Another champion, bull rider Charles Sampson, took top honors at a bull riding event in San Francisco, California, and donated his $2,000 winnings to the Bay Area Red Cross earthquake relief effort in the aftermath of the devastating quake that shook the San Francisco Bay area in 1989. Two years later, rodeo clowns at the same rodeo chipped in the proceeds of T-shirt sales to a relief fund for the victims of the disastrous Oakland and Berkeley fires. Similar tales of compassion and sacrifice are commonplace in rodeo.

Rodeo is a sport that places a premium on individual achievement, but seldom does a cowboy make it to the top without the help of others. When a cowboy is down and out, the rodeo tradition is to offer help. Auctions and other fundraisers have often been used to help the families of fallen cowboys no longer able to support themselves through arena earnings. But now rodeo organizations such as the Professional Rodeo Cowboys Association (PRCA) in Colorado Springs have begun to respond to the needs of members whose livelihoods have been impaired or cut short by arena accidents. The PRCA established the Justin Cowboy Crisis Fund to aid the families of injured competitors who can no longer compete. The first recipient was bull rider Chuck Simonson, who was paralyzed from the waist down while competing. He was awarded a truck that enabled him to continue his ranch work and a special saddle that helped him to train horses. A small response to a tragic situation, perhaps, but typical of a culture that believes in self-sufficiency.

Spontaneous philanthropy is just one example of the values that pervade rodeo society. Although it might seem old-fashioned to use the word "sportsmanlike" to describe the world of rodeo, the word has meaning to both fans and competitors. And it is this sportsmanlike ethos, as well as the danger and excitement of the contests, that compels people to engage in the sport.

Conversely, "sportsmanship" is a word whose meaning has suffered severely in the world of high-profile modern sports. From illegal college football recruiting practices to the illicit use of drugs by professional athletes to baseball Hall of Famer Mickey Mantle's admission of a lifetime of alcohol abuse, sports figures have lost much of their luster in the public's eyes. They no longer inspire a sense of high moral purpose; instead, their shortcomings only give us reason to overlook our own shortcomings. But modern rodeo athletes have somehow remained insulated from the abuses of public trust that seem endemic to higher-profile athletics.

We do not say that rodeo does not have its detractors or even that all rodeo cowboys are above reproach. Animal activist groups have taken to describing rodeo as "a culture of cruelty," and a percentage of the public would like to abolish the sport or severely restrict certain rodeo events. Furthermore, some people see the perpetuation of the cowboy mystique as a glorification of masculine dominance, a state of mind that runs contrary to changing views of male and female roles in society. Sociologist Michael S. Kimmel, in his article "The Cult of Masculinity: American Social Character and the Legacy of the

Cowboy," uses the image of the American cowboy (and by extension, the rodeo cowboy) as a metaphor for the aggressive character of American social and political behavior. Kimmel argues that society would be wise to abandon the cowboy myth as an archetype of the American character:[1] "The disappearance of the cowboy as the model of American masculinity will be a gain, not a loss. His disappearance as an individual hero, a template for individual role making, may help free United States' men from the constraints of a compulsively competitive masculinity and create new options for men as nurturing fathers, expressive husbands and lovers, and generous, sympathetic friends."

Others, such as Elizabeth Atwood Lawrence in her 1982 book, *Rodeo: An Anthropologist Looks at the Wild and the Tame,* take a similar tack. Lawrence contends that rodeo is an expression of the western determination to dominate animals through force: "As an outgrowth of ranching, rodeo embodies the frontier spirit as manifested through the aggressive and exploitative conquest of the West, and deals with nature and the reordering of nature according to the dictates of this ethos."[2] This viewpoint succinctly states the opinion of most animal rights activists, who would like to see rodeo competition ended permanently.

Journalist Dirk Johnson also seeks to strip rodeo cowboys of their mystique. Traveling on the road with numerous rodeo roughstock riders, Johnson examines the financial hardships and family pressures that these men face in pursuing their livelihoods as professional rodeo cowboys. Johnson's book *Biting the Dust* revisits the often-used theme of the struggling rodeo cowboy counterposed against the mythic conception of the cowboy as an American hero.[3] Johnson and others overlook the many benefits that these men and their families derive from being a part of the supportive rodeo culture. Furthermore, Johnson evaluates the cowboys against a modern standard that is perhaps not of the cowboy's choosing. While the cowboys may not be successful in society's measure—that is, in monetary terms—they are accomplished in their own minds and in the minds of their peers.

Rodeo in America: Wranglers, Roughstock, & Paydirt sets out to describe rodeo cowboys and the larger world that makes their lifestyle possible. We believe that although rodeo does draw heavily from the mythology of the cowboy, this mythology—so ingrained in the lives and the actions of the rodeo cowboys and cowgirls—contributes to their lives in a mostly positive way. This book is primarily about rodeo cowboys, though women figure in peripheral ways. Right or wrong, there are relatively few women compared to men competing in professional rodeo outside of barrel racing. For this reason, the masculine pronoun and the word "cowboy" are used throughout the book unless we are speaking specifically of women.

To many in the rodeo business, the word "mythology" would seem inappropriate. For those caught up in the sport, the cowboy is not a myth or a silver screen hero from the past. He is a neighbor, a friend, a family member, or the individual himself. They do not see a separation between past and present, myth and reality, but a continuum.

Rodeo cowboys do not live in a historical time warp. They inhabit the same world as the rest of us. They travel on the same jet planes, struggle with the same financial worries, agonize over their children's futures, and wonder if they are spending enough time with their families. To these cowboys, rodeo is a sport, a passion, and a means of earning a living and of accomplishing something with their lives. Rodeo is a lifestyle, the cowboy's pathway to the American dream.

A BRIEF HISTORY OF RODEO

It seems arbitrary to assign the birth date of the sport we now call rodeo to a particular period in history. Ever since humans began to domesticate animals, they have participated in contests that pit man against beast. Pictographs of Minoans, whose culture flourished on the island of Crete a full millennium before Christ, show men and women performing acrobatics with bulls. The Romans built coliseums for spectacular public exhibitions involving men and animals, including horse and chariot races. In Western Europe, the knights of the Middle Ages held mock battles to display their courage and riding skill. Spaniards brought their equitation to the New World, where noblemen held riding contests and exhibitions of horsemanship. Likewise, Russian Cossacks and Arabian Bedouins were known for their daring horsemanship, and Native Americans also competed on horseback at their gatherings.

Every rodeo today borrows elements from these cultures. In rodeo arenas, one can see bloodless bullfighting that the Minoans might have appreciated, chuckwagon races that would impress the ancient Romans, and feats of horsemanship that originated with the mounted warriors of both the Old and New Worlds. Native Americans continue to play a role in rodeo as producers, hosts, honored guests, and contestants.

Even though rodeo borrows from many cultures, what separates it from all other exhibitions involving men and beasts is the presence of a uniquely North American character: the cowboy. The origins of rodeo are inextricably intertwined with these men who worked cattle on horseback.

Cattle were brought to the New World by the Spaniards in the 1520s. As the Spaniards moved north from Mexico into what is today the American Southwest, they brought their cattle herds with them. Spanish noblemen and missionaries claimed vast tracts of land for the Spanish crown, and cattle ranching became an important industry, particularly in what is now the state of California.

In Spain, only those of noble birth were permitted to ride horses. But in the wide-open ranges of the North American continent, working cattle on foot was impractical. So the Spanish nobles and Catholic padres taught their servants and Indian religious converts to ride horses. These mounted herdsmen came to be known as *vaqueros*, the Spanish word for men who tend cattle. Later, English-speaking cattlemen corrupted the word to buckaroo, a name synonymous with cowboy in parts of the American West.

At first the Spaniards in the Southwest kept cattle mainly for their hides and tallow, but when gold was discovered at Sutter's Mill in the 1840s, the cattle became a source of meat for the thousands of miners who flocked to Northern California to hunt treasure. Many of the men who failed to find their fortunes in gold turned to cattle ranching, learning their skills from the vaqueros.

Meanwhile, in Texas, the feral cattle that had crossed the Rio Grande multiplied virtually unchecked. Their number grew appreciably during the 1860s, while the United States was embroiled in the Civil War. Following the war, soldiers as well as ex-slaves came to Texas in search of opportunity. They quickly realized that there was money to be made from the huge herds of Longhorn cattle roaming the Texas plains. But to get the cattle to the rail heads of Kansas and Missouri, where the cattle could be shipped by train to the eastern markets, the cattlemen needed laborers—men on horseback. They hired itinerant soldiers, unemployed drifters, Mexicans who lived along both sides of the Rio Grande, and former slaves to gather up the herds, brand them, and move them north. These men came to be known as cowboys, and their trade was cross-fertilized by the Spanish vaqueros, whose saddles, clothing, woven rawhide ropes, and language were adapted to the cowboys' needs.

Cattle drovers plied their trade on the open plains for a mere thirty years, and their hey-day lasted only from the early 1870s through the 1880s. The number of range drovers probably numbered no more than 20,000 individuals. And yet these men, many of whom were in their teens and twenties, came to symbolize the spirit of a young nation yearning for wide open spaces, prosperity, and adventure. The reputation of cowboys as the romantic characters of the plains grew large in proportion to their actual numbers and importance. The cowboys' egos were boosted by the nickel presses of the east, which expanded and amplified their antics in stories of bravery and infamy that captured the imaginations of the United States, and eventually the world.

By the 1880s, the long cattle drives to the rail heads were losing their importance, since the rail lines had been extended across the entire continent to towns throughout the West. By then, cattlemen had replaced the wild Longhorn cattle with a hardy and docile immigrant from England, the Hereford. By fencing off the range land, the cattlemen could raise their herds and sell the cattle to stockyards located nearby in towns alongside the railroad tracks. There was no longer a need to move the cattle to distant ranges.[4]

RODEO'S TRAILBLAZERS

But even as their way of life was changing, the old ways dying off, the cowboys were creating a new sport to celebrate their skills and heritage. Although the word "rodeo" was not widely used until the early twentieth century, cowboys of the 1880s were already competing in "cowboy tournaments" that usually included bronc riding and steer roping. The first recorded event was a bronc riding contest held on the eastern Colorado plains near a town called Deer Trail. The year was 1869, and the contest involved cowboys from two rival outfits, the Hash Knife and Mill Iron. Each outfit bet on its best rough string riders. There were no entry fees, no paying spectators, and no rules. The cowboys judged each ride, which probably lasted until the cowboy was thrown to the ground or the horse quit bucking. An Englishman, Emilnie Gradenshire, won the event and a new suit of clothes from the cowhands in his outfit.[5]

The Pro Rodeo Hall of Fame endorses the Deer Trail event as the first recorded rodeo contest. But a number of towns have also claimed the distinction of holding the earliest rodeo, and their claims are largely based on how one defines the word itself. The community of Prescott, Arizona, contends that its townspeople staged a rodeo-like contest on the Fourth of July, 1864. Other "firsts" claimed by Prescott include the first paid admission to a rodeo (1888) and the first presentation of a rodeo award, a medal presented to Juan Leivas.[6] Similar contests undoubtedly took place at other frontier towns and on the open plains. But unlike the contest at Deer Trail, these competitions went unrecorded. Not until the 1880s would the formal contests we now call rodeos became commonplace.

The word rodeo is borrowed from the Spanish *rodear* (meaning a surrounding). Cowboys understood a rodear as a mustering of cattle, such as the one at the beginning of a drive. It was at these gatherings that the cowboys roped and branded cattle and rode the unbroken mustangs that served as their mounts on the long drives north. If many outfits were involved, the cowboys sometimes bet their wages on their outfits' best bronc busters or ropers. Similar gatherings occurred at the end of the trail, when the cattlemen gathered at the stockyards and held contests of skill. In the northern ranges of Wyoming, Montana, and western Canada, it was not uncommon for dozens of outfits to come together to round up the cattle that grazed on the open range. Contests of skill undoubtedly took place.

In the 1880s, various western towns began to hold formalized cowboy competitions. What separated these contests from the informal events staged by cowboys themselves was the presence of paying spectators, usually townspeople who came to watch the festivities. The earliest rodeos went by various names: round-ups, stampedes, cowboy tournaments, and in the Southwest, fiestas.

Residents of Alpine, Texas, claim that their town held the first spectator rodeo in 1882—six years before a similar spectator rodeo was held in Prescott, Arizona. Another Texas town, Pecos, also claims to have held the first rodeo, a bronc riding and steer roping contest that took place on July 4, 1883. The West of the Pecos Rodeo, held each year over the Independence Day weekend, is said to be the longest-running rodeo in existence. Two Colorado towns, Montrose and Denver, staged rodeo-like competitions in 1887. The Montrose contest was noted in the town's newspaper, largely because a woman was nearly trampled to death by a bronc. There were no arena fences then to contain the bucking animals.[7]

Prescott claims that their rodeo was the first organized rodeo featuring a prize purse, an organizing committee, and gate admission. These, its supporters contend, are the essential ingredients of modern professional rodeo contest. The Prescott Frontier Days Rodeo continues today and is among the top twenty-five rodeos sanctioned by the Professional Rodeo Cowboys Association. It, too, takes place over the Fourth of July weekend.

WILD WEST SHOWS

About the time the early rodeos were held, more ambitious promoters created Wild West shows, elaborate productions that celebrated life on the western frontier. William F. "Buffalo Bill" Cody, originator of the most famous Wild West show, first appeared on stage in Chicago in 1872. His early melodramas played to audiences in small towns and large cities, including a stint on Broadway in March of 1873. But Cody did not hit his stride as a producer and promoter until some years later, when he returned to his homestead in North Platte, Nebraska. In 1882, as the Fourth of July approached, Cody was chagrined to learn that no special festivities were planned for North Platte. He resolved to give his town a show, and he devised a program that would include shooting, riding, and bronc busting. He expected a hundred entrants, but more than a thousand showed up for the contest. Cody quickly realized that he had a salable commodity and set to work creating a show that he could take on the road.

Cody's first show premiered the following year in North Platte. Then Cody and his troupe packed up and headed east, playing to appreciative audiences up and down the Atlantic seaboard. Before long, Cody's Wild West show had dozens of imitators, but Bill Cody was renowned as the original master showman. Buffalo Bill's Wild West and Congress of Rough Riders played to packed houses in prestigious venues, including London and the famed Madison Square Garden in New York City. The Madison Square Garden Rodeo would eventually become one of the biggest and most famous rodeo competitions.

Other famous Wild West shows, or Bill Shows as some of the cowboys called them, included the 101 Ranch Wild West Show and Pawnee Bill's Wild West Show. It was while working for the 101 Ranch that a black cowboy named Bill Pickett first demonstrated the art of wrestling a steer or bull to the ground, sometimes using his teeth to grip the animal's snout and pull him over. Pickett is said to have learned this trick while watching bulldogs harassing cattle in the course of their work. Pickett's "event" came to be known as bulldogging and later, steer wrestling. It is the only rodeo event seen today that can be attributed to a single individual.[8]

Much of the showmanship in modern rodeos can be traced to the Wild West shows. Rodeo events such as trick riding and fancy roping and traditions such as the grand entry were standard features in the Wild West shows. Another tradition, the rodeo parade, probably originated with the Wild West shows as well. When the show came to town, usually on a freight train, the performers and crew paraded the livestock to the arena, and to help attract customers for the show the next day, the performers dressed for the parade. The same strategy was used at many of the early rodeos, and contestants were required to ride in the parade. If a cowboy failed to appear, he could be disqualified from the competition.

Cowboys who performed in the Wild West shows were paid performers; rodeo cowboys, on the other hand, usually relied on earning prize money.

Still, it was not unusual for a Wild West show performer to jump ship and try his hand at rodeo or for rodeo cowboys to get hired by the Wild West shows. Show innovations also went back and forth as promoters looked for novel ways to attract audiences.

Because of the high cost of producing and promoting the Wild West shows, many of the producers folded their productions and began producing rodeos instead. Rodeos were particularly profitable. Not only did the spectator pay to see the show, the cowboys paid to compete. But in many cases, a local rodeo committee composed of townsmen and ranchers organized and promoted its own rodeo, hiring independent stock contractors to provide the animals. Local rodeo committees remain the principal organizers and promoters of rodeo competitions today.

Typical of rodeo organizers were the townsmen who organized the Cheyenne Frontier Days Rodeo. In 1897, Colonel E. A. Slack, who owned and edited the *Cheyenne Daily Sun*, proposed that the town host a celebration to be called Frontier Days. Slack and fellow businessmen had attended a potato celebration in nearby Greeley, Colorado, and Slack felt that Cheyenne should have a grand celebration of its own.[9] In just three weeks, on September 23, 1897, Slack and his hastily organized committee put together its first rodeo, which featured horse races, bucking bronc riding, and a steer roping contest. Spectators traveling from out of town got special rates on the Union Pacific Railway, which also provided sleeping cars for out-of-town visitors unable to find other accommodations.

The following year, the festivities were expanded to include Indians from the Shoshone tribe, who staged a mock attack on a wagon train. As the nineteenth century drew to a close, Cheyenne's Frontier Days was well on its way to becoming the biggest spectator rodeo of that time. By 1902, Cheyenne's Frontier Park had 20,000 visitors in one day, a crowd that would be considered large even by today's standards. Such was the fame of the Cheyenne rodeo that it came to be known as "the daddy of 'em all." Indeed, many communities in the early 1900s drew inspiration for their local events from it.

Two other successful rodeos spawned during that era were the Pendleton Round-Up and the Calgary Stampede. Pendleton, located in northeastern Oregon, held its first "rodeo" in 1909. The roping and riding contest was loosely structured, but the seeds for the future were planted. A young cowboy named Lee Caldwell, then seventeen, won the first bronc riding event in Pendleton. He later went on to become one of the most celebrated of early rodeo cowboys, winning all of the major rodeos of his day.[10]

The Pendleton Round-Up was officially incorporated in 1910, and like

Cheyenne, it drew spectators from throughout the West. Trainloads of people came to town for the event. In 1911, crowds topped 25,000. By 1913, there were more than 50,000 people in Pendleton for the rodeo—an impressive number considering that the town's population was about 5,000. Many of the visitors stayed in the Pullman sleeping cars of the fifty special trains parked in a yard during the rodeo. Others slept in barns or in the homes of towns-people, and many slept out in the open or in tents supplied by the Oregon National Guard.[11]

Pendleton prided itself on having the best bucking horses of any rodeo and became a show place for the great bronc riders of the era. Besides Caldwell, there was Yakima Canutt, a cowboy who later became a Hollywood film star and stunt rider. But perhaps the most popular cowboy at Pendleton, at least in 1916, was an Indian named Jackson Sundown.

Sundown was a strong, handsome Nez Perce Indian, the nephew of the famous Chief Joseph. Sundown competed in all of the events, but his fame as a bronc rider had become legendary throughout the Pacific Northwest. It is said that he once rode a bronc through the streets of Pendleton, crashed through the door of a dry goods store, and came out the back still mounted. In 1916, Sundown rode a horse named Angel at the Pendleton Round-Up, re-ceiving adulation and cheers from both the whites and the Indians assembled there. He was awarded the bronc riding title for the ride. Sundown was then fifty years old.

As rodeo's popularity was growing in the United States, Canadians also became enthusiastic about the thrilling new sport. In March 1912, a 27-year-old cowboy named Guy Weadick arrived in Calgary. He had been one of the original performers in the 101 Ranch Wild West Show in 1908 and had performed his rope tricks on the vaudeville circuit in New York and at the Orpheum theater. Because of his show business connections, Weadick began writing a column for *The Billboard*, the showmen's magazine. After seeing the popularity of cowboys in early motion pictures and Wild West shows and witnessing first hand the growing fame of vaudeville performer Will Rogers, Weadick felt that rodeos were falling far short of their potential. He vowed to create "the greatest outdoor show in the world," with prize money of $100,000. It would be called "The Stampede."[12]

It took considerable cajoling to gain the financial support Weadick needed for such a show. After he was turned down by all of the prominent busi-nessmen in Calgary, Weadick very nearly gave up. Then he met with A. D. Day from Medicine Hat, Alberta. Day, a prosperous rancher with a hobby of collecting bucking horses like other men collect stamps, was enthusiastic about Weadick's big-time rodeo proposal. He pledged his bucking string and $10,000 of his own money if Weadick could gain the support of the people of Calgary. When the Calgary newspapers spread the news of Day's backing, Weadick had little trouble gaining the $100,000 needed to produce his rodeo. H. C. McMullen, a general livestock agent for the Canadian Pacific Railway, introduced Weadick to several financiers, businessmen with deep roots in cattle ranching. Soon four other men, in addition to Day, had put up $25,000 each to produce the rodeo.

Weadick launched an advertising campaign that blanketed western Canada and the entire United States and plugged the event in his *Billboard* magazine column. The contests included many of the standard rodeo events —saddle bronc riding, steer roping, steer wrestling, and bareback riding— along with several that are now rare—women's saddle bronc riding, men's and women's trick roping, men's and women's trick riding, and cowboys' and cowgirls' relay races. Thousands flocked to Calgary and watched the rodeo, despite an almost steady downpour of rain. One cowboy said, "I saw more people sitting in the rain at Calgary than I ever saw anywhere else sitting in the sun." [13]

WOMEN IN EARLY RODEO

Women played an important role in the early rodeos. They were tough competitors, riding broncs or roping and tying steers weighing 1,000 pounds. They were as much the stars of the rodeo as men. Bertha Kapernick (Blancett) was the first woman to ride broncs at the Cheyenne Frontier Days Rodeo, putting on a bronc riding exhibition in 1904 after cowboys stopped the competition due to inclement weather. Kapernick's display was so well received that the cowboys had little choice but to continue with the scheduled competition despite the muddy arena conditions. Two years later, Cheyenne added cowgirl bronc riding and relay racing contests to their program. [14]

In many cases, women's times and scores in these early rodeos were competitive with men's, which infuriated some of the cowboys. At Pendleton, a popular cowgirl named Prairie Rose Henderson was the first to ride a saddle bronc in competition, finishing just a few points behind the winning cowboy. In 1914, Bertha Kapernick came within a dozen points of winning Pendleton's prestigious all-around title. Mabel Strickland, perhaps the finest bronc rider among the women of the 1920s, also roped steers, following a tradition first begun by Lucille Mulhall. At Pendleton one year, Strickland roped and tied a steer in eighteen seconds, a time that few cowboys of that era could match. [15]

Women remained prominent in rodeo competition until the 1930s. The death of a bronc rider named Bonny McCarroll, as well as other rodeo-related deaths involving women, caused many of the rodeos to put an end to women's roughstock riding events (no records were kept regarding men being killed in arena-related incidents). Because of this and other reasons—which we discuss more fully in a later chapter—most women's events were eventually dropped from the rodeos. Today, all-women rodeos are beginning to gain popularity, but it is unlikely that women will ever receive the recognition enjoyed by the pioneering cowgirls of rodeo's earliest days.

ORGANIZING PROFESSIONAL RODEO

As rodeo contests spread throughout the country, it became possible for cowboys and cowgirls to make their living strictly through competition or in the Wild West shows. With the evolution of professional rodeo came the need for standardized rules of competition. Prior to 1929, most rodeos had their own rules, which resulted in confusion and misunderstanding among the cowboys and organizers. So the more prominent and prosperous rodeo committees joined together to draft uniform rules of competition and rules for the conduct of the rodeos. They also set schedules in order to avoid, as much as possible, conflicting competition dates. Although several of the major rodeo producers never joined, those that did called their new organization the Rodeo Association of America (RAA).[16]

One advantage of a confederation of rodeo committees was that world championships could be determined. Before the RAA was formed, several rodeos touted their winning cowboys and cowgirls as world champions, and it was impossible to determine who was the top rider in a particular event. The RAA devised a point system based upon prize money, with one point awarded for each dollar in prize money won. At season's end, the cowboy who had won the most money in a particular event was declared the world champion. This system is still used by the Professional Rodeo Cowboys Association.

Despite the significant advance that the new organization represented, the alliance between cowboys and rodeo committees remained an uneasy one. Promoters often made promises to the cowboys that they simply did not honor once the cowboys arrived for the rodeo. Cowboys also complained that at several rodeos, their entry fees were being used to shore up the promoter's profits rather than returned to them as the prize purse. Cowboys also objected to judges picked from among the local citizenry. In many cases, these judges had never ridden a bucking horse or roped a steer, and they tended to favor local cowboys over the professionals who came to town to compete.

The conflicts came to a head in 1936. A rodeo promoter named Colonel William T. Johnson was staging two big contests, one at Madison Square Garden in New York and the other at the Boston Gardens in Boston. Johnson had promised a certain purse at both competitions, and he honored his commitments for the Madison Square Garden show. But when the cowboys arrived in Boston, they found that the purse was considerably less than they had bargained for. They protested. Johnson felt certain that the cowboys would back away from their demands, since they were far from home and in need of the money. Instead, the cowboys went on strike. They drafted a petition listing their demands, which was signed by sixty-one cowboys. Johnson tried to stage the rodeo with scabs, mostly Wild West show performers and cowboys who were competing in Chicago. But when the replacements learned of the situation, only a few showed up for the first performance of the sixteen-day rodeo. Johnson was told by the management of the arena that unless he squared things with the cowboys, there would be no more performances. Johnson quickly made amends, raised the prize money, and acceded to the cowboys' other demands.[17]

Empowered by their actions, the cowboys formed their own association, calling themselves the "Cowboys' Turtle Association." Legend has it, they settled on that name because they had been so slow to stick their necks out and get organized. But the Turtles, once formed, quickly became an important force in the development of fair rodeo competitions. They approved competitions, created rules for the fair promotion and conduct of rodeo contests, and began naming their own world champions. In 1945, the Turtles changed their name to the Rodeo Cowboys Association (RCA). In 1947, the Rodeo Association of America (by then called the International Rodeo Association) had folded, and the rodeo committees were organized under the RCA. Thus began the modern era of rodeo that continues to this day under the direction of the Professional Rodeo Cowboys Association (PRCA).

In the next chapter we present a detailed discussion of the seven standard rodeo events and the mechanics of judging each one. Those rodeo fans who are already well acquainted with the basics might wish to turn directly to Chapter 3.

"There are rodeos that are famous for their hecklers. Some places are really hard to be around—either the fans know too little about rodeo, or they know too much. I like it that people are involved, but you have to stand by your judgment. You darn sure want to make certain the money goes to the right cowboys."

—PRCA Pro Official Jade Robinson

2

RODEO

EVENTS &

JUDGING

At first glance, rodeo seems like a simple series of individual contests. In the roughstock riding, the cowboys ride bucking animals. In the timed events, they either throw a steer to the ground or rope and subdue a calf or steer. But in order to determine who carries out these tasks with the greatest skill, and therefore wins honors in competition, the sport has evolved a complex set of rules that can be difficult for the newcomer to grasp. Understanding these rules is crucial to understanding what takes place inside the rodeo arena.

In modern rodeo, there are seven standard events; four are *timed events*, and three are *roughstock events*. The timed events include calf roping, team roping, barrel racing, and steer wrestling. The roughstock events are saddle bronc, bareback, and bull riding.

Rodeo events developed through a series of stages. The earliest rodeos and Wild West shows always featured saddle bronc riding and some form of cattle roping—either team roping, calf roping, or single steer roping. Dozens of other events were created by promoters and added to enliven the early shows. Especially popular were wild horse races, in which teams of cowboys would rope and saddle range colts and then attempt to ride them to a finish line. Another popular event was wild cow milking, which involved roping a range cow and trying to milk her. The first man to squirt a few drops into a bottle and return it to the judges was the winner. Both of these events remain popular added events at rodeos today, but they are not recognized by the Professional Rodeo Cowboys Association (PRCA), the largest sanctioning body of professional rodeo competitions.

Other early rodeo events included relay races, trick riding contests, trick roping, and horse races. Steer wrestling, a popular exhibition event, made its debut in the first decade of the twentieth century and was fairly common by the 1920s. Bareback riding was also a standard rodeo event by that time. Improvements in equipment (the handheld rigging) helped to make this event immensely popular with rodeo fans, assuring it of a long-term place in the sport.

Bull riding began in these early rodeos. At first, the cowboys used a saddle to ride steers or bulls. Eventually, the saddles were replaced by ropes or saddle surcingles (the cinch used to hold a saddle in place on a horse). As time went by, braided ropes with leather handholds became the standard bull rider's equipment. A heavy cowbell was added to the rope to help release the rope from the bull's back if the cowboy fell off. The noise of the bell was also said to encourage the bull to fight more ferociously.

Bronc riding, calf roping, and team roping are holdovers from the work of the early cowboy. In the course of their ranch work, cowboys rope cattle in order to brand and castrate them, to doctor them, and to catch strays in the open. In Texas, where mesquite brush forced the cowboys to rope quickly before the cattle could hide in the brush, the cowboys began tying their ropes to their saddles to bring the cattle to a quicker standstill. The same technique was used when ropers had to work a cow on the ground single-handedly. It became the hard-and-fast method used in modern calf roping. In other parts of the West, a roper would "dally" his rope—wrap it around the saddle horn. This technique allows the roper to ease the cow to a stop and release it if necessary. Dally roping is still seen in modern team roping.

STANDARD EVENTS IN RODEO

Although there was a great deal of experimentation in the earliest days of rodeo, today's rodeo events are standardized throughout the Professional Rodeo Cowboys Association, the International Professional Rodeo Association, the Canadian Professional Rodeo Association, and in most amateur associations as well. Standard events of PRCA-sanctioned rodeos include calf roping, team roping, (women's) barrel racing, steer wrestling, saddle bronc riding, bareback bronc riding, and bull riding. In Canada, competitions also include wild cow milking, a concession to that country's early rodeo history.

THE TIMED EVENTS

Calf Roping. In this event, the cowboy's objective is to rope and tie a running calf as quickly as possible. Mounted on a fast-running horse—typically an American Quarter horse—the calf roper backs into the roping box. With his horse in position, the roper nods his head, signaling for the calf to be released. The calf is given a head start, called a "score," of five to thirty feet depending on the size of the arena. Once the calf reaches the end of the score, the cowboy and his horse begin their pursuit. As the competitor approaches the running calf, he swings the loop of his rope above his head, then casts it.

A calf roper can rope any part of the calf, but the most common catch is the head catch. The roper yanks the slack out of his rope, which is tied to his saddle, and his horse slides to a stop. The roper runs down along the rope, which is held taut by the horse. He then grabs the calf by the flank and throws it to the ground. (If the calf was jerked to the ground by the catch, it must be let back up or picked up—"daylighted"—and rethrown before it can be tied.) With a six-foot rope called a "pigging string," he trusses three of the calf's legs together. Under ideal conditions, this process takes place in nine seconds or less.

Team Roping. Team roping involves partners, a header and a heeler. The header's job is to rope the steer's horns. The heeler then comes in to rope the heels. The run begins with the ropers positioned in separate stalls on either side of the chute. When the header nods his head, a steer is released from the chute. The header rides out and loops the steer's horns, then dallies his rope around the saddle horn. He must veer off to his left (to get out of the way) before the heeler can move into position behind the steer and cast his loop. The heeler strives to catch both legs. If he only manages to catch one leg, the team is penalized five seconds. After the heeler dallies his rope, both contestants must face each other, with the steer stretched between them. A winning run in team roping often takes place in under five seconds.

A partnership in team roping, in the words of one contestant, is like "being married." Similarity in roping styles and compatibility in personal habits (since partners must live in close proximity, practice, and travel together) are two important factors in choosing a partner. "It's a lot harder to travel together," notes one team roper, "if you can't stand each other." Most partners go for a balance of personality types. "Cowboys traveling together have to develop a 'give-and-take' type of thing," comments a heeler. It is more difficult to heel than to head, so heelers miss their throws more often. "The header has to always praise his heeler and bolster his confidence," says one team roper, "since the percentage of the time the heeler misses is high." As a result of these potential problems, team ropers change traveling partners more often than competitors in the other timed events.

Barrel Racing. Barrel racing is the only all-woman event in professional rodeo. Though women are not barred from any PRCA event, they have not competed in large numbers, except in barrel racing. Most PRCA rodeos feature barrel racing, although it is regarded as an optional event. It is overseen by the Women's Professional Rodeo Association (WPRA), a separate rodeo organization. In Canadian rodeo and in the International Professional Rodeo Association, however, women's barrel racing is treated as a standard event.

In barrel racing, the horse and rider enter the arena at a run. They must complete a specified clover-leaf pattern around three barrels. After dashing around either the left or the right barrel, the racer crosses over to the opposite barrel, makes her second turn, and then runs to the barrel furthest from the start line. After taking a turn around this final barrel, the horse and rider dash back across the starting line. In barrel racing, electronic timers are used instead of the stopwatches used in the bucking stock events. Judges add five seconds for each barrel that tips over. Depending on the arena, winning runs range from sixteen to eighteen seconds.

Steer Wrestling. Steer wrestling began as an exhibition event. In steer wrestling, the cowboy must jump from a running horse and wrestle a steer (weighing over 500 pounds) to the ground. The steer wrestler is assisted by a hazer, who rides alongside the steer to keep it running in a straight line. Riding on the opposite side of the steer from the hazer, the bulldogger jumps from his horse, grabs the steer's horns, and falls to the ground, using his momentum to help topple the steer.

The steer must fall with its feet positioned on one side. If the steer's back legs and front legs are splayed in opposite directions, the rider must get the steer to his feet and bring him down again before time is called. A good run in steer wrestling takes place in about four seconds, though it can take longer in arenas where the steer gets a longer head start.

Steer Roping. A fifth timed event, single steer roping, is staged at some rodeos, usually in lieu of the team roping. The event is similar to calf roping, but instead of a 300-pound calf, the roper must topple a steer weighing twice as much. To do this, he first ropes the steer's horns. He then veers to the left and flips his rope along the steer's right side and behind his hind leg, between the hip and the hock, jerking the steer down. The fall generally knocks the wind out of the steer, and if luck is on the side of the cowboy, the steer remains on the ground. The steer roper dismounts, runs down the rope to the toppled steer, and trusses three of the steer's legs, exactly as he would in calf roping. A fast time in steer roping ranges from ten to fifteen seconds, depending on arena conditions.

The steer roping event is now uncommon and not as well accepted as calf roping outside the cattle-producing states of Oklahoma, Wyoming, New Mexico, and Oregon. These competitors have higher travel expenses because competitions are spaced farther apart. In other words, a competitor must cross several states to make any kind of living steer roping whereas a calf roper could do quite well staying in Texas, California, Colorado, etc. Steer roping is illegal in many states, including California, and was widely outlawed around the turn of the century due to injuries to the steers. Though ploughed arenas, lighter cattle, and shorter scores have reduced the injury rate considerably, steer roping has never returned to most places. Tripping a steer also requires a lot of space. For these reasons, steer roping is not held at the National Finals Rodeo, the PRCA's championship-deciding event. For the past decade the National Finals Steer Roping (NFSR) has been held each November at the Lazy E arena in Guthrie, Oklahoma.

Guy Allen, a rancher from Vinita, Oklahoma, has dominated the obscure and relatively low-paying steer roping event. With ten world championships, Allen is by far the most successful single-event world champion in the history of the PRCA.

THE ROUGHSTOCK EVENTS

At the timed event end of the arena the goal is to be quick. But rodeo roughstock riding focuses on style, not speed, and each cowboy develops a distinctive riding style that he hopes will impress the judges. As one saddle bronc rider observed, "Your riding style is an extension of your personality. Who you are, the way you present yourself, and the technique you use in riding, are all part of this style."

Saddle Bronc Riding. Of the three roughstock events, only saddle bronc riding has roots in ranching life. The horses used in the trail drives were usually horses that had been taken off the range and broken (tamed) before being assigned to some puncher's string. Since each man needed eight to twenty horses to use on the trail rides, broken horses were in constant demand. Men who specialized in training young, fresh range colts were called bronco busters or bronco peelers and were highly respected among their peers. When different outfits came together on the trail or in a cow town, they would sometimes bet on whose bronco buster was the best man. Corralling their most ornery horses, the men would snub the animals to posts, rails, or saddles. Each horse would be blindfolded, and the bronc buster would climb aboard. When the blindfold was removed, the ride began. Generally, these early contests would last until the bronc rider was thrown or had ridden his horse to a standstill.

Bronc riding was the standard contest at early rodeos, but as time went by it became more refined. Since riding a horse to a standstill often took away the animal's desire to continue bucking, a time limit was imposed on the event. At first the limit was ten seconds, which remained the standard until the late 1940s, when the time was shortened to eight seconds. Bronc riders were judged on their showmanship and allowed to spur and quirt (whip) their horses with abandon. Later, the quirts were outlawed as cruel. Riders were also prohibited from touching the horse with their free hand, since this allowed riders to steady themselves, which was not considered sporting. Saddle bronc riders now hold their free arms in different positions, depending on how they carry their upper bodies. "Most guys try to keep their hands out, rather than up," notes one saddle bronc rider.

Today, saddle bronc riders are required to spur above the break of the horse's shoulders on the first jump out of the bucking chute. Failure to "mark" (or spur) the horse out of the chute results in disqualification. After leaving the chute, the rider tries to spur the horse by reaching forward with his feet as the horse's feet touch the ground, then sweeping his feet towards the back of the saddle as the horse bucks. Failure to spur the horse and to time the spurring properly results in a low score. A good spurring motion is a requirement of a good ride.

Bull Riding. The average bull rider weighs about 150 pounds; the average bull weighs ten times that. A bull can easily jump over a five-foot fence or lift the back end of a car off the ground with his horns. To master animals of this size and strength, the cowboy relies on his sense of timing, anticipation, and balance. His only handhold is a specially plaited rope that runs around the girth of the bull, just behind the front legs. This rope is held tight only by the cowboy's grip. The cowboy is not expected to "mark out" the bull coming out of the chute nor spur the bull during the course of the ride. However, high marks are usually awarded when a cowboy spurs his animal. A bull that goes into a spin often allows the bull rider to demonstrate this spurring action, and a spinning bull is generally regarded as a desirable animal to draw in a rodeo.

If the cowboy can maintain his position in the middle of the bull, he is still not out of danger. Bulls commonly try to hook cowboys with their horns, tilting their heads back or from side to side to get at the cowboy. Bull riders maintain this middle position by leaning forward over the center of the bull, a movement known as "posting." Keeping his eyes focused on the neck of the bull, positioning his legs near the bull rope, and leaning forward allow the bull rider to hold position.

Once a bull rider has completed his ride, he loosens his bull rope and looks for a safe place to land. To protect the fallen riders, and those bull riders needing assistance to get off the bull, professional bullfighters distract the animal long enough for the cowboy to jump off, get to his feet, and scramble to safety.

Bareback Riding. Bareback riding has been compared to operating a jack hammer with one hand, but cowboys will say it's not that easy. In bareback riding, the cowboys hold onto the horse with a rawhide "suitcase" handle attached to a triangular piece of laminated saddle leather. They wedge their hand so tightly into the handhold that, if you listen closely, you will hear the leather squeaking. When the rider is ready, he leans backward and nods his head. As the chute gate swings open, the bareback rider must reach forward with his feet to spur the horse on the first jump. As in saddle bronc riding, failure to mark the horse on the first jump results in a disqualification. Bareback riders are also judged on their ability to spur their horses, although the spurring style is different than in saddle bronc riding. In bareback riding, the rider must time his spur strokes with the horse's bucking motion, reaching forward toward the horse's neck, raking his spurs upward toward his crotch as the horse leaps, then gaping his legs wide to set the spurs in the horse's neck again as the animal's front feet crash to the ground.

JUDGING IN RODEO

At the Pikes Peak or Bust Rodeo in Colorado Springs, a cowboy hunkers down onto a saddle bronc in the bucking chute. He mashes his hat down on his head, then quickly nods. The gate swings open, and the horse rears high, his front hoofs pawing the sky. The horse's feet slam to the ground, and the cowboy is thrown forward, almost over the horse's head. Again the horse rears, then takes two leaping lunges forward.

The cowboy fights to stay aboard, pumping his hand back and forth and trying to find a rhythm that doesn't exist. The horse arches his back and comes crashing to the ground, and the cowboy rakes his spurs forward, setting them in the horse's neck. On the next buck, the horse leaps straight upward, and the cowboy leans back over its rump. Now the horse lines out straight, bucking and kicking.

The cowboy senses the pattern, and he sweeps his feet forward then backward, nearly clicking his spurred boot heels together at the back of his saddle as the horse reaches the top of his arc, then snapping his feet forward as the horse's hoofs touch ground. After a few more bucks, the buzzer sounds. As the audience cheers wildly, the cowboy grabs the rein with both hands and weathers a few more bucks before taking a flying leap to the ground. The cowboy sprawls on the dirt on his hands and knees, then scrambles for the arena fence.

Both the cowboy and the cheering audience watch the scoreboard. After a few seconds, a score of 67 flashes on the board. The audience's cheers turn to boos as they chide the judges. The cowboy looks dejected as he walks back to the bucking chutes. The announcer tries to make light of the situation by telling the audience: "If you didn't like the score, go right ahead and tell the judges. They're staying at the Holiday Inn, rooms 205 and 206."

T he job of the rodeo judge, like that of most sports officials, is a thankless one. A rodeo judge scoring a roughstock event has only eight seconds to consider the ride and about five seconds to render a decision that can mean either a big pay-off or a big disappointment for a cowboy. In the timed events, the judge must simultaneously consider the actions of cattle, horse, and rider, looking for infractions of the PRCA rules that fill a twenty-four-page manual with very small print. As any judge will attest, there are a lot of technicalities in an eight-second ride. A mistake can be the difference between a cowboy enjoying a steak dinner and making a downpayment on a new truck, or settling for a hot dog and a rusty pickup that has gone 200,000 miles.

At the earliest rodeos, the cowboys themselves often judged the contests. In many cases, a cowboy who was injured or disabled was given the job of judging, and he was expected to be fair to all competitors. By the 1920s, this system no longer served rodeo well. There were many cowboys who were trying to make a living at rodeo, traveling from town to town and living off their earnings. When they showed up for a show, these professional contestants often found that the local judges favored local cowboys. Rodeo committees sometimes tried to solve this problem by bringing in impartial outsiders or townsmen who were not affiliated with the rodeo, but this only made things worse. These judges had no way of understanding the sport, and their decisions reflected their lack of knowledge.

Along with a fair system for awarding prize money, early cowboy organizations fought hard for a uniform system of judging. When the Cowboys' Turtle Association was formed in 1936, the cowboys established a judging system that required competitors who were members of the association to officiate at sanctioned rodeos. Since that time, the rodeo cowboys have worked to improve the sport's judging system by refining the rules and raising the level of professionalism among rodeo judges. Perhaps the biggest single improvement was the creation of a system of professional judges similar to the officials programs of professional football, baseball, and basketball.

The PRCA's Pro Officials Program, established in 1981, is administered from the PRCA national headquarters. Officials must pass rigorous tests to attain full-time positions. All pro officials must have competed in PRCA rodeo and attained full membership as competitors before becoming officials. They must attend an in-depth training program, apprentice with already sanctioned judges, and take part in annual seminars. But the most important requirement for being a rodeo judge is to love the sport. After all, as one official says, "None of us are getting rich doing this." Typically a rodeo judge receives $85–$100 a day to officiate at the smaller rodeos, plus $85 for judging "slack" (the overflow competition that precedes many rodeos) and $40 for daily expenses.

Over the years, according to rodeo officials, the PRCA and particular rodeos have experimented with the number of judges. On one occasion, six judges were used. Another time, two pro officials were used to judge the cowboy and two to judge the livestock. Neither of these "innovations" proved satisfactory. Now the number of judges varies, depending on the size of the rodeo. At smaller PRCA-sanctioned rodeos, two judges are employed. In the roughstock events, each judge scores both animal and rider, awarding a maximum of 25 points to the horse, 25 to the rider. When the two judges' scores are tabulated, the maximum possible point total is 100. To provide high-quality officiating at the largest, most lucrative rodeos, the PRCA went to a four-judge system in 1991. With four judges keeping tabs on the roughstock riding, the total scores are tabulated and then divided in half to yield a comparable score based on the 100-point maximum. For the top-paying rodeos, along with the year-end National Finals Rodeo competition, eight judges are contracted through Wrangler Jeans and the PRCA for the entire year. Rotated through the fifty top-paying rodeos, they are guaranteed to judge twenty rodeos a year.

ALL-TIME TOP SCORES IN THE ROUGHSTOCK EVENTS

To many cowboys in the Professional Rodeo Cowboys Association, a bull or bucking horse would have to perform like gymnast Nadia Comaneci for its rider to score a perfect 100-point ride. Or so it seemed.

Wade Leslie, a little-known bull rider from Moses Lake, Washington, made rodeo history when he scored the PRCA's first perfect 100 points at the Wild Rogue Rodeo, October 25–27, 1991, at Central Point, Oregon. Although Leslie's bull, Wolfman Skoal of the Growney Brothers Rodeo string, performed neither back flips nor triple somersaults, it was a wild ride indeed.

"The bull was doing everything to buck him off—mixing it up, but always spinning left. Going faster, going slower. Jumping high in the air, then going close to the ground," said John Growney, one of the bull's co-owners. "We knew we'd seen a really great bull ride, but I never thought it would be a 100."

Few cowboys, in fact, thought that the PRCA's notoriously difficult judges would ever grant a perfect score. Not even Wade Leslie: "Raymond Lewis—I had a lot of people say that they didn't think they'd ever see him score a guy that would be 100. He's kind of a tough judge and he don't give points away. If you stub a toe, he's dang sure gonna dock you points."

But Leslie didn't stub a toe, and Lewis, one of two PRCA judges at Central Point, felt he'd scored the ride correctly. "I had no doubt in my mind, and the other cowboys there thought it was not out of line at all," said Lewis, who credited both the bull and rider for a picture-perfect performance. "It was un-believable. I've never seen a bull jump like that and hit the ground and spin like that," said Lewis of the ride.

If there exists such a thing as bovine destiny, Wolfman Skoal seemed pre-determined for greatness. Besides a patrilineal relationship to Oscar, one of only three bulls inducted into the Pro Rodeo Hall of Fame, Wolfman is also a grandson of Red Rock, a Hall of Fame inductee owned by Growney. Red Rock went unridden in 312 attempts before being mastered by world champion Lane Frost in a special exhibition ride, a ride that many feel deserved a perfect score.

Although Growney only began campaigning Wolfman hard earlier in the 1991 season, the bull had already established himself as a tough opponent. Before Leslie's ride, only bull rider Casey Allred had managed to hear the bell aboard Wolfman, scoring 90 points at a rodeo in Canby, Oregon.

As for the other side of the match-up, Leslie seemed an unlikely candidate to earn rodeo's best-ever score. A farrier from a town with the whimsical name of George, Washington, Leslie only competed part time. Fame had mostly evaded Leslie in his seven-year professional career. Before the record-smashing ride, his main career highlight was a bull riding and all-around victory at the 1988 Columbia River Circuit Finals Rodeo.

Despite the seemingly uneven pairing, Wolfman, a small black bull with a distinctive mask, proved the perfect match for the 5-foot 2-inch Leslie. According to Growney, a bigger rider might not have been marked so high for the simple reason that he would dwarf the smallish bull. But the 1,300-pound bull proved a whirling dervish underneath Leslie's small frame. "The bull's only 1,300 pounds, and that's a small bull in the rodeo world," said Growney. "But Wade's a small guy—I'll bet he only weighs 130 pounds. So it was a perfect combination."

Leslie's winning ride was shown later on "The George Michael Sports Machine," a nationally syndicated sports program. Leslie had appeared on the show years before, but the cameo was less triumphant. In his rookie season at Cheyenne's Frontier Days Rodeo, Leslie's second bull ejected him in under two seconds, hit Leslie in the chin with a horn, then tried to hook Leslie as he came down. Then the bull slipped in the deep arena mud and tumbled on top of Leslie, burying the rider completely. In the video that aired on Michael's show, all that could be seen when the bull got to his feet was Leslie's hat.

Wade Leslie's historic 100-point bull ride is only one of the outstanding performances listed in the PRCA's record book. Denny Flynn scored 98 points on Steiner's "Red Lightning" in Palestine, Illinois, in 1979, and Don Gay recorded a 97 pointer on RSC's "Oscar" in San Francisco in 1977. The highest saddle bronc score—95—was earned by Doug Vold, who rode Franklin's "Transport" in Meadow Lake, Saskatchewan, in 1979. Kent Cooper of Albia, Idaho, earned 93 points on Kerby's

"Hang'em High" in Vernal, Utah, in 1980. Joe Alexander holds the highest score in the bareback riding, 93 points, earned atop Beutler Brothers and Cervi's horse "Marlboro" in Cheyenne in 1974. Ty Murray of Stephenville, Texas, holds the next highest score, 92 points. He hit the mark on the Flying 5 Rodeo Company's "Bordertown" in San Francisco in 1991.

Seeing one of these historic rides is a memorable experience for a rodeo fan. For a cowboy to earn 90 points in any of the roughstock events, he must maintain the control of an Olympic figure skater while riding an animal that is bucking and shaking like a rabid dog in an earthquake. It does not happen often. An average bronc ride will earn a cowboy 70 to 75 points. At many rodeos, any ride from 75 to 79 points will earn a cowboy a paycheck. A first- or second-place finish is almost assured to the cowboy who scores 80 points or more.

In marking the bronc riders, the judges consider the cowboy's exposure and control. Exposure refers to the chance the bronc rider takes in giving the horse the opportunity to buck him off, and control refers to the command the rider has over the spurring motion. In saddle bronc riding, for instance, the judges award points for the length of the stroke. A stroke that extends from the shoulder of the horse rearward to the back of the saddle increases the score. Spurring must be done with each buck for the full eight-second ride. Horses buck anywhere from eight to thirteen times in those eight seconds. The rider loses points if his toes are not turned outward with his spurs (which are dulled and do not injure the animal) in contact with the horse, or if the spurring action is not continuous throughout the ride. The rider can be disqualified for losing a stirrup; touching the horse, saddle, or self with a free hand; or changing hands on the buck rein. The buck rein is for balance only, not to help the rider hold himself on.

In bareback riding the mark-out rule is similar, but the rider's scoring zone and spurring action is different from that of the saddle bronc rider. The zone is at or ahead of the area where the bronc's neck emerges from the shoulders. The spurring action is up and down, with the rider usually lying back along the horse's spine. (In saddle bronc riding, by contrast, the spurring motion is fore and aft, and the rider sits upright atop the horse.) Lying far back on the horse with the riding arm fully extended increases the rider's exposure. A straightened riding arm allows the bucking animal a greater opportunity to toss the cowboy, as a quick turn by the horse can unseat even the most skilled rider in that position. Bareback riders who place their feet very high on the horse's neck are also awarded higher points, since they are taking the chance of being thrown off if the horse ducks or drops its head, dislodging the feet from their position. It is also difficult for the cowboy to repeatedly reposition his feet near the horse's neck throughout the eight-second ride.[1] An additional disqualification or fine for the bareback rider may occur if the rider's hand hangs up in the bareback rigging. This can happen if the rider wedges his gloved riding hand too tightly into the rigging in order to stay atop his mount.

In bull riding, the rider scores points by maintaining body control and position regardless of the moves the bull makes. Recoveries look spectacular to the audience but usually lose the rider points because the contestant has gotten "out of shape" and had to recover. Spurring is not required in bull riding, but the cowboy accumulates additional points by spurring that is more than just moving one's feet or grabbing for a new hold. Such spur action usually occurs when a rider is atop a spinning bull with the foot to the outside of the spin (away from the inside or "well") doing the spurring.

In scoring the animals in the roughstock competitions, the judges look for high kicking action with the animals' hind legs fully extended (particularly so with horses). The higher the kick the better the score, since high-kicking animals are far more difficult to ride. The strength and force of the animal's bucking efforts are also awarded points. Other considerations include how hard the animal tries to throw the rider; how hard the bull, for instance, kicks, lunges, and hits the ground. Bulls that change direction are scored higher, since spinning animals are harder to ride than ones bucking in a straight line. Likewise, bulls that "belly roll" or "sunfish," exposing their bellies, add another dimension to the up, down, sideways bucking action and are awarded more points.

In the timed events—calf roping, steer wrestling, and team roping—one professional official is usually in the arena, mounted, while the second one stands near the timed event chute from which the steers and calves are released. The mounted official is the flagman. His duties are to pass on the legality of the catch, throw, or tie and to indicate time to the timers by bringing his flag down sharply. If he waves the flag back and forth, he indicates that the contestant is disqualified. The judge posted near the chute is called the score-line judge. He makes sure the stock gets a fair start out of the chute and that the cowboy does not break the barrier—the rope across the roper's and dogger's box—until the stock has had its predetermined head start. All of the PRCA judges are men, although women are not restricted from earning judges' cards. Several roughstock riders interviewed expressed a preference for judges who have been timed event competitors. If the judge is inexperienced, they said, roughstock contestants can sometimes get away with "grandstanding" with a flashy performance on an animal that is not bucking particularly well. They also felt that roughstock competitors would think they could get away with similar antics if women judges were working the rodeos.

Many PRCA contestants pick up extra money judging collegiate and high school rodeos, pocketing $200 for their weekend efforts. Likewise, many professional cowboys who have been injured are hired part time to judge non-professional rodeos. And recuperating cowboys who have been fully trained as PRCA judges often judge PRCA-sanctioned rodeos on a part-time basis before re-entering competitions themselves.

FAIRNESS IN JUDGING

"If you let judges' opinions get to you, you'll have to quit. If you get that attitude where you want to complain all the time, then you're going to have a bad day every day. You've just got to find something positive in whatever you do and just say to hell with whatever the judges think. Besides, if you've got a bad attitude and cuss some judge, he just might be at the next rodeo judging your next ride."
—*PRCA bareback rider Mike Hammer* [2]

As this bareback rider attests, rodeo is not a sport in which athletes complain to judges. But among themselves, cowboys often lament the shortcomings of the professional judging system. One commonly heard complaint is that the top judges tend to associate with the top cowboys, traveling to the same rodeos and staying in the same motels. Familiarity, they argue, predisposes judges to award higher points to their cowboy friends. In rodeo, this tendency is known as awarding "name points." The pro judges, though, are quick to address this "reputation factor," claiming that they simply judge each ride on its own merits. "The one thing you can't be in this business is opinionated," says PRCA judge Tommy Keith.

Pro officials admit that they, too, are concerned about favoritism. Most claim that they try to avoid fraternizing with the competitors, but it's hard to do in a sport where officials, rodeo personnel, and cowboys are constantly thrown together. "Rodeo is still somewhat connected, and we can be part of the crowd," states one Canadian judge. "It is not like in baseball where umpires are often hurt [by the occasional player or fan]. We don't necessarily make new friends, but we keep our old ones."

An American pro rodeo official, George Gibbs, shares similar views. "I take my job real serious, as a man's livelihood is dependent upon my decision. I will talk to the guys, but I will not go out and drink with them or socialize with them too much. I spend a lot of time in my hotel room or I socialize with other judges. Judging can be a rather solitary occupation."

Another common complaint among roughstock riders is the spur out rule. Ideally, each judge must see the cowboy's spurs touch the front of one side of his horse as he leaves the chute, but a judge may miss seeing a poor spur out or he may flag a proper spur out incorrectly. That is one of the reasons why there are two judges, one for each side. It is not uncommon for one judge to mark the ride and the other not when a cowboy marks out on one side but misses on the other. In rodeo there are no instant replays or officials' consultations to change a decision, which is one reason cowboys are reluctant to appeal an unfavorable call.

Cowboys also point out that judges often reward smooth, easy rides with higher scores than the wild, gritty rides that the audience loves. "In the past, the judges in the bareback and saddle bronc events would like horses that changed direction and were more electric to the eye," says saddle bronc rider Clayton Price. "Now the preference among judges is to give the highest marks to the horse that is easy to ride and the one that allows the contestant to make his spur ride. The cowboy wins by the livestock he draws."

Rodeo fans also seem dismayed by the tendency of the professional judges to reward a technically correct ride over the wild ride they equate with the cowboy bronc rider. Pro official Jade Robinson explained his thinking about the topic: "A green or wild horse doesn't have the degree of difficulty, in the sense of power, that you see in a horse that has an even drop and kick style. Even if a wild horse looks hard to ride, it may not be as powerful or difficult. And it says in the rule book that a cowboy has to spur the horse to score points. It's like boxing. Some judges like the guys who lay a lot of leather on. Others like the guys that box, who stand back and jab, picking their shots."

Pro officials find it particularly distasteful to levy fines for rules infractions, but they are responsible for the public image of the sport. Judges may overlook minor infractions, but they generally come down hard on flagrant rule violations. When they do recommend to the PRCA that fines be levied, the charges are reviewed, and fines can be appealed to the director of rodeo administration through a three-step process. According to Lewis Cryer, the commissioner of the PRCA, some $448,000 in fines were levied in one recent year. Many of these fines resulted from the cowboy's failure to notify PROCOM, the computerized rodeo entry system, that he would be "turning out" at a specific rodeo—that is, not showing up.

Contestants can also be fined for deliberately injuring or abusing the animals. One calf roper had a particularly difficult time tying his calf, and in frustration, deliberately kicked the calf's head as he returned to his horse. The cowboy was fined $250 for that incident. At the same rodeo another calf roper was fined a similar amount for letting his horse drag the calf after it had been tied.

In recent years, the pro officials have been particularly concerned with charges of animal abuse, and in the rare instances where a cowboy has violated rules designed for the humane treatment of livestock, officials have been unyielding. Because of pressure from animal activist groups and the possibility of legislation that may further restrict—if not eliminate—the event of calf roping in rodeo, the PRCA began to experiment with a "no jerk down" rule in that event. If the cowboy ropes the calf in a way topples the calf head over heels, he may be fined (usually $100 for a first infraction). Jerking the calf down typically knocks the air out of the animal, making it less likely to kick and therefore easier to tie.

But jerking the calf backward (an action that is seldom, if ever, shown on telecasts of the calf roping event) is viewed as inhumane treatment by some critics of rodeo. They assert that more calves sustain injuries (usually to their legs or necks) in this form of catch. In 1995, California's state legislature considered a proposal by several animal rights groups to jail a contestant for six months upon his second jerk down offense. Although the legislation ultimately failed, California still maintains the strictest laws of any state regarding the calf roping event.

In response to legislation, the PRCA evaluates its rules. As one PRCA official noted, the PRCA has been upgrading its rules on the humane treatment of livestock since the 1940s. It has also requested independent studies that have shown that fewer than .001 percent of rodeo animals are injured in competition.

"The first conquest is cowboy versus stock, when you overcome the fear of the animal. The second is cowboy versus cowboy, when you get over worrying about the other cowboys and your competition. The third conquest is cowboy versus self, when you must learn to stop beating up on yourself. Each of these issues are important at different stages in your career."

—Clayton Hines, PRCA and Canadian saddle bronc rider

3

GROWING UP

COWBOY

hen Ty Murray was two and a half years old, his father put him on his first calf. "My dad would run along beside me, holding onto my belt loop," Murray recalls. "Sometimes I wish he was still running along beside me." A professional rodeo cowboy, Ty Murray currently holds the record for winning the most money in the shortest period of time: his arena income topped $1 million in only his sixth year of professional rodeo competition.

Murray began his career like so many other cowboys—with a dream. "All I can remember ever wanting to do was be a rodeo cowboy," says Murray.

"He didn't need us," his mother recalled after her son had won the third of his many world champion all-around titles in 1992. "He was destined to be here. I knew when he was one and a half and he rode my sewing machine top. He never wanted toys. Everything was connected with rodeo. We were poor, but we did our best to help him out. His dad worked, and I hauled him [to rodeos]. At age six he wanted a little trampoline. By ages seven and eight he traveled and rode with other kids. That's the way we did it with Ty. It was always fun."

Although Murray became an exceptional rodeo athlete, the path he took was the most common path for professional rodeo athletes. And Murray *did* need his parents.

SOCIALIZATION INTO THE SPORT OF RODEO

"We're the original breed. We were here long before all this new stuff came out.
We believe in simple living, the way it was before. It's not really the way you dress,
it's the way you feel. It's a thing of the heart."
—*A 16-year-old cowboy comparing his identity with that of his*
more urbanized schoolmates [1]

Cowboys do not learn their craft quickly. To compete successfully in rodeo takes years of hard work, dedication, and practice. Most cowboys were taught how to rodeo by family members at home on the ranch or learned by participating in one of the many youth-oriented rodeo training programs.

In a 1991 survey of 611 PRCA contestants on the rodeo circuit, more than a third indicated that they had been active in rodeo before high school, and about 80 percent had competed actively as high school students.[2] Three-fifths of the group had competed in a college rodeo program, and one-fourth had participated in at least one specialized rodeo training school. Nearly all of the respondents (91 percent) reported that they had always wanted to be cowboys.

It is a common assumption that rodeo cowboys come from ranching backgrounds. Furthermore, most are thought to follow family members, usually parents, into the sport of rodeo. Material gathered in this survey tends to support these assumptions. Most of these cowboys did come from ranching backgrounds. In fact, over three-fourths said that they had been exposed to some type of farming or ranching in their youth. The remaining fourth, however, had not grown up in ranching families and had little, if any, ranching background. Cowboys involved in the roughstock events—particularly bull riding—were least likely to have come from ranching backgrounds.

When asked if other family members competed in professional rodeo, two-thirds indicated that other family members had once competed or were currently competing in rodeo. This pattern was particularly characteristic of those cowboys who had reached the National Finals Rodeo (NFR), the sport's most significant competition. About 80 percent of the NFR cowboys, compared to 65 percent of the other professional rodeo cowboys surveyed, reported that other family members had competed in the sport of rodeo. This finding indicates that rodeo success is strongly correlated to being raised in a rodeo family. More than half—53 percent—of the parents of NFR qualifiers had competed in rodeo, compared to 39 percent of parents of the non-NFR cowboys. And a higher percentage of siblings and other relatives of the NFR-qualifiers had competed in rodeo (59 percent) compared to the relatives of the non-NFR cowboys (41 percent).

When asked where they had first learned their professional rodeo skills, more than half (56 percent) reported receiving their training at home with the help of family members. But this tradition may be changing. A number of respondents said they had learned their rodeo skills in high school or collegiate-level rodeo programs (14 percent), while others (30 percent) indicated that they had learned their rodeo skills in some other fashion—in specialized rodeo training schools, from their peers, or while serving in the military. It seems apparent that rodeo is no longer entirely dependent upon traditional ranch-raised competitors.

Given that the agrarian lifestyle in America has been on the decline at least since the 1940s, it should be no surprise that a portion of today's rodeo athletes have come to the sport via pathways other than ranching. In all likelihood, that trend will grow even stronger. But will the increasingly urban society produce enough cowboys to keep traditional rodeo alive? Rodeo's success will depend on the socialization of today's youth and the ability of rodeo organizations to grab—and hold—the attention of young people.

SOCIALIZING INFLUENCES

The socialization process begins at birth and continues throughout an individual's life cycle, but the early years—birth to adolescence—are the critical years when basic values are formed. They are also critical years for the socialization of the athlete. The study of socialization into sports is concerned with who gets involved in athletics and why. Research studies indicate that numerous people are involved in the process of socializing young athletes: their parents, other family members, coaches, peers, and the media or popular culture.

Families make the most important contributions to a youngster's life. Having parents or older siblings who have competed in sports is a key determining factor in an adolescent's athletic participation. Ty Murray's family followed this pattern. He had a mother who rode bulls and competed in barrel racing, a father who competed in bull riding and trained race horses, and an uncle, Butch Meyers, who was a world champion steer wrestler. Murray also came from a family with an unusually high level of achievement in rodeo. When Meyers came home in 1980 with the champion's buckle, 11-year-old Ty Murray said, "I can't wait until I get mine."

But Murray's case does little to explain why a third of today's rodeo cowboys come from families with little or no connection to rodeo, and why a fourth come from families with little or no involvement with large animals. Evidence suggests that these cowboys are drawn to the sport as a result of other socializing influences, particularly popular culture—the mystique of the cowboy, the popularity of country western music, and the western lifestyle. That popular culture can generate interest in rodeo became evident with the surge in PRCA membership that occurred within a few years of the release of the popular movie *Urban Cowboy* in 1980. The cowboys themselves often marveled at how many people, such as Bobby Delvecchio of the Bronx, had became interested in bull riding as a result of that film. A similar resurgence in rodeo's popularity has been gaining momentum throughout the 1990s, a time when Hollywood produced several popular westerns, such as *Lonesome Dove*, *My Heroes Have Always Been Cowboys*, and *8 Seconds*. Other contributing influences include the expanding coverage of rodeo on cable networks, the frequency of rodeo as a theme in country music, and the shifts in the fashion industry toward western attire.

Undoubtedly, many of today's rodeo athletes began their careers through a fascination with cowboys in general and rodeo cowboys in particular. Ben Holm, a 2-year-old rodeo spectator at the Brawley (California) Cattle Call Rodeo, exemplifies this pattern. Ben lives in the upscale Southern California community of La Jolla. According to his mother, Diana Holm, Ben insisted she drive him the 100 miles to the rodeo so he could watch the bull riding. "He watches rodeo we tape on TV," says his mother. "He's been to six rodeos. I want to raise him the All-American way."

Like a veteran cowboy—or at least a privileged guest—Ben Holm fraternizes with the cowboys behind the bucking chutes. When asked about his favorite bulls, Ben, decked out in cowboy boots, jeans, western shirt, and cowboy hat, tells the assembled bull riders, "I like Tick Tock, Glamour Boy, and First Blood the best!" Ben's knowledge of the livestock, some of the most notable bulls in rodeo, impresses the cowboys. His mother beams with pride, and her enthusiasm goes beyond merely indulging Ben's desire to see rodeos. She also allows him to ride goats—exactly the type of skill-building exercise that Murray and other cowboys from traditional rodeo families engaged in as youngsters.

Whether support comes from traditional ranching families or from the heart of urban America, rodeo provides a sense of value and self-worth to many youngsters. Ben's mother's attitude demonstrates the commonly held belief that rodeo somehow helps to impart core values in its participants. But what counterbalances this positive effect, in the minds of many parents, is the inherent danger of the sport. People who have not been affiliated with rodeo are not likely to involve their kids in a sport that involves great risk, particularly when that risk promises little financial reward for most of its athletes.

But for young people touched by rodeo, the will to overcome its dangers can be strong. It is nearly always true that early success in sports is an indication of future athletic accomplishment, and so it is in rodeo. Most of the top cowboys in professional rodeo, whether they came from South Dakota or south Los Angeles, placed in their first competition. The thrill of that first win carries them through much of the learning process and motivates them to continue in the sport. A bad first experience, on the other hand, often causes a youngster to give up on rodeo in the beginning.

Not all rodeo cowboys receive enthusiastic family support, even if their parents once competed. Some parents actively discourage their children's participation. Others seem to compete with their offspring, refusing to share important skills and knowledge. One 23-year-old bareback rider, Rick Bradley, talks about how his father "barely showed [him] the ropes" when he first started practicing rodeo. Although his father had competed professionally, he refused to come to local rodeos to watch his son compete during the young man's rookie season in the PRCA. His mother, who was separated from her husband, also avoided attending her son's rodeos, with the exception of a few competitions that were less than half an hour from her home.

Often rodeo cowboys wish to discourage their offspring from a career that they experienced as difficult, low-paying, and dangerous. Parents who were badly injured, or whose rodeo careers quickly fizzled, fear that their children will make the same mistakes they made. About 11 percent of cowboys surveyed indicated that they would discourage their children from becoming rodeo cowboys. An additional 23 percent said that they were unsure of whether they would want their children to become cowboys. Still, about two-thirds of the rodeo cowboys—particularly those with notable careers—said they would encourage their children to take up the sport.

Often, top cowboys acknowledge their parents as key contributors to their overall success. Roy Cooper, the eight-time world champion calf roper, steer roper, and all-around champ, says that his father sacrificed his rodeo career in order to provide support for his kids. In his book *Why We Win*, Cooper wrote, "I figure my dad probably gave up his rodeo career so that my brother and sister and I could learn to rope. My wanting to rope is probably one of the good things that has happened for my dad."[3]

The five-time world champion bareback rider Bruce Ford has taught his three children to compete in rodeo and is nearly as busy today hauling his children to rodeos as he once was traveling to rodeos himself. Ford said that he once had a conversation with eight-time world champion bull rider Don Gay. Both agreed that they would not fall victim to "Little League Syndrome," the desire to push their kids to excel in a sport that they themselves enjoyed. Both cowboys said that their huge successes in rodeo gave them a sense of fulfillment and that if their kids wanted to go in other directions, they would support those decisions.

FROM MUTTON BUSTER TO BRONC BUSTER

For some youngsters, the starting point in rodeo is when they enter the "mutton bustin'" competition. The kids are given head gear and placed on a sheep inside a miniature bucking chute. When the chute gate is opened, the kids hold on to the "woolly" as long as they can. In some instances the youthful competitors are sons and daughters of rodeo contestants and are decked out in matching attire, even wearing matching miniature contestant numbers on the backs of their cowboy shirts.

Not all youngsters are eager to compete in these events, though the clowns and rodeo announcers try to make the best of touchy situations. In one mutton bustin' contest, a 3-year-old was plucked from his sheep by a rodeo clown at the end of the contest. An announcer asked the boy if he wanted to ride again. The kid shook his head vigorously and told his father, "You do it, daddy!" Other kids are even less enthusiastic about the sport. While most enjoy their first moment in the limelight, some walk away from the experience in tears. But for some kids, that first trip on a sheep is the beginning of a rodeo career.

In a sense, professional rodeo has its own farm system for competitors. Youth programs include National Little Britches Rodeo, Junior Rodeo, as well as high school and intercollegiate rodeo associations. Serious competition for youths begins as early as age eight, when they are old enough to join the National Little Britches Rodeo Association (NLBRA). Formed in 1952 by a small group of dedicated people, Little Britches has grown to nearly 5,000 members participating in 150 rodeos throughout North America. Youngsters can stay with Little Britches until age eighteen, competing as they get older in standard rodeo events such as bareback, saddle bronc, and bull riding, calf roping, steer wrestling, and team roping. Nonstandard events include girls' goat tying, flag racing, dally ribbon roping, and a trail riding course. The organization holds its own national finals each summer, for the past few seasons in Colorado Springs, Colorado.

Junior Rodeo, a comparable organization, is divided into three age groups: five to twelve, thirteen to fifteen, and sixteen to eighteen. At the junior level, boys and girls compete in approximately the same number of events. However, girls almost invariably compete in timed events whereas boys are also offered the opportunity to ride bucking horses, bucking steers, and in the older age groups, bucking bulls. As the youngsters progress through high school and college rodeo, girl's and women's events continue to be restricted. Although there are opportunities for women at the professional level to compete in the roughstock events, realistically only barrel racing offers a viable financial career for rodeo cowgirls.

Ty Murray, for example, progressed through the ranks of junior, high school, and college rodeo before going on to a career as a top professional. Similarly, his girlfriend, Julie Adair, was a women's collegiate all-around champion. But the young woman, now in her twenties, notes that her professional career options in the PRCA are limited to barrel racing or being a corporate spokesperson for rodeo events.

For many of the cowboys, the progression from junior rodeo to high school rodeo trains them in full-time competition. "I came up through the junior rodeos — the American Junior Rodeo Association and the New Mexico Junior Rodeo Association — and high school rodeo," recalls Roy Cooper. "When I was eleven, my mother probably hauled me to 40 or 50 rodeos. When I was twelve, I went to something like 60 rodeos, and I only missed four calves. When I was seventeen years old, I went to 140 rodeos. I actually nodded my head 140 times."[4]

HIGH SCHOOL RODEO

The National High School Rodeo Association (NHSRA) offers a competitive environment for youth ages fourteen to eighteen. Headquartered in Denver, the organization represents about 8,000 youth across the United States and Canada. Each July, some 1,300 NHSRA cowboys and cowgirls vie for national titles at the NHSRA-sponsored High School Finals Rodeo, first held in 1949. The top four contestants from each state's finals qualify to participate. In one recent year, contestants at the High School Finals represented thirty-seven states and two Canadian provinces. Although teenagers from as far away as Hawaii and Florida compete, the majority hail from western and midwestern states. High school rodeo is most popular in Texas and Oklahoma, two states that contribute many contestants to rodeo at all levels. Besides sponsoring the national High School Finals Rodeo, the NHSRA now awards over $114,000 each year in college scholarships. About sixty NHSRA scholarships of $500 each are awarded to graduating high school seniors to help defray college expenses. Corporate sponsors award additional scholarships to top high school competitors.

In most cases, the rodeo cowboys who will go on to collegiate and professional success get acquainted at the week-long high school state finals. "High school finals were fun because people stayed in tents and camped out," recalls PRCA bull rider Sean McRoberts of Lathrop, California. "I remember chasing each other with water balloons. It was like a week of summer camp for all the high school cowboys. My closest friends and traveling partners on the PRCA circuit are those guys I met while competing in high school rodeo."

Some PRCA cowboys express concern about the caliber of the current high school contestants. "The quality of high school rodeo has gone way down," says one top bareback rider. "Several young bareback riders were injured recently because they just weren't ready to rodeo," notes another.

Youth rodeo takes its toll on its practitioners. Bareback riders often injure their tailbones, which then require surgical fusion. Hyper-extended elbows caused by repeated stress are another common injury. Saddle bronc riders often require surgical repair of torn knee ligaments, and bull riders suffer injuries of all kinds. For the youthful competitor, high school injuries often end promising careers in rodeo. Gary Leffew, a professional bull rider who operates a school for bull riders, voices a common concern: cowboys are starting too soon, before their bodies have fully developed and are able to withstand the repeated strain of roughstock competition. But the nature of the sport makes it almost mandatory that cowboys begin rodeoing no later than their teenage years.

Besides dealing with injuries, young competitors must often cope with the inadequacy or lack of training facilities and on-going instruction. Unlike colleges, high schools rarely have on-campus training programs, a factor that often discourages kids and their families. Many youngsters choose to drop rodeo in favor of mainstream high school sports.

In high school, an economic differentiation develops between those who compete in the roughstock events and those who compete in timed events.

In the initial stage of youth competition, almost any horse or pony can carry the rider to first place. The competitive demands of the timed events, however, call for better and better horses, so that a winning junior rider must own a superior horse by the time he or she reaches high school. Only fit, well-trained quarter horses are adequate, and they can cost anywhere from $1,000 to $25,000. The family must also own horse-keeping facilities, stock trailers, vehicles for hauling, and often camper rigs to support their child's rodeo interests. For these reasons, timed event competitors are more likely to come from families with substantial economic resources than roughstock competitors.

For many cowboys, high school marks the end of their participation in rodeo competition. At this juncture, cowboys who wish to go on have two choices. Some can find work and continue to rodeo at an amateur level, and perhaps even go on to professional careers in rodeo. Others, particularly those that excelled in high school, go on to compete in college rodeo programs. Often it is the rodeo scholarships earned at the junior level that make it possible for them to attend college. Accomplished high school riders are aggressively recruited by rodeo coaches. They may be granted scholarships at any of the 120 college rodeo programs offered throughout the country.

INTERCOLLEGIATE RODEO

Many of today's rodeo cowboys honed their skills in college rodeo—a decided difference between cowboys of today and those who rodeoed only a few decades ago. Results of our study of 611 PRCA contestants indicated that three-quarters of them attended or graduated from two- or four-year colleges. Most majored in agriculture or animal sciences, followed by managerial, professional, and business fields. Although the roughstock contestants were less likely to have graduated from college than the timed event contestants, the majority of top cowboys had attended college.

Sul Ross State University in Alpine, Texas, hosted the very first college rodeo in November 1948. The first College National Finals Rodeo (CNFR) took place a year later at the Cow Palace in San Francisco. Although women began competing in college rodeo in 1951, it was not until 1961 that the women's efforts were counted toward collegiate team titles. Today, more than 300 college competitors from around the country meet each June to compete in the College National Finals Rodeo. Held since 1974 on the Montana State University campus in Bozeman, Montana, this premiere college rodeo event is sanctioned by the National Intercollegiate Rodeo Association (NIRA). Each year more than 30,000 people attend the four-day competition. Collegiate contestants compete for national titles as well as scholarships.

Through grants and scholarships, the NIRA has brought a college education within the reach of students who might otherwise find it beyond their family's means. The U.S. Tobacco Company awards $1,500 to each CNFR event champion, $800 to second-place winners, and $400 to third-place winners. Men's and women's all-around champions receive $2,500.

To be an NIRA member, students must take at least twelve credit hours each semester and maintain at least a 2.0 grade point average. The collegiate contestants accumulate points during the season at the sanctioned rodeos within one of eleven regions. These points determine the ranking of the competitors in each event as well as the leading teams of nine contestants (six men and three women) in each region. Men compete in the roughstock events of bareback, saddle bronc, and bull riding and the timed events of calf roping and steer wrestling. Women's events include breakaway calf roping, barrel racing, pole bending, and goat tying. Team roping is open to both genders. As of 1990, the top two Canadian collegiate performers in each event were also invited to participate in the CNFR.

Collegiate contestants who have gone on to compete in the PRCA tend to speak fondly of their college rodeo experiences. For many, college rodeo is viewed as excellent preparation for a professional career. "College rodeo is good in that it helps you get over your nervousness before your event," states 1995 Sierra circuit saddle bronc champion Clayton Price of Norco, California, who attended the college rodeo program at Pierce College near Los Angeles. "In college, coaches want guys entered in several events so they don't have time to worry about any one particular event. It gets you relaxed for your specialized event. In other sports, there is a coach or a trainer looking over you at all times. But in most college rodeo programs, it is not that sophisticated. What I learned in the program was how to set goals and try to achieve them." Bareback rider Casey Vollin of Salinas, California, participated in the rodeo program at nearby Hartnell College. He says: "College rodeo gets you used to all of the competition and the hustle and bustle. You learn how to handle it better because you've been exposed to it earlier."

Unlike other collegiate athletes, rodeo cowboys can and often do compete in professional associations while maintaining scholarships and collegiate eligibility. Furthermore, eligibility extends to six years beyond high school graduation, with a four-year period of competition allowed within that time frame. Three of those years may be at a junior college, where many collegiate rodeo programs are based. Collegiate competitions are nearly as rigorous as professional events, and collegiate cowboys with professional aspirations can also enter selected PRCA-sanctioned rodeos—those that accept contestants who are completing their permit card or have received their card and are competing as rookies in their first year of PRCA competition.

Ty Murray followed this route. In 1989, Murray won *both* the collegiate rodeo all-around championship and PRCA all-around world championship, competing for Odessa College in Texas. The previous season, Murray had been the PRCA-Resistol overall and bareback riding rookie of the year while also competing in college. But Murray is the only cowboy to win collegiate and PRCA national titles in the same season. "I'm glad I went to college," Ty Murray says. "It's a great stepping stone. Coming straight out of high school and going straight into the pros is a big step."[5] Ty Murray's roommate in college was Jim Sharp, who won the 1986 NIRA bull riding championship while attending Odessa College. Sharp would go on to become a two-time PRCA world champion bull rider.

Most collegiate rodeo programs involve more than just training and practice. College credits are given for courses that focus on the history of rodeo, rules, judging, and rodeo production and management. West Hills College in Coalinga, California, has an exemplary rodeo program. With three on-campus arenas, it attracts some seventy-five student athletes from across the United States and Canada. Begun in 1982, the program became so successful that the college decided to drop its football program in 1990 and add additional funding to the rodeo program. At one point, two full-time rodeo coaches—one skilled in the timed events and one in the roughstock events—trained the students.

"We would practice three or four hours a day," recalls Casey Minton, a graduate of the West Hills rodeo program. "We each would rope twelve calves a day. Guys that just practice on their own at home on the ranch typically do not put in that much practice. Best thing I can say about college was leaving home. At home it was your own responsibility to train. When you are at college, it gives you the right frame of mind. At home there are other influences." In just his second year out of college, Minton won PRCA's prestigious Linderman Award in 1993. The annual award is named for Bill Linderman, a world champion in both timed events and riding events, who died in a 1965 plane crash. It honors the cowboy considered rodeo's best all-around hand. To qualify for the award, a contestant must win at least $1,000 in each of three events, including a roughstock event and a timed event.

Besides the classroom content, students in college rodeo programs are responsible for practicing eight hours a week. The roughstock animals are frequently loaned by local stock contractors who want to try out their new bucking stock. Cowboys at West Hills College, for instance, "test drive" about fifty horses and fifty bulls each year. Those that buck are integrated into the stock contractor's high school, college, and professional rodeo strings.

California stock contractor Cotton Rosser, an earlier graduate of a four-year college rodeo program at California Polytechnic State University, San Luis Obispo, assists with several different West Coast rodeo programs. "I wouldn't have gone to college without rodeo," claims Rosser, who also was a top competitor in the very first College National Finals Rodeo in 1949. "Growing up in Long Beach, I didn't have the ranching background to help pay for school. Now my involvement with college rodeos is a way of giving it back. I tell the coaches to buy whatever stock they need and want, and I'll pay for them."

Once referred to as the Notre Dame of Rodeo, the multifaceted program at Cal Poly, San Luis Obispo is fairly typical of rodeo programs that have developed across the country. Besides offering training and practice in the various events, a class in rodeo production requires students to raise $50,000 each year by contacting local sponsors and holding fundraisers to help defer the costs of the program. They also stage the semiannual on-campus rodeo.

According to the program's rodeo coach, PRCA calf roper Clay Robinson, 80 percent of the rodeo athletes graduate from college, compared to only 50 percent of those involved in other athletic programs on campus. "Our program promotes academics," notes Robinson, when interviewed in 1991. "The positive thing about rodeo is it encourages them to be good students. Fifteen of this year's group of students are going on to graduate school."

RODEO TRAINING SCHOOLS

It's a gray, overcast morning at the Korkow Ranch about twenty miles outside Pierre, South Dakota. For days it has rained, and as the cowboys gather at the arena to begin the morning's lessons in roughstock riding, they look up at the sky, hoping for a break in the dreary, monotonous weather.

There are seventy-three student riders, ranging in age from preteens to early thirties. Most are from the Dakotas, though some have traveled from as far away as Texas and California. Many are dressed in clean, new outfits—shiny leather boots, new hats, pressed jeans and shirts. But the older, more experienced riders wear worn-out jeans, tattered cotton flannel shirts.

They are divided into groups according to their interests: bull riders, bareback riders, and saddle bronc riders. The bull riders head for a smaller, round arena where sand is being brought it to fill the huge puddles that have formed overnight. The bronc riders wait on a hill for their turn to ride later in the morning. World champion bareback rider Wayne Herman, a native of North

Dakota, hops onto a flat-bed truck with the bareback riders. His group heads for the large rectangular arena.

The bareback arena is a mud bog, but that doesn't seem to bother Herman. "It slows the horses down some and makes for softer landings," he says. Mercifully, the sun comes out, and the riders' spirits seem to rise.

On the first day of the school, the instructors meet with the students and spend several hours going over equipment. The saddle bronc riders, in particular, receive a lot of attention. "Even the more experienced riders have [their equipment] all wrong," says bronc riding instructor and National Finals Rodeo qualifier Tom Miller.

Pink-cheeked and fair-skinned, sixteen-year-old Judd Schomp has a face that has never been nicked by a razor. He's wearing a bright western shirt, clean white Resistol hat, and shiny-bright rodeo chaps. Climbing onto a sorrel bronc in chute number five, Schomp eyes the foot-deep mire of the saddle bronc riding arena. He visualizes a perfect ride that ends in a clean dismount onto a waiting pickup horse.

With the confidence of a world champ, the young cowboy from Chamberlain, South Dakota, nods for the gate. Seconds later, he's taking a full-body mud bath. The kid picks himself up, disgustedly wipes a handful of mud off his ruined wardrobe, then hustles over to Miller. "You spurred the horse out well and held a good position for the first few jumps. You just got behind the saddle," Miller tells him. Schomp is reminded that only the other day, he was still having trouble getting his ride underway.

"It's not a money-making project," says Jim Korkow, a second-generation stock contractor who puts on the school each year. For Korkow, the rodeo school is an investment in the future. For the past decade, the Korkow family has graduated a few dozen aspiring cowboys like Judd Schomp into the ranks of junior and amateur rodeo. Their efforts assure that there will be a steady crop of new riders at the dozen or so junior, college, and amateur competitions the Korkows haul livestock to each year.

Out at the bull riding arena, two South Dakota men, John Scarrot and Clint Filipek, are in the arena, practicing the skills of rodeo bullfighting. As the riders come crashing out of the chutes, Scarrot and Filipek rush in to distract the bulls, throwing body fakes like veteran football running backs. The only two student bullfighters at the school, they get lots of practice, running and dodging the bulls as the twenty-five or so fledgling bull riders take ride after ride.

"I'm really enjoying it," says Scarrot. "Allen [Olson, the bull fighting instructor] said the other day that I have no fear." Twenty-eight years old, the *former high school football player is beginning his career at an age when many bullfighters are nearing retirement. Later, a bull hooked Scarrott, smashed into him, and trampled him in the mud. Scarrott got back up and fought on. "It didn't humble me," he says, "but it gave me more respect for the bulls."*

When the bull riding concludes on Sunday, Scarrott is sweaty, sore, and just plain exhausted. But his enthusiasm hasn't flagged. "I want to play a part in rodeo. I think this is what I can do best—be there to protect the cowboys," he says. After the school, the instructors are so impressed with his athletic ability and his attitude that they talk to Korkow about him. Korkow offers the aspiring bullfighter a chance to work at some amateur rodeos later in the season.

Clint Filipek, the other bullfighter, also receives an offer for work. And at the end of the day, Filipek, too, gets hit by a bull. But like Scarrott, he remains stoically enthusiastic. "Getting hurt, that's just part of rodeo," he says as he is taken to the hospital with a separated shoulder.

In addition to learning rodeo skills at home or in junior to college-level rodeo programs, more than one-third of the PRCA cowboys surveyed indicated they had enrolled, at one time or another, in one or more specialized training schools. Numerous rodeo training schools are held throughout the year across North America, often organized by world champions or National Finals Rodeo qualifiers. These schools, one to four days long, cover, in the words of one saddle bronc rider, "the basics." Typically, the student riders receive instruction in properly fitting their equipment, strength and flexibility training, and mental preparation before they actually practice the specialized skills of their events. Timed event competitors also work on training their horses, a critical skill.

Roughstock training courses often feature training exercises such as riding mechanical "bucking bulls" like the one shown in the film *Urban Cowboy* and those found at bars and nightclubs throughout the urban West. Lacking one of these costly machines ($3,000–$6,000), the riders may practice on 55-gallon drums suspended in the air with ropes, as seen in the film *My Heroes Have Always Been Cowboys*. When the ropes are pulled, the drums respond much like bucking animals. One well-regarded bull riding instructor, Gary Leffew, instructs riders in English equitation—jumping and posting—activities that he contends require the balance skills cowboys will need to successfully ride a bucking bull or bronc.

Although champions often attract students to their schools, teaching success has more to do with the instructor's ability to communicate and to motivate students than with his achievement in professional rodeo. Champions Leffew, Bruce Ford, Jim Shoulders, and Roy Cooper have all enjoyed long and successful side careers as instructors, not only because of their reputations as top cowboys but also their renown as able teachers. Ford, who has conducted riding schools for more than fifteen years, often found himself competing at the National Finals Rodeo against his former students. "I guess I am teaching them too well," Ford said during one National Finals in which no fewer than seven of his competitors were former students at his school.

It is not unusual for students to attend a rodeo school each year as they progress through the ranks of junior rodeo, and some students attend several schools over the course of a season. Often, they are looking for the proper "fit"—a school where the method of instruction and the student's personality complement each other. "The roughstock riding schools that are any good are ones where the teacher lets your style develop," notes saddle bronc rider Clayton Price. "[A skilled teacher] gets you to refine the basics, gain a positive outlook, and encourages you to become goal-oriented. Over the years, I've been to three such schools. The best part of the schools for me was working on my attitude."

Ability levels vary greatly among the participants at most rodeo schools. Many kids, and even adults, simply want to give rodeo a try, perhaps with the goal of participating in rodeo as a hobby or simply as a one-time thrill like bungee jumping. Others come to the schools with experience and the desire to improve their skills. Even seasoned veterans, perhaps in a competitive slump, attend the schools to be critiqued and get encouragement before returning to competition. Some young students don't even know how to saddle a horse, much less ride a bronc. But, in the words of one teacher, "The easiest guy to teach is the one who is 'off the street.' The ones that have won some money are already influenced into a particular riding style, and they are a little harder to get through to."

Rodeo schools are the biggest training ground for the modern rodeo cowboy. Several timed event champions began working with other cowboys back in the 1940s, and all-around champion Jim Shoulders pioneered the roughstock riding schools in the early 1960s. Besides teaching basic skills, today's schools usually focus on positive mental attitudes—in other words, sports psychology. Bull rider Gary Leffew of Santa Maria, California, is often credited with pioneering the concept of mental conditioning. His success as a bull rider in the sixties and early seventies was credited with revolutionizing the training methods of rodeo athletes. His methods are partly responsible for the new level of professionalism among top athletes in the sport today. "You need to maintain a tough attitude," says Leffew. "There is a moment of truth when riding bulls. You make up your mind to be great. You conquer your fear by having confidence in what you can do. This mental toughness you've got to develop, and that comes from knowing the limitations of the bull. After all, there are only so many moves the bull can make. Nothing feels better than when you ride that unrideable bull."

One reason for the success of specialized rodeo training schools is the changing demographics of the American public. Rodeo cowboys of the 1920s through the 1950s usually learned their skills on ranches and farms. Bucking animals were plentiful, and the young cowboys grew up breaking and training range livestock. During and after World War II, however, the United States shifted from a rural, agricultural economy to an industrialized economy. With fewer ranches and fewer ranching families came fewer opportunities for youth to learn basic ranching skills such as roping and riding. Furthermore, changes in horse breeding practices made bucking horses less common. As breeders sought to make gentler horses suitable for the emerging postwar recreational riding market, aspiring cowboys had a harder time finding practice broncs.

Rodeo schools emerged, in part, to fill this void. In the timed events, rodeo schools offered intense training sessions and expert instructors who could help the students to avoid the bad habits they often learned from ranch roping or riding. In the roughstock events, rodeo schools offered the basic tools needed to learn the sport: bucking animals.

World champion bull rider Don Gay of Mesquite, Texas, a riding instructor himself, commented on the importance of bull riding schools, but his words apply to all rodeo instruction: "After being exposed to the fundamentals at a riding school, of course, the student will not instantly be an accomplished bull rider. He merely has the tools provided him to begin mastering those fundamentals. At least he will not have to listen to the 'has beens' or 'never was' that hang around the bull riding jackpots giving out advice."

"The way I see it, looking back now, a guy needs to take care of his business, remember and keep your goals—always try to achieve them, and don't ever forget them—and stay away from the parties as much as you can. It's not for the parties or the girls."

—World champion bareback rider Clint Corey [1]

4

GOING DOWN

THE ROAD

Cowboys' dreams of competing in professional rodeo, qualifying for the National Finals, and winning the gold buckles that proclaim them world champions usually begin when they are very young. Some covet that gold buckle even before they are sent off for their first day of grade school. But only a few ever realize their dreams. There are about 5,700 full-fledged competitors in the Professional Rodeo Cowboys Association (PRCA), rodeo's major league. Only 120 of them qualify for the National Finals Rodeo, the PRCA's championship-determining event held each December in Las Vegas. Of those 120 contestants—15 from each event—7 are awarded world titles at the conclusion of the competition. (Only one women's championship is awarded at the NFR, to the top-ranked barrel racer in the Women's Professional Rodeo Association.)

As in any professional sport, the climb to the top in rodeo depends on talent, training, and raw desire. Luck plays a role, and the dangers in rodeo games makes injuries inevitable. As Jim Shoulders, a rodeo cowboy whose competitive career began in the 1940s and stretched over three decades, once commented, "It's not a question of if you'll get injured, just when and how badly." Shoulders was the perfect example of what it takes to be a contender and a champion. The son of a Tulsa, Oklahoma, mechanic, Shoulders came to rodeo at age sixteen and won the bull riding event at the first competition he entered. He was a "natural," a man gifted with enough athletic ability to make him a standout in any sport he tried. He was a fierce competitor, dedicated to improving his skills, and he was tough. He was known to ride despite injuries—broken bones, torn muscles, and damaged ligaments—that would have sidelined less determined cowboys. Shoulders won sixteen world titles in his career, a record that still stands in the Professional Rodeo Cowboys Association.

BECOMING A PRCA RODEO COMPETITOR

Riders can make the long climb to the top of professional rodeo on several different paths. Generally, the most successful riders in collegiate rodeos go on to compete in the PRCA. These contestants make up the largest group of PRCA cowboys. Another large component of PRCA contestants emerges from the ranks of amateur rodeo. They graduate either from state amateur associations or from informal "jackpot" competitions in which groups of competitors effectively wager against one another, awarding the jackpot to the winning rider.

Some contestants come to PRCA competition after a few years in another professional rodeo association. Canada, a country whose rodeo tradition roughly matches that of the United States, has its own national rodeo association, the Canadian Professional Rodeo Association (CPRA). Cowboys who compete in this association participate in a system that is in most ways identical to the PRCA's. In fact, points earned in CPRA rodeos count toward PRCA championships if the contestant is a paid member of both associations. Because Canadian riders compete against their PRCA counterparts, their competitive experience is as rigorous and challenging as that of any cowboy in the United States. Canadians also have the added benefit of competing for national titles within the CPRA.

A few competitors cross over to PRCA competition from a rival association, the International Professional Rodeo Association (IPRA), headquartered in

Oklahoma City. Founded in 1961, the IPRA began as a splinter association founded by competitors disgruntled with the PRCA. Today, the IPRA sanctions more than 500 rodeos per year and has a membership of approximately 6,000. Despite its name, the IPRA is primarily a regional association that has been successful in developing rodeos in the southern and eastern United States (areas of lesser importance to the PRCA, which dominates rodeo throughout the West) and in maintaining a large following in Oklahoma. Although the IPRA also names world champions each year, the association does not enjoy the prestige of its larger and more established rival, the PRCA.

No matter which pathway a cowboy takes toward becoming a PRCA contestant, the process of becoming a member of the organization is the same. Cowboys must prove that they are worthy of full-fledged membership through the permit system. In order to obtain a permit to compete at selected PRCA rodeos, a cowboy must be eighteen years old and pay a set fee ($185 in 1995). Once he obtains a permit, he tries to win a set amount of money—$1,000 in 1995—to "fill his permit," which qualifies him to become a full-fledged member. Some cowboys manage to fill their permits after only a few rodeos, but others may take years to win the required amount of money. In most cases, the riders working to complete their permits compete at rodeos close to their homes to reduce expenses.

Once they have filled their permits, cowboys become full-fledged PRCA members. The primary benefit of full membership is the privilege of competing at any PRCA-sanctioned rodeo. (Because the most lucrative rodeos frequently attract a thousand or more contestants, permit riders are generally not allowed to compete at these events.) Cowboys must then decide whether to continue competing close to home or to head out on the road to the major events. Ambition and finances are the primary decision-making factors.

The PRCA regular season begins in early November and runs a full year, nonstop. Some people talk about "the rodeo circuit," but the term is misleading. Cowboys don't travel an established circuit; they choose from many rodeos. In a given week, there may be anywhere from two or three rodeos to forty. Some cowboys travel only to rodeos close to home. But those who hope to win a world title or at least to qualify for the National Finals travel all across the country to as many of the big competitions as possible. In a typical season, it is not unusual for them to travel more than 100,000 miles.

Of the roughly 800 rodeos sanctioned by the PRCA each year, about 25 offer purses in excess of $100,000. Since the goal of serious rodeo competitors is to make as much money as possible in a single season, these cowboys tend to enter the rodeos with the largest purses. But not always. Sometimes a cowboy has a better chance of picking up a check at a small, less competitive affair. Knowing when to enter small rodeos and when to take a chance at a more lucrative but also more competitive major rodeo is one of the keys to managing a professional rodeo career.

THE ROOKIE SEASON

For the rookie cowboy, figuring out which rodeos to enter is perhaps the biggest challenge of the rodeo season. "I had it made in my rookie year," said Jim Sharp, a bull rider who holds the record for most money won in a rookie season (1986). "I didn't have any pressure because I was going with Tuff Hedeman, Lane Frost, and Cody Lambert. Tuff did all the entering and all I had to do was show up and ride. If you can take the pressure off that first year, you'll have a good one."[2] Buddying up with experienced cowboys is a common solution to first-year problems. Benefits include learning how to "take care of business"—managing travel and expenses—and psychological support.

In the roughstock events the buddy system also means access to reliable "intelligence"—insiders' information about the abilities and patterns of the bucking stock. Veteran cowboys, like other athletes, gather as much information as they can about their opponents—the animals. In rodeo, collecting this information is known as "keeping a book," but in other sports it's more commonly referred to as scouting. Some cowboys actually maintain diaries or even extensive video tapes on the performance of certain animals, but all of them share information about the abilities and quirks of the livestock. Cowboys talk about stock by number rather than by name, since the name often changes when the animal is sold to another stock contractor and it can also vary from rodeo to rodeo. The rookie gains a competitive edge if he travels with a partner who possesses this valuable livestock knowledge.

One of the biggest mistakes rookie riders make is buddying up with other rookies. "Younger guys get caught up in the contagion of winning or rodeoing and so they enter everything they can and frequently get too spread out," says one PRCA veteran. A better strategy, he says, is "mapping out what rodeos to go to and figuring out expenses. They are trying to go to the least amount of rodeos and make the most money. Guys only have to go to fifty rodeos to be competitive."

As in any other sport, first-year competitors can expect to be the brunt of the veterans' jokes and pranks. In this way they are initiated into the competitive society. One common prank involves the large "war bags" (or gear bags) that the cowboys use to carry their equipment. On occasion, just before a rodeo, a rookie cowboy will reach into his bag and find that along with his chaps, spurs, and athletic tape there is — Surprise! A snake. Since most cow-boys have a basic fear of snakes from growing up in rattlesnake country, the reaction is usually explosive.

At the San Francisco (Cow Palace) Grand National Rodeo, saddle bronc rider Jeff Shearer discovered just such a snake in his gear bag. It had been placed there by a ranch hand back home. When he realized that it was only a common garter snake, Shearer decided to have a little fun himself. As the lights dimmed during the singing of the "Star-Spangled Banner," Shearer tossed what appeared to be the snake into the air above the assembled cow-boys. They scurried away from the get-ready area, tripping over one another and their equipment in the tight quarters. When the lights came back up, they looked a bit sheepish. Shearer's snake was only several pieces of rawhide string. Undoubtedly, the snake had already found its way into another rookie's gear bag.

Practical jokes are standard fare during the long, dull trips across the coun-try. Another favorite is to fill a rookie's gear bag with lettuce and other "ripe" produce harvested from a trash bin behind a grocery store. Among timed event cowboys, a classic prank is to send a rookie to a fast-food restaurant for take-out, knowing that the only transportation available is his horse. Dealing amicably with such pranks helps to ease a rookie's acceptance into the pro-fessional rodeo fraternity. Humor is a common way of relieving tension and a distraction from the inherent dangers of the sport.

Like athletes in other sports, many rodeo cowboys are superstitious. For good luck, a cowboy should not place his hat on a bed, eat peanuts, wear yel-low, or quit roping practice on a miss. "It's just a mind game," scoffs saddle bronc world champion Billy Etbauer. Still, he heeds the superstition about the hat on the bed. "I used to get my butt chewed out for putting my hat on the bed," he says, though he can't explain why it is associated with bad luck. "I just put it anywhere but the bed."[3]

Another cowboy tells of driving alone on a remote rural highway when he saw a black cat race across the road. He stopped. "I waited forty-five minutes before another car came along, passed me by, and drove over the spot where the cat had crossed, before I continued on my way."

Many cowboys have rituals they follow each day of competition, such as how they pack and unpack their gear bags, how they put on their spurs and bootstraps, or which shirts they wear. Others, however, consciously avoid such rituals. "When I started rodeoing professionally, I didn't want to have any rituals," says Richard Bucher, a saddle bronc rider from Woodland Hills, Cali-fornia. "I didn't want anything to control me. I'd see a shirt and start to take it out, realizing I had done well in that shirt, and I'd say, 'No.' I'd put it away, not wanting it to haunt me."

THE COWBOY READYING AREA

It is 6:45 P.M., fifteen minutes before the start of the Reno Rodeo. The ready-ing area behind the chutes, where the cowboys gather, is guarded by rodeo committee members who screen those trying to gain access. Already it's filling up with rodeo contestants. Most sip coffee to stay warm in the unusually brisk evening in late June. Some jump up and down to keep their muscles from tight-ening up.

The horses for the first event, bareback riding, are being moved from the hold-ing pens down the lane leading into the bucking chutes. Several of the bareback riders grab their rigging as the horses are secured into the individual chutes. Meanwhile, the saddle bronc and bull riders, whose events will follow later in the evening, busy themselves with chatting, attending to their equipment, or exercising, oblivious to the action taking place in the chutes a few feet away.

The three Etbauer brothers, a triple threat in saddle bronc competition and perennial NFR-qualifiers, arrive dragging their saddles and gear bags be-hind them. They busy themselves finding out about their evening's draw and how these horses have done in previous nights' outings. Other cowboys huddle around them, passing a Copenhagen snuff can among themselves. Bareback rider Mark Garrett walks over and shakes Dan Etbauer's hand.

Five minutes before the beginning of the rodeo, thirty cowboys have gathered behind the chutes, the spot one rodeo committee member refers to as "the cow-boy shrine." Grouped more or less by rodeo event, by friendship, and perhaps even by skill level, they are performers offstage awaiting their grand entry for the dance of rodeo.

Behind the bucking chutes, before the rodeo begins, there is an easy camaraderie among the contestants. The exchange between two veteran bareback riders is typical: "Wild Wes Ward!" shouts NFR-qualifier bareback rider Bob Logue as he pumps the other cowboy's arm. The cowboys grin and talk excitedly, as though they had not seen each other in several months. In fact, both men were at the very same rodeo the previous afternoon. Similar interchanges are repeated at each rodeo as the cowboys assemble, share information about how they did in the previous day's per-formance or at another rodeo, mention what stock they have drawn for that given day's performance (or "perf"), and share any knowledge they have of the stock another cowboy has drawn. The rookie cowboys, not yet part of these inner circles, can often be found on the sidelines, quietly observing the friendly camaraderie of the more seasoned contestants who, in the course of preparing for their respective rides, touch base with many, if not most, of the other top contestants in the readying area.

There is pageantry involved in getting ready for a ride. At every rodeo, cowboys go through set patterns. Many arrive early at the rodeo grounds, park their vehicles in the contestant parking area, and look over the draw sheets (or day sheets) to see how previous contestants have done. The timed event contestants arrive early, using the time before the performance to exercise their animals, either inside the rodeo arena or in a special warm-up area.

After paying their entry fees, the roughstock contestants move to the readying area set up behind the bucking chutes. Cowboys in the three roughstock events warm up in slightly different ways. Like peacocks strutting their stuff, bareback riders pace up and down doing exaggerated kicking-out exercises, movements similar to those they will make when they're on their horses. Saddle bronc riders, meanwhile, sit on their saddles and perform their stretching exercises, kicking out with their feet in their stirrups. The bull riders drape their bull ropes over a panel siding, put rosin on them, then work the ropes with their gloved hand to assure a steady grip during their rides. Some bull riders do deep knee bends and other light calisthenics to limber up before their rides. Since bull riding is often the last event of the rodeo, many bull riders arrive late, preferring to remain at home or in their motel rooms until just before their competition.

Earlier on the day of a competition, cowboys often relax by going bowling or miniature car racing or perhaps taking in a movie. Some competitors walk through the exhibits and carnival area during the hours before a rodeo performance. Or they may play cards or watch television in their rooms— anything to keep their minds off their rides later that afternoon or evening. "Most contestants are nervous before their event," explains one saddle bronc rider. "Most guys focus on some other issue during the day to reduce the nervousness. Some try and keep busy. Most try to store up that energy, bring it under control, and tap into it during their rides."

Dressed in casual clothes, many competitors blend into the fair crowd and walk through the exhibits and carnival area during the hours preceding or following a rodeo performance. At the Cow Palace one year, world champion Ty Murray was getting his boots shined at a shoe stand on the main concourse. The majority of rodeo fans passing by on the packed concourse did not even recognize Murray as he sat on the elevated stand. Half an hour later these same fans would be screaming themselves hoarse as he competed in the rodeo.

In many respects, the rodeo subculture is a clique, a closed society to those not yet truly part of the scene. To be accepted by the veteran cowboys, a rookie must earn their respect. "It's always been this way around rodeo that until you do something extraordinary, nobody really remembers your name," notes PRCA stock contractor John Growney from Red Bluff, California. "But the second you do something out of the ordinary, like ride a real good bull, all of a sudden they call you by your first name. We're all guilty of that in rodeo, and we're guilty of that in life as well."

For most rookies, the first year is difficult. The more ambitious want to qualify for the National Finals Rodeo and get rookie of the year honors in their event. But as entry fees, travel, and lodging whittle away their savings accounts, many rookies find the goal increasingly unattainable. Some will be forced to return home and find work, thus having less time available to go to rodeos.

But a talented few—those whose network of friends and supporters proves effective or whose luck strikes at the right moment—pile up earnings at the rodeos they compete in. Often, a timely win at a major rodeo—such as the National Western Stock Show Rodeo (held in Denver), the Houston Live-stock Show and Rodeo, or the Cheyenne Frontier Days Rodeo—provides enough money to carry a rookie through most of the season and to push him to the forefront of the rookie ranks. The added recognition leads to acceptance into the upper echelon of rodeo's competitors, easing the rookie stigma. Most rookie cowboys realize that it takes a while to establish oneself and become accepted by the veteran cowboys. As one rookie bareback rider explains it: "It all takes time. It takes about five years of 'paying your dues' before you get your reward in rodeo. Right now I'm just biding my time. I think this is a good attitude to have."

One cowboy whose rookie season was astonishingly successful was Joe Beaver, calf roper and 1995 all-around world champion from Huntsville, Texas. Beaver hit the professional rodeo ranks in 1985 and proceeded to do the unthinkable. Not only did he win the overall rookie of the year and calf roping rookie of the year titles and qualify for the National Finals Rodeo, Beaver also won the world title in calf roping. Beaver and another calf roper, eight-time world champ Roy Cooper, are the only cowboys to win rookie titles and world titles in the same year.

Winning the rookie title is a strong indication of future success in professional rodeo. Close to 50 percent of the rookie title holders have gone on to win world titles.

TAKING CARE OF BUSINESS

Cowboys are quick to acknowledge that the rigors of competition mature the newcomer. As one PRCA saddle bronc rider notes, "Because you are traveling at a young age, you mature earlier. You learn how to take care of yourself and learn to take care of business." That includes taking care of the specialized equipment a cowboy uses in the arena. Depending on his event, a competitor's gear bag or horse trailer will hold a variety of materials for making quick repairs to saddles, bull ropes, boots, gloves, and bareback rigging. The veteran cowboy carries rolls of adhesive tape, rosin for preparing the bull rope, safety pins to affix his contestant number, a protective vest for bull riding, protective pads to cushion his tailbone from blows in bareback riding, and plenty of aspirin. Cowboys will also pack their looser-fitting riding jeans as well as their riding boots inside the bag, changing clothes just before and after their event.

In the three roughstock events, the flank strap—the wool-wrapped girth strap that is tightened by the flank man as the animal leaves the bucking chute—is provided by the stock contractors. If the strap breaks, the rider gets a reride. But if the equipment that the cowboy provides breaks during the course of a ride, no reride is awarded. For this reason, and for safety, it is imperative that the cowboy check his equipment before each performance.

In saddle bronc competition, for instance, the contestant provides the bronc rein. "You may vary your bronc rein, depending on how you feel on a given day," notes one bronc rider. "You spot or mark your rein by using a piece of mane or piece of string so that if you lose your rein in the chute you can quickly get your mark back. You measure your rein based on the type of horse that you've drawn. If you know that a horse bogs, or lowers its head, then you give it more rein, and mark your rein accordingly. There are a variety of ways to measure your rein—to the end of the horse's mane, or over its head and to one eye."

The frequency and cost of equipment replacements vary by roughstock event as well. Bull ropes are replaced every eight months. Bronc riding equipment, on the other hand, seldom needs replacing. Competition bronc saddles are not used for ranch work, usually not even for breaking colts. A good bronc saddle will last for many years—a single saddle, well cared for, often outlasts the careers of several bronc riders. When a cowboy purchases a new competition saddle, often from an established saddle maker who charges over $1,000, he may sell his old saddle to a fellow competitor. Rookie cowboys talk about the saddles they have purchased from the more experienced veterans the way they talk about blood lines in livestock.

"Your saddle becomes an extension of you," one saddle bronc rider says. "If you lined up twelve bronc riders and blindfolded them, they could all find their saddles." Saddle bronc riders often replace their stirrup leathers after a certain number of rides (usually between twenty and sixty) because stiff leathers will snap back. Some cowboys reinforce their stirrup leathers to give them even more snap.

Besides the saddle and stirrups, bronc riding equipment includes chaps and boots. Chaps may help a little—but not much—in saving a cowboy's legs from bruises and abrasions, but their chief function is to help keep the rider in the saddle. Leather on leather, especially when combined with rosin, is much less slippery than denim on leather. Custom-made chaps—costing up to $300—vary in style and color. Decorative chaps add flash to the ride, so many cowboys now use fluorescent colors and design their own chaps.

Each event requires a different type of chaps. Bronc riding chaps are made of heavier leather than bull riders' chaps, with more material to the outside of the chap or leg to cover the legs and help exaggerate the spurring action. Since the rider is stroking his spurs up and back, the movement of the longer leather chaps may make the spurring action look more extensive than it actually is. Bull riders' chaps, by contrast, are usually made light for mobility in getting away from the bull. Bareback riding chaps are made in the middle range, sometimes heavier on the bottom of the chap since the contestant wants his feet to snap back down during the course of his ride. Barrel racers wear "shot-gun" chaps, laced up the side or zipped up to look like a pair of slacks. Some of the women also wear shin guards, wrapped on the outside of their pants legs, to protect themselves from the injuries associated with hitting the side of the barrel. The only other cowboys who wear chaps in the rodeo are the pickup men, who wear heavy chaps padded with foam rubber and even more covering to the side since they will be plucking the riders off their mounts and may get kicked by the bucking broncos or by the riders themselves. The pickup men also wear shin guards.

Like the chaps, the gloves that cowboys wear vary from event to event. A bareback rider's glove (worn on the hand that is shoved into the rigging) is thick compared to a bull rider's glove. It's so thick, in fact, that the bareback rider actually cannot close the fingers on his riding hand. With his other fist, he pounds as much of his fingers around the rigging and inside the "bubble" (a strip of rawhide perpendicular to the rigging handle) as he can. This explains why some bareback riders get caught up in their rigging at the end of the ride—they have packed the gloved hand too tightly into the handle. If a rider gets hung up, the pickup man riding alongside works to free his hand. A bareback rider typically gets fined if he has packed his hand too securely and gets caught. It sounds like double indemnity—you get hung up and beat around, then fined a hundred dollars to boot. But the reasons—safety for the rider and better treatment of the horses (and pickup men)—are valid.

In bull riding, some competitors take a "suicide wrap" by fitting their bull rope between two of their fingers and wrapping it back around and over their glove and bull strap. If the bull rider is jerked down away from his riding hand and twisted around by the bull during the course of his ride, he may get hung up in his bull rope. When this happens, the bull rider must maintain his composure and footing, and try to lunge back atop the bull to extricate his hand from the bull rope. Often times the bullfighters will jump in to rescue the rider, positioning themselves on the opposite side of the bull and grabbing hold of the bull rope to free the contestant. Other times, the action of the spinning or bucking bull will dislodge the rider's caught hand.

Most of the roughstock competitors guard their equipment and gear bags like prized treasure. Even so, their gear is often lost or stolen. Since many of the veteran cowboys travel by private or commercial plane, their equipment often gets misplaced. "The saddle bronc riders lose their saddles on flights all of the time," notes bareback rider Robin Burwash. "The ground loading crew don't like to handle the big equipment and leave the saddles on the tarmac, so the cowboys' saddles never get there when they do. There is nothing worse than to arrive at a place only to find that your saddle was not loaded, and you've got to rodeo that afternoon."

Other cowboys report gear bags stolen from their trucks or from the rodeo grounds. "My gear bag got stolen while I was having dinner at a Sizzler restaurant after the rodeo," explains bareback rider Chad Waldhauser from Ramona, California. "It cost me $800 to replace it. I called all the suppliers and they rushed replacements to me. I was able to get going again within two weeks. In the interim I borrowed some high school kid's stuff." At one rodeo in Iowa, calf roper Tod Slone's horse was stolen when the lights were dimmed for the national anthem. The search ended seven years later, when the horse turned up at another competition in Denver.

THE RODEO LIFE

Bareback rider Clint Corey stands in line at the concession stand at the Pikes Peak or Bust Rodeo in Colorado Springs. He waits patiently as several other customers order their soft drinks, popcorn, and giant salted pretzels. Finally, Corey steps up to the young girl at the front of the booth.

Corey orders a hot dog ("rodeo steak"). He opens the white wrapping paper, pumps the handle on a mustard jar, and squeezes out relish from a plastic packet. Then he stands at the top of the stairs and eats his hot dog while he watches the rodeo clowns perform in the arena.

Clint Corey is a small man with a handlebar mustache that droops down around his mouth. His small stature marks him as a roughstock rider. In the previous week, he has traveled thousands of miles to half a dozen rodeos and slept very little. It's been several weeks since he was home, despite the recent birth of his daughter, Bailey Ann. He has just come from a rodeo in Sikeston, Missouri. He is entered the next day at a rodeo in Omak, Washington, and plans to take the opportunity to see his family, if only for a day or two.

Corey's rodeo career has been highly successful. He competed in the International Professional Rodeo Association in his native state of Washington but soon switched to the PRCA. In his rookie year, Corey qualified for the National Finals Rodeo and stunned the rodeo world by finishing as runner-up to the world title holder. In 1991, he won the PRCA bareback world title. In 1995, Corey qualified for his eleventh consecutive National Finals Rodeo, finishing the year second behind three-time champ Marvin Garrett.

Clint Corey is a world champion cowboy, but none of the rodeo spectators at the concession booth recognize him. He's seldom bothered by autograph seekers. In fact, he enjoys signing autographs and is always pleased when small children ask him what he does. Cowboys often say of Corey, "He's one of the nicest guys you'll ever meet in rodeo."

*L*ife at the top of the rodeo game is neither glamorous nor financially rewarding. A cowboy of Corey's stature can expect to stay in cheap hotels, dine at truck stops and fast-food restaurants, and take an occasional trip home to be with loved ones. Those cowboys who only dream of being like Corey sleep in the beds of their pickups, minding their money so that they can afford the entry fees.

But even though rodeo offers many hardships and meager rewards, it still attracts competitors. Why? One reason is the allure of the rodeo cowboy's freedom. As one bull rider says, "To be free is to be able to go where you want, when you want, and how you want."

The American fascination with travel and independence runs deep. Through travel we believe we will be set free, released from the shackles of everyday life. A line from a Temecula, California, rodeo program illustrates the importance of independence to rodeo: "Regardless of the risks involved, the rodeo cowboy chases his goals in a style he considers essential. Working and sweating for a possible steak dinner is infinitely more palatable than working nine-to-five for a guaranteed burger." Those involved with rodeo often speak of the independence that keeps the competitors on the road. "You're your own boss," said T. J. Walter, a twelve-time NFR bareback rider who is now director of rodeo administration with the PRCA.

For many cowboys, the independent way of life, the adrenaline-pumping excitement of mastering a rank horse or bull, the seamless link between horse and calf in the timed events, the flash dance of a horse's hoofs around the barrels, and the roar of an approving crowd make up for a life of sacrifice and hardship. At any rate, the alternatives look bleak. Ranching and farming have spiraled beyond the means of most young men, and the return on a substantial investment in land is never guaranteed. Fluctuations in the value of cattle and crops have ruined generations of agricultural families, a fact that is all too familiar to today's cowboys. Often the only work available to these men is a service job or construction work in their home towns.

Rodeo is the means for these young men to pursue their dreams and, if they are successful, to achieve some financial stability. Although many more cowboys attend college today than ever before, often as the result of their rodeo abilities, seldom do they go directly into the working world after graduation. Instead, they continue to pursue the glories of rodeo competition. Once they are caught up in the freedom of the sport, it becomes ever harder for cowboys to imagine another way of life. For others, the appeal of rodeo is the lessons it teaches. For one former bull rider, now a blacksmith in Dodge City, Kansas, rodeo represents a "rite of passage" to greater maturity. "One thing I got out of rodeo was an appreciation for life," he says. "You don't appreciate life until you come close to losing it. That's what war does for a young man. Rodeo did the same thing for me when I was twenty years old."

IF THIS IS TUESDAY, THIS MUST BE TEMECULA

A professional cowboy has 750 or more rodeos to choose from. The PRCA rules state that roughstock competitors can enter as many rodeos as they wish, though only 125 designated rodeos count towards national ranking. Timed event competitors, who must consider the costs and logistics of moving horse(s) and trailer from one rodeo to the next, may enter a maximum of 100 rodeos that count toward their rankings.

Cowboys must pay a great deal of attention to their schedules. The basic source of information on upcoming events is the *Prorodeo Sports News*, a tabloid published by the PRCA. Cowboys comb the pages of this newspaper the same way stock brokers study the *Wall Street Journal*. In fact, the *Sports News* is as critical to the success of the rodeo cowboy as the financial pages are to an investor. Although the *Sports News* carries articles that track the exploits of top riders, the most important information for the cowboys is probably the fine print in the middle of the publication. There the PRCA-approved rodeos for the next two or three months are listed, along with entry fee scales (which fluctuate by event and by the amount of money added to the purse by rodeo committees and corporate sponsors) and the location, dates, and times of each rodeo. Also included is a list of sponsors, who often offer bonuses or series points that can augment the cowboy's income but do not affect his championship point total.

Some rodeos offer "slack" performances—competitions run outside the regularly scheduled performances to accommodate the surplus of cowboys who may have entered that rodeo. Cowboys with tight travel schedules often prefer these contests. Listings include information on slack performances and whether or not permit holders can compete. The names of the stock contractors are noted (and for the larger rodeos, subcontractors), an indication of the quality of the bucking animals. Also noted are special qualifications or restrictions on entries (often pertaining to cowboys' earnings or rankings) as well as the deadline for calling PROCOM, the central entry system in Colorado Springs, to enter the rodeo.

One cowboy explains the system that he and his traveling partners use to decide which rodeos they will enter: "The first thing a cowboy looks at is the amount of money added [to the prize purse]. Then, how much it costs to enter the rodeo. The stock contractor is important mainly because a lot of cowboys will avoid a stock contractor who doesn't have a consistent herd of animals. These rodeos become a kind of drawing contest."

Cowboys entering rodeos also focus on the dates and location of the rodeo. A PRCA roughstock contestant says: "I ask myself, do I want to drive all that distance? Or, how am I going to get there? What is the cost involved? How is this rodeo grouped in reference to other rodeos I may be going to that weekend?" Another cowboy complains: "There are five different rodeos [in

California] being run at the same time this weekend. This makes it difficult for cowboys to schedule since it is too competitive. Rodeo committees probably don't even look at their competition. They could have opted to schedule their rodeo on a noncompetitive weekend and more cowboys would turn up. Last weekend, for example, there were no rodeos scheduled in this area."

Because of the complexity of the PRCA rodeo calendar, the association has created a centralized computer entry system called PROCOM, an acronym for Pro Rodeo Communications. With a call to PRCA headquarters, contestants can get complete information about the rodeos they wish to enter and enter the lottery for specific rodeos' dates. Most rodeos will only schedule twelve to fifteen entries per event, so not all contestants get their first choice of rodeo. The lottery determines who gets scheduled for which performance and who is relegated to slack. Before the PROCOM system was adopted in 1976, cowboys entered rodeos by calling individual rodeo secretaries. Commonly, the cowboys had to stop several times each day to make a connection, since phone lines were often jammed with hundreds of callers.

Though PROCOM has proven helpful to cowboys, it is not flawless. Unlike the rodeo secretaries, who generally work for stock contractors, many of the PROCOM operators are college students hired to handle the busy summer scheduling season. Their lack of familiarity with the rodeo business can lead to confusion. For example, when world champion bareback rider Deb Greenough called PROCOM one year to find out the number of the horse he had drawn for a major rodeo, he was given his contestant number instead. The cowboy, who would have to drive from Cheyenne, Wyoming, to Salinas, California, for the rodeo, had to base his travel decision on the animal he was to ride. Misled by the erroneous information, the cowboy drove all night to the California Rodeo. It was not until he arrived that he realized the mistake.

One aspect of PROCOM that has helped the cowboys considerably is a system of preferences that allows several cowboys to enter rodeos as a group. By grouping their entry dates, they are able to share car rides in what amounts to a national cowboy car-pooling system. Roughstock cowboys also receive considerably more information about the animals they have drawn for a given rodeo compared to the timed-event contestants because of a quirk in the PROCOM system. Days before the rodeo, a stock contractor submits a list of the bucking animals that will be at that rodeo. The roughstock riders entered there can then find out which animal they have been assigned in the random lottery known as "the draw." If the animal is reputed to be a poor performer, one that the cowboy has little chance of scoring high points on, he may opt not to appear at that rodeo—a decision known as "turning out." It is primarily an economic decision: if a cowboy does not feel he has a reasonable chance of winning, it is better for him to forfeit his entry fees than pay travel expenses. "Ninety percent of a roughstock rider's decision is the draw," notes bareback rider David Sherod. "Once you have a good animal you have to take the advantage. It's like field position in football. If you get it, you take advantage."

The draw is not as critical in the timed events. However, a calf roper or steer wrestler who knows that he has drawn a bad animal, one that balks as it leaves the timed event chute or ducks away from a rope, is at a decided disadvantage. Unfortunately for these competitors, the PROCOM system does not give them a chance to learn which animal they have drawn. Their draw is decided only an hour before the contest, when the rodeo secretary essentially draws the names of the cowboys and the numbers of the livestock from a hat or box. In most cases, travel distances and prize money play a much bigger role in the travel choices and rodeos entered by timed event specialists than is the case with roughstock riders.

A problem unique to rodeo is cowboys not showing up to compete. At smaller rodeos and at rodeos scheduled during the sport's peak months—June through August—many rodeos find themselves short of competitors. "Every rodeo has some turn outs," explains Lewis Cryer, commissioner of the PRCA. "The cowboys enter an inappropriate number of rodeos, often entering several on one weekend. They may do well at one rodeo and make the finals. Not anticipating that they would do so well, they also entered another rodeo on that same date. Choosing to remain for the higher pay-off at the rodeo in which they qualified for the finals, they turn out of the other competition."

Rodeo administrators, stock contractors, and rodeo committees all complain about turn outs. They are especially bothersome to the rodeo committee that promotes a particular star athlete, only to find that the cowboy elects not to show up. But Dave Appleton, a popular Australian cowboy who moved to the United States and won the world champion all-around title in 1988, explains the situation from the cowboy's point of view. "It's a letdown for the fan that's come to see me ride, and that's sad," said Appleton. "But that's a fallacy of rodeo. I'm not paid a guaranteed contract. I'm paying my own bills. I'm not like a football player or basketball player that has a guaranteed contract. My next contract is only as good as my next ride."

One result of the turn out problem is that professional rodeo does a poor job of promoting its biggest stars. This is one of the reasons why a world champion like Clint Corey is seldom recognized by the fans in the stands. But to the professional cowboy, entering rodeos is about economics, the chance to win money and accumulate points towards national standings. Each dollar earned at PRCA-sanctioned rodeos equals one point in the rankings, and world titles are decided by the amount of money won at the end of each rodeo season. Given the year-round dash for points, it's no surprise that publicity (which seldom benefits a cowboy financially) takes a back seat to making it to the next show.

PRIZE MONEY IN RODEO

Prize money, the rodeo "purse," comes from three sources: contestants' entry fees, the rodeo committee at each rodeo, and sponsors, either local or national. Nearly half of all prize money comes from contestants' entry fees — that is, out of the cowboys' pockets.

ENTRY FEES

Rates are set by the PRCA, but the amount of the fees varies. One factor in determining entry fees is the number of cowboys who will be allowed to enter each event at a given rodeo, adding to the pot. Another is the added money provided by the rodeo committee and sponsors. In bull riding, for instance, if the funds from the rodeo committee and sponsors in 1996 were between $500 and $999, the cowboy paid $40 in entry fees for one go-round (one bull ride per contestant) or $60 in entry fees for "two head" (competing at two separate performances during the rodeo). If the monies were between $1,000 and $1,999, the entry fees increased as well: $50 for one head, $75 for two. For added monies ranging between $2,000 and $2,999, a bull rider would pay an entry fee of $80 for a single head or $90 for two head, and so on.

Entry fees vary by event as well. Typically, bareback and saddle bronc riders pay a comparable graduated fee; calf ropers and steer wrestlers pay a comparable entry fee. However, team ropers each pay a separate entry fee, and barrel racers pay their own set fee. Entry fees in bull riding are treated separately since many more bull riders enter rodeos than competitors in the other six events. Prize money in bull riding is distributed by daily performance standings as well as overall rodeo standings. Both go-round (or day money) and overall pay-out are awarded to the top three winners per event in most rodeos. In larger rodeos, prize money may be paid to the six or even the ten top finishers.

RODEO COMMITTEES

Each rodeo is required to contribute money to the purse at its own rodeo. The PRCA determines the amount required of each rodeo committee, primarily on the basis of paid attendance. Secondary factors include money raised by local sponsors and concessions.

The purse in many professional rodeos is sweetened by corporate sponsors. Rodeo committees across the country compete for such sponsorship, knowing that the added money is the key in attracting top contenders. The corporate sponsors connected with professional rodeo—U.S. Tobacco, Wrangler, Coca-Cola, Coors, Resistol Hats, and Dodge Trucks, to name a few—also award their own year-end bonus money to cowboys who have entered and won at specially designated rodeos. Such corporate bonus money can greatly increase a cowboy's annual earnings. A rodeo committee assumes that corporate sponsorship will attract the top cowboys—those who are accumulating prize money not only towards national standing but also towards standing in the corporate-sponsored competitions that award additional money and prizes at the end of the season. The Original Coors Chute-Out Pro Rodeo Series, for example, lists in the *Prorodeo Sports News* the fifteen contestants in each event leading the point standings at those rodeos designated as Coors-sponsored. If a cowboy is doing well in a particular series, he may choose to enter the rodeos affiliated with the series, even if it means traveling long distances. Rodeo committees, therefore, use sponsorship to offset the problem of rider turn out, assuming that the top cowboys are likely to come for the bonus series standings and the pay-out.

RELYING ON EACH OTHER

"Cowboys usually travel with someone else who competes in their events. Most timed event contestants take longer to get from one rodeo to another because they take their horses with them. Most drive pickup trucks and travel in pairs. Competitors in roughstock events usually travel four to a vehicle, and they often stop only long enough to compete. As soon as they've ridden, they all pile back in the car and head off to another rodeo. Although the buddy system was devised to ease the financial strain of traveling, it has had the added effect of cultivating long-lasting friendships. Cowboys who compete against one another are often close friends."
—*1992 Oakdale Saddle Club Rodeo program, Oakdale, California*

The professional cowboys who buddy up to enter rodeos and cut expenses and for camaraderie also compete against each other for prize money and berths at the National Finals Rodeo. Not only are cowboys in this situation forced to rely on their chief rivals, but their chief rivals are often their closest friends. The fact that competitors travel together from arena to arena in order to compete against one another is a phenomenon that sets rodeo apart from other professional sports.

A particularly poignant example of this dilemma occurred at the 1994 San Francisco Grand National Rodeo. The final event of the season, the Grand National often decides which cowboys will be among the qualifiers for the National Finals Rodeo and which will simply go home. Such was the case for a band of Canadian bareback riders. The four cowboys, who had traveled together throughout most of the 1994 season, were ranked in the standings from thirteenth in the world to eighteenth. With more than $5,000 on the line for the top finisher, it was a wide-open competition. The winner would go to the NFR.

"We all travel together," said one of the cowboys, Canadian champion Robin Burwash of Okotocs, Alberta. "We all planned to be at the NFR, to be higher in the standings and not have to fight it out. We even talked about splitting up our money if only a couple of us got in, but nah. We've got the Canadian Finals next week, and there'll be a chance for all of us to win some there."

With a strong finish at the Cow Palace, Burwash managed to qualify for the NFR, and Bill Boyd, despite a lackluster performance, retained his lock on an NFR berth. Traveling partners Shawn Vant and Darryl Cholach were not so fortunate. It was a long ride home for the four Canadians, two of whom were quietly elated that they had made the NFR, and two of whom were profoundly disappointed that they had not.

Traveling all season with the same companions—a partner, a group of competitors, or family members—has its advantages. Contestants who travel consistently together provide moral support for each other, offer words of encouragement to a group member who's in a slump, and critique each other's rides or techniques. As world champion saddle bronc rider Robert Etbauer, the eldest of the three Etbauer brothers, explains: "The three of us and Craig Latham all go to the same rodeos, and there's no hoping for the other guy not to do well, even though we're all in the same event. We're all going for the same thing. I hope they make a good ride, and when I'm up, they hope I do well, too." According to Robert Etbauer: "We just drive each other and expect a lot from each other. If one of us makes a mistake, the other guys will sure tell you the truth. If I have a weak spur out, those guys will tell me about it. You don't always want to hear it, but it makes us better bronc riders."[4]

Traveling with cowboys who share the same positive view of the sport also gives a competitor an edge over contestants who go it alone or are not "teamed up" with the right group. Fred Whitfield, a Texas calf roper, admits that although he preferred to travel by himself, when he was in a long slump it helped him to get in the truck with veteran Roy Cooper. "He made me focus on what I was doing and that made me want to rope again," says Whitfield, winner of two world championships.

Buddying up also offers cowboys a chance to unwind, to relax a bit, and to spell one another from driving night after night to rodeos strung out all across North America and from having to make all of the arrangements. Even the most minute details can be burdensome. Worrying about who will look after a cowboy's personal belongings while he's competing, for example, can be a major concern, especially when he's been going for five days straight and had just a few hours sleep in all that time.

Cowboys maintain their sense of camaraderie by downplaying their interpersonal rivalries and focusing their energies on defeating the animals and not defeating or psyching themselves out. In this way, they are able to help one another, even when offering advice to one's travel partner can mean doing oneself out of a paycheck.

It's a hot day in Victorville, California, a small town located in the high desert, halfway between Los Angeles and Las Vegas. Bareback riders Marv Hurley and Jimbo Thibert are sitting side by side, getting ready for the first performance of the day. They present a striking contrast—the Felix Unger and Oscar Madison of rodeo partners. Hurley is flamboyant, short, and as cocky as a fighting rooster. Thibert is quiet, reserved, and wears thick eye-glasses—in fact, his eyesight is so poor that he can't see the pickup rider's approach until he's right alongside him. Thibert helps Hurley wrap athletic tape around his neck. Hurley has torn the cartilage in his upper arm, and the tape helps hold the torn ligaments in place.

The two partners take their turns riding. Thibert's horse rears in the chute and revolts against the chute gate, which opens too slowly. He scores 68 points, a low mark, but perhaps adequate for this small competition. Then Hurley takes his ride, which is equally unspectacular, earning an identical 68 points.

Later that evening, the pair return to the arena for round two. They repeat the taping ritual. Then Hurley paces back and forth on the catwalk behind the bucking chutes, saying over and over to no one in particular, "I love rodeo, I love rodeo." Other cowboys pace, too, stretching and jumping up and down on the rickety wooden platform. The motion causes the slats to give, unsettling the horses in the chutes. Thibert gets ready to ride, but the flank man tells him to wait while he adjusts the horse's halter, which is loose. (The flank man acts like a corner man in a boxing match.) Hurley comes over to give Thibert advice on how to ride the horse.

The grandstands are full. Thibert slaps his cheeks as the national anthem plays. He takes his seat on the horse. Hurley says, "Here, let me help you." Thibert sticks out his chin, and Marv playfully but forcefully slaps his partner's cheeks a couple of times to get the adrenaline flowing.

Thibert is now ready to ride his horse, whose name is Be Aggressive. He cracks out of the chute, but his horse is anything but aggressive. Still, the judges score him 70 points, and he moves into the lead for the rodeo. Hurley then takes his ride. This time, the judges reward a better ride, a better horse, and Hurley receives a 76 to capture top honors in the bareback event. "Marv is just too good," one cowboy says at the end of the ride.

The two traveling partners meet behind the chutes. Quietly, they pack their bags. Thibert is disappointed that he has lost the match, but he keeps his feelings to himself. Hurley is quiet, too. In a few minutes, the pair will head for another rodeo.

It is a scenario that plays out at rodeos all over the country. When a cowboy is beaten by one of his pals, he seldom sulks, and when a cowboy wins, he makes a point never to rub it in. As one saddle bronc rider who spent an entire season neck-and-neck for the world title with his traveling partner says, "You never wish anything bad on the other guy. You just hope that you do a little better."

"Last year I was at a match calf roping and this man came up to me and said, 'Boy, I wish I could rope like you.' I said, 'No, you don't.' And he said, 'Yeah, I really do. I'd give anything to rope like you.' I told him, 'No, you wouldn't stay out there, under a floodlight and rope a dummy until there were blisters on your hands. You wouldn't do that day after day. And you wouldn't give up your family life to be on the road 200 days a year. So you don't wish you could rope like me.'"

—World champion calf roper, steer roper, and all-around cowboy Roy Cooper [1]

5

RODEO COWBOYS

OR PROFESSIONAL

ATHLETES?

weathered sign on the outskirts of an Oklahoma plains town reads "Welcome to Checotah, Home of the World's Best Steer Wrestlers." On the sign are listed the names Benny and Willard Combs, Billy Hale, Ote Berry, and Roy Duvall. The names represent several generations of world champion cowboys whose careers span five decades of rodeo history.

Roy Duvall is fifty-two years old and still competing at the top of his event. In 1994, he competed at the National Finals Rodeo in steer wrestling for the twenty-fourth time in his career—easily the record for the most NFR qualifications in a single rodeo event. The majority of his competitors there had not even been born when Duvall saddled up for his first National Finals in 1966.

Even in his fifties, Duvall has the physique of a football player. His chest is broad and his arms are stout. He weighs 250 pounds, mostly muscle, and is six feet tall. Today, Duvall and his nephew, Sam, are in Duvall's home arena practicing in the rain and the mud. Roy Duvall carefully backs his horse into the roping box, looking over his shoulder as his horse tucks its haunches into the padded corner of the open stall. Once the horse is in position, Duvall takes a deep breath and concentrates on the steer waiting in the metal chute to his right.

Duvall nods his head and a helper pulls a lever. The short-horned corriente steer breaks into the arena, and almost instantaneously the Duvalls are in pursuit. Sam aligns his horse alongside the steer to keep it running in a straight line while Roy approaches the steer from just behind its left shoulder. His horse matches the steer's speed. Its hoofs make sucking sounds in the mud as it strains to keep up with the steer. Duvall leans from his saddle toward the steer. Pressing down on the steer's near horn with his massive arm, he slides out of the saddle and drops to the ground. With his other arm hooked under on the steer's far horn, Duvall plants his boots in the muddy ground and slides for a few feet like a water skier on a lake. With a grimace, he brings the steer to a near stop, using the animal's forward momentum to drive its head toward the ground. With a twisting motion of his body, Duvall topples the steer onto its side and falls to the ground alongside it. All this takes place in less time than it takes to sprint 100 yards, less time than it takes for you to read this paragraph.

Duvall's horse is brought back to him. He steps into the stirrup and swings a leg over the horse's back. Another steer is already loaded into the chute, ready for the next run. When not on the road or competing, Roy Duvall and his nephew practice every day, rain or shine. Duvall's older brother, Bill, helps with the sessions and with training new horses. Duvall says he runs eight to ten steers in every practice. Missing a day of practice is as inconceivable to Duvall as it would be for an Olympic athlete. "We train horses every day, and we have all our lives," he says.

Duvall was an athlete long before the fitness revolution, and he trains the old-fashioned way. He owns a pair of running shoes, he says, but he never uses them. "My wife bought me some jogging pants and tennis shoes years ago. I ran to the barn and my legs cramped up. I ain't seen them since," he says. Duvall doesn't bother to stretch. "Shoot, I might cramp a muscle," he says. Make no mistake, though. Roy Duvall is an athlete, and a great one.

TYPES OF RODEO COWBOYS

Of the some 5,700 cowboys who enter PRCA rodeos each year, only a small minority are full-time competitors who make a living competing in their sport. In a recent year, fewer than 380 PRCA cowboys earned more than $10,000 in competition. When expenses are factored in, the number of cowboys earning anything approaching a decent income grows even smaller. The bulk of PRCA contestants might best be described as amateurs, athletes who do *not* make their primary living from their sport.

In rodeo, the competitors all identify themselves as cowboys, but a number also identify themselves first and foremost as professional athletes. In the minds of both the public and the cowboys themselves, there is confusion about whether rodeo cowboys are, in fact, cowboys or athletes. The cowboys who move to the top of the sport tend to think of themselves as athletes while those who participate in the sport primarily for pleasure do so as an expression of their desire to identify with the mythology and traditions of the American cowboy.

Although any division seems arbitrary, for the sake of analysis, we have identified four distinct types of modern rodeo cowboys: *traditionalists, weekend warriors, professional athletes,* and *elite athletes.* The vast majority of rodeo cowboys might be called hobbyists. They compete infrequently, seldom earning enough money to cover their expenses. These hobbyists include the traditionalists (25 percent of those surveyed), who tend to be enamored of the cowboy lifestyle rather than the rigors of athletic training, and the weekend warriors (35 percent), cowboys who take competition seriously but must hold down full-time jobs, limiting their overall ability to compete. By contrast, the professional athletes (25 percent) and the elite athletes (15 percent) are full-time rodeo competitors who devote most of their energies to their rodeo careers. The main distinction between these two last two groups is that elite athletes have been more successful.

THE TRADITIONALISTS

Accounting for one-fourth of the surveyed group of 611 PRCA cowboys, traditionalists identify with the mystique of the cowboy and the Old West and socialize their children into carrying on this tradition as well. Their homes are generally in rural areas, where they live the cowboy lifestyle passed down to them by earlier generations. Their livelihood stems from the family farm or ranch or from blue-collar occupations such as construction or other trades. They are less likely to have attended college, opting to remain at home or go directly into a trade.

The traditionalists surveyed were quick to agree with the statements, "I have always wanted to be a cowboy" and "I would encourage my children to become cowboys." They also strongly disagreed with the statement, "I consider myself to be an athlete rather than a cowboy." In many ways, traditionalists are the mythical cowboys of a bygone era, and some perpetuate the myth of the hell-raising, rabble-rousing drifters of cowboy lore. Dressed for all occasions in a cowboy hat and worn-out western gear, this type of cowboy best fits the Hollywood stereotype of the down-and-out rodeo cowboy. In the 1991 film *My Heroes Have Always Been Cowboys*, the story line followed the plight of a rodeo cowboy down on his luck, prone to drinking and carousing, who is unfaithful to his loved one and barely able to make ends meet. As he drifts from rodeo to rodeo, his hope for salvation is a chance to ride an infamous bull and win a big pay-off so that he can keep the family ranch. Such is the dream of the traditionalist rodeo cowboys.

Some of the professional and elite rodeo cowboy-athletes, on the other hand, are concerned about the image that some of these traditionalists convey, noting that the media is too quick to stereotype *all* rodeo cowboys in this fashion. "The macho, chauvinistic attitudes of the amateur cowboy hurt us all," notes one top PRCA saddle bronc rider. "This macho image is reinforced by the media and shapes what the public thinks of the rodeo cowboy. The macho thing can affect your performance, actually hurting your ride. You get so focused on being tough that you don't ride well."

Other top-ranked PRCA cowboys distinguish between the "every day" cowboy or ranch hand, who fixes fences, "works the spread," and occasionally rodeos, and the "modern" rodeo cowboy. "There's the rodeo athlete and then there's the cowboy," notes Phil Smith, an NFR-qualifier in bareback riding from Emerson, Arkansas. "Rodeo cowboys spend time competing. Real cowboys work on the ranch. The image of the [rodeo] cowboy is changing. No longer is the cowboy 'getting drunk and getting into fights.' The modern rodeo cowboy is better educated, more articulate, and better able to communicate with sponsors and with the public."

The traditionalists enter competition to impress family and friends, to trade war stories, and to take part in the social scene that swirls around the rodeo. While the full-time cowboy-athlete is almost always pressed to depart quickly for the next rodeo, traditionalists "belly-up" to the bar, spending time recounting their near-rides and "wrecks," and their occasional successes. "The modern rodeo athlete sees rodeo as an art form," notes saddle bronc rider Clayton Price. "By contrast, the 'wannabe' is the local town guy who brags his head off, and then has a hundred different excuses why he couldn't make his ride. Professional guys will explain why they made a mistake."

More than a third of the cowboys surveyed fit the description of a weekend warrior: men who reported that they compete in rodeos only as a "weekend hobby," entering mostly rodeos close to home. Choosing to compete in their regional circuit, they seldom, if ever, enter rodeos outside of their region. Of the four types of rodeo cowboys, weekend warriors are the most likely to believe that rodeo is becoming "too much of a big business." Most agree that they could not make a living as a rodeo contestant.

Weekend warriors often have other responsibilities apart from rodeoing. Frequently in their late twenties to mid-thirties, these men hold down weekday jobs and provide financially for themselves and their families. They seldom place in the rodeos they enter, so any money they invest in competition is likely to be forfeited simply for the pleasure of competing.

Of the four groups surveyed, the weekend warriors were the least likely to indicate they had first learned to rodeo in high school and college. Most acquired basic rodeo skills solely in training schools. Few weekend warriors come from rodeo backgrounds, and many may live in urban or suburban settings. Rather than learning rodeo from their families, most gravitated to rodeo through other contacts, perhaps picking it up in the military, through coworkers, or by attending informal buck-out sessions (at ranches belonging to stock contractors, cowboys can pay a few dollars to ride a bucking horse or bull). Timed event competitors often gain experience through local riding clubs, where groups of horsemen pool their money to purchase practice animals and lease arena facilities.

Many weekend warriors in the PRCA graduate from other rodeo organizations such as the military, police and firemen's rodeo associations, state rodeo associations, and in a few cases, the International Professional Rodeo Association. They may continue to compete in these associations as well as PRCA-sanctioned events as they fill their permit card.

Most weekend warriors fill their card and qualify for full PRCA membership by competing in the small, lower-paying contests that take place mostly in rural communities. Some find it difficult to win even at these rodeos and never fill their permits. All but a handful of weekend warriors lack the rodeo skills and practice time necessary to be competitive on a national scale. But some persevere, competing week after week at small-town rodeos and attending buck-out sessions until they gain confidence, perfect their skills, and progress to more competitive, higher paying professional rodeos. Few succeed at the highest levels, though. For most weekend warriors, winning money or a buckle (awarded to the champion of each event in some competitions) at any rodeo is a primary goal, and once accomplished, the win often marks the high point of their rodeo career.

Much of the money that supports professional rodeo is generated by the membership dues and entry fees paid by the thousands of weekend warriors. In effect, their entry money subsidizes the more professional rodeo athletes. "The top fifty guys win 60 percent of all the money awarded in prizes," notes PRCA Commissioner Lewis Cryer. "What does it leave? A lot of guys that don't make money. The top fifteen guys in each event averaged 36 percent of the prize money. The cream rises to the top."

Even among weekend warriors, there is a division of abilities. A very small minority is capable of competing on the level of the top-ranked riders. For those with the necessary talent, jobs or family commitments make it impossible for them to make the year-round effort required to advance in the standings and go to the National Finals.

But in many cases, these savvy weekend warriors are able to work the system to their financial advantage by traveling short distances, thus saving money on travel expenses and facing off against competitors whose ability levels do not match their own. If successful, they may set aside earnings to mount brief runs at the biggest rodeos. Winnings from one or two major rodeos can then be tucked away in savings or invested in a ranch or business. Since the expenses of this type of rodeo campaign are small in comparison to a full-out, year-round effort, a talented weekend warrior may actually net more money over the course of a strong season than a top cowboy who squanders much of his profit in an attempt to qualify for the National Finals.

Often, cowboys from the elite ranks slip into the category of weekend warriors when they grow tired of life on the road. This is most common in the timed events, where a career can stretch over several decades. An elite team roper who slows his career down to the leisurely pace of the weekend warrior can still expect to trump his less-seasoned competitors well into his fifties.

Perhaps more typical of the weekend warrior, though, is Dennis Swearingen, a saddle bronc rider in Southern California who took up the sport at age twenty-nine. He raced cars but switched to rodeo after deciding that auto racing was too expensive. A graphic artist by trade, Swearingen, now in his second year of PRCA competition, is till trying to fill his permit. He has entered the Simi Valley Days Elks Rodeo. On a hot Sunday afternoon in October he gets bucked off his bronc and slammed into the dirt in front of his hometown crowd. But he does not seem to mind. "I got what they call 'sent over the dashboard,'" says Swearingen with a characteristic grin. A few weeks earlier, he broke his ankle while competing, and he described this Sunday's mediocre performance as "a confidence builder" that helped him get over any fears from his most recent accident. Swearingen planned to compete in three rodeos the next weekend.

For reasons of status, many weekend warriors try to pair up with fellow competitors who have graduated from these ranks to join the more established professional rodeo athletes. The more successful competitors, however, may find themselves in a bind between loyalty to friends from the ranks of the weekend warriors and dreams of pursuing their own independent careers. One Sierra Circuit team roper spoke about facing just such a dilemma when he had to select his team roping partner. Since he had been successful, he was finally able to enter the "higher league" of rodeo competition. But he also wanted to maintain contacts with friends and previous traveling partners. "It's hard to pick your riding and traveling partner," he notes. "Some guys just want to enter rodeos to say that they have competed in a rodeo that weekend. I call these the 'Monday morning cowboys,' who try to improve their status by attaching themselves to a 'career cowboy' who really does want to win and enjoys the competition."

The successful cowboy at this transitional stage in his rodeo career is also concerned about not dropping back down to a less competitive level. "It's almost like a tug-of-war sometimes," he says. "As a career cowboy you need to keep focused and not lapse into the Monday morning cowboy type. What eventually separates you is effort and talent. After establishing credibility with the top guys, you don't take steps backward. The circuit system helps a lot, and going to rodeos and beating those other guys keeps you focused."

The Circuit System. To accommodate the vast pool of part-time rodeo cowboys, the PRCA in 1975 set up a circuit system composed of twelve regional circuits, each of which encompasses an area ranging in size from one state to thirteen. Every PRCA cowboy in the United States resides within one of these circuits. Californian Dennis Swearingen, for instance, competes in the Sierra Circuit. When competing at rodeos within his circuit, a PRCA cowboy accumulates points toward circuit championships. If enough points are earned, a cowboy may qualify for his circuit's annual finals event. Depending on the circuit, a cowboy must compete in no less than twelve rodeos or 20 percent of the rodeos in his circuit in order to qualify for the circuit finals. Though they may only compete part time, some circuit competitors are as serious about rodeo as their full-time counterparts.

Quite a bit of cash is at stake within the circuit system, and part-time cowboys who do well at the circuit level can advance to regional and national finals. Every circuit's top fifteen cowboys in each event are invited to compete in that region's circuit finals, held just before or soon after the conclusion of each regular rodeo season. It is at these regional finals that circuit champions are determined. Top-ranked cowboys from each of the twelve circuits also qualify to compete at the Dodge National Circuit Finals Rodeo (DNCFR) held each March in Pocatello, Idaho. With more than $300,000 at stake, the DNCFR is one of the most lucrative rodeos that take place each year. It is this large purse that attracts many cowboys—from weekend warriors to elite rodeo athletes—to circuit-level competition. For some cowboys who compete only at the circuit level, the trip to the DNCFR may mark the only time that season that they venture out of their home state to compete.

Since the ranks of the weekend warriors are sizable, it is important to understand the attraction that rodeo provides these men and their families. Many of the weekend warriors are simply at the early stages in their careers. Others see rodeo as an activity their entire family can enjoy, traveling together on weekends to "watch Dad ride."

Rodeo, perhaps, serves as a kind of magic looking glass for these cowboys. By passing through this looking glass each weekend, these cowboys step into another world. Rodeo sweeps them away from relationship problems, from mundane nine-to-five weekday jobs, from loneliness. Rodeo allows each of them to shed a Clark Kent identity and turn into Superman. It provides them the opportunity to experience a unique way of life—or subculture—with its own set of rules and values. For a few hours several times a month these weekend warriors can live out their fantasies, encounter danger, and experience the "ultimate adrenaline rush," as one bull rider defined his event. And, more importantly, rodeo provides them with an opportunity to meet other people like themselves and creates a unique fraternity.

THE PROFESSIONAL ATHLETES

Professional rodeo athletes are the cowboys ranked among the top fifty money-winners in each event. They consider rodeo a full-time career. However, if their bankrolls shrink and their luck turns bad, they may occasionally step back from rodeo to re-group and take jobs to earn money before returning to full-time competition. Or, realizing that their chances to qualify for an NFR berth are slim in a given year, they may opt to pull back and compete only in their circuits. Or they may decide to enter only those rodeos that offer them the opportunity to win a substantial pay-off. Another strategy is to enter smaller rodeos where they have a good chance of defeating their less-skilled counterparts. The lower level of competition with the weekend warriors and traditionalists assures the rodeo athletes an easier paycheck, provided their draw in livestock offers the potential for a high mark or a competitive time. Once bank funds are replenished, these rodeo athletes return to national circuit level competition, entering the higher-paying rodeos.

Dropping out of rodeo for a time has its downside, though, particularly if the break is lengthy. As in any professional sport, it may take an athlete some time to come back after time away from competition. If the hiatus was due to an injury that prevented the cowboy from practicing and keeping in shape during his convalescence, the comeback is even more difficult. "Even with guys that ride good, if they take a year off, it is really tough to get back into the sport," notes one top saddle bronc rider. "Your body just isn't prepared to take the physical pounding. You just can't jump back in and compete against guys who've been rodeoing all the time that you've been gone."

In addition to the problems of finances and injuries is the problem of losing streaks. "With 125 rodeos, you will eventually get on a losing streak where you are not doing well," says saddle bronc rider Clayton Price. "Losing forces you to become humble and you lose whatever chip on your shoulder you might have had if you had previously been winning a lot. If you become too cocky, and the stock throws you off, it forces you to get or regain respect [from the other cowboys]. The cockiness doesn't last too long. The losing streak takes care of that."

Results of our study indicate that the professional athletes were trained in high school and college rodeo and are likely to have won state or national titles as youth competitors. They are familiar with the mechanics of their sport and often train rigorously in order to stay in shape. The professional athletes, one-fourth of the group surveyed, agreed with the following statements: "I train as much for the sport of rodeo as other professional athletes train for their sport" and "I consider myself to be an athlete rather than a cowboy." They also agreed with the view that rodeos have become too much of a big-time business and indicated that they find themselves struggling to make a living as they compete full-out on the national circuit.

Near the end of the year-long rodeo season, many of these cowboys find themselves "on the bubble"—holding down positions twelve through twenty in the world standings in their respective events. This situation can lead to a frantic schedule of rodeo competition as they hit nearly every available fall rodeo in hopes of "shoring up" their year-end standings and becoming one of the top fifteen qualifiers in each event who go on to compete at the National Finals Rodeo.

That these professional athletes come to view professional rodeo as too much of a big-time operation is not surprising. This complaint stems from the fact that the expenses they incur, and the time spent in traveling to so many rodeos, eventually take their toll. Physically and mentally exhausted at the end of so demanding a pace, these rodeo athletes—including some who are successful in qualifying for the NFR—may end their regular rodeo season penniless or in debt. Even qualifying for the NFR, where prize money in 1995 was $3.2 million, is no guarantee of financial security. As in any rodeo, a cowboy must place at the NFR to win a pay-off. And it is this frustration and economic hardship, particularly acute in the minds of those rodeo athletes who are trying hard to support themselves and their families, that leads to criticism of the sport.

THE ELITE ATHLETES

In the early seventies, the director of the association's media department, Randy Witte, began using the word "professional" in press releases and media materials. Bob Ragsdale, who was then serving as Rodeo Cowboys Association president, thought the word had a good ring to it and would set the RCA apart from the smaller, less prestigious rodeo associations. Unbeknownst to Witte, Ragsdale suggested adding the word "Professional" to the rodeo association's name, and the association's board of directors approved the name change in 1975.

"As soon as they adopted the new name, all the other organizations added the word professional, too," says Witte. "The International Rodeo Association became the International Professional Rodeo Association. The California Rodeo Association became the California Professional Rodeo Association. The Canadian Rodeo Association became the Canadian Professional Rodeo Association, and so on. So I thought that all I'd done by using the word professional was muddle the English language."

"There's always been a lot of guys who were real top hands, that could rope on the ranch in the open and then go to the arena and beat everyone else too," continues Witte, now the publisher of *Western Horseman*, the world's largest all-breed horse magazine. "A lot of them never leave their homes, but I would consider them professional. Professionalism [in rodeo] has always been a matter of degree—there's a lot of guys who will say it's a matter of attitude. The professional is the guy who pays his bills and takes care of business and doesn't rob banks as he goes down the road."

In fact, professional rodeo cowboys—those who actually make a living from the sport—make up a very small percentage of PRCA cowboys. Those who do have been classified here as the elite athletes. These cowboys typically have ambitions of qualifying each year for the National Finals Rodeo and consistently rank among the top fifteen cowboys in their respective events. Of the 5,700 PRCA members who enter at least one rodeo in a given year, less than 1 percent will qualify for the NFR.

The survey clearly identified the distinctive traits of this group of top competitors—15 percent of the group surveyed. These cowboys demonstrated a strong business sense, viewing their profession as more than just competition and more than just a way of life. They viewed it as a money-making venture as well. They agreed with these statements on the questionnaire: "I wish that rodeos could be grouped together and scheduled in such a way that it would cut down on my traveling expenses," "It takes a lot of money in order to compete as a cowboy on the rodeo circuit," and "One must have a sponsor in order to compete successfully in today's rodeo."

With their profits from competition and product endorsements, these elite athletes had the luxury of money to invest in business ventures that would provide them with a livelihood after they retire from rodeo. Many had used their earnings to purchase cattle ranches. Others were developing businesses as craftsmen, making saddles, chaps, spurs, or handicrafts associated with the cowboy trade. Still others looked for business opportunities in the western apparel industry, as corporate representatives in rodeo-related business, or in other occupations affiliated with the sport. Most indicated a strong interest in remaining involved with the sport of rodeo after their competitive careers had ended.

The elite athletes tended to be slightly older than the other three groups of professional rodeo cowboys. Compared to the roughstock competitors, timed event elite athletes were more varied in age. Whereas four-fifths of the top roughstock riders were in their twenties, only half of the top timed event cowboys were in their twenties; the rest were older. Only 2 percent of the roughstock elites were in their forties, and none were in their fifties or older. By contrast, 12 percent of the top timed event cowboys were in their forties, and 4 percent were fifty or older.

Injuries in the roughstock events frequently limit a competitor's professional career. Careers in the timed events last longer, particularly in team roping, where the cowboy need not even dismount from his horse during a run. Knee and shoulder injuries common to steer wrestling make that event the most dangerous of the timed events, although steer wrestlers generally enjoy longer careers than roughstock competitors.

A second distinct pattern was that the elite cowboys tended to enter fewer rodeos than the cowboys in the next lowest tier. By entering mainly the top-paying rodeos, the elite athletes maximized their opportunities to qualify for the NFR while minimizing their expenses. With a less cluttered calendar, they could devote more energy and attention to other business ventures.

The elite athletes had generally been trained in college, not only in perfecting their rodeo skills, but in managing the business end of their careers. For some, this meant they had majored in business or rodeo management rather than animal sciences or agriculture. Others who specialized in agribusiness planned to convert their rodeo earnings into large-scale ranching.

However, not all the elite athletes fit this model. Younger individuals—and those primarily competing in the roughstock events—rodeo full-out, hoping to obtain a "nest egg" for future business ventures. But here, too, distinctions can be drawn between the elite group and the other professional rodeo athletes. The elite athletes, confident in their skills and talents, can establish a front-runner position early in the season at big winter rodeos, or around the Independence Day holiday. With these early season wins, many elite cowboys lock up berths in the NFR, which enables them to take time off from professional rodeo and devote their energies to other financial pursuits. Still, free time is relative. Nearly every cowboy spent at least 200 days each season traveling and competing.

Of the 611 PRCA cowboys who responded to the survey, 112 (20 percent of those sampled) had qualified for the National Finals Rodeo. The NFR cowboys—elite athletes by definition—were older, more likely to be married, and had spent more years competing in professional rodeo. They also won prize money in a higher percentage of the rodeos they entered than nonqualifiers did. For instance, over one-third of the NFR cowboys reported having won money in over half of the rodeos they had entered in the preceding year, compared to one-fourth of those who did not qualify for the NFR. Consistency was a critical dividing point between the cowboys who could earn a living in the sport and those who could not.

This group of rodeo elites also had competed in rodeos throughout the country, in every regional rodeo circuit. In fact, 31 percent of the NFR-qualifiers reported having competed the preceding year in all twelve rodeo circuits compared to just 11 percent of the non-NFR-qualifiers. The elites were also more likely to have won a purse greater than $5,000 at one rodeo (excluding the National Finals)—79 percent of these elites reported having earned this amount at one rodeo compared to only 10 percent of the non-NFR-qualifiers.

The NFR-qualifiers reported higher expenses, even though they might have gone to fewer rodeos in a season. This apparent contradiction results from the considerably higher expenses associated with the top competitions.

Entry fees are high at the big events, and since they generally take place in large urban areas and run for longer periods, lodging expenses are higher as well. At a major competition, a cowboy will compete several times in preliminary rounds, and if he does well, he will also return for the rodeo's finals. If several important competitions have overlapping schedules, the cowboy is forced to travel between the different competitions, often driving hundreds of miles in a single day, and thousands of miles during a hectic week. These expenses add considerably to the elite cowboy's travel costs.

If the distances between rodeos are great, cowboys will even schedule commercial flights or contract private airplanes. These "high-end" cowboys, as one charter pilot referred to them, may spend several thousand dollars in the course of a week-long run. It is a calculated risk whose pay-off remains uncertain until the end of the season, when the cowboy finds out if his efforts result in an NFR qualification. "It seems crazy for a cowboy to spend $800 on a plane ticket to go to a rodeo where he only wins $30," says a many-time NFR bull rider. "But that $30 may be the difference between qualifying for the NFR and not qualifying." Since so many contestants now fly from rodeo to rodeo, many cowboys choose to live close to big cities rather than on farms or ranches so that they are close to airports. In Texas, for instance, many top cowboys live in the suburbs or small towns near the Dallas–Fort Worth airport, in communities such as Keeler or Stephenville. The local media even refer to these communities as "cow burbs."

The NFR cowboys were significantly more likely to report greater costs than other PRCA members. In fact, 19 percent of the NFR cowboys claimed competition expenses in excess of $50,000 for the preceding year while only 1 percent of the non-NFR-qualifiers claimed such high expenses. It is true that the NFR cowboys win more money. But it is also true that their costs to rodeo are much higher than average. In 1994, for instance, the top five cowboys in each of the three roughstock events participated as follows: bareback riders averaged 70 rodeos, bull riders averaged 78 rodeos, and saddle bronc riders averaged 88 rodeos. Furthermore, only 272 cowboys (out of 5,700 who entered at least one PRCA-sanctioned rodeo in 1994) competed at 75 rodeos or more—down from 321 in 1991.

"Rodeo now is not necessarily about the stars since the stars are going to fewer rodeos," said Commissioner Lewis Cryer in reporting these figures to an audience of rodeo committee members at the association's 1994 convention in Las Vegas. "Ty Murray [the PRCA all-around champion and leading money winner] this year earned $165,000 by only going to 60 rodeos. He

averaged $2,750 per rodeo. But he also spent $30,000 this year in order to make that $165,000 and qualify for the NFR," said Cryer.

But even with the high costs involved, four-fifths of the NFR-qualifiers (81 percent) agreed with the statement, "One can make a living as a rodeo contestant." By contrast, two-thirds of the non-NFR-qualifiers (66 percent) agreed, a surprisingly high percentage considering the fact that they were not making a lot of money at rodeo. Clearly, there is a gap between what the cowboys consider to be a paying profession and the reality of the economics of rodeo. Cryer brought the reality into clear focus when he told a group of students at a university seminar: "The last guy in 1990 on the list who made money earned $11.14. And many cowboys didn't make any money at all. The top guy on the list [Ty Murray], some 3,938 guys later, made over $200,000. Even with $18 million in prize money, a lot of cowboys aren't making much money."

One can conclude that the hope of making money, of becoming one of the handful of elite cowboys whose earnings exceed their expenses to the point that they achieve a comfortable income, motivates most rodeo athletes. The fact that so few actually achieve this goal is a major challenge to the sport's continued well-being and growth.

6

SUPPORT

PROGRAMS &

HEALTH

ISSUES

orld champion all-around cowboy Ty Murray does not wear sponsor emblems on every square inch of his body like the racers at the Daytona 500. But as rodeo's best-known athlete, Murray has become rodeo's highest-priced billboard for corporate advertising. On his chaps, the Texas roughstock ace wears a representation of the famous MGM Lion. On his shirt, there's the familiar logo of Wrangler, the company that makes the jeans worn by more than 90 percent of PRCA cowboys. Murray also endorses Resistol Hats, another major rodeo supporter.

Murray is rodeo's biggest beneficiary of sports marketing, a relatively new trend in rodeo that has long been a fixture in other sports. Although he will not disclose how much his name is valued by companies eager to be associated with rodeo, he admits that his endorsements pay far more than the quarter million in annual arena earnings he has averaged for the past six years.

Though they are reputedly a stoic bunch, rodeo cowboys have long been concerned with the physical, psychological, and economic difficulties their sport presents. The growth of rodeo in recent years has made more resources available to help its athletes: individual and corporate sponsorships assist cowboys financially; advances in athletic conditioning, the development of a rodeo sports medicine program, and improvements in equipment reduce rodeo injuries; special programs address health-related concerns such as drinking, drugs, and the use of chewing tobacco; and support programs offer financial, religious, and emotional assistance to cowboys and their families in times of need.

FINANCIAL SUPPORT PROGRAMS

Rodeo endorsements are nothing new. Jim Shoulders, a sixteen-time world champion, began endorsing Wrangler jeans as early as 1949 and has endorsed them ever since. What *is* new is that since 1990, cowboys have been allowed to wear sponsor patches on their arena clothes and on their saddle blankets. It is this arena exposure that is beginning to attract corporate America. By 1995, about 100 cowboys had become involved in the PRCA's patch program, which allows the cowboys to work out individual sponsorship deals with companies or corporations. Ty Murray's experience notwithstanding, the typical rodeo cowboy can expect a sponsor to provide only modest financial support—a few thousand dollars—or merchandise, such as the use of a truck, vouchers for free meals, or a supply of ropes for the team roping event.

Bareback rider Wayne Herman, who won the world title in 1992, was among the first rodeo cowboys to take advantage of the patch program. Prior to the 1991 National Finals Rodeo, Herman worked a sponsorship deal with local McDonald's franchisers in the North Dakota area. At the NFR, Herman wore chaps and a shirt emblazoned with golden arches. Each time that Herman appeared in the contest, his sponsor received valuable national exposure on ESPN, the network that televised the competition.

Interviewed for an article in the *Fort Worth Star-Telegram*, Herman explained why individual sponsorship was an important trend in professional rodeo. Even a modest amount of sponsor support could greatly improve a rodeo cowboy's bottom line, he said. A rodeo cowboy who qualifies for the

National Finals can expect to pay $30,000 in expenses. On typical earnings of $45,000 a year (the average for a cowboy who finishes the season ranked between tenth and fifteenth in his event), the cowboy makes a net profit of just $15,000. "If a guy could get someone to spend $30,000 on them, that would double their net income," Herman said. "I realize that spending $20,000 to $30,000 is not a lot to athletes in other major sports. But it's a big deal to us. It's a big deal to us for someone to spend $10,000."[1]

Still, only a handful of cowboys can attract such money, or even more modest levels of financial support. Top cowboys are seldom asked to endorse major products because they aren't recognized by the general public. But a successful campaign can help to create a following. World champion bull rider Charlie Sampson's endorsement of Timex watches, which ran in *Time, Newsweek, Entertainment Weekly*, and other national magazines in 1993, increased the rider's public recognition. Capitalizing on Sampson's long string of horrific injuries, the watch company was able to tie Sampson into its well-known slogan, "It takes a licking but keeps on ticking."

In recent years, the PRCA has been able to increase its public visibility with a series of televised rodeos, the ESPN Wrangler World of Rodeo. Underwritten by one of the PRCA's major sponsors, the telecasts feature a dozen top rodeos, including the National Finals Rodeo in December. The Nashville Network, a country music cable television network, televises rodeos from the Mesquite arena and the Professional Bull Riders Tour on a weekly basis. Occasionally, rodeos are telecast on the Prime Ticket cable network, and several rodeo segments have appeared sporadically on the syndicated sports program, *The George Michael Sports Machine*.

For the most part, though, rodeo still reaches a relatively small segment of the American public, and network scheduling is typically sporadic. But the people who watch rodeo are what marketers call a "niche market"—a small, specialized market. Rodeo fans usually like horses, listen to country music, and wear western clothing—niche markets already being exploited by commercial sponsors. So even though rodeo athletes may excel at attracting a particular type of customer, they are still not considered good marketing "vehicles." A rodeo performer spends only a few seconds in front of the camera during his run, and even then, it is hard for the spectators to see him in detail.

Rodeo competitors often receive low levels of media coverage, particularly in newspaper sports sections. Many sports editors do not regard rodeo as a legitimate sport, and when rodeo coverage is offered, it is often assigned to a second-string reporter unfamiliar with the sport. Often, coverage of rodeo is relegated to the special interest sections of the paper, where emphasis tends to focus on rodeo as a lifestyle rather than a sport. Only in a few cities such as Dallas, Fort Worth, Calgary, and Oklahoma City does the sport of rodeo receive serious year-round coverage. Papers in these cities assign sports writers to cover professional rodeo full time, and they publish weekly—if not more frequent—rodeo-related stories. Other cities that host major rodeo events, such as Denver, Houston, Reno, and Las Vegas, cover rodeo only during their local competition.

Sporadic rodeo coverage is the norm throughout most of the United States. In most areas of the country, because of the general media indifference toward the sport, rodeo athletes remain anonymous to all but the most ardent rodeo fans. As Katherine Weisman notes in her *Forbes* magazine article "Don't Let Your Babies Grow Up to Be Cowboys," "When the rodeo comes to town once a year, few spectators recall who wins each event."[2]

These problems have not gone unrecognized in the sport, but officials of the PRCA seem at a loss as to what to do about them. In the mid-1980s, an attempt was made to restructure the sport in order to promote its top stars. Teams of cowboys, each chosen from among the top athletes, were outfitted by well-known corporate sponsors. Each sponsor agreed to underwrite one of five rodeos, supplying $100,000 in prize money in exchange for guaranteed television exposure. The select rodeo cowboys were paid to compete, and they also received bonus prize money. In exchange, the cowboys made themselves available in the selected communities where these rodeos were held for several days of promotions and interviews, and elaborate media information packets were distributed to publicize the cowboys on the tour.

The project's goal was to raise the cowboys out of anonymity and put them in touch with an audience. The team approach to rodeo, it was thought, would give the fans a focus—something to root for. Each team in the Pro Rodeo Tour had its own easily recognizable sponsor colors, decorative shirts, and logos. The chaps worn were all custom-made and similar. "People liked it since they associated the team with a product as opposed to a particular athlete," noted Rodeo Hall of Fame stock contractor Cotton Rosser. "Most people are loyal to their region, identifying with the sports teams from their areas. But with cowboys it is hard to have regional identity. Football players would probably be categorized in the same way as cowboys, but [as a fan] you focus on the team instead. You could have had a distinctive style for a given rodeo team in much the same way that pro football teams have their different styles."

Despite an enthusiastic response from the top cowboys, the program rapidly developed opposition from nearly all sides. Major rodeos would not agree to go along with the sponsors' demands, fearing that Pro Tour events would detract from their own competitions. As a result, most of the Pro Tour rodeos were held in markets with a tepid rodeo following. As one Pro Tour contestant, saddle bronc rider Derek Clark, noted, "In the cities that we traveled to, there was not a nucleus of people who understood or identified with rodeo, so the audience turn-out was low."

Cowboys who were unable to share in the largesse of the Pro Rodeo Tour complained that they were being left out. Because the PRCA is a membership organization, it was forced to defend its program to these disgruntled members. Rank-and-file PRCA members expressed little confidence in the new structure, and the Pro Tour concept became a divisive issue that separated the top cowboys from the bulk of the PRCA membership. R.J. Reynolds Tobacco Company, the major supporter of the Pro Tour, eventually withdrew its support. This sent the PRCA into a financial crisis that nearly bankrupted the association. Since that time, the PRCA has been reluctant to make any drastic changes to the sport's organizational structure.

Cowboys who participated in the Pro Tour, however, felt that it was a major step in the right direction and failed only because it was poorly organized and executed. "Every cowboy on the Pro Tour saw the potential," says 1988 world champion all-around cowboy Dave Appleton, who competed on the tour. "Problem was, everyone in the PRCA got a chance to vote. Guys became upset who were passed by, and those who weren't ready complained as well. If the contestants had stepped forward to address the companies' concerns, they might have done things differently. We, perhaps, missed our chance."

Today, the cowboys are on their own in trying to attract individual sponsorships. This, too, is a problem, since most of the cowboys lack the time and business savvy to cultivate corporate sponsors. Recently, independent business people have stepped in to represent cowboys in sponsorship negotiations. Some top cowboys have hired managers to help them get sponsorship packages. Others, particularly those residing on the West Coast, have hired agents with connections to the film industry, television shows, and commercial advertising agencies.

Another promising avenue for financial gain has been the recent formation of outside players' associations made up of professional roughstock riders. These groups now control several stand-alone bull riding competitions. Entries are limited to members of the groups, who each share in a portion of the proceeds of tickets sales, concessions, licensing agreements, and television contracts. In 1995 the Roughstock Team Rodeo competition was introduced. Each of the ten teams is composed of three top PRCA cowboys, a bareback rider, a saddle bronc rider, and a bull rider. Each team has its own corporate sponsor and competes for total team points.

If these breakaway ventures prove successful, they may very well challenge the PRCA's hegemony over the supply and quality of cowboys competing in rodeo today. They may also create a new kind of professional rodeo athlete unhampered by the constraints of the PRCA's traditional membership structure. Another added bonus of these breakaway organizations is that they market their select rodeo events to new audiences. Often, fans who attend bull riding and roughstock competitions have never attended a traditional rodeo. Many are drawn into local competitions by the fast-paced action of the bull riding and roughstock competitions telecast over cable television. These competitions are generating a new audience of rodeo fans who graduate from the roughstock events to full-fledged PRCA contests.

Although rodeo has not been successful in promoting individual cowboys and securing individual sponsorships for its athletes, it has enjoyed modest success in attracting and holding corporate support for the sport itself. Beginning in the 1950s, the PRCA has signed contracts with corporate sponsors promoting items that market research has shown appeal to rodeo fans and competitors. Companies with long-standing sponsorship arrangements with the PRCA include Wrangler, Dodge Truck, Resistol Hats, and the Justin Boot Company.

Dodge Truck Rodeo is directly involved with some 120 PRCA-sanctioned rodeos each year. Local dealerships, seeing the potential benefits of involvement with local rodeos, apply to the corporate headquarters for cosponsorship. If selected for the Dodge Truck Rodeo Series, the local dealer will pay a set fee. Some money goes to the national corporation to run the program, and the rest goes to the local rodeo committee to assist with expenses, the stock contractor, and the rodeo announcer who will promote the product during the rodeo. Since many rural rodeo fans and blue-collar rodeo fans in urban areas drive trucks, the Dodge Truck program benefits from its relationship with rodeo. Sales of Dodge trucks increase during the weeks preceding and following a competition. This type of direct feedback is often crucial, since it allows the sponsor to gauge the effectiveness of the dollars spent on sponsorship activities.

Wrangler awards special rodeo tickets to people who purchase their jeans from a local Wrangler jeans supplier. A western wear store uses national sponsor money to buy a block of discounted tickets, which it presents to customers. In this way, the rodeo benefits from increased ticket sales, and Wrangler is able to calculate how much new business is generated in a given rodeo market.

Other corporate sponsors have been attracted to professional rodeo as a means of getting around restrictions on advertising their products. The Federal Communications Commission prohibits commercials for certain products—hard liquor and tobacco products, for example—from airing on network television. To get around restrictions, the makers of these products borrow marketing techniques from auto racing competitions, since the demographics of the audiences for the two sports are similar. The manufacturers display signs advertising their products around the inside of the rodeo arena, including the bucking chutes, in much the same way signs are hung on the motor speedway sidings and barriers. In this way, television cameras covering rodeo cannot avoid panning these strategically displayed signs as they follow the competitive action taking place in the arena. This practice is being scrutinized by trade regulators in the federal government.

The PRCA has been able to demonstrate a substantial return on sponsorship investment for the majority of its major sponsors. Wrangler, which spends 15 percent of its marketing budget on rodeo activities, has an almost complete saturation in the rodeo market. An estimated 98 percent of rodeo cowboys wear only Wrangler jeans, though there are no rules stating that they must wear this company's products in the arena. "A benefit of rodeo that you don't see in other sports like football or basketball is that the cowboys wear many products that the customer will also use," says Louis Russo, director of western marketing at Wrangler. "Those guys are out there wearing hats and boots, which is great if you make hats or boots." Not to mention jeans.

Russo's point is not lost on other rodeo sponsors. Justin, the world's largest maker of quality western boots, sponsors several rodeo programs, including the highly regarded Justin Sports Medicine Program, which supplies sports medicine assistance to the rodeo athletes at most of the top PRCA rodeos. In most cases, the cowboys return the support by buying this manufacturer's products. Resistol Hats, the largest maker of western hats, also provides substantial financial support to rodeo. Again, cowboys and audiences tend to support this brand above all others. At PRCA-sanctioned rodeos across the country, announcers no longer refer to cowboy "hats"—they refer to them as "Resistols."

Crown Royal is one PRCA sponsor whose success contradicts the claim that rodeo fans are a niche market. "I was surprised that we became involved in rodeo, thinking that it was a blue-collar sport," notes Richard Bailey, Northern California marketing director for Crown Royal's parent company, the House of Seagram. "But horse people and polo, whether they are connected with rodeo or not, are the affluent target group we want, and they support our product. It seems that the more affluent rodeo fans appreciate that a status product like Crown Royal would associate with rodeo. This is contrary to what the New York marketing experts thought. They didn't think we would fit in with the rodeo crowd."

With the success of Crown Royal's rodeo sponsorship, perhaps other corporate decision-makers will consider marketing upscale products to affluent rodeo fans. PRCA Commissioner Lewis Cryer is not particularly optimistic, though: "We have the toughest time attracting sponsors. The marketplace is very discerning. What every sponsor comprehends is cost per exposure. If you can't move the product, they won't participate."

MEDICAL, HEALTH CARE, AND SAFETY PROGRAMS

The Industry Hills Charity Pro Rodeo is held in mid-October each year, several weeks before the close of the rodeo season. With an added purse of $1,500 per event, the rodeo—which takes place in the equestrian center in a middle-class, suburban community in Southern California—attracts several of the top cowboys in the "worry hole" who are scrambling in the final weeks to secure an NFR berth.

Troy Dunn, PRCA cowboy from "down under" in Queensland, Australia, plants himself in front of the first chute, eyeing the horse he has drawn, Desert Storm. Already taped, Dunn does his warm-up exercises, holding on to the slats that serve as the narrow platform from which he will soon set his bareback rigging and climb into the chute to mount his horse. As Dunn kicks out in exaggerated fashion, he grimaces from the pain of bruised ribs, which he's wrapped in athletic tape.

Dunn is in the hunt—but for a berth in bull riding. "Why is he competing in the bareback event?" one cowboy asks another. "This close to the end of the season, it's crazy. He should just stick to bull riding."

As the rodeo starts, Dunn, whose horse will be the first in the competition, settles down onto Desert Storm. But the horse wants no part of this and rears back on him inside the chute, the area where many injuries to roughstock riders take place. Dunn has to be assisted off the horse. He is holding his chest, nearly doubling over.

But in the classic gesture of "cowboying up"—shaking off an injury—he climbs back on after spitting to see if he is coughing up blood. Dunn asks for his hat, still clutching his chest with pain. However, on this second try, Desert Storm sits down inside the chute. Dunn is given an option of a reride, which he takes. The chute gate is opened and the horse races out into the arena. Two cowboy hats remain in the bottom of the chute, belonging to the cowboys who had tried, by fanning motions with their hats, to get the horse to stand up so that it could be ridden.

At the conclusion of the bareback riding event, many of the bareback riders have taken off their riding gloves. They drop their swollen hands to their sides, and several have trickles of blood dripping from their hands to the ground. (The rubbing motion and tightness of grip causes scabs to develop on the little finger side of the riding hand—scabs that are often torn off during the ride.) "It will be really sore tomorrow," bareback rider Marv Hurley says as blood drips from his swollen and callused hand. "There's no use putting ice on it as it will just come off again. You get used to it."

Troy Dunn is walking around feeling his rib cage. As the steer wrestling takes place, he is busy readjusting his bareback rigging and retaping his riding arm. No one comes to assist him or asks how he is feeling. Several cowboys watch him out of the corner of their eyes, but no one walks over to where he is. Dunn's reride horse does not have a good day, and though the cowboy gets a score, it is not sufficient to place him in the money.

Returning from his ride to the cowboy readying area, Dunn busies himself with his bull rope and psyches himself up for the bull riding event. In this event he is more successful. He scores high enough to win some money, which moves him closer in the hunt—one he will be successful in, as later in the month Dunn will qualify in bull riding for his first National Finals Rodeo.

"When a rodeo cowboy gets injured, the paychecks stop. There never was any salary to start with, much less 'injured reserve,' and the cowboy must get back on the rodeo [trail] as a simple means of economic survival. If you're hurting, you don't go home. You just get in that car or plane and try to heal on the way to the next one."
—Eight-time world champion bull rider Don Gay

When Don Gay was competing hard in the 1970s and early 1980s, there were few medical resources for rodeo cowboys. When they showed up injured at a hospital or doctor's office, they might have asked, "Doc, what can I do to get better?" The common response was, "Quit rodeoing and take up a safer sport, like sky diving or downhill skiing."

Although the situation has changed for the better, rodeo cowboys still compete with injuries that would sideline other athletes. At the 1994 National

Finals Rodeo, for example, bareback rider Clint Corey competed with a broken ankle. Several cowboys suffered from concussions, abrasions, pulled muscles, damaged rotator cuffs in their shoulders, and torn knee ligaments. One cowboy, bull rider Brent Thurman, died as a result of head injuries suffered in the final round of competition. It was the first fatality suffered in the history of the National Finals.

JUSTIN SPORTS MEDICINE PROGRAM

Cowboys today have it better than ever before in terms of health care services. In 1982, the Justin Boot Company of Fort Worth, Texas, initiated a sports medicine program that has made several major improvements in the way rodeo athletes train and in how they recover from injuries. Prior to that time, a major problem was the lack of medical professionals with experience in the patterns of rodeo injuries and the unique situation of athletes who must continue to compete, even when seriously injured.

Justin helped to fund a fledgling program begun by Dr. J. Pat Evans, an orthopedic physician and former team doctor for the Dallas Cowboys (NFL) and Dallas Mavericks (NBA). Evans and a sports medicine specialist, Don Andrews, pioneered the concept of a mobile sports medicine facility that could travel to major rodeos, providing information, training equipment, and advice to the cowboys as they went down the road. Most of their initial efforts focused on helping cowboys avoid injuries by teaching them to tape their bodies properly, to use stretching to prevent common joint, muscle, and ligament sprains and strains, and to employ strength training to improve overall fitness and muscle strength. Additionally, the program's physicians advised injured cowboys about when they can return to competition with a reasonable chance of not reinjuring themselves. Evans maintains a clinic in Dallas, Texas, where he treats cowboys with serious injuries that require surgical repair. It is not unusual to find several top cowboys waiting in his office on a given day.

The Justin Sports Medicine Program travels to some fifty rodeos per year. At nearly every major competition, cowboys can find one of the two forty-foot trailers emblazoned with a bucking horse and the Justin logo parked behind the bucking chutes. These $125,000 centers—the first of their kind—are loaded with medical equipment and supplies that previously were impractical or impossible to transport from one rodeo to another. They hold ultrasound and electric muscle stimulation units, hot and cold therapeutic packs, adjustable weights and a mini trampoline, treatment and taping tables, and video and audio cassettes that provide continuing education in preconditioning and rehabilitation. Each unit and its staff offer on-site medical attention, including a cardiac life support system that can be removed from the center and wheeled into the arena for emergencies.

The mobile units also contain computers that record injury statistics and store individual medical histories for easy access by the attending physicians. Statistics gathered show that injuries to the spine area, including the lower back, neck, and mid-back regions, are the ones most frequently treated by the "Justin Heelers." In fact, one-fifth of the injuries (21 percent) are of this type. Injuries to knees, shoulders, and thighs (groin pull) are also common.

Over one-third (37 percent) of the cowboys treated are involved in the bull riding event. This is not surprising, considering the risk for injury in this event. But it is not the bull riders themselves who sustain the highest level of injuries; it is the men who help them—the bullfighters and clowns. Although they make up less than 1 percent of the pro rodeo population, these men incur almost 10 percent of the injuries in rodeo.

Besides the bull riders, event-related injuries are most common to bareback riders (23 percent of the total injuries seen by the Justin Sports Medicine staff). These are followed by injuries to saddle bronc riders (16 percent), steer wrestlers (8 percent), calf ropers (4 percent), and team ropers (1 percent). To avoid sports-related injuries—or so it seems—it pays to stay atop one's horse and stick to the team roping event.

Other medical personnel are also required at all rodeos. Paramedics and at least one ambulance must be on-site at all PRCA-sanctioned rodeos. But it is often the Justin Heelers who first get to the fallen cowboy inside the arena. According to Gene Andrews, whose brother Don was one of two men to initiate the program in 1980, "The cowboys recognize us. Generally we are disguised as cowboys in that we are wearing western clothes whereas the paramedics are in their [usually white] uniforms. With any injury I try to get out in the arena quickly, primarily to get their buddies away from picking them up by their belt buckles."

A medical chain-of-command exists at the top rodeos when both the Justin Heelers and the paramedics are available. "If the cowboy is 'down and out,' or if there is any question of the injury being a spine, neck or head injury [injury to the central nervous system], then we do not handle it but wait for the paramedics, as they have the proper equipment," says Gene Andrews.

Besides the Justin Sports Medicine Program, a new service, the Wrangler Sports Chiropractic Program, provides some rodeos with chiropractic services. Dedicated to "providing athletic excellence for the cowboy," in the words of Dr. Ed Corley, the national event coordinator, this program coordinates locally based, volunteer chiropractors with those rodeos requesting the service. The selected chiropractors set up their treatment tables near the cowboy readying area and provide complimentary adjustments to those rodeo athletes who want them.

Such programs have become quite popular. At one rodeo, for instance, as many as three chiropractors could be seen busy at work adjusting bareback and bull riders as well as bullfighters and clowns. Even several rodeo committee members, and one of the rodeo photographers, stood patiently in line an hour or so before the rodeo, awaiting their turn to be treated. Once the line had dwindled to a few, one of the chiropractors, dressed in the standard-issue pullover shirt with the Wrangler Sports Chiropractic Program logo on the front, honored a request by the rodeo announcer to adjust his horse's neck. This the chiropractor did as the announcer sat astride his mount issuing commands. Nearby, those cowboys busy stretching and exercising in preparation for their competition laughed as they watched the horse getting adjusted.

IMPROVEMENTS IN EQUIPMENT

Nearly every professional rodeo contestant can count on spending some of his career sidelined because of injury. In the 1993 National Finals Rodeo, for instance, three past world champions went down during the competition — bull riders Ted Nuce and Tuff Hedeman and saddle bronc rider Billy Etbauer. Hedeman's injury proved to be the worst. Following an eighth-round spill, Hedeman was completely paralyzed. Carried from the arena by stretcher, he was taken to an area hospital where he underwent surgery to remove a bulging disc in his neck. Fortunately, the paralysis was only temporary. A year after the accident, Hedeman returned to the arena to compete again.

Roughstock riding will always be dangerous. That's part of the appeal. Professional cowboys often invent their own equipment to protect themselves from injury or re-injury. It is not uncommon for contestants to fashion their own braces to support weakened knees, necks, and ankles, and rodeo fans have become used to seeing cowboys with these protective braces in the arena. But a recent movement towards safety equipment seems to be taking hold. New on the bull riding scene are protective vests, which may reduce the number and severity of injuries and perhaps even save lives. These vests, constructed of leather sheets covering impact-absorbing panels, are similar in design and function to the bulletproof vests worn by police officers. When a cowboy is gored or stepped on, the vest spreads the impact over a broader area than would be the case if the rider were unprotected.

Protective vests are not really new to the rodeo arena. Some bullfighters have been wearing them since the early 1980s. But use of the vests by top professional bull riders, and some riders in the other roughstock events as well, is just now becoming widespread. And according to the bull riders who wear these vests, it is about time. "I think they're the greatest thing that's come along," says world champion bull rider Cody Custer of Wickenburg, Arizona. "I've lost a few friends who were hit real hard. I wish these vests would have come out ten years ago." Ty Murray concurs: "I think it's long overdue. Every other sport that has any contact whatsoever has precautionary measures."

Three styles of vests are currently vying for attention. One has a hard polyethylene plastic shell covering a dense foam core and is similar to the type often used by bullfighters. Another is a soft model worn inside the shirt and is similar to the style used by racing jockeys. And the third is a leather or denim soft vest, a hybrid that looks like a traditional cowboy vest but has the safety features of a jockey vest. All three weigh only a few pounds and are designed to be nonrestrictive.

In fall 1993, Murray, Custer, and many of their friends and fellow competitors began wearing this "body armor," as the vests are sometimes called. Murray strapped on a padded leather vest and won the Houston Livestock Show and Rodeo bull riding competition, putting to rest any skepticism that the vests might restrict the bull riders' freedom of movement. "I can't see that [the vests] restrict your ability whatsoever," says Murray, who now wears his regularly. Today, virtually all top-ranked PRCA bull riders wear the vests.

As career-ending injuries and deaths in bull riding continue to occur, though infrequently, the protective vests have become even more widely used for practice sessions and competition alike. California-based bull rider Jimmy Vann, thirty-two, died after being stepped on by a bull at the 1994 Red Bluff (California) Round-Up. The eleven-year veteran of the PRCA suffered a crushed sternum and broken ribs that punctured his heart. Although it is pure speculation that a protective vest might have spared this cowboy's life, the death underscored the need to protect bull riders' internal organs.

Because the vests are so new to the bull riding scene, the only evidence that they will reduce serious injuries is anecdotal. Former world champion freestyle bullfighter Dwayne Hargo, who wears a hard-shell vest, is convinced that his vest has saved him from broken ribs: "I've been whacked in the front and back and not even realized how hard those hits were. You can see the scars where the bull has hit the vest, and my feeling is that those could easily have been broken ribs."

Now that these vests have the approval of rodeo's top stars, college and junior riders have started wearing them as well. Bull riding champion Gary Leffew requires protective vests at his popular bull riding schools. "I believe these chest protectors will cut down on fatal injuries," Leffew says. "To cut down on the death rate, that's my objective."

The vests have not met with the resistance that other safety gear, such as helmets, have encountered among rodeo cowboys. Bull rider Cody Lambert says, "I can see how some guys might think it's soft to wear them, but it's a matter of business. In rodeo, you can't feed your family if your ribs are broke."

Changes in professional rodeo have been likened to changes made over the years in other professional sports, such as football. J. D. Casey, writing in a recent issue of *Rodeo News*, points out how football's evolution into a sport with a much higher level of contact brought about improvements in football equipment, such as pads and helmets. And though the added equipment changed the look of the original game in dramatic ways, the game remained essentially the same.

"Today, rodeo champions are athletes," Casey quotes one PRCA competitor as saying. "They've taken the basics of things they've always worn every day, such as chaps and hats and boots, and kept those traditions. But because rodeo is a sport, the equipment has had to evolve and keep up with the sport itself. People will adjust [to seeing the new equipment]. They will still enjoy the sport."[3]

TRAINING TECHNIQUES AND PREPARATION

Because professional rodeo athletes must compete and win in order to make a living, improvements in training techniques are welcomed if they improve the rodeo athlete's performance. Most of the top cowboys have developed personal and individualized routines that they go through just before competition to help ensure readiness, consistency, and improvement. Some use visualization techniques to prepare for their rides. "When you've got only eight seconds in the arena, you have no time to think your movements through," notes one observer. "They have to be a reflex action. To do that, you have to review the event over and over again in your mind and get really psyched up."

Top NFR-qualifier bareback rider Bob Logue discusses a typical day preparing for a ride: "On the day of competition, I will think about my upcoming ride, but in a relaxing way. I usually do this about ten times. I will start out by visualizing coming to the rodeo arena, fixing my gear, getting the horse ready in the chute, the gate opening and my riding the horse, dismounting, walking from the arena, gathering up my gear, and leaving the rodeo grounds."

In his early years of PRCA competition, Ty Murray ran five miles a day to stay in shape. "I might not do something physically connected to rodeo every day," Murray says. "But I at least think about it. I go over the fundamentals in my mind every day."

Conrad Gonzales, a California-based steer wrestler who is also a professional fireman, must find ways to keep in shape for both rodeo competition and his strenuous job: "Before, I was doing power bodybuilding, but I didn't have much flexibility off the horse. But now I'm doing weight lifting for endurance, reps, and super sets to build up strength and flexibility. I work out six days a week, between one and a half and two hours, early in the morning. To relax my mind, I go play golf."

Many cowboys use golf as a form of relaxation. NFR-qualifier in bareback riding Rocky Steagall explains how golf has helped him in various ways: "I golf a lot. If it wasn't for golfing, I think I'd go crazy. It's helped me settle down. I used to have a bad temper. Once you golf a lot, you lose your temper."

Some rodeo cowboys stay in shape by using devices to assist with toning muscles for a specific event or improving eye and foot coordination. Both bareback and saddle bronc riders use a "spur board," a stationary wooden contraption that allows them to practice their spurring motions as well as proper placement of their feet. Still other cowboys prepare for their rides by watching tapes of the bucking stock they have drawn. "Sometimes it's kind of nice to watch a tape," notes Mark Garrett, an NFR-qualifier in bareback riding. "But if you get into a habit of watching, you can over analyze it. If you handle basics, it will work out. You can get too analytical and you start fighting your head. Basics is all it is, and that's what makes you consistent on every kind of horse."

Cowboys who have experienced serious injury often must recondition themselves before re-entering competition. In 1991, the year after becoming Canadian bull riding champion in his rookie year, Daryl Mills broke his riding arm. While he was waiting for his arm to heal, Mills returned to his father's cattle ranch in Pink Mountain, British Columbia, an isolated community that the *Pro Rodeo Canada Media Guide* describes as "84 miles north of people!" "I taught myself how to ride again," Mills said when interviewed in 1991. "I rodeoed holding on to my other arm. I went home and built myself a bucking barrel between three trees, and taught myself all over again. I also practiced riding horses with my other hand. I got on a couple of cows, did okay, and decided to re-enter. I am just trying to make the Canadian Finals this year."

Three years later in 1994 Daryl Mills was crowned PRCA world champion in bull riding.

Successful cowboys must learn to handle the downside of rodeo, injuries, and slumps. "You draw bad, you ride bad, it's hard to think it's not your fault," notes California bareback rider Casey Vollin. "It's hard to get good medical advice. I went to a doctor once who, it turns out, was an animal rights activist. He told me to get out of rodeo. You just have to have enormous faith in yourself and your abilities and know that the dry spell will eventually be over."

When a cowboy gets on a "bad roll," his attitude often gets sour as well. The seasoned cowboy eventually will "walk it through." As one saddle bronc rider notes, "With the proper encouragement from fellow riders, a guy can ride through the bad times. But, frequently, when times get tough you don't have the range of support such as coaches and trainers that you would receive if you were competing in another professional sport." Past successes will often keep a cowboy going, since they serve as a reference point. For the younger guys, however, focusing on past successes may prove detrimental. Those who were successful in college may take winning for granted and feel that they will continue to progress and win. When that doesn't happen, some lose interest.

SUBSTANCE ABUSE

Even with improvements in athletic conditioning and the desire of many cowboys to see themselves as athletes and treat their bodies accordingly, rodeo cowboys are not immune to social ills occurring in society at large. One area that has come under considerable scrutiny in recent years is substance abuse, including alcohol, drugs, and smokeless tobacco. Some rodeo fans, though supportive of the sport, are quite outspoken about the athletes who abuse such substances and the rodeo committees that encourage such behavior at their events. Many fans wish the rodeo athletes would be positive role models and abstain from excessive drinking and the use of chewing tobacco. Others complain about the heavy promotion of alcohol and chewing tobacco at events touted as "family entertainment."

Rodeos held as community events and produced on public property have been particularly vulnerable to such criticism. In 1991, a former public official in Ramona, California, challenged the use of park grounds for the local rodeo since it was sponsored by Coors brewery and Copenhagen Skoal tobacco. (Coincidentally, Ramona was the residence of five-time saddle bronc champion Casey Tibbs, a man legendary for his flamboyant carousing.) The district board ruled that the organization that had leased the rodeo grounds had the right to allow any sponsor it chose and any activity it wanted, so long as it was legal.[4]

Other communities in Southern California have also debated the merits of alcohol at public functions. In Brawley, supporters tried in 1994 to get the city council to lift the ban of no alcohol on public property so that beer could be served for the first time in the Brawley Cattle Call's thirty-eight-year history. The supporters were defeated, as they had been in years past. Religious groups and other opponents organized and packed city hall, claiming that allowing beer at the Cattle Call would send an unwanted message to the youth of Brawley. "How can adults tell kids that alcohol is bad and then turn around and permit it to be sold at the community's premiere social event?" asked one of the opponents to lifting the ban.[5]

DRINKING AND DRUGS

Many rodeos serve alcohol. For a number of rodeo committees, the profits generated by the sale of alcohol is the margin that guarantees a financially successful rodeo. Booze, then, or at least beer, is readily available at most rodeos, a situation that has led to drinking problems for some cowboys. But as one competitor pointed out, the sport is too competitive at the very top for an athlete with a drug or drinking problem to remain competitive for long.

The drinking behavior of rodeo cowboys is no different than athletes in other sports who "unwind" with a few beers after their sporting event. Some would even argue that the rigors of competition and travel for the pro rodeo athlete, as well as the true nature of most rodeo cowboys, preclude heavy drinking. Even so, the public's image of the cowboy, fueled by Hollywood stereotype, is that of a hard drinker and carouser.

Those cowboys who do consume alcohol try to "take care of their own," watching out for an inebriated friend. But often such drinking escapades become the fuel for the next day's story, since cowboys—like college fraternity boys or military personnel after a night on the town—are quick to share their "war stories" of drinking bouts, hangovers, and wild behavior. One bull rider describes an evening of celebration after placing in a top-paying rodeo: "I went drinking. I got a ride from the dance back to the parking lot, and went to sleep in my pickup. I put a camper on it this spring so I could sleep comfortably. But this morning I woke up at 10 A.M. when the sun was shining in. I didn't make it to the camper. I slept in my front seat, curled up like a pretzel. That was a waste of money."

Sometimes the drinking exploits of cowboys are the running jokes used by announcers in a rodeo. Such accounts, according to the critics, only glorify objectionable behavior. Most jokes go something like this: a cowboy, on winning $8,000 at a rodeo in Oklahoma City, was asked by the announcer what he was going to do with the money. "Well," the cowboy replied, "I'm going to spend $4,000 on women and whiskey." "And the other $4,000?" the announcer asked. "I'm going to spend it foolishly," the cowboy replied. At one rodeo, the talk behind the bucking chutes concerned the plight of a cowboy who had been arrested for drunk driving the night before. "He did a 360 degree turn and got picked up by the police," said a fellow bronc rider about his friend and occasional traveling partner whom he had bailed out of jail before the rodeo. "His bail was posted at $3,500 because he had outstanding warrants on him for traffic tickets. He called me at the motel this morning to come get him. Fortunately, his girlfriend had wired him $1,000 yesterday before this all happened. He's up in Ogden and Cheyenne this week, so he wasn't taking care of business."

Many people buy cowboys drinks, particularly at community social events, and because a cowboy often travels to a rodeo by himself, he may not have a designated driver. Others who drink rely on the teetotaler in the group to transport them. On occasion, the combination of drinking and driving by cowboys has caused severe injuries and death. In 1991, three top bull riders who had all qualified for the NFR the preceding December were involved in a serious accident. One of them, Johnny Shea, was killed when the pickup truck the three were riding in went off the road late at night and hit a tree.

In recent years, opposition to substance abuse has become more vocal. In Oklahoma, where rodeo is especially popular, Mothers Against Drunk Drivers (MADD) have attempted to outlaw beer ads at all sporting events, including rodeo. Another group in Oklahoma, led by a woman whose son has cancer of the mouth, has campaigned against the smokeless tobacco industry.

The PRCA is sensitive to the issue of substance abuse and alcohol among contestants and rodeo fans. In 1994, it presented an alcohol risk management seminar at its annual convention. Noting the increasing risk of liability when individuals who have been served alcohol subsequently become involved in accidents, the seminar suggested rodeo committees take action to limit risk. In principle, such a program encourages rodeo committees to assume responsibility and take action before a problem develops. By limiting the number of drinks that can be purchased, by training all employees and volunteers to adhere to safety guidelines, by raising the price of alcoholic beverages, and by documenting every alcohol-related incident, rodeo committees can demonstrate that they take the problem of excessive drinking seriously.

Drug abuse, though difficult to judge, has never been considered a major problem among professional cowboys, and it has decreased in recent years, according to several top rodeo cowboys. "In the late sixties and seventies," notes one veteran, "some cowboys smoked marijuana and experimented with psychedelic drugs. But the cowboys generally stayed away from hard drugs."

But according to another observer, this pattern changed somewhat in the mid-eighties. "In 1986, a cocaine problem blew through rodeo," claims a female rodeo photographer who had dated several of the cowboys during this period. "The cowboys were totally naive about drugs. They were unprepared to deal with it. It wiped a lot of guys out financially and in terms of their rodeo careers. Many of them ended up becoming 'Broke Dick Riders' [a phrase describing someone who has been at the top]. They're now 'has beens,' trying to live through their memories."

From time to time, stories circulate among the cowboys about top-ranked contestants who take drugs. But on balance, younger cowboys seem to shy away from illicit drugs, perhaps because they have observed first hand what drug abuse has done to careers of cowboys slightly older than themselves. "Drugs are not part of my generation of cowboy," says one young bronc rider, summing up the pattern.

Collegiate rodeo programs have also tried to play a constructive role in preventing drub abuse. One rodeo coach comments: "I fight it by scheduling practice sessions early in the morning and on a frequent basis. The cowboy who stays up all night partying ain't gonna do well at practice. Rodeo is a commitment, and I don't want the partiers around. Those cowboys serious about professional careers in rodeo have to make choices."

In September 1993, the National Intercollegiate Rodeo Association introduced a program to combat substance abuse. The program, called RAWHIDE (Rodeo Athletes on Wellness Helping Individualize Drug and Alcohol Education), encourages the rodeo athlete to make the kinds of choices that will enhance his performance. "We're trying to create an atmosphere that encourages positive lifestyle choices for NIRA athletes," says Pat Beard, coordinator of the program. RAWHIDE sponsors seminars in each of the NIRA's eleven regions, emphasizing positive alternatives to substance abuse, such as fitness and education, and urging the cowboys to remain "drug free." The efforts appear to be paying off. Results of a recent survey of the 2,500 NIRA members indicated that less than 1 percent of the rodeo student-athletes use drugs.[6]

Cowboys are not known for taking performance-enhancing drugs such as steroids, a common pattern found among athletes in other professional sports.

But pills can be found in a cowboy's gear bag. Most contestants carry pain-killers to dull the discomfort from injuries. Others take amphetamines, such as speed, to keep themselves awake during all-night drives to the next competition.

SMOKELESS TOBACCO

If there is a "drug of choice" among rodeo cowboys, it is smokeless tobacco, known as chew or snuff. Although the Marlboro Man may symbolize the American cowboy to people throughout the world, today's cowboy is far more likely to be packing a round can of chewing tobacco than a pack of smokes. Estimates of the extent of smokeless tobacco use vary. Wayne Wise, rodeo announcer from Loveland, Colorado, claims that between 50 and 60 percent of the contestants chew tobacco. "I do it because of nervous energy," says Wise.

Other cowboys contend that fewer cowboys are using smokeless tobacco than they did several years ago. Still others, though they continue to use snuff, wish they didn't. "It's a bad habit. I've got to quit," says 1992 world champion saddle bronc rider Billy Etbauer of Ree Heights, South Dakota. Etbauer no longer chews when he rides, though, because a buddy of his "about choked to death" when he was competing and chewing.[7]

But nicotine — whether delivered through cigarettes or chew — is addictive, and tobacco use is a hard habit to break. Since one can of snuff delivers as much nicotine as sixty cigarettes, the tobacco-chewing addiction is even more pernicious than cigarette smoking. Even with a barrage of programs, publicity, and medical reports warning of the health risks involved, using smokeless tobacco is common among rodeo cowboys. Furthermore, U.S. Tobacco, makers of the Copenhagen Skoal line of smokeless tobaccos, has been a major corporate sponsor of rodeo at both the collegiate and professional level. For several years, tobacco companies have been under attack by legislators in Congress. Proposed "get-tough" changes in 1995 ban tobacco companies from sponsoring any sporting events under their product names and restrict paraphernalia such as hats and shirts carrying tobacco brand names. To counter this legislation, representatives of the tobacco industry have set up special booths at rodeos, encouraging rodeo fans to mail in cards expressing their opposition to any restrictive federal legislation. If such bills pass, tobacco might have to stay out of auto racing and pro rodeo. "We're on line for controversy," said Ted Maynard, a representative of U.S. Tobacco, when interviewed in 1992. "But we've decided to make a stand and continue to support the two biggest grass roots sports in America. You can't get any more grass roots than rodeo and auto racing."

Campaigns against smokeless tobacco have varied in their approach over the years. In 1991, a group of students at Cal Poly, San Luis Obispo, were awarded a grant from the California Department of Health Services for a "cessation program" aimed at education and at getting fellow university students to give up tobacco. At the annual spring rodeo, the students set up a booth and distributed literature explaining their "Snuff-Out Tobacco" campaign. "This is the first rodeo we've done," said Liz Cofer, a student organizer of the campaign. "The sponsorship by Copenhagen of Cal Poly rodeos in past years is what led to the project. This year we asked that they not hand out free samples at the rodeo. A lot of students use smokeless tobacco. It's been an issue on campus. The rodeo seemed to be a logical place to begin."

The California Department of Health Services has also sponsored freeway billboard signs critical of the tobacco industry and its promotional tie-in to the cowboy lifestyle. "Kids Love Cowboys. Unfortunately, so does the Tobacco Industry," read one such sign, prominently displayed on a freeway close to a PRCA-sanctioned rodeo in Indio, California. Other anti-chew campaigns have targeted a similar audience. One ad, sponsored by the Tobacco Control Coalition, displayed the circular imprint of a snuff can in the back-pocket of a pair of jeans. Under the imprint were the words, "The First Warning Sign of Cancer."

Clearly, the health risks of smokeless tobacco are considerable. The recently published results of a twelve-year study of 135,000 men found that users of smokeless tobacco were 1.4 times as likely to die of heart disease as those who did not use tobacco in any form.[8] Smokeless tobacco has been linked to oral and throat cancers, mouth sores, gum disease, and tooth loss. Other studies have found that the number of people using smokeless tobacco has increased in recent years, primarily due to the influx of male users between the ages of eighteen and thirty-one.[9] An earlier 1985 survey of male college baseball players found that 40 percent used smokeless tobacco regularly, whereas only 3 percent smoked cigarettes. Because of the popularity of smokeless tobacco among professional baseball players, major league baseball joined forces in 1991 with the National Cancer Institute to publish a public service pamphlet offering a "9-Inning Game Plan" for kicking the habit. Several top baseball players were quoted in the twenty-page brochure, giving personal testimony about why they had decided to give up the product. In all likelihood, similar efforts will one day be targeted at rodeo cowboys.

OTHER SUPPORT PROGRAMS

The rodeo community is tight-knit. Most competitors who travel long distances on the national rodeo circuit get to know each other's families. They often bunk at fellow competitors' homes or at the homes of their parents, other family members, or friends. Parents of a rodeo contestant soon get used to feeding armies of cowboys when rodeos are held nearby. Some homes or ranches, because of their strategic locations near busy freeways and certain regions of the country, see many such visitors as the contestants criss-cross the nation during the long rodeo season. Joy Murray, Ty Murray's mother, says: "Rodeo is all just one big family. You fall in love with all the kids. You holler for all of them. You want them all to make the whistle and let the judges decide. And we are all there to support each other if any one of them should get injured."

ASSISTANCE ORGANIZATIONS

In recent years, organizations have been developed to assist rodeo cowboys and their families during hard times. In 1991, the Justin Cowboy Crisis Fund was established to provide financial relief to rodeo participants injured in the arena. Since then, the nonprofit organization has collected almost $1 million and paid out more than $850,000 in assistance.[10] In 1994, over $136,000 was distributed to cowboys injured in the arena. The fund is open to all professional rodeo cowboys and cowgirls, no matter what organization they belong to, who have been injured in arena participation or while practicing and can demonstrate financial need. In the event of a death, aid is given to the surviving spouse and children.

Another organization, the Cowboy Assistance Foundation, was formed in the early 1990s by nineteen cowboys and independent businessmen from Texas. They not only wanted to help members in a time of crisis; they also wanted to provide the cowboys with rehabilitation, education, and scholarship opportunities. Programs sponsored by the foundation are open to all members of the rodeo community, including contestants, contract personnel, laborers, and rodeo committees involved in the sport. Financial assistance is based on educational needs, illness, death of a family member, or a career-ending injury. Operational money is generated from membership drives—individual, rodeo committee, and corporate—and benefit rodeos, ropings, and other charity events.

Besides assisting cowboys with career changes when their rodeo years are over, the Cowboy Assistance Foundation has developed a substance abuse and awareness program open to individuals participating in rodeo at any level. It also plans to work with local police departments and public safety officials in increasing awareness of driving safety for horse and stock trailers and to help local veterinarians assure animal safety and well-being.

RELIGIOUS SUPPORT

In 1974, a handful of Christian cowboys, with the help of the nationally known Fellowship of Christian Athletes (FCA), founded a cowboy chapter that is now known as the Fellowship of Christian Cowboys. Tired of the "love 'em and leave 'em" image of cowboys that both the music industry and Hollywood had created, the group aimed to combat this stereotype and to offer fellowship. Organizers of the Fellowship of Christian Cowboys also hope to attract younger cowboys and cowgirls involved in youth associations by offering prayer, religion, and fellowship—as well as involvement with rodeo and animals—as an alternative to the drug- and alcohol-influenced lifestyle that now attracts many teens. In our survey of 611 PRCA competitors, two-thirds of the cowboys indicated a religious preference, and 17 percent of the sample group defined themselves as Christian cowboys.

Today, a religious service—"Cowboy Church"—is held at a number of rodeos throughout the country, and about twenty pastors are involved with the special ministry to rodeo cowboys. Services attract contestants and their families, as well as rodeo committee members and others, and provide moral support and friendship for Christian cowboys. Both before and during a rodeo performance, it is common to see several Christian cowboys form a circle and join hands in a quiet moment of prayer. Christian fellowship is also conducted each night after the performance of the National Finals Rodeo.

Reverend Coy Huffman, one of the pastors in the Pro Rodeo Ministries program, conducts services in the grandstands several hours before Sunday rodeo performances at around fifty different rodeos each year. A former rodeo competitor himself, he also works as a chute boss for several stock contractors and rodeo committees. In a typical sermon, Huffman will point out the parallels between biblical passages and the everyday challenges in the life of the traveling rodeo cowboy. Cowboys in attendance often share conversion stories with those assembled. At the California Rodeo at Salinas one year, a several-time world champion team roper talked about losing his mother to cancer when he was fifteen. "I rebelled afterwards, turning to rodeo, marijuana, and partying for three years," said this cowboy, addressing over 400 worshippers assembled in the large grandstand. "But at eighteen I returned to the religious foundation my Mom had given me, and I prayed for a change. Over the years I have had the good fortune to find a Christian wife and together we have raised three children. Rodeo has been good to me, but so has the Lord."

Outward demonstrations of religious faith are not unique to rodeo athletes. An article in the *Los Angeles Times* describes "public displays of religious faith in the arenas and the locker rooms" and maintains that the postgame "prayer huddle" has become a popular new formation in the National Football League.[11] A Catholic priest interviewed for the article was asked, "How do you preach to these [football] guys?" His answer could serve to explain rodeo cowboys' interest in spiritual matters as well: "These are young men trying to keep their lives together and make their careers work. Most are people at a very interesting point in their lives. They live on the edge in a way most of us will never experience. One injury can end a career, and all the big money will end, too. Consequently, people are driven to seek what is beyond their career. People ask, 'Am I just a modern gladiator? What am I worth?' And they begin a search for a spiritual foundation that goes beyond [their sport]."[12]

Finding a meaning to life may ease the inevitable transition that all athletes must one day face: the end of their careers. Although Senior Rodeo has provided opportunities for some to extend their participation in rodeo, injuries and other problems force many professional cowboys into retirement long before they are ready. A career-threatening wrist injury in 1991 forced all-around world champion Dave Appleton to give up rodeo for sixteen months, and, in his own words, "pour myself into the world outside of rodeo." In *Prorodeo Sports News*, Appleton wrote about his break from rodeo:

Looking back at that day [of my injury], I think maybe the good Lord was telling me, "Cowboy, I've been giving you all the signals to start doing something outside of rodeo because you can't rodeo forever." I'm very thankful for what I've achieved in the rodeo arena, and I will always try to be a good ambassador for the sport of rodeo. But, strangely enough, one of the best things that every happened to me was tearing up my wrist. Now I know there is life after rodeo.[13]

7

STOCK

CONTRACTORS

& ANIMAL

WELFARE

John Growney is a small, slim man with stringy, muscular arms. Were it not for the silver strands near the temples of his crow-black hair, you might mistake him for one of the competitors at the Chief Joseph Days Rodeo, a small four-day rodeo competition in a mountainous ranching community of Joseph, Oregon. Growney is walking through the arena dirt, opening a blind gate that leads to the area directly behind the chutes. As he steps through the gate, he surveys the roughstock riders slipping on their gloves, strapping their spurs to their boots, or otherwise fussing with their equipment. Some of the riders are tense, probably thinking about their rides.

"Boys," he says, "I don't mind if you ride 'em for eight seconds, but after that buzzer sounds, you'd better show the audience some fantastic wrecks."

The cowboys laugh, the tension dissipates, and Growney's watery blue eyes twinkle. He walks over to some cowboys from Hawaii, bull riders who have come to the mainland to try their luck in professional rodeo. He puts his hand on the shoulder of one young man, talks to him for a moment, then starts to walk off. The young bull rider says, "Hey John, what can you tell me about my bull Ram Tough?" Growney turns back slowly and looks the cowboy in the eye.

"He usually takes a couple jumps out, then turns back to the left. Watch for the turn back and be ready for him when it comes." The cowboy thanks the man, and Growney walks away to check on the bareback horses in the loading chutes.

John Growney is a rodeo stock contractor, one of about seventy-five men (and a few women who have inherited the operation from their husbands) who provide livestock—bucking horses and bulls, steers, calves, saddle horses—to Professional Rodeo Cowboys Association competitions. He's come up from his headquarters in Red Bluff, California, driving several hundred miles to set up camp for six days in a mobile home on the rodeo grounds.

When he's not caring for his livestock—several hundred animals in all—or giving directions to his employees and other contract help, Growney hangs out at his trailer. Cowboys come by to visit, sitting in cheap plastic chairs haphazardly strewn atop a carpet of astro-turf. Growney may offer them a beer or a soft drink, and if the barbecue is burning, he invites them down to a supper of chicken, salad, and canned beans.

Growney is a cowboy's cowboy, a man who is seemingly always available to the competitors. A friend. During the rodeo, he works behind the chutes, making sure that each bucking horse or bull is lined up properly, the equipment adjusted correctly. Other contractors ride in the arena or pound the walkways behind the chutes, bossing the action, hurrying the cowboys up. Growney is patient. He wants the show to go quickly, but he also wants the cowboys to get a fair ride.

STOCK CONTRACTORS

It is a balancing act, the job of the stock contractor. On the one hand, he has an obligation to the rodeo committee to ensure that the rodeo goes smoothly and efficiently. On the other hand, he must deal with the cowboys. They need time in the chutes to prepare themselves mentally and physically to battle bulls that can weigh a ton, broncs that can kick through a board two inches thick as though it were a match stick, or a calf roping horse that is too excited to remain quiet in the roping box when it is time for the cowboy to make his run.

A cowboy wants to defeat his adversary in the arena; stock contractors, on the other hand, secretly hope that their bucking animals will win—that they will plant the cowboy in the arena dirt. Most stock contractors are open in their admiration of the man who rides their bull or bronc, and they are equally open in their pride if their animal wins. In the roping events, the stock contractors are not so concerned. As long as the animals run straight and true, they are satisfied. But a stock contractor's reputation among the cowboys, and among the rodeo committees, in part depends on the strength and wiliness of his bucking animals and their ability to test the cowboys to the extent of their abilities.

Stock contractors handle myriad responsibilities associated with each of the rodeos they work. Some produce the rodeo itself and provide all the equipment—arena panels, bucking and roping chutes, and sometimes even the grandstands. Producers also arrange for all contract personnel, such as novelty act performers, bullfighters and barrelmen, secretaries, timers, announcers, pickup riders, chute bosses, and flank men. They place advertising in newspapers and on radio stations, print handbills, and sell tickets. If they need extra stock, they will also hire additional stock contractors to provide animals.

Only a handful of stock contractors, however, are equipped to handle all of the varied tasks of production. Most are satisfied simply to supply animals and arrange for contract personnel, leaving the rest up to the rodeo committee. Stock contractors are hired by independent rodeo committees, often made up of business people, civic club members, the local chamber of commerce, and other community groups who handle the production details. The rodeo committee may write its own contracts with rodeo personnel but will usually confer with the stock contractor about those choices or perhaps leave the choices entirely up to the stock contractor. The rodeo committee also leases an arena if one is not already owned by the organization.

Rodeo committees often form close personal relationships with their stock contractors. For example, the Pikes Peak or Bust Rodeo in Colorado Springs has worked with Fowler, Colorado, stock contractor Harry Vold for more than two decades. Former rodeo committee president Ryer Hitchcock, a vice-president of a stock brokerage firm, boasts that "all of our contracts with Harry Vold have been made on a handshake. We've never needed a written contract."

According to PRCA Commissioner Lewis Cryer, there are several different classes of stock contractors. Some handle only small shows, both professional and amateur, usually in their region of the United States. Others travel the country, working the small to mid-size events and subcontracting their top stock to the big shows. Cryer refers to half a dozen stock contractors as the "big show" stock contractors, capable of handling all aspects of the very largest professional rodeos. "These top stock contractors have successfully divided up most of the big rodeos," Cryer says. "Mike Cervi has all the big indoor shows. Harry Vold has the big outdoor shows. Cotton Rosser, Benny Beutler, and Neal Gay have the rest of the big shows. No one can buy them out, and their operations will likely all be divided out once they pass on."

These large-scale operators are not without their critics—often the rodeo contract personnel or stock contractors who are not getting large slices of the big rodeo pie. One announcer, for example, speaks of the various stock contractors he had worked with over the years, singling out one contractor as "a showman who saves big money by gypping the little guy." Another he rated as "fair," another as "egotistical and authoritarian," and yet another as "famous for running his rodeos with metronomic precision." "Most of them try and take advantage of you," says another rodeo announcer. "You survive by playing their game. I don't like to do that, but that's called 'taking care of business.' As rodeo goes, unfortunately, we will have to cater more and more to them."

One cowboy pointed out the role the stock contractor's personality plays in his success. One contractor, he says, will attract cowboys to even the most insignificant rodeos simply because he is relaxed and humorous, while another irritates the cowboys by pestering them, forcing them to hurry in the chute, and being over-protective of his stock. In many cases, cowboys will bypass that contractor's rodeo unless the money is too alluring to pass up.

An especially sensitive area of trust between stock contractor and cowboy is the stockman's evaluation of his animals. Bad information breeds ill-will. One cowboy compares the relationship to that between a race car driver and his mechanic: "The mechanic knows the car better than the driver, but he's not out there getting into the car. The stock contractor knows his stock, but he doesn't get on the stock." Some contractors are evasive because they prefer to see their animals win, forcing cowboys to seek the advice of their peers. That's why a stock contractor like Growney, who tries to give the cowboys a fair evaluation of his stock, is a favorite among the rodeo roughstock riders. •

Most contractors earn praise from cowboys and rodeo committees. Many are former rodeo cowboys themselves, and they understand the needs of the contestants. But they also know that the rodeo fans and the rodeo committees help pay the bills, and they are ever mindful of their needs as well. How they balance their responsibilities to the different groups varies. Rodeo men take pride in their individualism, and each stock contractor has his own brand of showmanship.

California stock contractor Cotton Rosser, a former rodeo contestant whose operation is based in Marysville, California, takes his cues from circuses, ice shows, and the earlier Wild West shows. A typical Flying U Rodeo features an elaborate grand entry, perhaps with a horse and a pretty flag girl rising out of a huge cowboy boot or an ersatz Liberty Bell to the strains of the "Star Spangled Banner." Fireworks almost inevitably play into the show, as well as spectacular trick riders and fancy ropers and sometimes a circus-like trained animal act. Rosser would rather cut corners elsewhere than fail to give audiences a spectacular rodeo presentation. For this reason, he has been chosen to produce the openings at the National Finals Rodeo in Las Vegas for nine of the past eleven years.

In many ways, Rosser is like the stock contractors who worked the famous arenas all across the country during rodeo's Golden Age, the 1940s and 1950s. He was just a cowboy then, trying to earn his pay riding broncs and bulls, roping calves, and throwing steers. When he severely injured both legs in a farm threshing machine, his rodeo pals held some fund raising auctions and raised enough money for Rosser to open a western wear store. Eventually, Rosser's legs healed, his business grew, and he was able to start a stock contracting firm. With the financial help of a business partner, Rosser's Flying U Rodeo Company has grown to be the largest stock contracting firm on the Pacific Coast.

Rosser is a gruff man with a florid face that can bulge with anger one moment and break into a warm, crooked-toothed grin the next. Because of his accident, Rosser has a pronounced limp in his slow, laborious walk. Perhaps to compensate, he rides his colorful Paint horses throughout each of his rodeos. He cuts an impressive figure on horseback, sometimes roping the livestock after their runs and leading them out of the arena—a showy flourish typical of a man who loves a good show. "I used to go to Madison Square Garden and ride there," he says, "and [Gene] Autry would bring in the Longhorns and do 'Ghost Riders in the Sky.' God, they were show people!"

Rosser may be the last of that dying breed. Rising expenses—higher transportation costs, higher feed costs, higher salaries and benefit packages for employees, and soaring insurance rates—have caused many stock contractors to scale down their productions. Even Rosser, stock contractor to some of the largest rodeos in the country, grouses about production costs. "There is a huge expense in putting on a rodeo," he says. "In Long Beach, for instance, we had to haul in 600 tons of dirt to put on the arena floor and twenty tons of steel to set up the chutes and sidings. I just paid the ambulance drivers $120 an hour for being here at today's rodeo."

Cost-cutting measures have taken their toll. The contract acts that were once a part of almost every rodeo—trick riding teams, animal trainers, Mexican charros, and fancy rope artists—have been cut from many of the smaller shows. Today, clowns often take up the slack between events. Announcers grumble about contracts that barely cover their expenses. Trailers may go without new tires longer than safety and prudence would suggest. Still, stock contractors and rodeo committees do their best to provide as much entertainment as their budgets allow.

The locale often dictates the level of extracurricular activities needed to keep the audience entertained. In some cases, particularly in the rural areas of Colorado, Utah, New Mexico, and Wyoming, audiences are very knowledgeable about rodeo. They are content to sit through no-frills rodeo performances simply because they love the competitive events. Rodeos in or near large cities, on the West Coast, and in states where rodeo has not gained a large following tend to be more elaborate productions.

The work day for a rodeo stock contractor is nearly twenty-four hours long. Check into any rodeo in the country and you're likely to find a situation like the one in the desert community of Indio, California.

It's 11 A.M. on opening day of the town's annual Date Festival and as part of the festivities, a rodeo will be held this afternoon. Cotton Rosser's Flying U Rodeo is providing the livestock, and two men from his crew, Julio Moreno and Jeff Shearer, are working in the arena. The men, who will serve as pickup riders during the rodeo performance, are setting up the rope that triggers a barrier and signifies a fair start in the roping events. Known as "the score," the rope sets the distance that an animal must travel before the barrier is released, allowing the cowboy to ride out of the chute in pursuit. Official Bill Dunn watches their work, measuring the score to make sure it conforms to the PRCA rules established for the competitions.

Dunn fills out a standard form that all PRCA rodeo officials must complete, providing particulars about arena conditions, the length of the score, the contestants entered, and other information that will later be transmitted to the staff at the PRCA national headquarters in Colorado Springs. In the event of a rule dispute or a legal challenge, the form serves as evidence. Its main function, though, is to keep track of the competition times and scores. Julio Moreno glances at the sheets, looking over the numbers of contestants who will be competing in the timed events this afternoon: fifteen calf ropers, fifteen steer wrestlers, and eleven pairs of team ropers.

As the crew members take care of arena details, one remarks that only halter-broken bucking horses will be performing at this rodeo. (Some broncs are not halter broken and cannot be lead easily with a rope. They must be herded or pulled out of the arena.) "With the portable arena," he says, "it's easier to move the horses in and out of the arena." *A minor detail, something that most people wouldn't consider. A contractor must deal with hundreds of similar details at every rodeo—details that make the difference between a poorly organized competition and a clockwork-smooth production.*

In the parking lot are three semi-trailers, one for the rodeo equipment and two large "pot" trucks—huge aluminum-sided trailers with two levels, designed for carrying livestock. Additional rigs—pickup trucks paired with large stock trailers—carry a dozen horses each. The company also brings several motor homes, where employees sleep and take meals during their stay at the rodeo.

In addition to the vehicles owned by the Flying U, there are vans, pickups, and trailers owned by the various contract personnel—announcers, clowns, and others in the arena parking lot. Typically, a rodeo requires dozens of contract employees and an army of volunteers. In most rodeos, the volunteers participate simply because they enjoy rodeo. Serving on the rodeo committee or working alongside a stock contractor gives them a chance to be part of the cowboy heritage of the West.

"It's these weekend warriors that keep rodeo going," says Cotton Rosser as he sweeps a hand toward a group of volunteer helpers who have assembled around him. "This is their hobby. Like me, they say, 'This is what keeps me from having to play golf.'"

Some contractors have adapted well to the changing times. Mack Altizer, a Sonora, Texas, stock contractor, owns the successful stock contracting outfit Bad Company Rodeo. Altizer, the son of world-champion calf roper Jim Bob Altizer, combined his passion for rock music with rodeo. The result is a rodeo featuring high-amplitude sound systems blasting popular rock and rap music throughout the performances. Altizer prides himself on a party atmosphere featuring wild clown acts that appeal to college audiences. Each bucking animal is named for a popular song, such as "Bad to the Bone," the classic George Thoroughgood rocker. Each animal's namesake song plays as the bull or bronc busts loose from the chute and bucks across the arena. In keeping with the rock and rodeo atmosphere, Altizer promotes his rodeos like rock concert tours, complete with T-shirts, bumper stickers, and other promotional items popular among young audiences more familiar with Lollapalooza than the Lone Ranger.

Stock contractors are also distinguished by the names they give to their bucking stock. Each of the roughstock animals has both a number (which is the number drawn by the contestant via the PROCOM entry system) and a name. In a way, the names contractors select for their animals reflect the age of the stock contractor. Contractors from the older generation often name their livestock after family members and friends or choose popular names; the younger generation of contractors tends to name bulls after contemporary rock or country western songs, country musicians, and hard-rock groups.

Rosser and Altizer represent the extremes of rodeo showmanship—the fading traditions of the Old West shows from which rodeo originated to the high-tech, high-amplitude entertainment now found at sporting events like NBA basketball and NHL hockey. Most stock contractors fall somewhere in between, reflecting the traditional presentation of rodeo favored for the last two or three decades. Typical of these stock contractors are the Honeycutts, owners of the Honeycutt & Sons Rodeo Company of Alamosa, Colorado. Like most rodeo stock contractors, Roy Honeycutt depends on his family to handle the daily operations. Sons Jerry and Scott serve as pickup riders, the men who pluck the bareback and saddle bronc riders from the pitching horses. Their wives both serve as timers, recording event times and scores.

In addition to providing stock at fifteen PRCA-sanctioned rodeos, the Honeycutts contract rodeos for the National Old Timers Rodeo Association, high school rodeos, and amateur competitions in the vicinity of Phoenix, Arizona. In the summer, the stock is kept in Colorado; in winter, it is hauled to Arizona. "When we started business [nearly three decades ago], we owned one horse," says the family's matriarch, Virginia Honeycutt. "We went into a partnership, then had our own company for seventeen years. We leased everything. Now there are a lot of rules and regulations. You have to have so many animals and go to so many rodeos."

Virginia Honeycutt describes her company's method of getting the rodeo off to an exciting start: "A fast, snappy opening. Fast horses and pretty girls." With variations, this kind of opening is used by most stock contractors today. Typically, the flag girls, usually local or state rodeo pageant queens and their courts, enter the arena on horseback. Sequined outfits blaze as the young women ride at high speeds around the arena. Often, local dignitaries or special guests ride into the arena in parade formation, perhaps followed by the contestants on horseback. Flags bearing the logos of the rodeo sponsors may be presented, again on horseback, and certainly the state flag and the U.S. flag will pass through the arena before the flag-bearing horsewomen stop at center arena for the singing of the national anthem. Such an opening is known as the grand entry—a traditional prelude to an exciting rodeo.

The Honeycutts are typical stock contractors in other ways, too. Most stock contractors were born into the business and grew up around rodeos and livestock. When a company's founder dies or grows too old to handle the day-to-day operations, the company is handed down to the children. The Honeycutts, for example, count three generations of stock contractors in the family.

Dan Russell and his father, Dan, Sr., also fit this pattern. The Russells own Western Rodeos of Folsom, California. In the past ten years, the Russells have owned some exceptional bucking bulls, including three winners of the Bucking Bull of the Year Award, a prestigious award given to the owner of the bull voted most challenging by the top thirty bull riders. Similar awards are given to the owners of the top saddle bronc and bareback bronc. The Russells won three consecutive bucking bull awards for the phenomenal Pacific Bell, 1988 to 1990. Another Western Rodeos bull, Rocky, won the award in 1993, and a third bull, Grasshopper, took the award in 1994.

To win a bucking bull or bucking horse of the year is the stock contractor's equivalent of owning a winning Super Bowl team. In addition to working the California rodeos, the Russells take stock to the Cheyenne Frontier Days, the biggest outdoor competition. For this rodeo, they typically select fifteen of their best bulls and fifteen of their best horses from the nearly 500 head of bucking stock they own to use at Cheyenne. Other contractors, as many as six, take their very best stock to Cheyenne as well. Because of the prestige of this massive outdoor rodeo, stock contractors consider it an honor to have their stock there—like sending stock to the National Finals Rodeo. At Cheyenne and other large events, such as the Denver National Western Stock Show, the Houston Livestock Show, and the San Francisco Grand National Rodeo, it is typical for a number of stock contractors to provide stock to ensure evenly matched pens of top-quality bucking stock.

RODEO ANIMALS

Livestock—bucking bulls and horses, roping cattle, and the saddle horses used in the grand entry and throughout the rodeo—are the stock contractor's most valued assets. Acquiring good bucking stock and roping cattle is a year-round job for the average rodeo stock contractor. He attends three, four, or more bucking stock auctions each year, gatherings where buyers watch animals buck, then bid for them. Prices can be quite steep. At the 1994 National Finals Rodeo bucking stock sale, for instance, John Growney paid $13,500 for a 4-year-old bucking mare named Baldy. Another stock contractor paid

$12,000 for a 9-year-old bay gelding for the B Bar J Rodeo Company of Cleburne, Texas. The top bull at the annual sale went for $6,700—a high price for tough hamburger. According to one contractor, to purchase a complete string of quality bucking stock would cost approximately $1 million.

Typically, top-caliber PRCA stock contractors buy the higher quality (and higher priced) stock, selling their weaker stock to the contractors who service the smaller rodeos and amateur events. But a stock contractor who works a variety of rodeos must be mindful of his entire herd, looking for a balance of animals, some fearsome and others downright tame. With such a herd, he can provide stock to a range of rodeos—youth competitions, high school and college competitions, small-town professional rodeos, and the big events, including the National Finals Rodeo.

Up until the 1940s, it was possible for stock contractors to buy animals from ranchers or farmers, with plenty of rank bucking animals to choose. Ranchers who discovered a bucking colt in their string would call up a stock contractor, typically allowing the man to try the horse at a few rodeos before a deal was made. Sour saddle horses and farmers' draft animals that had gone bad supplied more bucking stock. Furthermore, bands of wild horses still roamed parts of the West, and some of these horses were inclined to buck. At some rodeos and bucking stock auctions, the promoters would simply run the feral horses in from the range, and the cowboys would ride them. (Feral horses are domesticated animals that have been released into the wild. During the Great Depression, tens of thousands of horses were simply abandoned because their owners could not afford to keep them.) The supply of bucking stock on the open range was so great, many stock contractors thought it would never diminish. They were wrong.

By the 1950s, bucking horses were in short supply. Ranchers began fencing off more and more pasture land, shooting the wild horses they considered a useless nuisance. And since rodeo had also become more popular, stock contractors had further depleted the pool of range horses. Working livestock was replaced with trucks and tractors, and rogue horses became scarce. A post–World War II market for horse meat also opened up, and instead of going to rodeos, outlaw horses were sent to packing plants and canneries, their flesh shipped to hungry citizens in some parts of wartorn Europe. All of these factors contributed to a tightening market and a scarcity of bucking stock, but perhaps the most disastrous change was in animal breeding practices.

Horsemen who grasped the principles of genetics discovered that bucking stock is often genetically predisposed to buck. That is, orneriness in a bucking horse is often passed from one generation to the next just as the desire to run is passed from the great thoroughbred racing horses to their offspring. Horsemen began breeding for gentle dispositions, and the result was fewer and fewer horses that felt inclined to buck.

"BORN TO BUCK" PROGRAMS

It seemed that the depletion of the wild horse pool and the urbanization of the United States would spell disaster for the stock contractors. Most stock contractors continued to search out bucking animals, for they knew no other way to acquire them. However, a Montana stock contractor named Ernest Tooke reasoned that if horses could be bred for tameness, they could also be bred to buck.

Tooke bought a draft horse named Prince and an Arabian stallion named Snowflake. These two proved to be mean bucking broncs, and when crossed with mares that Tooke owned, they produced horses with similar dispositions. While not all of the offspring bucked, Tooke soon discovered that his chances improved if he put the stallions with mares that also liked to buck. Within a few years, Tooke was selling bucking stock to contractors throughout the country. By crossing Snowflake's offspring with Prince, Tooke was able to improve the size, strength, and bone structure of his horses, creating a draft horse–type bucking animal with a characteristic look. In only a few years, the cowboys learned to recognize Tooke's horses simply by their appearance, and the science of breeding bucking horses was born.

Today, virtually all PRCA stock contractors breed bucking horses. Many breed bucking bulls as well. Although raising horses is usually more expensive than buying them, it has become a necessary part of stock contracting. One of the most successful breeding programs in rodeo is run by stock contractor Harry Vold. Vold is by far the most successful stock contractor in rodeo, controlling some of the biggest rodeos in the business, including Cheyenne's Frontier Days Rodeo. His stock is so well respected, his rodeos so appreciated, his approach so professional, that he has been chosen the PRCA's stock contractor of the year for nine consecutive years, beginning in 1987.

Each year, Vold raises about seventy-five colts on his sprawling 25,000-acre ranch near Pueblo, Colorado. Although Vold buys most of his bulls, he does raise authentic fighting bulls for his rodeos' American bullfighting competitions. Vold is known for his exceptional saddle broncs, which have won a total of eight bucking horse of the year titles. All told, Vold's bulls, saddle broncs, and bareback horses have won eleven bucking stock of the year titles.

Vold is especially proud of a horse named Bobby Joe Skoal, whom cowboys voted the top saddle bronc three consecutive times. Bobby Joe Skoal was the first winner that Vold had raised entirely on his ranch. Vold's livestock manager, Scott Walton, points out that there are no blueprints for breeding success. "We just breed out good bucking mares to the bucking studs," says Walton. "I would say that three or four colts out of a batch of ten might grow up to buck. That's about 35 percent. If you breed something to buck, it doesn't always work that way. You hope for the best, but you just never know." The "failures" are often broken as saddle horses for use in parades and grand entries, as well as for use on Vold's Red Top Ranch.

While Vold has achieved great success with horses, California stock contractor John Growney has had similar success with bulls. Growney works with another man, Don Kish, whose main concern is breeding top-quality bucking bulls. Growney was fortunate enough to own a bull named Red Rock, one of the greatest bulls in rodeo history. Red Rock went unridden throughout its entire career until it was retired in 1987. Growney brought the famous bull out of retirement in 1988 for a promotion called "The Challenge of the Champions," a special series of bull rides that pitted Red Rock against 1987 world champion bull rider Lane Frost. In the seven-round series, Red Rock defeated the champion on the first three rides. Frost finally puzzled out the bull's style, and on the fourth trip, he became the only man in history to ride the bull. Frost went on to win the series four to three over Red Rock. (Soon after the completion of the series, Lane Frost died after being gored by a bull at the Cheyenne Frontier Days Rodeo.)

Kish and Growney developed a breeding program built around Red Rock, one of only three bucking bulls ever inducted into the Professional Rodeo Hall of Fame. They crossed the bull with the offspring of another Hall of Fame bull named Oscar. The result is a line of bucking bulls with pedigrees that go back to two of the three most celebrated bulls in rodeo history. (The third Hall of Fame bull was Tornado, owned by sixteen-time world champion Jim Shoulders. Tornado was laid to rest at the Cowboy Hall of Fame in Oklahoma City, Oklahoma.) Growney and Kish now name each generation of bulls, calling one, for example, "The Wolf Pack." This current generation includes a bull called Wolfman, who has helped increase Growney's fame as a stock contractor. It was this small, brindle-faced bull who teamed with a little-known bull rider named Wade Leslie for rodeo's first (and to this date, only) perfect 100-point ride.

Bulls like Red Rock or Wolfman can create a promotional and marketing boom for a media-savvy stock contractor like Growney. "I will bring Wolfman to half of my rodeos this year," notes Growney. "Some rodeo committees ask for him specifically. When Red Rock became famous, I would take the bull to fifty rodeos and promote the bull aggressively. Most of the time he was bucked twice a weekend. Some rodeos are paying me an extra $1,500 to bring Wolfman to their rodeo this year. Copenhagen Skoal Pro Rodeo is interested in promoting both Wolfman and Outlaw as 'The Skoal Bandits.' It looks as if the bulls can market the stock contractor and introduce new ways to promote rodeo competition."

Few stock contractors, however, have the marketing savvy of John Growney —or notorious bucking animals like Red Rock and Wolfman. To breed a truly amazing animal athlete, whether it be Wolfman or Secretariat, requires a lot of know-how and a large degree of luck. Growney and Don Kish started breeding bucking bulls because it was nearly impossible to get the quality they wanted on the open market. "In terms of the percentage of bulls that will buck, you are lucky to get more than one out of ten bulls to buck that you buy at a sale. Because of our breeding program, we're now getting 70 percent to buck," says Growney.

Like most stock contractors, John Growney grows very attached to certain animals in his herd. After Red Rock retired from both bucking and breeding, Growney turned him out into a green pasture with a flowing brook. To this special retirement community, Growney later added a second champion bull, Mr. T. This huge black-and-white animal was owned by Wyoming stock contractor Pete Burns. Mr. T had gone unridden for more than 170 trips before finally being mastered at Cheyenne's Frontier Days by a bull rider named Marty Staneart. But Staneart's ride, one of the greatest feats in rodeo history, was overshadowed by the death that same day of world champion Lane Frost—the man who had defeated Red Rock. Burns and Growney agreed that Mr. T had earned a retirement in the mild climate of Red Bluff rather than the harsh, cold, windy winters of Wyoming.

Both Mr. T and Red Rock died in 1994 and were buried in the same pasture. When Red Rock was buried, Growney said, "He was one of the most famous people in Northern California." Similarly, when the three-time bucking bull of the year Pacific Bell was laid to rest at the ranch of California stock contractors Dan and Linda Russell, Linda said, "I cried. He was family."

LEVELS OF STOCK

Besides extensive breeding or Born to Buck programs, it is not uncommon for a large scale stock contractor to purchase, for instance, sixty new bulls in early winter from several different places. He tries out these "green" bulls by providing stock to the colleges to practice with or to be used in military and police rodeos. Those bulls that show promise or potential are kept and rotated into the main herd.

Rodeo animals buck because it is their nature. As a rule, roughstock animals seem to actively dislike contact with people. Contrary to popular opinion, bucking horses are not wild horses. Most come to rodeo because they have not performed well in other endeavors—as pickup horses, in one of the rodeo's timed events, as race horses, or as pleasure horses.

The stock contractors constantly evaluate their herds, looking for consistency in their bucking stock. It takes about a two-year tryout period before a stock contractor knows whether or not he has a good bucking animal. "We can buck our 2-year-olds at high school and college rodeos and see what they do," states John Growney. "Then, when they're used to rodeo and really bucking well, we'll turn them loose in the pros at age five." Average bucking animals are sold at stock sales or to other contractors to be used in amateur-level rodeos. Many animals that lack the capacity to become good bucking bulls will be "retired" from rodeo altogether.

The top cowboys are quick to comment on the bucking potential of the new stock. Between the bareback and saddle bronc riders, for instance, there may be a difference in opinion about a horse that turns back while bucking and one that chooses, instead, to buck forward in a straight line. As one cowboy noted, "In bareback, a horse that turns back is one you can deal with since you have the rigging to hold on to, and you can get a good score. But in saddle bronc, a horse that turns back is dangerous since you can't hold on, and they kick you when you fall."

The newer roughstock frequently act up in the bucking chutes, having not yet become accustomed to the procedures. The bulls try to turn around inside the chute, tails slapping back and forth, and get reputations as "chute fighters." Most of the new bulls have not been officially named, awaiting the stock contractor's decision to keep them. Sometimes they are transported to rodeos but not bucked to give them experience being moved and being in noisy crowds. Other times the new stock will be tried during slack outside of official competition by those cowboys wishing to ride for practice.

Stock contractors with two or more strings of roughstock animals will weigh several factors in deciding which string to take to a particular rodeo, primarily where the stock will be penned at the rodeo grounds. Those roughstock horses that are halter-broke and can be lead by hand can be fed in less constrained areas. Those that are not must be kept and fed in pens. Another factor is the length of the rodeo, which may vary from two or three performances to ten or twelve days. The most important factor, though, is the skill level of the contestants. A stock contractor providing animals for training programs for beginners, junior and high school rodeos, and the like will bring the *bloopers*—the easier stock in the herd, such as a bull that will merely lope down the arena. The cowboys with greater skills—those competing in college-level rodeos, military and police rodeos, International Rodeo Association (IRA) events, and the smaller, lower-paying PRCA-sanctioned rodeos— will likely ride a stock contractor's *average* stock. These animals are consistent but not spectacular—the ones a cowboy can make a ride on and maybe place.

The third level of stock is referred to as *rank* stock. These animals are tough, unpredictable in their movement patterns. They include the "eliminator" stock, hardest of all to ride. Rank animals, if they can be ridden, give the contestant the winning edge, the higher scores. These are the animals, along with the flashy average stock, that are brought to the top-paying PRCA rodeos.

For the livestock used in the timed events, the stock contractor looks for consistency in the herd, so that each competitor gets an "even playing field." Generally, about 70 percent of the calves or steers are consistent enough that the contestant can successfully complete his event. At bigger rodeos, however, the consistency may be lower since more animals are needed.

In steer wrestling, great care is taken in selecting the right animal for competition. The best steers are small and they run hard; they are also light in the back, heavy in the shoulders, and have a good neck base. The steers must also be in good health and are checked by a veterinarian before and after they are shipped from the ranch to a rodeo. Steer wrestlers particularly like steers with horns at least eight inches long so the steers cannot slip out of the cowboy's reach.

The roughstock must be "out" (used in rodeos) at least eight times during the course of the year in order to be evaluated by the top cowboys who select the bucking stock for the National Finals Rodeo. A string tires when it is transported too often from rodeo to rodeo, and a contractor can sense the state of his animals by how well they perform in the arena. Contractors who provide bucking stock for several different rodeos—sometimes three or four rodeos per weekend—hold back their top stock, sending younger horses and bulls (their third string) to the lesser paying rodeos. Bucking off a cowboy builds the green stock's confidence level, and over time, these animals will be moved into the better strings and out of the amateur ranks.

The stock selected to compete in the National Finals Rodeo by the top thirty cowboys in each event is the "cream of the crop." Animals will be grouped together for each of the ten performances into separate "pens" selected by the event director in each of the three roughstock events. The event director—chosen by the top cowboys and a current or former contestant in that event—groups each pen for consistency of style. For instance, at one performance of the bareback competition, cowboys may ride horses from the "souped-up tweet" pen—horses that are especially flashy. The consistency within each of the pens of horses is critical—it assures every contestant an equal chance of winning on most every horse.

At one recent NFR, the event director for the bareback riding competition, C. R. Kemple, discussed the improved quality of stock: "We're getting better bucking horses, stronger bucking horses, and they look more spectacular to the crowd. I hope to keep the consistency the same for each performance. [Both animals and cowboys] are getting higher scores because horses today are bucking better. The horses that make it to the finals have to be more fit, better fed, and better athletes."

Of the bareback horses used in PRCA-sanctioned rodeos throughout the country during the year, some 100 horses will make the NFR cut. All 100 will be used during the ten performances, with the event director rotating the stock throughout the week. Most of the bucking stock will be used only once, with the best-performing livestock used in the closing performances.

Besides the "souped-up tweet" pen (or "tweetie pies"), which measure the cowboy's style and ability, there is a "tweet" pen of even nicer horses less likely to buck the cowboys off. Other pens in the bareback riding event during the NFR include the "television" pen—a group composed of flashy, athletic horses; the "jam-up" pen—the good, solid horses that buck hard, true to their set pattern, from one rodeo to the next; and the "eliminator" pen— those horses that eliminate cowboys from the competition because they duck, dive, and spin to test the cowboy. These horses are extremely rare and often the pride and joy of the stock contractor, though they're no fun for the cowboy. At the NFR, each of the three roughstock event directors schedule their eliminator or TV pens on different nights. The saddle bronc riders, for instance, like to ease into the tougher animals so that the third night is their eliminator pen. For the bareback riders, the first night is "juice" night, when the riders are still fresh and their arms and backs are not sore.

In bull riding, the event director for the NFR competition, Bryan McDonald, begins with the easier to ride bulls in the first performance, followed the second night by the "spur" pen—those good, honest bulls with a set pattern. In the third night he shifts to the eliminator pen—the bulls that do not have speed or finesse but are "cheap shots" and try a little bit of everything. The fourth performance features the "fast spinner's" pen. The fifth pen is the "rank" or TV pen, the bulls ordinarily saved for the last performance at seasonal rodeos, the performance that is usually televised in the big rodeos. The sixth pen of bulls at the NFR is a mixture of every kind of bull.

Eliminator pens for both horses and bulls are those animals that have not been ridden much during the year. In this pen, for example, is the bull that reverses its spin, or the bull that belly rolls before it turns back. Or the horses that hop and skip, change direction, and have an irregular quality or timing in their bucking. Often in the roughstock events, the animals that are victorious in the eliminator pens are voted stock of the year in their event.

At the NFR, the draw in the timed events is run somewhat differently from that at other rodeos. The cowboys draw their animals for only two nights at a time. After the second night of competition, the pens are switched and the calves and steers are placed into rotation so the competitors are less likely to know specifically which animal they have drawn in future performances. With the timed events, the eliminator pen is made up of steers and calves that are difficult for the cowboy to make a good run with.

No matter what its reputation, an animal's performance can be affected by arena conditions. A horse with a reputation for bucking in a particular way may not perform accordingly under certain weather conditions, for example. If an outdoor arena is soupy after a heavy rain, the bucking horses often will skip-hop across the arena, trying to keep out of the mud puddles. Many horses dislike jumping in the mud—they don't like the mud splashing on their bellies and legs. In the mud they have the tendency to jump further apart. Sometimes the mud scares them or makes them mad. After they skip, they do not buck as well.

The contractors are concerned with keeping the animals in top shape for rodeo competition. "The bulls that buck well usually do not fight the other bulls," says John Growney. "For those that have a tendency to fight, we separate them so that they will not attack each other. The animals have a real strong pecking order. Our job is to keep them healthy. Other bulls turn on the loser of a fight between bulls."

Upon arrival at the rodeo grounds, the stock is worked in the pens behind the chutes. Often before the first performance they are brought down the lanes into the bucking chutes, released into the arena, and driven out through the "catch pen" (or "stripping chute," where the cowboy's equipment is removed from the roughstock). This trial run helps familiarize the animals with the arena set-up. The seasoned bulls learn their way around quickly and look for the exit gate as soon as the ride is over, but getting the green stock to head for the catch pen can be a laborious task. Once through the stripping chutes, the animals are led back to their holding pens.

The better the animal, the more often it is hauled to rodeos. Traveling together in the large transport trucks seems to help the stock become an elite string and explains why they will pair up and pen together in the fields back on the ranch. "Even the NFR stock pairs up on its own, as does the mediocre stock," notes Growney. "Maybe being secluded on the ranch, or traveling together in the trucks, bonds the stock together. But they pair up by their ability. We watch for this, as it is easier to load the stock for traveling purposes if we know which ones have buddied-up."

Back on the ranch, the roughstock are placed in open fields. They need to be out where they do not see human life. The more contact they have with humans, the more spoiled they will become. As one contractor noted, "Unless you have about 500 acres, you can't raise the stock in the correct way. The more the stock is close to humans, the more likely they will not have that independence, that sense of freedom."

In the large-scale operations, a stock contractor may bring as many as three big semis filled with livestock to a rodeo. At the four-day Prescott rodeo one year, Harry Vold transported ninety horses and forty bulls for the three roughstock events, along with calves and steers for the timed events, fighting bulls for the bullfighting competition, and horses for the wild horse race. John Growney provided eighty-two horses and eighty bulls for a recent two-day rodeo in Oakdale, California. With good bucking horses costing anywhere between $3,000 and $10,000 each and rodeo bulls running from $10,000 to $20,000, the costs involved in providing an entire string of stock for a rodeo are quite high.

At the rodeo none of the stock will be used for more than two performances. That is why it is not unusual for a proven bucking horse to compete in rodeo for twenty-five years and for a superior bucking bull to compete for twelve years. The prime bucking age for rodeo bulls is three to nine years old.

ANIMAL ACTIVISTS AND ANIMAL WELFARE

"The rodeo is where terrified baby cows run away from lariat-swinging horsemen just before their bodies are snapped backwards by a noose fastened onto their

necks, burning, bruising, and sometimes breaking those necks. The rodeo is where
frenzied [horses] gyrate violently, not because that is their nature, but solely
because of the 'bucking strap'—the spurs belted onto their flanks. The rodeo is
where steers are team roped, one lasso around their legs, another around their
heads, yanked in opposite directions, swung in the air, and slammed to the
ground, and where on occasion their horns crack and splinter.

The rodeo is about intimidation and abuse of those weaker than us. It is
about brutality and cruelty and injustice, forcing fear and pain on the innocent,
defenseless beings and violating the basic principles of freedom and peace. As a
violent and exploitative part of our culture, rodeos should not be tolerated. It
should be boycotted and put out of business."
—Baron L. Miller, *in a letter to the editor in a Northern California newspaper* [1]

The animal rights movement began in the late 1800s in England with
the antivivisectionists, who were dedicated to eliminating the use of animals
in medical and scientific experiments. In the late 1800s protests were held
in New York City over the use and treatment of horses in horse-drawn bug-
gies. Animal rights groups have protested rodeo for the past century as well.
In 1895, the Denver Humane Society had local police arrest a man who was
demonstrating steer roping at a public event. In 1923, protests by the Calgary Humane Society and cattlemen who wished to protect their livestock
from injury led to a ban on steer wrestling at the Calgary Stampede. The
"complete abolition" of rodeo was also advocated by the Washington State
Humane Society as early as 1926.[2]

In most cases, however, animal advocacy groups have not made rodeo their
primary target. Though their agendas vary, many groups want to regulate or
ban hunting, trapping, whaling, and fishing. Some oppose the use of animals
in zoos, circuses, scientific experiments. They also oppose "factory" farms
and furriers. Some condemn the use of animals in entertainment such as
films and television, and some oppose the purposeful breeding of wild and/or
companion animals. Since rodeos do not attract the media attention of many
of these other activities, and because rodeos already have humane rules and
a defensible humane record, rodeos are not among the most desirable of tar-
gets for these organizations. At times, however, they have taken a stand on
rodeo-related legislative movements.

Estimates of the number of such organizations range from a low of 700 to
a high of 7,000. According to one observer, these animal rights groups have
some 10,000 dues-paying members and raise from $50 million to $100 million to affect public opinion and lobby state and congressional legislatures.

People for the Ethical Treatment of Animals (PETA), one of the largest of the national organizations, had a budget of $8.8 million in 1990.[3]

In recent years, the ideas of animal activist groups have been sympathetically received, which can be explained, in part, by simple demographics. In 1776, 90 percent of the U.S. population lived in rural areas. By 1920, that number had shrunk to 36 percent. By 1990, only one in five Americans resided in the country. The fact that Americans increasingly grow up in urban areas has meant that fewer and fewer people have had experience working with, or living around, horses and cattle.

As rodeo has evolved, the people charged with overseeing the sport have done their best to dispel the opinion that the sport is institutionalized animal cruelty, and that the animals are purposely abused for the sadistic enjoyment of humans. They have also made necessary rule changes to improve the physical well-being of the animals. And yet, in recent years the critics have continued to target rodeo, becoming even more vocal as the sport has become kinder and more humane.

Typically, rodeo stock contractors point out that they have a substantial economic interest in maintaining the health of their animals. If an animal gets injured, the stock contractor cannot use that animal and therefore loses money. One of the biggest misconceptions about the treatment of rodeo stock is that pieces of wire or glass are placed inside the flank strap to make the horses buck. "Some also say that the flank strip squeezes the horse's genitals and that isn't true," Growney points out. "The flank strip is there to annoy the horse, just so they'll move from where they're standing and kick. No one can make horses buck if they don't want to. From a purely business standpoint, horses won't buck if they don't feel good. And giving them the best hay, grain, and medical care makes them feel good."

Working with animals is one of the most gratifying aspects of the rodeo stock contractor's job. The affection John Growney has for his animals is apparent in his voice as he talks about his love of the sport of rodeo. "God's greatest gift to man is the horse," observes Growney. "And the rodeo horses, well, they're the one's who won't conform. They're a special breed."

Stock contractors are proud of their care and routinely invite animal rights protesters to inspect their livestock facilities. Their reasons for this invitation are not entirely pure; most stock contractors know they will not persuade animal rights activists to support rodeo. But by bringing them into the back pens, they can keep them from public forms of protest. Still, some activists actually come away from these inspections with a changed attitude about rodeo animals and their care after a public relations tour with a stock contractor.

California stock contractor Cotton Rosser, owner of the Flying U Rodeo Company in Marysville, likes to recount his experience with an animal rights activist who came to inspect the livestock at the National Finals Rodeo. Rosser took the woman on a full tour of the facilities and even invited her to the prestigious competition, seating her in his own luxury skybox for the evening. After seeing the behind-the-scenes care of the livestock and sitting through an entire performance of the rodeo, the woman told Rosser, "I agree that the animals are well cared for, but you should take better care of the cowboys."

The PRCA has hired a full-time public relations spokesperson known as the "humane officer" to respond to negative media coverage of rodeo live-stock. In addition to tracking legislation that could affect rodeo, the representative of the world's largest rodeo association works with other rodeo and livestock associations to fight back against legislative moves that could harm the rodeo and livestock industries. It is also the humane officer's responsibility to work with rodeo committees to train their staff members to respond to protests, to handle media inquiries, and to deal with acts of protest that might adversely affect rodeo audiences and rodeo facilities.

Humane treatment of animals has been a concern of rodeo organizers for decades, almost since the creation of the sport. The PRCA established rules regarding the humane treatment of animals in 1947. Those rules have been continually updated and strengthened. There are now more than forty rules geared specifically toward the humane treatment of rodeo livestock. Some stock contractors argue that the rules have become financially burdensome. But for the most part, the stock contractors support them, mainly because the alternative could be far more severe: the restriction or even abolition of rodeo in some states.

Most stock contractors seem befuddled by the negative criticism that is stirred up by animal activists. Harry Vold, several time PRCA stock contractor of the year, notes, "These animals work about a minute and a half each year. They have an easy life—good food, medical care." And, as he and others point out, what other purpose could these outlaw animals serve? "If it were not for rodeo, these animals would be sold for slaughter," says Vold.

The PRCA publishes a humane facts pamphlet outlining the care and treatment of professional rodeo livestock, assuring the public that the animals used are top athletes. By inspecting every animal before it is selected for competition, the PRCA ensures that only healthy livestock is used. If an animal becomes sick or injured between the time it is drawn and the time it is scheduled for competition, it will not be used.

A 1988 survey of on-site veterinarians at some of the PRCA's top rodeos indicated the injury rate for animals was so low that it was statistically negligible. In 6,933 outings, just twelve animals (less than .2 percent) were injured.[4] It is statistically more likely that a calf, steer, bull, or horse will be injured at a ranch than in the rodeo arena. Even so, animal activists often argue that one injured rodeo animal is too many.

This zero-tolerance attitude is one reason why rodeo organizers feel that they will never satisfy animal activists, because no matter what steps are taken to protect the animals, some will inevitably get injured. Adverse publicity about injuries to animals during high-profile rodeos has increased, making the rare injuries seem far more common than actual statistics indicate. In 1995 at the California Rodeo at Salinas, three serious injuries to animals (two of which occurred in non-PRCA-sanctioned events such as the wild horse race) resulted in pressure on the rodeo committee to become even more diligent about animal safety—this, despite the fact that several hundred animals performed without incident.

PRCA rules require that a veterinarian be either on site or on call for every performance and every section of slack, in the event an injury does occur. Many of the PRCA's competitors and committee members are also veterinarians and can render medical treatment. Rodeo committees also have a contingency plan set up to move any injured animal from the arena to a location where it can be attended to. This is a recent trend among rodeos and was partly initiated to remove an injured animal from the public's eye as quickly as possible, thus avoiding disturbing publicity.

Animal activist groups frequently express concern about the equipment used in rodeo, particularly the flank straps, spurs, and electric prods used on the roughstock animals. Given that most animal rights activists do not work with livestock and have no working knowledge of large animal anatomy, the activists often misidentify the body areas that are touched by the bucking strap. Much of the early animal rights literature claimed that the straps contacted the sensitive genital areas of the stock—in fact, the straps are positioned well in front of the genital areas of male animals and, of course, many of the bucking horses are mares.

The flank strap enhances the bucking action, serving as an irritant. Since the strap crosses the horse's or bull's back and stomach, it is natural for the animals to try and throw the strap off with their hoofs as they jump and kick. This is an instinctual response to having something on their backs, such as an attacking mountain lion or other predator. According to large animal veterinarians, the bucking straps cause no injury to the animals. PRCA rules strictly regulate the use of the strap, which must have a quick-release buckle and must also be lined by sheepskin. Sharp or cutting objects are never placed or used in the strap's construction. The horse's kidneys are protected by its ribs, and the flank strap does not injure internal organs.

The spur rowels used in pro rodeo's three roughstock events are required to be dulled and to be loose in the two bronc riding events so that they roll easily over the animal's thick hides; dulled locked rowels are used in bull riding. Spurs that meet PRCA guidelines have blunt rowels—the star-shaped wheel on spurs—that are about one-eighth of an inch thick so they cannot cut the animals. If a rider uses spurs that do not meet these requirements, he can be disqualified from competition.

The electric prod is a device developed by the cattle industry to move animals humanely, replacing the sharp-ended prods common to the industry a few decades ago. In PRCA rodeos, electric prods are occasionally used to move the rodeo livestock into the chute area. The PRCA rules regulate the use of prods, requiring that they be used as little as possible. Animals may be prodded only on the hip or shoulder area. Powered solely by flashlight batteries, the prod is used for only a fraction of a second, producing a startling but noninjurious shock.

Not all people who question rodeos are animal activists. As one observer noted, rodeo doesn't "address the obvious tough question, though, and the one that seems to bother a lot of people. Rodeos are obviously not pleasant for the animals, even though they may not actually be hurt. The flank strap irritates them enough to make them thrash and buck wildly. For a calf, being yanked backwards from a full run by a rope around its neck has got to be a nasty experience. How can we really justify this? And lumping everyone who might be worried about this under the umbrella of animal rights activist seems too easy and an oversimplification."

Even with the safeguards, most animal rights organizations continue to oppose the sport. At times, the opposition has led to violence. This was the case with rodeo champion Jack Roddy, whose livestock barn was burned to the ground by activists in the late 1980s. At some rodeos, activists have disrupted the competitions with protests. Picket lines outside rodeo arenas are common in certain communities, particularly those located near large urban centers.

To avoid trouble, some rodeo committees have tightened security. Others have designated areas where protest groups can assemble. "We have security looking out at the stock yards," states Robin Reynolds, committee member of San Francisco's Grand National Rodeo. "We will always have one or two days where protesters show up. We have set up three authorized zones where they can have their freedom of speech. If they pay their ticket and come in, we don't mind them watching. But if they cause problems, we will escort them out."

Animal activists view calf roping as rodeo's Achilles' heel. The act of roping and trussing an infant animal is often viewed as brutal, despite the fact that injuries to calves at PRCA-sanctioned rodeos number less than .1 percent. Because of the sensitivity to the animal welfare issue, the PRCA has responded to spectators' and animal activists' concerns about calf roping with rule changes that have made the event more cosmetically appealing. One rule dictates that calves may not be flipped over backward or thrown from their feet when roped, a practice referred to by cowboys as "jerking down" the calf. At designated rodeos, cowboys are now fined if they jerk a calf down.

In communities where displeasure with calf roping is strong, some stock contractors and rodeo committees simply keep the event away from the audience's eyes. Calf roping at some rodeos is scheduled as the final rodeo event so that people may leave early if they so choose. Or the calf roping event is held separately from the regularly scheduled rodeo performance. Calf ropers argue that these steps are unnecessary and detrimental to the sport over the long run. Still, some stock contractors frankly admit that they would rather upset the cowboys than lose or offend spectators.

Some of the actions taken by animal activist groups have been disruptive. At the La Fiesta De Los Vaqueros Rodeo in Tucson, Arizona, one year, activists smeared epoxy glue in all of the gate locks, thus preventing people from entering the rodeo grounds and parking lots. In Orange County, California, in 1991, twenty-two protesters paraded inside the rodeo grandstand area shortly after the opening ceremonies, to the boos of the rodeo fans. The matching orange-colored sweatshirts worn by the activist group, with the phrase "Rodeos Hurt Animals" on the front, clearly identified their cause.

"We are against any form of animal exploitation," said Ava Park, organizer of the demonstration and founder of the Orange County People for Animals (OCPA), interviewed shortly after the first protest. The next year, the protest was repeated. Hoping to avoid such disruptions in the future, the Orange County Fair board allowed the OCPA to set up a booth just outside the rodeo arena in exchange for an agreement that no protesters would disrupt the competition.

In 1995, four years after OCPA's first demonstration, the group claimed a victory. "Last roundup for some rodeo events: competition and complaints mean calf roping and steer wrestling are out" ran a headline in the *Orange County Register*. It marked the decision of the rodeo committee and stock contractor to change the format of the 70-year-old rodeo. Although there were other reasons for making the change, the decision to exclude these timed events and produce an amateur-level rodeo focusing on only rough-stock competition was due, in part, to complaints from animal rights activists.

Those who do not understand large animals and their needs are vulnerable to the manipulation of the facts by the activists. Often, the published literature distributed by such groups incorrectly refer to steers as cows, and calves as bulls. Descriptions of equipment are also misleading. One brochure published by the Humane Society of the United States claimed that metal is used in the bits of bucking horses, the implication being that the metal injured the animals' mouths. In fact, bits (metal bars placed in the horse's mouth to enable the rider to control the animal) are never used in rodeo roughstock events. Halters, which are wide, flat leather or nylon head restraints that fit over the horses' noses, are used in the saddle bronc riding, while no head restraints of any kind are used in the bareback riding. Factual errors such as these are common in the literature of the animal rights groups, and the inaccuracies are upsetting to people trying to defend the sport or rodeo.

"Some people who oppose rodeo and other animal uses are well-meaning individuals who want to do something to prevent animal cruelty," says Bob Ragsdale, a former rodeo competitor and past president of the PRCA. "Unfortunately, their views are often based on sensationalized material designed by people who can't be credited with the same worthy intentions."[5]

Media representatives have often been misled by factually questionable information furnished by animal activists. Just like the animal activists themselves, few reporters have experience with livestock, and this lack of knowledge makes it difficult for them to separate truth from fiction. News reporters always prefer the controversial to the common; injured animals are therefore more newsworthy than healthy animals.

In 1991, a segment on NBC's *I Witness Video* showed a bull who broke a leg in a rodeo in Pittsburgh, Pennsylvania. This video created such a public outcry that rodeo was subsequently banned in the city. But as humane officials appointed by the Society for the Prevention of Cruelty to Animals (SPCA) pointed out, the rodeo had an excellent record with few instances of injury to the animals. The bull's broken leg was the exception, not the rule.

In 1994, television footage of horses being tripped in a Mexican-style rodeo on the ABC show 20/20 led to legislative action in California and Texas banning the event. Although horse tripping (known as *mangana*) is seldom condoned by American rodeo officials or competing cowboys, the initiative that ended up stopping the practice in California also included attempts to ban calf roping and steer wrestling. These amendments were later taken out of the legislation, which likely would have been defeated had the ban on traditional rodeo events remained in place. As a result of the negative media attention brought by video cameras, some rodeo committees now ban their presence.

Particularly hard hit by animal rights activism is the Mexican form of rodeo, the *charreada*. Several of their main events, in which horses are roped either on foot or on horseback, have been outlawed in California. A movement to ban them in other states—Texas, New Mexico, Arizona, Colorado—is now being orchestrated by animal rights groups. *Charro* (cowboy) organizations claim that they are the victims of an attack on minority and rural culture that the urban majority does not understand. Animal activists—some of whom are Latino—counter that the charros are justifying cruelty when they argue political correctness. Under a banner headline, "A Question of Culture or Cruelty?" a 1994 article in the *Los Angeles Times* documented how animal activist groups had been successful in portraying charros as "horsemen who abuse animals for sport."[6]

Initial efforts in 1993 to pass a bill that would ban tripping horses died in the California Assembly's Committee on Agriculture, mainly due to pressure from American rodeo organizations, who feared a backlash that would spread to their sport. But such a bill was passed the following year, in part because of the activists' successful efforts in getting support for the ban from groups ranging from the California Veterinary Medical Association to the California Council of Police and Sheriffs to the United States Equestrian Team. By that time, the PRCA and other rodeo groups had withdrawn any support for certain charreada events, which, association spokespeople point out, are not condoned at PRCA-sanctioned contests.

Much of the negative media coverage regarding rodeos has focused on incidents in amateur rodeos, which are not necessarily required to adhere to the same high standards of livestock care established by professional rodeo. Because of the lack of humane rules enforcement, the generally poorer condition of the livestock, and the lack of know-how on the part of competitors and stock handlers, animal injuries at these rodeos may be unreasonably high. This, in turn, attracts more criticism and more opportunity for the discovery of poor or neglectful treatment. The negative publicity about these shows has generated a public backlash that has hurt rodeo at all levels, including PRCA-sanctioned competitions.

Even though pro rodeo has defended the sport for the past several decades, more concerted efforts have emerged in response to the serious challenges raised by the activist groups. In June 1992, the PRCA began a regular column, "Animal Welfare Issues," in the *Prorodeo Sports News*, which includes a regular update on the activities of animal rights groups. Supporters of rodeo have begun to fight back by warning the public about animal activist groups, and the PRCA has also begun to work with amateur and youth rodeo associations, encouraging them to adopt the PRCA's humane rules and to enforce them at their events. In this effort, the PRCA has also organized seminars on how to take better care of livestock and how to deal with animal injuries when they occur.

Many people in rodeo believe that the animal activists will eventually lose favor with Americans, and signs of this already seem evident. "Animal Activism is another enemy lurking on our soil. Think about it America. Listen up USA!" proclaimed one freeway sign in Orange County in late 1994. Groups supporting rodeo have been developed to educate the public about ranch animals and to combat the animal activists. One such organization, Friends of Rodeo, was formed in 1992 by Kenny Ross of Dallas, Texas, to preserve rodeo, horse shows, trail rides, and other equine events that the organization considers part of the nation's heritage. The organization raises money to fund legislative efforts and education programs in support of the rodeo industry. Friends of Rodeo supports the PRCA's goal of educating amateur and youth rodeo organizations about humane rules and supports the PRCA's efforts to compel these organizations to adopt the PRCA's humane guidelines.

Several stock contractors, both amateur and professional, now conduct informal chute tours before select rodeo performances. Individuals or groups who have questions and wish to learn more about the sport are given the opportunity to observe rodeo livestock in the holding pens, walk around the cowboy readying area behind the bucking chutes, and handle equipment such as the flank strap and spurs. The success of such ventures has led to organized Chute Tours programs. The PRCA realizes that providing educational opportunities and practicing good animal welfare will help counter the criticism raised by the activist groups. Besides urging its members to conduct themselves and their rodeos in a professional manner, the association also remains committed to supporting new rules that will help protect both the animals and the sport.

Rodeo pageantry on parade in Cheyenne, Wyoming.
(Photo by Gavin Ehringer)

Contestants at the National Finals Rodeo in Las Vegas line up during the
grand entry, the traditional opening of a rodeo performance.
(Photo by Ken Opprann)

Rodeo star Ty Murray welcomes rodeo fans to his home-away-from-home:
the MGM Grand Hotel and Casino in Las Vegas.
(Photo by Ken Opprann)

A bull rider wearing a comical cowboy shirt seems preoccupied.
(Photo by Ken Opprann)

A competitor prepares mentally and physically for his next ride.
(Photo by Ken Opprann)

Ty Murray stretches just prior to one of his rides.
(Photo by Ken Opprann)

Sitting on the fence by the bucking chutes, a rider waits his turn.
(Photo by Ken Opprann)

Bull rider Aaron Semas tapes his wrist in preparation for his speciality event.
(Photo by Ken Opprann)

Bareback rider Roger Lecasse gets ready for his event at the Cow Palace in
San Francisco, despite torn ankle ligaments sustained in a collision during
a previous ride.
(Photo by Ken Opprann)

Behind the chutes, a saddle bronc rider gets ready for his next "go."
(Photo by Ken Opprann)

A bull rider straps on his spurs.
(Photo by Ken Opprann)

A saddle bronc rider breaks from the bucking chute.
(Photo by Ken Opprann)

Robert Etbauer, two-time World Champion Saddle Bronc Rider, is only the most recent of a long line of winners in that event from South Dakota.
(Photo by Dan Hubbell, courtesy of PRCA)

A bareback bronc rider demonstrates good form at the Pikes Peak or Bust Rodeo
in Colorado Springs, Colorado.
(Photo by Gavin Ehringer)

Adam Carrillo (pictured) and his twin brother Gilbert are two of the most widely
recognized elite bull riders in professional rodeo.
(Photo by Dan Hubbell, courtesy of PRCA)

Rodeo's danger is most apparent in the bull riding. At the 1994 National Finals, bull rider Brent Thurman was fatally wounded when a bull stepped on his neck and head. Bullfighters Joe Baumgartner and Lloyd Ketchum attempt to lead the bull away from the fallen rider.
(Photo by Ken Opprann)

As a baby, Rooster Reynolds rode in the NFR grand entry with his dad Benny. Three decades later, he competed in the steer wrestling event, wearing the World Champion All-Around Cowboy buckle Benny won in 1961.
(Photo by Dan Hubbell, courtesy of PRCA)

In 1995 Joe Beaver captured the World Champion All-Around Cowboy title as a timed event competitor. It was the first time since 1984 that the award had not gone to a roughstock ace.
(Photo by Dan Hubbell, courtesy of PRCA)

Only bull riding exceeds the popularity of barrel racing among rodeo fans, thanks in large measure to the achievements of world champions Sherry Potter-Cervi and Charmayne (James) Rodman, a ten-time winner.
(Photos by Dan Hubbell, courtesy of PRCA)

Performer Gerardo "Jerry" Diaz performs the traditions of the Mexican charro in rodeo arenas throughout the country. Here, he displays his rope artistry at Denver's National Western Stock Show. (Photo by Gavin Ehringer)

A Native American drummer performing in Cheyenne, Wyoming. (Photo by Gavin Ehringer)

Rodeo clown Charlie "Too Tall" West.
(Photo by Ken Opprann)

A rodeo fan's innovative effort to obtain tickets.
(Photo by Ken Opprann)

One of the many vendors that ply their wares at contemporary rodeos.
(Photo by Gavin Ehringer)

Rodeo queens act as spokespersons for the sport. Here, Wendi Lund of Canada and Jennifer Douglas of Texas pose for a publicity photo at the National Finals Rodeo. (Photo by Ken Opprann)

Films like 8 *Seconds*, the story of bull rider Lane Frost (portrayed here by Luke Perry), help to keep rodeo in the public eye.
(Photo by Louise Serpa, courtesy of New Line Cinema)

Rodeo careers often begin at a young age. Here, Lyle Etbauer plays with his three sons—Robert, Dan, and Billy. All three have gone on to have great success in professional rodeo.
(Courtesy of Bev and Lyle Etbauer)

A young cowboy practices his roping at a rodeo in Hayward, California.
(Photo by Ken Opprann)

In the professional circuits, every rodeo competitor must wear a cowboy hat and long-sleeved shirt, or be fined by the PRCA. Here, a hat vendor steams a crease into a hat for one of the competitors.
(Photo by Ken Opprann)

Tools of the trade: a crumpled shirt, a contestant's number, and a bull riding glove.
(Photo by Ken Opprann)

CONTRACT

PERSONNEL,

CLOWNS, &

BULLFIGHTERS

J ohn Payne, a ranch cowboy, was working on an electrical power box. He knew little about electrical wiring, and his ignorance proved almost fatal. An improper connection caused 10,000 volts of electricity to surge through his arm and exit his body through his abdomen. For several minutes, Payne's heart quit beating. Other ranch hands tried CPR to keep him alive, and miraculously, his heart began beating once again. Doctors were able to save Payne's life, but at the cost of his right arm.

After the accident, Payne earned his living by gathering wild cattle in the South with the help of a pack of trained dogs that he'd taught to ferret out the cattle from the thick brush. One day, Payne visited a friend, stock contractor Walt Alsbaugh, and Alsbaugh took Payne to one of his rodeos. As Payne stood watching the contract act, he told Alsbaugh that the act was poor and that he could do better. Alsbaugh told Payne to prove up or shut up, and Payne took *the bait. At home, he went directly to work creating an act that he felt would impress rodeo audiences. He realized that his strong suit was working with cattle, dogs, and horses. What he came up with was nothing short of amazing.*

At the start of his show, one of Payne's assistants drives a one-ton truck-and-trailer rig decorated with thousands of flashing lights into the rodeo arena. On the truck's hood is a set of six-foot-wide cattle horns, and on the side of the trailer are the words, "The One Arm Bandit and Company." Payne rides into the arena on horseback, cracking a bull whip with his one arm while his horse darts around the arena, guided only by the horseman's leg cues. A small herd of cattle is released from the trailer, followed by Payne's pack of black-mouthed cur cattle dogs. With Payne cracking his whip and shouting directions, the dogs herd the cattle around the arena. To demonstrate the dogs' amazing stock-handling abilities, Payne has the dogs drive the cattle back to the trailer and climb, via a small ramp, to the trailer's roof. Payne then jumps his horse onto the ramp and rides to the roof of the trailer himself.

As the audience looks on, Payne then stands up on the saddle of his horse. More than twenty feet above the ground, balanced precariously atop his horse, Payne cracks his whip. The audience cheers wildly, and Payne raises his hat to salute them. Meanwhile, the rodeo announcer recounts the story of how Payne overcame his handicap, developed his amazing act, then went on to become the most celebrated performer in rodeo, the PRCA Specialty Act of the Year.

CONTRACT PERSONNEL

Contract personnel like John Payne make a huge contribution to rodeo. They arrive early for the rodeo, do much of the advance publicity, help the rodeo committee fine-tune the production details, and give the audience memories that remain long after the competition ends. Ask an audience member new to rodeo what his or her favorite part of the rodeo was and the answer is likely to be the contract acts. This response is doubly true for children, who can appreciate a clown and his performing duck much more easily than they can appreciate a great bull ride.

Each year the PRCA publishes an extensive directory of contract personnel. Besides the rodeo producers and stock contractors, the fifty-six-page directory includes the names and addresses of the specialty acts, rodeo announcers, timers, secretaries, laborers, photographers, clowns, barrelmen, and bullfighters. Though they do not all share the limelight (only the specialty acts, announcers, clowns, and bullfighters strive to entertain the crowd), the contract personnel are the key to a lively and entertaining rodeo.

People often compare rodeos to circuses—a fair analogy in some ways, particularly when it comes to the contract acts. Just as a circus is made up of more than stars, rodeo is more than cowboys. If the cowboys are like the high-wire artists and animal tamers of the circus, the contract personnel are like the carnies, clowns, masters of ceremonies, and ticket sellers.

SPECIALTY ACTS

Today's specialty acts vary according to the budget and the needs of the rodeo committee and the audience. Some of the more traditional rodeos employ the trick and fancy ropers and riders, staples of rodeo since Buffalo Bill's Wild West shows. The riders race at top speed around the arena doing a variety of acrobatic maneuvers, including the Cossack Drag with their heads hanging to the ground close to the flying hoofs of the horse, or the Hippodrome Stand, standing atop their mounts with arms fully extended. These acts, which may only last a few minutes, take lifetimes to perfect. It is not unusual for a trick rider to begin his or her apprenticeship before entering grade school and to develop the routines for a decade before actually taking the show on the road.

Trick roping is a throwback to a bygone era in which a cowboy's ability to perform fancy rope tricks in order to catch livestock on the open range was nearly as important as his ability to ride saddle broncs. Trick roping and riding were competition events as late as the 1930s, and many of today's artists perform stunts named for the pioneering cowboys and cowgirls who competed in these events at these early rodeos.

RODEO ANNOUNCERS

The responsibility of the rodeo announcer is clear. He must inform and entertain the audience while providing a running commentary on the contestants' scores and times. Some announcers work on horseback inside the arena, stopping by the arena fence to chat with members of the audience. Others are located in crow's nest booths, near or above the bucking chutes, where they can keep a close eye on all the rodeo action.

Although there are over 100 card-carrying announcers in professional rodeo, only a small number work full time and are able to make a living at their profession. "It is a very competitive business with a dozen or so getting most of the jobs," said Wayne Wise of Loveland, Colorado, in 1992. "In a typical year I will work about 75 rodeos, but the big name announcers will work over 200 rodeos. This is the beginning of my fifth year and I'm close to getting into the good pack." Wise now announces the Bull Riders Only tour as well as PRCA-sanctioned rodeos.

The fans' enjoyment of the rodeo depends in great measure upon the announcer, who must be able to convey to the audience information about each contest event and the rules involved as well as information about the contestants themselves. The announcer is a master of ceremonies who sets the pace for the action in the arena. He announces the cowboy out of the chute, describes the action taking place, and reports the judges' scores. His knowledge of the bucking stock is important, too. But what separates the best announcers from the pack is charisma, the ability to involve the audience members in the rodeo action.

One of the top rodeo announcers in the PRCA is Bob Tallman, who has worked the NFR and also covers rodeo for television and radio. He has twice been selected as the PRCA's announcer of the year. "I had the desire for the lifestyle of a cowboy, but I didn't have the dedication to be one," commented Tallman in an article written for the *Reno Gazette-Journal* in 1991. "When I found out that I had a blessing to exploit the mannerisms and the talent of my friends by talking I said, 'Heck this has got to be a great way to get rich.' And I was able to keep the lifestyle."[1]

RODEO TIMERS AND SECRETARIES

Rodeo timers use stopwatches to keep the official time in the timed events; they also sound a buzzer after the required eight seconds in the roughstock events. The rodeo secretary records the times, figures the pay-off, and pays the winning cowboys; the secretary also stays in communication with the PRCA and assists judges in drawing stock.

"It's a lot of work," says Mildred Farris, five-time PRCA Rodeo Secretary of the Year. "But being around rodeo people makes it all worthwhile. Everywhere we go, it's sort of like a family reunion." Farris works over twenty-five rodeos a year, including the big winter rodeos that last up to two weeks. "We live out of our motor home when we're on the road," says Farris, "and during performance days at rodeos I'm working from 6 in the morning until 11 at night. At Fort Worth, I won't see one of the performances because I'll be in the office all day. But usually—especially if I'm working as a timer and a secretary—I get to see quite a bit of the rodeo."[2]

Before the rodeo, the secretary often handles the finances, accepting the entry fees paid by the contestants. Because the rodeo secretary is often left with sizable amounts of cash, most large rodeos now post an armed security guard and arrange for daily bank deposits. Permit holders generally pay their entry fees in cash, though some first-year PRCA members pay their fees by check. Some new proposals would have all contestants pay their entry fees by credit card or directly to the PRCA in a centralized banking account. Winnings would be posted to the contestants' individual accounts. The cowboys seem opposed to these changes, however, because the rodeo secretaries have been their bankers for years. Many cowboys arrive at a rodeo without having had the time or opportunity to stop at a bank or they are from out of state. Either way, they often rely on the rodeo secretary to cash their personal checks.

Some rodeo secretaries have hired out as business managers to assist cowboys with their financial records. "Most contestants don't know how to balance their accounts, even when the PRCA has provided them with an account book. They have their mothers, wives, or girlfriends do their books," says one rodeo secretary. "Some complain that the secretaries are tyrants, but there are reasons for that. Some cowboys are babies. The ones who don't win any money are the most difficult. The top guys are real professional. They are in the business of rodeo and know how to take care of business," she notes.

Being a rodeo secretary has its unusual moments. One saddle bronc rider recounts this incident: "A calf roper competed with a wooden leg. As he got off his horse to race after the calf, his wooden leg came off. The crowd gasped, thinking he had broken his leg or worse. They thought the guy's leg had come off. People were crying, screaming for the ambulance. In fact, people were so upset, the rodeo secretary had called for an ambulance before everyone realized what had really happened."

CHUTE LABORERS

The chute laborers are hired by the stock contractor to assist with transporting, feeding, and readying the livestock for the rodeo. Some are hired to do specific jobs, but all are involved with several facets of the rodeo operation. During the rodeo, one of the laborers opens the chute gate once the contestant nods his head to signify that he's ready for the stock to be released from the chute.

The *flank man* helps the cowboy adjust his equipment before the ride and pulls the flank strap in the roughstock events. "I'm one of the 'behind the chutes' guys," says Dave Keipe, a flank man who has worked for several stock contractors and works construction when he's not going to rodeos. "We're the unsung heroes of rodeo. We're up at 7:30 A.M. to get the pickup horses or the grand entry horses washed and saddled." Most of the chute laborers get $15 to $25 per performance plus expenses, or they earn a set amount, such as $150 for a weekend's work. "It gets me down the road," says Keipe.

The *pickup men* help the bronc riders in getting off their horses following successful rides and help free bareback riders who get hung up in their rigging. They also chase the bulls out of the arena. Most pickup men are former rodeo competitors themselves. Being a pickup man allows these cowboys to stay close to the animals and the excitement. Still, accidents can occur. "I got bit once," says Mike Corey, one of the pickup men at the California Rodeo at Salinas. "A stud grabbed me by the leg. You can get kicked and you can get bit, but normally everybody fares pretty well if you're just experienced." [3]

Between 150 and 200 PRCA pickup men help on about 50,000 bareback and saddle bronc trips each year in some 2,250 performances at PRCA-sanctioned rodeos.[4] The PRCA's pickup men are sponsored by Dodge Truck and wear bright red padded chaps with the Dodge logo. Some also use catcher-like shin guards to protect their legs and ankles. These "rodeo lifeguards" must be able to rope, read livestock, and react instinctively to any arena situation. They must also be adept at handling a horse.

Although the cowboys praise the pickup men for rescuing them, the pickup men credit their horses with getting the job done. Kenny Clabaugh from Arvada, Wyoming, a pickup man for twenty years who has been selected on six occasions to work the NFR, says: "Your horse is 95 percent of it. If you ain't got a good horse under you, you got nothin'." [5]

The *chute boss* oversees the entire operation inside the arena. He indicates the order in which the cowboys and their mounts will be released from the bucking chutes and hurries the events along. Coy Huffman, a chute boss who has worked for several rodeo contractors and committees since 1980, explains his duties: "Typically, I arrive in town a day ahead of time. I look over the day sheets to see which stock will be used on which day. Working together with the stock contractor, we'll then set up the arena. At the end of the perf we'll go over the rodeo and make any changes that are necessary for the following day. We're constantly looking for ways to get the audience's attention so as to hold their interest and make the rodeo more exciting."

PHOTOGRAPHERS

Rodeo photography is a profession open to both men and women. Some photographers develop a long-term association with specific rodeo committees and are hired to serve as their official photographers, snapping pictures to be used in the rodeo program and for promotional purposes. Other "shooters" make a living selling rodeo photographs to magazines, advertising agencies, or creating stock images for photo companies. But the majority of full-time rodeo photographers sell their work primarily to the contestants. At nearly every PRCA-sanctioned rodeo, one or two photographers set up their vans near the bucking chutes, displaying the photographs or negatives from previous competitions. Rodeo fans are also invited to stop by the photographers' vans and purchase the rodeo pictures.

Sandy Wares of El Cajon, California, is the oldest PRCA-member rodeo photographer active in the business. Now in his seventies, he has been shooting pictures of cowboys and their rides for nearly forty years. Before that, he was a photographer in the navy. "The cowboys don't buy as many pictures as they used to," says Wares. "The champions, unless it's really an outstanding picture, don't even look. The punk'in rodeos (junior, amateur-level, and small-time rodeos) are fun to shoot since people buy the pictures."

Wares has survived nearly every possible accident or "wreck" during his long career. "At one time or another, I've been run over by everything in the arena, including barrel racers and judges," comments the photographer. "I've only been hurt once real bad and that was by a bulldogger. I got hit in the arm and had to have it operated on. Another time, a horse ran into me and knocked me out cold. The medics rushed in to check me out. They dragged me back behind the chutes, but I was okay."

In recent years, professional rodeo has gone high tech with the addition of elaborate sound systems, scoreboards, and video replays. Gogi Grant, owner of Sports Sound System, provided the elaborate music system at the Santa Maria Elks Rodeo in Santa Maria, California, one recent year. With a battery of six tape decks, Grant monitored a giant audio control board, coordinating his music and sound effects to the words of the rodeo announcer and the action taking place inside the arena. It took four large rigs to transport the sound speakers and system.

"I use the sound system for other sporting events as well, such as golf, but I enjoy rodeo because of the narrative dialog," explains Grant. "You can tell an entire rodeo story and history or a particular event with your music." Grant claims that having a good sound system at a rodeo increases rodeo sales, since the fans can hear the announcer and understand what is happening. "The varied western music creates a pleasant atmosphere," he says.

Equally impressive are the two Copenhagen Skoal Pro Rodeo scoreboards, first introduced in 1990. Besides providing rodeo spectators with detailed facts about contestants and rodeo events, the 20-foot-high, 40-foot-wide scoreboards record the cowboys' times and scores and give frequent updates on the standings in each event. The 2,200-pound scoreboards, made of steel and aluminum and modeled after those used in other professional sports, are transported to the top PRCA rodeos in a 45-foot trailer and lifted by cranes into position.

In 1992, Tony Llama Boot Company of El Paso, Texas, a subsidiary of PRCA national sponsor Justin Boots, introduced the first state-of-the-art video replay screens to professional rodeo. The two 8-by-11-foot screens enable fans to relive the excitement of a spectacular ride in slow motion and stop action. They also allow for the rodeo announcer to diagram the rodeo action, as football commentators mark plays on the television monitor for the viewing fans. Frank Scivetti, president of Tony Lama, says that the company saw the video replay screens as an opportunity to help enhance the fast-paced sport of rodeo: "It is our hope that the screens will give each spectator his or her own chute pass to the action behind the scenes giving everyone an exciting entertainment experience."[6]

CLOWNS, BARRELMEN, AND BULLFIGHTERS

Over 170 rodeo clowns and bullfighters work in PRCA-sanctioned rodeos. Some serve as *comics or entertainers*, performing animal and other specialty acts and acting as a sideshow to the rodeo. Others act as *barrelmen*, providing bull riders with a safety refuge behind the barrel and distracting the bull, who may be charging after the rider. Still others work as *bullfighters*, deliberately placing themselves between fallen rider and bull, or competing in their own specialized event of bullfighting.

Many of these men progress from bullfighter to barrel clown and comic as they get older. "I started fighting bulls when I first got in the business," stated Donnie Landis of Susanville, California, who has twice been selected barrel-man for the National Finals Rodeo. "My dad fought bulls and clowned for several years, and my mother was a rodeo secretary. I followed what my dad did. He was quitting as I was starting out. I fought bulls in high school rodeos. I never made the finals in the bullfights. Doing barrel work is easier on my body," explained Landis, now thirty-five.

COMICS OR ENTERTAINERS

The small contract acts seen at all rodeos include the clowns and their trained animals. The variety is almost endless. Since rodeo is seen in more small arenas than large ones, most of the acts are modest in size. Rodeo clowns who perform novelty or animal routines list their specific acts in the contract personnel directory and are hired by the rodeo committees because of the popularity of their acts. The novelty acts are scheduled during lulls in the rodeo action, often while the roughstock is being loaded into the bucking chutes and the cowboys are readying their equipment and preparing for their rides.

Typically, the rodeo clowns are contracted by the rodeo committee to arrive several days before the event so that they can assist in promoting the rodeo. Some go to the local schools and perform their clown or animal acts. For the grade-school youngsters, the clowns demonstrate how to apply the clown make-up. At high schools, the clowns usually address a student assembly about the sport of rodeo in general. "A major part of our job is communication with the public," wrote Butch Lehmkuhler, two-time PRCA Clown of the Year, in a special column to the *Prorodeo Sports News*. "We know that when we go to a rodeo, three or four days prior to it, our responsibilities include visiting old folks homes and shaking hands with old timers. Or maybe visiting a children's wing in a hospital. We also speak at various service club meetings."[7]

Lehmkuhler and others see rodeo promotions as a large part of their job. In the past, cowboys stayed in town for longer periods of time and were available to do promotions. But now the stars have limited time to engage in rodeo promotion, arriving just before their events and leaving shortly afterwards. As a result, contract personnel such as the rodeo announcers and clowns have assumed much of this responsibility. Most clowns develop a distinctive style of dress or make-up. Most are male, though a few female clowns have performed in amateur or women's rodeos. All seem to agree that the profession has changed over the years. As one clown notes, "It's becoming a science instead of just getting out of the way of the bull." Some put on rodeo clown schools for other aspiring performers. "A guy can go till he's sixty, but a lot of them can't or won't last that long," says one senior rodeo clown. Still, most rodeo clowns seem committed to the sport of rodeo and plan to stay involved once they retire from clowning and bullfighting. "When my clowning days are over, I want to market the right cowboys to the public such as through TV commercials," says Luke "Leon" Coffee, a three-time NFR clown and barrelman.

Others are quick to point out their concerns about the future of rodeo, agreeing that "rodeo has to go back to its roots." Citing the difficulties in motivating youth today, one urged that professional rodeo "cultivate the youngsters coming up," including those who might consider becoming rodeo clowns. Other clowns have pointed out that professional rodeo must maintain high standards. "Rodeo should be clean family entertainment. Filth has no place in rodeo," cautioned 69-year-old Wilbur Plaugher, the "Dean of the Rodeo Clowns," at a recent PRCA convention.

Many feel that while modern rodeo's emphasis on the seven standard rodeo events may have streamlined rodeo, it has hurt the contract act business. "Many of the big acts have left the rodeo industry for the circus or the Wild West shows," claims Jerry Wayne Olson, a third-generation rodeo performer. "Only about one-fourth of the PRCA rodeos now use specialty acts to any great degree. The rest of the rodeos are not taking care of business, so specialty acts have left rodeo because they couldn't survive financially. Too many rodeo committees try to cut corners by cutting out the specialty acts. They then wonder why their attendance keeps going down."

Like others in the business of rodeo, the clowns also expressed concern about making a living in their profession. "Each year it gets more and more difficult," says one clown. "I'm at the top of my form, but I'm still not making great, great money. It's difficult to earn enough to raise a family. Plus, you're on the road a lot." Others indicated they were thrilled to have a career that allowed them the opportunity to perform at rodeos. "I never thought it would be like this when I sat on my tractor as a young kid and dreamed," recalls Dale Woodard, a several-time NFR barrelman. "I thought I had a curse on my life in high school. But rodeo gave me something. Rodeo has given me a gift, and I just amuse people. I see myself as blessed. And to get paid for what you are gifted at is a double blessing."

During the PRCA convention each year, a special room is set aside where the contract act performers, rodeo clowns, and bullfighters set up elaborate booths to advertise their skills and availability. Some show video highlights of their performances at past rodeos. Rodeo committee members circulate among the various booths, interviewing the different performers, and sign them to contracts for the following year's rodeos.

"Eighty percent of my business is done at the convention," explains Dale Woodard. "But it is just a contract signing spot. Most of the rodeos I have already verbally agreed to, or we've had a handshake, before the convention begins. The monies I receive are fairly consistent from one rodeo to the next. You can hold the line on your charges. I try to stay away from being jacked around. I try to deal with solid people. I don't want to get there and be mad. I always wanted to work the big rodeos, but big rodeos don't need you as much because so much is going on with all the other events."

Rodeo clowns are constantly looking for new animals and novelty acts to add to their repertory. Most try to "lay out" for a year—that is, they avoid repeating their act at the same rodeo two years in succession. Many of the big-time rodeos change their specialty acts and clowns every year, believing that bringing in different entertainment guarantees repeat rodeo customers. Contract acts can also fill time at a rodeo if there are a lot of turn outs by the rodeo contestants.

Several rodeo clowns entertain the crowd with unusual and innovative novelty acts. Donnie Landis, for instance, rides out into the arena atop his "Leaping Llama," a stuffed animal he refers to as a "wild cantbeatalope." Loping around, doing unusual turns and spins, Landis concludes his popular act by having the "animal" spray a section of the audience with water. Another popular novelty act at rodeos in recent years has been the "Robo Bull" routine. In this act, a four-wheel all-terrain vehicle, decked out like a bull, races around the arena, snorting and puffing steam.

At other rodeos, a sheep dog jumps rope with a clown. Then later in the rodeo, after the barrel racing event, the clown orders the dog to race around the barrels. At the first barrel, however, the dog stops and lifts his leg to relieve himself, to the audience's laughter, before completing the barrel race. As the dog races back from the third barrel to the clown, he stops to relieve himself once again—this time on a cowboy hat that had been left lying nearby. The crowd laughs even more at this. Both of the dog's "pit stops" are part of the novelty act. Other clowns use a trained monkey, decked out in full western attire, who is strapped to the back of a sheep dog. The two race around the barrels in a pattern similar to that of the barrel racers. Later, rodeo fans can purchase photographs of the two animal celebrities.

Much of the repartee between the rodeo clown and the rodeo announcer is in the form of jokes. Some jokes border on the risqué, and others could be considered as sexist or as stereotypes targeting ethnic and homosexual minority groups. At some rodeos, the clowns are introduced to the audience in novel ways. One rodeo begins the performance with a black stretch limousine being driven into the arena. As it circles around to loud music and great fanfare, the announcer asks the audience, "Who is it, I wonder? Guess. It's 'The Three Stooges'!" Out pop the three rodeo clowns dressed in tuxedos. Other clowns go into the grandstands before the rodeo commences to meet with the fans and apply clown make-up to some of the youngsters. At some rodeos, families are encouraged to paint their children's faces to look like rodeo clowns. These youngsters are then entered in a contest for the best rodeo clown make-up. Between rodeo events, the rodeo clowns themselves choose the winners. Other rodeo clowns remain behind at the conclusion of the rodeo, signing autographs and having their pictures taken with the young rodeo fans.

Sometimes the clowns are teased good-naturedly by the cowboys sitting alongside the chutes. At one rodeo, during the barrel racing event, the first barrel racer's hat fell off as she made her turn around the third barrel. The bullfighting clown did not retrieve her hat, letting the ground crew run out to pick it up. But when the second barrel racer's hat also fell to the ground, the rodeo clown quickly ran out to retrieve it once she had completed her ride. When the clown returned with the hat to the bucking chute area, one cowboy teased, "Why didn't you go get the ugly girl's hat?" The clown, make-up and all, blushed and looked rather sheepish as the cowboys laughed at his predicament.

BARRELMEN

There is an art to being a barrelman, according to the clowns who assist the bullfighters. A barrelman must know when the bull is going to charge his barrel. He must also condition himself for the wear and tear of being inside the barrel when the bull strikes. "You don't want to be loose in the barrel when the bull hits," says Dale Woodard. "I quickly learned that lesson. I received a headache on the first day with the bulls when one of them hit the barrel and I wasn't totally secure inside."

"I watch the faces and eyes of the bull," continues Woodard. "I know when the bull is coming towards me and the barrel. It's like cops. You can see it in people's eyes before they shoot. You know when they are going to fire at you. It's the same thing with fighting bulls. You can see it in their eyes when they are about to charge."

Several barrelmen reinforce their barrels with Kevlar, a tough, light synthetic fiber used in bulletproof vests, flak jackets, and boat hulls. "I buy the raw material and put it on my barrel myself," explains one barrelman. "The hard part is getting the Kevlar. They apparently thought I was a terrorist. It took me the longest time before I was okayed to buy it."

It takes six weeks to make a barrel, which weighs close to seventy-five pounds. Customized to fit each individual barrelman, a barrel can range in price from $700 to $1,500. Although the barrels can be made of steel or fiberglass, which is then padded with special half-inch styrofoam and tape, the sturdiest barrels are made from aircraft aluminum. A typical barrel can last fifteen years or longer. Inside the padded barrel are pull or hold-down straps for the barrelman's safety.

Barrels used in the bullfighting competition are somewhat oddly shaped. Often they have a 22-inch flat spot on the side for stability on the ground, so that the bullfighter can use the barrel in jumping maneuvers over the bull. In effect, the bullfighter will position himself behind the barrel and run forward, jumping up on the barrel and over the bull just as the bull is charging forward and reaches the tipped barrel—which has been laid on its side and is held steady by a second clown. Other barrels are short for easier handling when placing them in front of the bulls.

One of the more colorful clowns on the PRCA circuit is Steve Tomac, who is also a state senator from St. Anthony, North Dakota. The 38-year-old has been a barrelman for twenty-two years. He started in high school, when a rodeo clown did not show and he took the job. At rodeos, he squats down inside the barrel with just his head—sporting an orange wig and green felt hat—sticking out of the top, focusing on the bucking chutes through gold wire-rimmed glasses. Tomac is older than many rodeo clowns but says he's not ready to give up his greasepaint yet: "The bulls will let me know when it's time to retire."[8] Tomac is quick to mention how rodeo has changed and is now recognized a professional sport. He also points out that the rodeo clown has helped with this new perception. "The image of the rodeo clown was one who did it with a bottle," states Tomac. "We've finally upgraded the clown's image and rodeo image to show we are citizens and civic leaders."

BULLFIGHTERS

At the early rodeos that featured bull riding or steer riding, the cowboys took turns helping their compatriots. When a cowboy fell, another cowboy had to dash in front of the bull and draw its attention from the fallen rider, giving the cowboy a chance to escape. As time went by, it became apparent that better protection was needed. Cowboys who had good stock savvy or a talent for clowning eventually replaced the volunteers. Over time, these pioneers became more and more skilled at handling the bulls. Some even gained formidable reputations for their lifesaving skills, and their moves influenced other aspiring bullfighters.

Bullfighting as a sport has developed continually over the last several decades and today is recognized as an exciting and dangerous event in its own right. It received its ultimate recognition in 1981 with the creation of the Wrangler Jeans Bullfight Tour, today's major league of bullfighting. More recently, the American Professional Bullfighters Association (APBA) was formed to monitor the sport and ensure professionalism. It also offers training seminars for aspiring bullfighters.

At about sixty PRCA contests each year, bullfighters get to compete for cash prizes and championship points. The bullfighters square off against Mexican fighting bulls, dodging and leaping and evading the bull's deadly horns for seventy seconds. They are judged by their ability to control the bulls, by their athletic skills, and their willingness to expose themselves to danger. The bullfighters score points by remaining close to the bull throughout the allotted time. Judges award points for daring, innovation, and control. The six PRCA bullfighters who accumulate the most points during the regular season qualify to compete for a national title and big prize money at the Wrangler Bullfight Finals held each year in conjunction with the National Finals Rodeo.

A rodeo bullfighter is a skilled athlete. "I'm not a clown," says two-time Wrangler World Bullfight Tour Champion Ronny Sparks. "I'm sorry, but I'm not out there in the arena to be funny. There's too much at stake. Twenty to twenty-five years ago, yeah, a clown and a bullfighter were the same thing to me. But not anymore. You've got a guy who's more of an athlete and a businessman out there. When I'm protecting cowboys, I'm all business. I'm a bullfighter."[9]

Both the traditional-style rodeo bulls and the Mexican-style fighting bulls are used in competition. Often the bulls are two or three years old, small, quick, and dangerous. Their horns have been smoothed or cut back so that the tips are the size of a fifty-cent piece. "The big traditional rodeo bulls are easier to deal with," explains one top bullfighter. "These Mexican bulls are faster and are bred to kill you. I saw one bull hook four guys. A big Brahma bull might hook but will only stay on you for a second. The Mexican bulls will stay around and charge you again. In this business, if you practice very much, you're going to get hurt." Most bullfighters agree that it is hard to keep the fighting bulls competing at top form. One notes, "The bulls quit when they can't catch us. Mexican bulls come on more. They bring the fight to you, forcing you to make a mistake."

Bullfighting has become immensely popular in recent years with the advent of the Wrangler Bullfight Tour. One of the most gregarious and beloved bullfighters on the circuit is Dwayne Hargo, who has competed in the Wrangler Bullfight Tour since 1986. In 1989 he won the world title. One writer describes Hargo's bullfighting maneuvers: "Dwayne Hargo stares and pulls just long enough for the wayward riders to flee the wrath of their angry horns. Just as a matador lulls his subject into a trance with his cape and concentration, Hargo keeps [bulls] from trampling or goring fallen cowboys by clownish antics."[10]

This account captures the essence of the role of the rodeo bullfighter. Without regard to his own safety and using whatever means necessary, the bullfighter must distract the bull long enough for the rider to scramble to safety. As one observer notes, "The bullfighter puts on a comical appearance with his clown make-up, brightly colored tights, and baggy shorts. But once a bull is released, his job is anything but funny."

Dwayne Hargo estimates that a top bullfighter who combines bullfighting competitions with steady work at rodeos can make between $60,000 and $70,000 a year. But he also notes that there's room at the top for only a couple dozen bullfighters. Hargo cautions those who wish to follow his career path: "A person right off the street can't just go in there and do it without getting into some kind of predicament." He advocates working with the animals, studying them, learning their habits. He feels that his animal sense coupled with his athletic skills helped him rise through the ranks. Hargo believes in rodeo schools and recommends that aspiring bullfighters attend not only bullfighting schools but bull riding schools as well. "Until I started sitting in on Gary Leffew's [bull riding] classes, I didn't realize everything that could go wrong. Knowing what happens to the bull rider helps me go out and do my job better," he says. Keeping fit and in good shape is also important, for as Hargo points out, "Your body is the bullfighter's tool."

Perhaps the hardest part of being a bullfighter is overcoming fear, and Hargo has advice on that topic, too. "A lot of times I get hooked by a bull, a bad bull. You have to have a little heart going for you to get out there and face them again. It's best just to get back out there and get on him, just like a horse," he says. For a bullfighter, heart—sometimes called courage—is the most important job qualification of all.

Hargo's comments are echoed by other successful bullfighters. "It takes a special type of person to be a bullfighter," says four-time Wrangler bullfighting world champion Rob Smets. "I get scared every time I walk into the arena, but the adrenaline-pumping fear also is part of the thrill and attraction of the sport."[11]

9

RODEO

COMMITTEES

& SPECIAL

PROGRAMS

t's high noon on the streets of Joseph, Oregon, a small ranching town in the northeast corner of the state. Four men on horseback are riding down Main Street. They stop and dismount. One leads the horses off to the side of the pavement, and the other three stroll over to the First Bank of Joseph, a two-story stone building shaded by trees and an elaborate white portico.

One of the men stations himself by the front door, and the other two enter the bank. A minute later, a woman screams. The two men come running out, bandannas pulled over their faces, and dash toward their waiting horses. But before they get halfway across the street, several gunmen positioned on the bank's roof begin shooting at the fleeing desperadoes.

The bank robbers return fire. A lawman steps into the street, shots barking from the six-shooter in his hand. The street fills with smoke as the lawmen and the robbers exchange fire. One of the robbers falls to the pavement, a second is captured. The third man, who is wounded, makes it to the waiting horses. He mounts, and with his co-conspirator, flees from the scene.

Hundreds of people have witnessed the botched robbery, and when it's all over, they begin to cheer. Of course, they didn't see an actual crime, but the reenactment of a bank robbery that took place in Joseph nearly a century ago. With a Paul Harvey "and now for the rest of the story" flourish, an announcer tells the crowd that one of the bank robbers who escaped, a local cowboy and sheepherder named Dave Tucker, was later apprehended. Tried and convicted, Tucker served his time and was released. Tucker (who is portrayed in the staged event by Joseph's mayor, Ken Roberts) remained in Joseph and became a prosperous businessman. He eventually worked his way up to vice-president of the very bank he robbed.

It's a story that the people of Joseph never weary of telling, and each year the reenactment plays a prominent role in the Chief Joseph Rodeo festivities, which also include a parade, the running of the horses down Main Street, an Indian encampment that includes several Pacific Northwest tribes, rodeo dances, an all-night pancake breakfast, and the rodeo itself.

In many towns, rodeo is more than a sporting event. It is a gala celebration, the single most important community event of the year. It is the means to recount history, to express civic pride, to commemorate major holidays, and to celebrate distinguished community members.

Though the cowboys provide the thrills and spills at the rodeo, the volunteers provide the manpower and the business savvy to make the rodeo happen. The promotion and production of a single small-town rodeo can involve hundreds of people, and a major rodeo may require several thousand volunteers. The Houston Livestock Show Rodeo, for instance, has a volunteer force of 9,000. In most cases, the volunteers receive no compensation beyond the satisfaction of a job well done, but their efforts benefit the community in innumerable ways.

RODEO FOR CHARITY

Charities and community groups benefit directly from the work of rodeo's volunteer army. Although there are several strictly for-profit rodeos in the PRCA, the majority of PRCA rodeos donate a portion of their proceeds to a community group or charity. The Pikes Peak or Bust Rodeo in Colorado Springs, for instance, has contributed money to several programs that help military families. The tradition began in the wake of World War II, when servicemen returned to Colorado Springs and began the difficult transition into civilian life. Over the years, the community has expressed its thanks for their service with more than $1 million raised through the rodeo. The effort is reciprocal: soldiers from nearby Fort Carson help direct traffic at the rodeo and provide security, the local chapter of the Veterans of Foreign Wars sells rodeo programs, and a platoon of army cooks sets up a field kitchen to feed tens of thousands of rodeo fans at a pancake breakfast.

KIDS DAY RODEO

Like several other rodeos across the country, the Industry Hills (California) Charity Pro Rodeo hosts a Kids Day Rodeo. Held during slack, where overflow competitors make their runs, on the Friday morning preceding the weekend performances, Kids Day attracts over 5,000 grade-school students. Bused in from local schools, many children dress in western gear or paint their faces like rodeo clowns. Unlike most slack competitions, which take place with no audience, the Industry Hills' slack offers kids a chance to go behind the scenes, learn about the animals, and meet the cowboys. It also has benefits for rodeo. Committee members point out an increase in rodeo attendance for the regular paid performances, as the children encourage their parents to bring them back on subsequent days.

One year the youngsters in attendance were divided into three sections and given a designated color to represent their "team." Likewise, the cowboys competing in the roughstock slack competition were loosely grouped into three teams. Each of the three sections, at the urging of the rodeo announcer and clown, cheered wildly for its team.

Besides watching the competition, children learned about their western heritage. Cowboys showed the kids what a cattle drive looked like, providing them with a taste of the Old West. Youngsters cheered enthusiastically throughout the demonstrations, for the most part unaware of the education they were receiving. PRCA rodeo announcer Randy Corley, during a lull in the action, told the kids, "If you're not having fun, you'll have to go back to school!" The youngsters, naturally, booed at that.

The Industry Hills Charity Pro Rodeo also helps educate the youngsters about the history of rodeo and the West in other ways. Some three weeks before the actual rodeo, an elaborate sixteen-page brochure is distributed to the teachers. The book includes ready-to-color rodeo scenes, connect-the-dot drawings, and a word scramble as well as the history of PRCA rodeo and the different rodeo events.

Industry Hills also sponsors a poster contest for two different age groups and displays the winning posters inside the entrance gate area throughout rodeo weekend. Besides receiving a financial award and free tickets for his or her family for the final Sunday performance, the winner's poster is included in the next year's rodeo program and billboard. Children attending the Kids Day Rodeo all receive a copy of the stock contractor's own rodeo-related program as they leave the grounds.

The Industry Hills Charity Pro Rodeo raises money to improve the lives of emotionally disturbed and developmentally disadvantaged children. In a ten-year period, the rodeo also raised more than a quarter million dollars for a local youth center and a gang intervention and prevention program.

Youth programs such as these are a major part of rodeos today. The intention is to give children a pleasurable experience in the guise of an educational program. In the short term, the rodeo committee hopes that by getting children interested, they can attract their families to the paid performances. In the long run, the committee hopes that they will remain interested in the sport, once they are exposed to it. And by teaching children about rodeo, the committee hopes that they will not be persuaded to regard rodeo as a cruel or exploitive form of entertainment, a charge often made by animal rights groups.

PRCA EXCEPTIONAL RODEO

Professional rodeo's involvement with programs aimed at youth with special needs—including children with physical, mental, or sensory impairments or learning disabilities—is not new. In an event similar to the Challengers program in professional baseball, the PRCA's Exceptional Rodeo program was initiated in 1983 in response to numerous requests from the professional rodeo cowboys themselves. The cowboys wanted a program that presented them as benevolent—one that was uniquely their own and uniquely rodeo. The recreational event—designed primarily for fun—pairs pro rodeo cowboys and cowgirls with disabled children inside the rodeo arena. At the beginning of an Exceptional Rodeo, each of the children receives a cowboy hat, bandanna, contestant back number, and a kid-sized lariat. Each child's professional cowboy or cowgirl helper guides him or her through the competition, providing some instruction and lots of encouragement. The children take part in many competitive events that mimic real rodeo contests: a goat relay; steer roping using dummy steers; eight-second rides on "Wimpy," the hand-rocked bull, and "Payday," the hand-rocked bareback horse; steer wrestling with "Cory Corriente," a stuffed doll; and a flag race (at a walk) on the back of a real horse. For most, the horseback ride is the most exciting moment, since so few of the children have ever had contact with a horse.

The forty-five-minute performance is announced by the rodeo's announcer. At the end, each child is individually recognized and awarded a trophy and an autographed picture of the child and his or her cowboy partner. Participating rodeo committees each pay a fee to cover the administrative costs of running the event. Thirty rodeos are selected each year to take part in the program. Exceptional Rodeos run either one day before, or a few hours before, a pro rodeo performance. The PRCA-affiliated Exceptional Rodeos have been immensely successful. The Brawley (California) Cattle Call Mini Rodeo for Special Kids, for example, attracts about 600 students enrolled in special education programs in the local community.

OTHER PROGRAMS

Another national program with links to professional rodeo is the Smokey Bear and the American Cowboy fire prevention program initiated by the United States Forest Service in 1988. After several decades of teaching the public to prevent forest fires, the forest service saw a similar need for grasslands fire prevention. For this reason, the Smokey Bear and the American Cowboy program was born. "The tie between Smokey and the cowboy couldn't be more natural," says Gene Dowdy, a former cowboy who helped create the campaign for the Forest Service. "No one is closer to the land than cowboys and Indians, and protecting the land is what Smokey is all about."[1]

Dowdy and another colleague from the Forest Service train several adults throughout the country to play the part of Smokey. Dressed in the familiar bear costume, Smokey and his cowboy helper appear at schools and in rodeos to make fire-awareness presentations to school-aged children. In addition, the Forest Service discusses with committee members the safety considerations in working around livestock and assists with their public relations, such as how best to work with the local news media. At the rodeos, the Forest Service employees set up booths to distribute coloring books, trading cards, and other fire prevention and rodeo-related materials. The program is so popular that PRCA rodeo committees compete to get Smokey Bear to attend their rodeos.

Other educational programs are also available to rodeo committees. One new program is called REACh, an acronym for Rodeo Education and Children. The brainchild of a former barrel racer and elementary school teacher, REACh provides local rodeo communities with education-oriented programs. The pre-show program instructs children and their families about the care that the rodeo livestock receive and explains the various rodeo events through a series of pictures and demonstrations. In this way, fans who come early and watch the REACh presentation are better educated about what they will be seeing in the performance. Several committees hosting rodeos in nonagricultural settings have found such instructional programs to be worthwhile.

Professional rodeo also attempts to reach inner-city youngsters. As part of a federally funded Cities in Schools program, several metropolitan rodeo committees participate in a Rodeo Corral program. It features a workshop about rodeo that directly involves students in mock rodeo events and allows them to see actual rodeo rides. One such inner-city outreach program was held in the Los Angeles Forum (home of the NBA's Los Angeles Lakers) in 1993 and attracted more than 500 black youth.

David Walker, an African-American cowboy and the promoter of the event, has tried to combine his rodeo experience with his concern for black inner-city youth. "I grew up as one of those kids and I want to help out," Walker explains. "I want to link inner-city kids with pro rodeo, teaching them the skills and helping them get an interest in rodeo. I want to inspire these kids to remain in school and work to follow their dreams."

At the special rodeo, plastic calves' heads were attached to bales of hay to give junior high school youth a chance to practice calf roping skills. The youngsters were shown the inner workings of the rodeo arena, including the bucking chutes and the roughstock pens. Later, a mini-rodeo was held, with volunteer cowboys from the local area and those who had arrived a day early before the scheduled PRCA rodeo demonstrating how the bucking horses and bulls are ridden.

Rodeo committees also raise money for programs like the new Western Wishes programs for children with terminal illnesses who express a wish to be around popular rodeo contestants. At the 1994 Reno Rodeo, for instance, 17-year-old Kara Wilson, who contracted Lyme's disease when she was ten and has been wheelchair-bound as a result, was linked with ten-time world barrel racing champion Charmayne (James) Rodman. Despite her condition, Wilson rides horses and practices barrel racing. She was able to make a special barrel racing run at the Reno Rodeo, cheered on by literally thousands of rodeo fans.

Through the help of Donnalyn Quintana, founder of the Western Wishes program, a number of youths with debilitating diseases like leukemia and Lyme's disease have been united with their rodeo heroes, including world champion bull riders Ty Murray, Tuff Hedeman, and Ted Nuce. Jody Ledbetter, a senior in high school and aspiring bull rider, had contracted stomach cancer. With the assistance of Western Wishes, he attended the 1994 National Finals Rodeo where he met his rodeo idol, world bull riding champion Ted Nuce. When Nuce won the 1994 NFR's ninth round by scoring 88 points on the famous Growney bull Wolfman, Ted Nuce gave the go-round buckle to Ledbetter.[2]

Clearly, rodeo's benefits to a community go beyond the simple economic impact of the competition itself. Because of the myriad programs designed to bring people into active involvement with the sport, rodeos tend to develop strong and loyal followings. Emphasis on youth participation is a particularly strong part of the rodeo promotion game, but it would be cynical and unfair to say that the motivation for the many youth events is ticket sales. In most cases, youth programs are initiated by individuals on rodeo committees who have a personal involvement with disadvantaged or disabled kids and see the rodeo as a way of reaching out to those youth in a constructive and supporting way.

THE WORKINGS OF THE RODEO COMMITTEE

For every cowboy who competes in a rodeo, there is a rodeo committee member who has spent months preparing the welcome mat. The PRCA recognizes their hard work and dedication by acknowledging the top indoor and outdoor (both small- and large-scale) rodeo committees. Voted on by the NFR-qualifiers, the awards are presented at the annual PRCA Awards Banquet held before the season-ending rodeo.

The promotion and production of the rodeo as a major sporting event require the collaboration of numerous committee members, often volunteers from a wide array of backgrounds. Hours of labor are required to put on these events, and often the only reward is the satisfaction of having presented a quality product. For these committee members, the rodeo is more than just a sporting event. It is a symbol of community pride. "Rodeo is not put on for rodeo's sake," explained PRCA Commissioner Lewis Cryer in remarks to a university class. "It is put on to make the community feel good. It gives a community a sense of civic pride. Most rodeos are tied in around some local community event, holiday, or occasion."

Naturally, rodeos also serve as a source of revenues for merchants and local governments. Not only do the charities benefit, but with the free-spending, festive crowds in the streets at rodeo time, so does the business community. Banks, hotels, restaurants, bars, and retail stores share in the celebration. For many communities, rodeo weekend (or rodeo week) is the biggest economic event of the year. In Brawley, California, for instance, the annual fall Cattle Call Rodeo generates more money than any other event held in the Imperial Valley. "Dollars earned in Brawley are turned over from three to five times," says Richard Bogue, chairman of the committee. "Motels and restaurants throughout the valley report a booming business during Cattle Call festivities. Managers of service stations also notice increased sales."[3]

Brawley is not the only community to notice the positive cash flow that hosting a PRCA rodeo generates. The thousands of rodeo fans who pack the grandstands and hundreds of contestants who ride and rope leave behind a lot of folding green. Exactly how much money the rodeo pumps into the local economy is difficult to gauge, because rodeos are so different. Some rodeo committees multiply the rodeo committee's budget times a factor of seven to estimate the amount of money brought into the local economy. Others note the amount of sales tax generated or hotel occupancy rates during the rodeo time period. And some committees have conducted surveys to estimate how much rodeo visitors pump into the local economy.

Whatever the actual figures, the overwhelming perception among communities sampled is that a rodeo is a financial blessing. Almost 80 percent of 385 residents polled one year by the California Rodeo committee in Salinas, California, said the rodeo had favorable local economic impact. And in a sample of fans in attendance at the rodeo, only 30 percent indicated they lived in the Salinas Valley. The majority of attendees were out-of-towners, and 40 percent of these fans indicated that they stayed overnight in the region. Eighty percent of the contestants, too, had stayed at least one night in the local area, and 70 percent had booked rooms in local motels.[4]

The tasks facing rodeo committee members are diverse. Attention must be paid to promotion, publicity, ticket sales, the design and printing of the rodeo program, the hiring of stock contractors and specialty acts, transportation and lodging, and the preparation of the rodeo grounds. Other committee members install and operate sound systems or act as gate men, parking lot attendants, or arena security. They write news releases, organize contests for beauty queens, attend endless meetings—all because they love rodeo and all that it represents in American life.

One upscale community in Orange County, California, decided to celebrate its fifth-year anniversary in 1991 by hosting a PRCA rodeo. The Rancho Santa Margarita Fiesta Rodeo—quickly dubbed the Yuppie Rodeo—budgeted $60,000 for the two-day event. One committee member, Charlie Ware, observes, "We learned through the school of hard knocks how to put on a rodeo. We had talked to people who had put on nearby rodeos to get ideas. We decided to focus on the family since we are a new bedroom community in the area."

The sold-out rodeo, which drew 240 participants from several states to compete for $15,000 in prize money and 7,000 spectators, was so successful that it has become an annual event. Anthony R. Moiso, president and chief executive officer of the Santa Margarita Company, welcomed the fans, many of whom were attending rodeo for the first time, to the inaugural rodeo: "Since the early days of the American West, rodeos have been the traditional way to celebrate important milestones and bring people together. Rodeos have joined neighbors and visitors for family fun, lots of conversation, great food, healthy competition, laughter, and excitement. Rodeos are one of America's oldest sports. Rodeos are where traditions are created."[5]

More established rodeos have developed such traditions. At the Calgary Exhibition and Stampede, Tony Mayer, active in the Western Heritage Society, notes a bit of folklore connected with that event. "The typical Calgary resident," Mayer states, "doesn't take off cowboy boots or hat during the entire [ten-day] Stampede Days!" Although Mayer may overstate the case a bit, many academics have discussed and written on the social impact of rodeo on townspeople.

Richard J. Ossenberg, in an article entitled "Social Class and Bar Behaviour During the Calgary Stampede," observes how middle-class citizens "let loose" during the Stampede. In a pattern similar to the King-of-Fools festival of the Middle Ages—which was subsidized by the aristocracy who actively participated in the "fun and games" in a temporary "inversion" of class structure—Ossenberg observes how the Stampede provides middle-class participants with an opportunity to step outside their traditional, more reserved social roles and indulge in binge drinking and more spontaneous expressive behavior.[6]

Frederick Errington, in a 1990 article "The Rock Creek Rodeo: Excess and Constraint in Men's Lives," notes how men who have "sacrificed their individuality to lead conventional lives" are likely to wonder from time to time if they have given up too much. This American dilemma, Errington claims, is confronted and temporarily resolved for some during the local Fourth of July rodeo. By participating in the tradition and ritual of the community's rodeo, the fifty-or-so members of the rodeo committee present themselves as the guardians of the American tradition.[7]

Often it is up to local historians to capture and convey the traditions associated with their respective rodeos, and over the years, several important books have been written by these rodeo historians. Milt Riske's 1984 *Chey-*

enne Frontier Days: A History of the "Daddy of 'Em All," Virgil Rapp's 1985 *Let 'er Buck! A History of the Pendleton Round-Up,* James H. Gray's 1985 *A Brand of Its Own: The 100 Year History of the Calgary Exhibition and Stampede,* and Danny Freeman's 1988 *World's Oldest Rodeo* on the Prescott Frontier Days Rodeo are just a few of the excellent historical accounts of some of North America's top, long-standing rodeos.

Not all rodeo committees, however, are wedded to the idea of maintaining tradition. One rodeo committee chairman for the high desert community of Victorville, California, argues that rodeo must change in order to continue to attract fans. "The focus on the upcoming generation is *participation* sports, not *spectator* sports," he says, noting the low turn-out for the afternoon's performance. "My own kids prefer skiing and fishing to watching rodeo. From what I've read in the fair-type trade papers, rodeo—unless it can change and inject itself with a new vitality—is dead in the water." He also points out needed areas for change. "From my observation, rodeo is too stereotyped. You can anticipate what's going to happen. You need to create different kinds of events. Eight years ago there were a lot more people in attendance than are here today. We're talking about a stereotype of audience and contestant. I've heard the same jokes and clichés for thirty years. It's time for a change."

Rodeo committees strive to improve the quality of their product by sharing information among themselves. Each year in December before the National Finals Rodeo, hundreds of rodeo committee members attend the three-day PRCA Annual Convention in Las Vegas. There they meet, contract help for their coming rodeos, attend seminars dealing with a variety of rodeo-related issues, and socialize. They also participate in the Association of Rodeo Committees (ARC). Begun in 1973, the ARC conveys to members important information about the PRCA and how to produce rodeos. It establishes and maintains uniform policies and procedures concerning the production of rodeos and assists association members in their dealings with the organizations representing professional rodeo athletes. Typically, the ARC informs members on how to conduct a press party, attract local sponsors, spend time with rodeo spectators to find out what they want, work effectively with contestants and contract personnel, and motivate and retain volunteer workers.

Unlike many professional sports, which have uniformly high production values, rodeos range from elaborate, highly structured entertainment events to casual, loosely run competitions that remind one more of a weekend barbecue than a professional sporting contest. Each rodeo committee takes into consideration the needs of its community, the economic resources at its disposal, and the level of dedication of its volunteers. A small-town rodeo in

Wyoming may offer townspeople only a straight-forward rodeo, whereas a town in California, where the competition for the entertainment dollar is higher, may feature an elaborate grand entry, several contract acts, a celebrity appearance, some audience participation activity, and a fireworks display. As Cindy Moreno of the Marysville, California, Flying U Rodeo Company says: "Out here, where people have Disneyland and Hollywood, you have to give the people something more than a plain old rodeo. You have to give them something really entertaining." Rodeos in urban areas also must work harder than their country cousins to help audiences understand the sport.

IMPORTANT RODEOS FROM THE CONTESTANTS' VIEWPOINT

From the point of view of the professional rodeo cowboy—particularly those in serious pursuit of an NFR berth—rodeos can be ranked according to four general factors: *prize money, prestige, season,* and *special perks.* Whether a particular rodeo attracts the top cowboys in the sport or not depends mainly on how highly it ranks in these four key factors.

A top-paying rodeo is one of the fifty rodeos with total prize money in excess of $70,000. Although rodeos that pay top prize money also tend to rank high in terms of prestige, cowboys hold some high-paying competitions in higher regard than others, partly because of the atmosphere surrounding the event.

Prestigious rodeos are those steeped in cowboy lore: rodeos with fifty or more years of tradition, such as the Cheyenne Frontier Days Rodeo, the Calgary Stampede, the California Rodeo, Prescott Frontier Days, and the Pendleton Round-Up Rodeo. The top cowboys often say that winning at one of these prestigious rodeos ranked as a high point of their professional rodeo careers. "My favorite rodeos are the 'sentimental' rodeos, the ones that are the oldest," says Derek Clark, a saddle bronc rider who has qualified for the NFR several times. "They're the ones with lots of tradition and pageantry, and not necessarily those that pay the big bucks."

Seasonal factors can also add to, or detract from, a rodeo's popularity among the cowboys. Early in the season, cowboys need to do well at a major competition in order to have the financial resources to continue to compete throughout the year. Later in the year, they need to rack up prize money to make a bid for the National Finals. Although rodeos take place every week of the year, the most crucial rodeos tend to cluster into three critical seasons:

winter, summer, and fall. The large-scale winter indoor rodeos include the National Western Stock Show in Denver, the Southwestern Exposition and Livestock Show and Rodeo in Fort Worth, the San Antonio Livestock Exposition Rodeo, and the Houston Livestock Show and Rodeo. A win at one of these lucrative rodeos (all are among the ten highest-paying professional rodeos) is crucial to a good start on the season.

As bareback rider Mark Garrett notes, "If guys do well at the winter rodeos, it takes the monkey off their back, since they are not pressured to go to so many rodeos the rest of the year. Guys are carrying a ton of bricks until they get into the top fifteen." Failing to place at one of these top-paying winter rodeos makes it imperative that a cowboy compete hard throughout the summer. Some cowboys, however, may drop out of competition for the year if they do not place high in the winter rodeos.

The "big run" summer rodeos, held from late June to late July, fall into the period that the cowboys call Cowboy Christmas—cowboys can attend so many events during this time that they are almost bound to win prize money. Nearly one-fourth of all PRCA rodeos take place in the two-week period before and after Independence Day. As one reporter for the *Prorodeo Sports News* put it, "A cowboy can virtually step out his front door and jump on a bucking horse."

On the downside, the hectic schedules (top cowboys will often compete at nearly a dozen rodeos during the week that surrounds Independence Day) make this time costly and exhausting. Still, cowboys stumble on, knowing that Cowboy Christmas is their best opportunity to win money. "The standings start taking shape about the Fourth of July, and it's nice to have those big winter wins behind you about that time," claims world champion steer wrestler John W. Jones, Jr., of Morro Bay, California. "If you're not in it after the Fourth, you might as well hang around the house and wait 'til next year."

"This is a very important week," says Todd Fox of Marble Falls, Texas. "There are guys who will make a bigger move this week than they do all winter. Several guys will come from nowhere to making the finals from this week right here. If a guy comes out of it with some momentum, it'll carry him through the summer and into the fall."[8]

Rodeos that take place over the busy summer season include the Reno Rodeo, Greeley Independence Stampede, Calgary Stampede, Cheyenne Frontier Days Rodeo, California Rodeo (in Salinas), and the Dodge City Days Round-Up Rodeo (in Kansas). All of these rodeos rank among the most prestigious competitions and attract virtually all of the top athletes in the PRCA.

The fall rodeos are the rodeos most critical to those competitors who are "on the bubble" or in "the worry hole"—holding down positions ten through twenty in the world standings. Due to the precariousness of their rankings, these cowboys must compete full-out in order to make the final fifteen cut and qualify for the NFR. The late-season, high-paying rodeos include the Pendleton Round-Up Rodeo, New Mexico State Fair Rodeo, and Pueblo State Fair. The most critical fall competition, however, is the Grand National (Cow Palace) Rodeo. Held in San Francisco, the Grand National completes the last rodeo of the PRCA season. It can play an important role in deciding which cowboys qualify for the NFR. As saddle bronc rider Dan Etbauer says, "This 'un makes or breaks ya."

While the top-ten-ranked cowboys slow down and rest in the fall season before the National Finals, any cowboy below tenth place in the world standings must rodeo as hard as time, money, and stamina allow as the season comes to a close. Every dollar is critical, as calf roper Joe Lucas discovered in 1989, when he missed qualifying for the NFR by one dollar plus change.

The Grand National is not the only rodeo held that final season-ending weekend. In 1991, after nearly two decades of inactivity as a rodeo site, Madison Square Garden hosted a professional rodeo, recalling the days when the Garden was a fixture on the rodeo circuit. Bull rider Art Watson of Bakersfield, California, "on the bubble" for a top-fifteen NFR spot, had not drawn well at the Grand National, and a ride of 71 on Destroyer failed to qualify him for the Sunday short-go. Along with several other bull riders, Watson caught a "red-eye" overnight flight to the Big Apple after the Saturday afternoon performance in San Francisco. Although Watson did not draw well in New York either, and failed to qualify for the NFR, he was glad he had competed at the Garden. "People that don't know much about rodeo always ask me if I've rode in New York, Calgary, and Mesquite," Watson says. "To them, those are the three big rodeos, even though there hasn't been a rodeo in Madison Square Garden in a long time. It was good to go there and compete. Now when they ask, I can say, 'Yes, I've ridden in New York.'"

Some cowboys also go out of their way to enter rodeos where the rodeo committee has a reputation of treating the cowboys well. The Dodge City Days Round-Up Rodeo takes particular pride in catering to the cowboys' needs. It has been recognized for its efforts, too. PRCA cowboys, stock contractors, and contract personnel voted it "Rodeo Committee of the Year" for many years. Noting the endless hours that the committee members put in preparing for their rodeo, Bill Austen, president of the committee, notes: "Each year we try to add improvements for the cowboys. We do not charge for electricity and water hook-ups, we have a cowboy lounge area, we have added washers and dryers at no charge, and we also have showers and restrooms that are open all night. This year we are working on setting up a hot tub in the back area for cowboys and cowgirls to soak those sore muscles and bruises."[9]

The cowboys are quick to express their appreciation for the special perks and favors extended to them by the rodeo committees. "They add a lot of money here, but a lot of rodeos add a lot of money," notes PRCA saddle bronc rider Butch Small, commenting on the Dodge City rodeo. "The main thing is, they treat you good. They treat you like they want you here. It doesn't take a whole lot to make a cowboy happy—a free sandwich, a free beer after the rodeo—it's not a lot, but it shows they're thinking of you."[10]

The most successful PRCA rodeos—those that attract the top athletes and reap the highest revenues—are those that address all four of the factors important to the contestants: prize money, community pride, schedule, attentiveness to cowboys' needs. To attract top competitors, a rodeo must first offer sufficient prize money (anything over $1,200 in added monies will make a top cowboy seriously consider entering a specific rodeo). Second, the rodeo should demonstrate a sense of community pride and/or tradition. Third, the rodeo should ideally be held during a strategic time in the year when it is of paramount importance for the top cowboys to enter the rodeo. And, fourth, the rodeo committee must consider and respond to the contestants' needs, extending a warm welcome and creating a friendly atmosphere to make their stay in the community a pleasant experience. All of these elements are part of the rodeo committee's larger goal of attracting a paying crowd. The expectation that quality competition will make for a more satisfying show is the basis for special consideration of the rodeo athlete.

10

WOMEN

AND

RODEO

At the Durango (Colorado) All Women's Rodeo, a slight, 24-year-old woman with long blond hair pulled a leather glove over her painted pink fingernails. She was about to climb aboard a 1,600-pound bull. It would not be a pretty ride.

Jo Burton, a former horse trainer from London, was among the fifteen women competing at the Professional Women's Rodeo Association (PWRA) competition. She had learned about bull riding while on vacation in Texas, where she witnessed several men's competitions. One of the rodeos featured female riders, and that opened her eyes.

Burton, also a former jockey, moved to the United States and established a relationship with reigning world champion women's bull rider Tammy Kelly. Soon after taking a class and practicing on several bulls at Kelly's arena, Jo Burton began competing in 1994, when she placed second in the PWRA's rookie standings.

At Durango, Burton climbed aboard a bull named *Medicine Man* for a thrilling six-second ride to the buzzer—the regulation time in PWRA events. After the ride, Burton was hunting for a place to get off when the bull threw her into a steel post, breaking her jaw and injuring her knee. But Burton stood up and saluted the crowd before leaving the arena.

"It doesn't matter if you're a guy or girl, you have to be tough in this sport," said Burton as she got into her truck. In pain, she drove through the night to her home in Chandler, Arizona, happy to know she'd placed second at the rodeo.

Sports have historically been a "male preserve." This fact has discouraged many women from seriously pursuing sports of any kind and resulted in the devaluation of the performances of serious women athletes. According to sociologists Howard L. Nixon II and James H. Frey, "The cultural message has been that females do not belong in sports, and this message has been reinforced by a number of structural hurdles that have denied females access to sports opportunities, resources, and rewards."[1]

Bil Gilbert and Nancy Williamson, in an earlier series on women and sport in *Sports Illustrated,* noted that three myths have been used to justify discrimination against females in sport: first, the belief that athletics cause physical harm to women and "masculinize" their appearance; second, the belief that women do not play sports as well as men and so do not deserve athletic parity; and third, the idea that women are not really interested in sports.[2] During the past several decades each of these myths has been disproven by research. Even so, these beliefs persist and continue to restrict the opportunities for women in sport, including rodeo.

CHANGING OPPORTUNITIES FOR WOMEN IN RODEO

In the early years, women in professional rodeo fared much better than women in other sports. According to historian Mary Lou LeCompte, rodeo cowgirls were among the first American women to succeed as professional athletes. Not only did they achieve international acclaim and financial success from the 1880s into the first third of this century, rodeo cowgirls also received overwhelmingly favorable and unbiased treatment from the press.[3] One reason for women's early success in rodeo is that they learned their craft while assisting family members on the ranch. On the frontier ranches of the American West, all the family members had to pitch in, and cowgirls learned to do "man's work"—from shoeing horses to branding cattle to breaking broncs—

at an early age. Traits of athleticism, independence, and assertiveness were invaluable for these pioneer women and professional athletes.

Just as they had on the frontier, women found a niche in rodeo. According to LeCompte in her important 1993 book, *Cowgirls of the Rodeo*, at least sixteen women competed in rodeos or Wild West shows as early as the 1880s. In these early rodeos, women competed against men in events such as saddle bronc riding and steer roping. Interviews conducted with female winners in the 1920s indicated that they were well treated by male competitors.[4] According to LeCompte, over 450 women enjoyed professional rodeo careers between 1890 and 1942. During the 1920s and 1930s, women's competition in bronc riding, trick riding, trick roping, or relay racing was included at about one-third of all rodeos. These events were particularly popular at the most prestigious rodeos, including the Calgary Stampede.

Several factors, however, began to weaken women's hold on rodeo participation. For one, women's role in professional rodeo was never as secure as men's, since it was the cowboy—and not the cowgirl—who was crucial to the image of the mythical West, the basis for the continued popularity of the sport. A second factor was a fatality at the 1929 Pendleton Round-Up Rodeo. Popular bronc rider Bonnie McCarroll was thrown and trampled to death. Although it was not the first fatality involving a woman, the ensuing media uproar persuaded the rodeo committee to permanently ban women from the event. Other rodeos quickly followed suit.

That same year a group of rodeo committees and producers formed the Rodeo Association of America (RAA) and established a format for rodeo events at their rodeos. Ignoring pleas that they sanction women's bronc riding and issue rules ensuring the safety of participants, the rodeo promoters effectively reduced women's participation. And when cowboys organized their Cowboys' Turtle Association in 1936, they excluded women. The net effect of these changes was to further restrict cowgirl bronc riding during the 1930s. By the early 1940s, the contest had virtually disappeared from major rodeos.

Besides these changes, other influences were also at work to remove women from the rodeo arena. LeCompte is particularly critical of the role that the popular movie matinee singing-cowboy star Gene Autry played in redefining women's role in rodeo during the 1940s. Filling a void in rodeo producing, entrepreneur Autry effectively took control of the rodeo industry and reshaped it to reflect his more traditional and strongly gendered values.

Capitalizing on his fame in motion pictures (and subsequently in television), Gene Autry enjoyed a virtual monopoly over the big-time rodeos of that era. Streamlining the rodeo competition to a mere five cowboy events,

Autry relegated women to more supportive roles such as "sponsor girls," who were selected for their glamour and dependency upon men rather than for their rodeo skills and independence. "Like the women in his western films," notes LeCompte, "rodeo cowgirls changed from genuine participants to mere props, whose primary purpose was to make the cowboys look good."[5]

Combined with the impact of World War II, which saw a steady decrease in the number of rodeos held nationwide as the country focused on other priorities, these changes severely curtailed women's role in professional rodeo. Although cowgirls had for many years been far ahead of other female athletes, this was no longer the case by the mid-1940s.

But all was not lost. According to LeCompte, by the late 1940s and early 1950s, rodeo cowgirls had begun a renaissance. They formed their own association, the Girls Rodeo Association (GRA), in 1948. Established by a group of Texas women, the group was eventually successful in lobbying for the inclusion of GRA-sanctioned barrel racing contests at a majority of professional rodeos across the country. But their greatest achievement was the eventual inclusion, after much lobbying, of barrel racing as part of the PRCA's National Finals Rodeo, beginning in 1967.

In the 1950s, as the GRA gained respect and barrel racing competition continued to grow in popularity, negative publicity concerning women's involvement with rodeo became less of a problem. Rodeo queen contests replaced the controversial sponsor contests, and women who are now selected as Miss Rodeo America or as one of the many state rodeo queens are judged equally on horsemanship, appearance, and personality.

The GRA was renamed in 1982, and since then the Women's Professional Rodeo Association has expanded its goals to include larger purses, bigger and better rodeos, and greater public recognition of women's rodeo. It also works with rodeo committees, encouraging them to prepare their rodeo arenas to lessen injuries to barrel horses and competitors due to bad ground conditions. As of 1995, about 1,850 women are involved in the WPRA, which recently moved its headquarters from Oklahoma City to Colorado Springs.

Although financial discrepancies continue to exist (in terms of amount of prize money available for women compared to men in rodeo), the WPRA has set up new programs—such as the divisional tour championships that allow women to compete in barrel racing in non-PRCA rodeos—where additional money can be won. The WPRA has also obtained its own corporate sponsors, such as Purina Mills and the American Quarter Horse Association, as well as those sponsors long affiliated with the PRCA (Resistol Hats, Copenhagen Skoal, Wrangler Jeans, Dodge Trucks, Award Design Medals, Coors Brewing

Company, and Coca-Cola). Furthermore, in a move to reclaim the status that women once held in men's rodeo, the WPRA in 1987 established an off-shoot organization, the Professional Women's Rodeo Association (PWRA). This separate division handles all-women events, including bareback bronc riding, bull riding, team roping, tie-down calf roping, and breakaway calf roping.

In the roughstock events, women may choose to hold on with both hands, they do not have to spur, and they ride for six seconds rather than the eight seconds in men's competition. But riding with two hands—under the assumption that women are not strong enough to use one—does not allow for shock absorption, and many cowgirls are jerked down on top their mounts. Because of this, Jonnie Jonckowski, a top roughstock contender for over fourteen years, was quoted in 1992 as saying, "They all had no teeth and scars on their chin."[6]

Compared to the opportunities for barrel racers, roughstock cowgirls continue to perform "at second-rate venues for third-rate pay."[7] By 1990 the world champion barrel racer earned thirty times as much as the all-around world champion cowgirl. Cowgirls bent on careers in rodeo, therefore, must continue to choose whether to become barrel racers, where they'll have a chance for financial success and wide media coverage, or pursue the roughstock and timed events as a hobby, with maybe half a dozen sanctioned PWRA rodeos per year. Those women who select and excel in the latter are invited to the PWRA All Women's Finals and Wrangler Divisional Tour Finals. Held since 1985 at the Lazy E Arena in Guthrie, Oklahoma, the annual All Women's Finals has recently moved to the Cowtown Coliseum in Forth Worth, Texas.

Since 1967, with the inclusion of the WPRA's barrel racing event into the PRCA's National Finals Rodeo, women have steadily worked to close the gender gap in rodeo. They are succeeding, in large measure because of the role the WPRA has played, but also because of the broader changes that have taken place in society during the past several decades.

BARREL RACERS

Barrel racing is one of pro rodeo's most exciting and colorful events. This fast-paced contest teaming rider and horse is easy to understand and ranks as a crowd favorite right behind bull riding. Barrel racing began as a friendly challenge of horsemanship skills between cowgirls and has evolved into a multi-million-dollar professional sport.

Charmayne (James) Rodman's legendary status as the queen of barrel racing is forever secure. Her run of ten consecutive world titles from 1984 to

1993 may never be rivaled, and who is to say that another gold buckle is not in her future? Despite the fact that her superhorse Scamper is now retired, Rodman has never dropped from among the front runners in the WPRA's world standings. And at twenty-six, Rodman is far from over the hill.

In 1984, the then 14-year-old rookie from Clayton, New Mexico, earned her first world championship, setting a new money-winning record of $53,500. That year, Charmayne James and Scamper won the rookie of the year honors as well and picked up an additional $20,750 in bonus money. Since then, Rodman has continued to rewrite the record books in professional barrel racing. She is quick to credit her gelding for her success: "Scamper is a gifted athlete and is quite a personality as well. He is so smooth, there are no wasted motions. If you ride him like you know how, it is not very hard, and his winning is what makes things look easy." [8]

But in 1994, with Scamper hampered by arthritis (the horse would be inducted into the Pro Rodeo Hall of Fame in 1996), other barrel racers quickly staked out their goal of winning a world barrel racing championship. At the NFR that year, rodeo watchers were already pondering whether Sherry Potter, the barrel racing sensation from Marana, Arizona, would be the next Charmayne Rodman. During the 1994 finals, Potter put in a stellar performance in which she and Troubles, her top barrel horse, placed in nine of ten rounds. Together, they bagged an NFR-record $57,816 in earnings. Only a tipped barrel in round four, which cost her the world title, marred an otherwise flawless maiden voyage at rodeo's most important and lucrative competition. As it was, Potter was just $5,000 plus change behind 1994 World Champ Kristie Peterson of Elbert, Colorado, when the final season's earnings were tallied.

Although Potter's outstanding performance during her rookie season may have surprised some, a look into her background reveals one truth: like her outstanding horses, Potter was bred and raised to win.

From her earliest days, Sherry Potter breathed arena dust. "One of my earliest memories is of going to steer ropings with my Dad," she says.

Sherry's parents, Mel and Wendy Potter, have been involved in rodeo in some way since they were high school sweethearts. The couple competed at the annual college rodeo in Tucson, Arizona, and in 1954 they each won all-around honors and were victorious in the mixed-pairs team roping event. After quitting graduate school, Mel Potter tried to make a living at rodeo. His biggest moment in the arena limelight came in 1959 at the very first NFR, where he competed in calf roping. By then, the Potters were already married and had a child.

In the mid-1960s, the Potters went into partnership in a rodeo stock con-

tracting company with famed quarter horse breeder Jack Brainard and rodeo announcer John Snow. Their company, Rodeos Inc., boasted some of the great bucking stock of the era, including the saddle broncs Major Reno and Tea Trader, voted the top bucking horses at the National Finals. During this period, Wendy took time out from her secretarial duties at rodeos to compete in barrel racing. In 1971, she was sixteenth in the world standings and was allowed to compete at the NFR at the last moment, when one of the top fifteen barrel racing qualifiers declined to enter the competition.

Sherry was born in Tucson, and she wasn't long out of diapers before she was on the back of one of her father's aged roping horses, Toad. She began competing in gymkhanas and junior rodeos on her first horse, a pony named Ginger. She still has that pony, who is twenty-three years old.

Sherry quickly graduated to bigger and faster horseflesh. In high school rodeo, she competed in all of the girl's events, and ironically, she won state titles in every event but barrel racing. She was the Arizona high school rodeo all-around champ three times and won top honors at the state finals in breakaway roping, goat tying, and cutting.

"I never won the barrel racing because I never had a tough horse. In fact, I never won a saddle for barrel racing until the National Finals," she says. However, Sherry did earn a rodeo scholarship to Central Arizona College in Casa Grande. During her first year, a fortunate change of horses altered her rodeo career.

Sherry's barrel horse, Danish, was crippled. Her father and mother began looking for another horse, and Mel came across a cantankerous gray gelding named Sir Double Delight. Mel liked the horse's pedigree but wasn't thrilled about his disposition — it was no accident that the horse's nickname was Troubles. But the owner agreed to lease Troubles to the Potters, and when Sherry climbed aboard at a rodeo in Spooner, Wisconsin, the pair clicked, winning their first rodeo.

It was already mid-season in 1994 when the Potters got Troubles, and Sherry had to make up a lot of ground in order to qualify for the National Finals. But big paydays at Cheyenne, Dodge City, and the San Francisco Cow Palace helped her lock up her first trip to the NFR. In the meantime, her father felt that she needed a back-up horse in case something went wrong with Troubles. He'd heard about another hard-running horse named Jet Royal Speed, nicknamed Hawk. The price was steep, but Mel felt that the horse was a good investment and lent Sherry the money to buy him.

At the 1994 NFR, much was made of the money that Sherry paid for her horses, and the criticism hurt her. "People have exaggerated the cost a great deal. But as my Dad points out, there's not one of these horses that we couldn't sell for far more than we paid for them originally" — not to mention that Sherry managed to win $105,000 that year, more than enough to repay her parents' loans. "These horses have paid their way," Sherry says. "If I weren't winning, I'd have to say I did the wrong thing."

Although Sherry prefers Troubles, she shuffles between Hawk and Danish at smaller rodeos. Her strategy in 1995 was to go to as many rodeos as she could, saving Troubles for the big-money competitions. Amazingly, all three of the horses are competitive against the best in the business. At the 1995 Dodge National Circuit Finals Rodeo, for example, Sherry cruised to third place over-all aboard Hawk, finishing behind world champ Kristie Peterson and NFR-qualifier Lindsay Hayes.

Now married to Mike Cervi, Jr., son of PRCA stock contractor and rodeo producer Mike Cervi, Sherry isn't shy about admitting that she hoped to win a world title. "That's my goal, to win the world. I am going to try my best to do it. And if I win, I can't say I won't get gold fever," she says, referring to the gold buckles that are given to rodeo's world champions. "But I know I won't go as hard as I am going right now." Although she loves rodeo and barrel racing, she's not yet certain that she'll make it a full-time career. For now, she plans to go back to college. But like her parents, she probably won't ever stray far from the rodeo arena. "I've always loved barrel racing," she says, "and this is what I've wanted to do all my life."

S herry Potter-Cervi arrived in Las Vegas for the 1995 National Finals Rodeo with $129,584 in season earnings — over $40,000 ahead of her nearest competitor, the 1994 world champ Kristie Peterson. In fact, Sherry's 1995 pre-NFR earnings totaled more money than any other rodeo athlete has won in a single event over the course of a season in the history of professional rodeo.

Her unprecedented earnings guaranteed Potter-Cervi the Number One back number awarded each year to the rodeo athlete who has earned the most money during the regular rodeo season. The numbers worn by the 120 competitors at the NFR are distributed in rank order based on amount of money earned during the season. This prestigious Number One had been worn the previous five years by all-around world champion Ty Murray, sidelined for the 1995 NFR after reconstructive surgery on both knees.

During the 1995 NFR, Sherry Potter-Cervi held on to her lead and edged out runner-up Kristie Peterson, the reigning champ, by $7,392. With some $157,172 in total prize money, Potter-Cervi's year-long strategy had paid off: the 20-year-old won her gold buckle. Charmayne Rodman, using her replacement horse, Magic, would finish the year further down the pack—in twelfth place.

SURVEY OF BARREL RACERS

As a part of our survey of PRCA cowboys, barrel racers at certain rodeos, including several of the big-time rodeos where the top fifteen PWRA barrel racers were competing, were asked to complete the questionnaire. Thirty-two women did so—a small sample but generally representative of the top contenders in 1991.

The responses of this group of women were then compared to the responses of the men. In general, their experiences in professional rodeo were more similar than dissimilar.

The differences were interesting if not entirely surprising. Women in rodeo reported having been involved with rodeo for fewer years than men, and a somewhat lower percentage of women than men came from ranching backgrounds. The cowgirls who were or had been in college were more likely than the cowboys to major in a field other than agriculture. Cowgirls reported competing in fewer rodeos during the preceding year than their male counterparts—in fact, none had competed in more than ninety. Cowgirls were even more likely than the cowboys to agree with the statement, "I train as much for the sport of rodeo as other professional athletes train for their sport."

Women also reported earning less money than the cowboys, though twice as many women reported winning money in over half of the rodeos they had entered. Where a fourth of the men reported winning over $5,000 at one rodeo, less than a tenth of the women won such lucrative purses. And cowgirls were significantly less likely than cowboys to agree with the statement, "One can make a living as a rodeo contestant." The vast majority of men thought they could make a living in rodeo, but less than half of the women agreed.

Obviously, economic parity is of concern to these women. Although improving, the amount of prize money available to women in professional rodeo is less than that for men, partly because women are not allowed to compete in many rodeo events. And though one can point to the year-end earnings of Sherry Potter-Cervi (whose winnings in 1995 totaled $21,892 more than the $135,280 pocketed by the top PRCA bull rider Jerome Davis), only a few women at the top of the barrel racing pyramid are earning the big bucks.

Besides economic concerns, other issues are important to barrel racers, from how they make their run around the barrels to the physical risks involved in rodeo competition. "The first barrel is the money barrel," explains one top contestant. "You have to turn on it clean and tight. If not, you are thinking about it as you approach the other two barrels and may lose your concentration. It is difficult to catch up if your run around the first barrel is off target."

"I've had my share of falls and had horses roll over me," she continues. "If a horse has a wreck, like running into and even tipping over a barrel, he frequently doesn't want to go back into the arena. Our horses are very temperamental. I treat mine like he's a 'big baby.'"

Rodeo cowgirls are not without their critics. Some criticism appears to stem from the male attitudes that continue to surround professional rodeo; other criticism stems from certain persistent and harmful myths. "Barrel racing is fine," observes one saddle bronc rider, when asked how most professional cowboys feel about women competing in the sport. "But we feel that the roughstock events are men's events. Roping events like team roping would be okay for women, too. But women who want to be in the rest of the events look pretty masculine and tough."

Ty Murray has also expressed disapproval of women competing against men in standard roughstock events. "Not ever, no way, *impossible*," Murray is quoted as saying. "They're not strong enough, they're not tough enough — until they prove me wrong, there never has been one."[9] Other criticism stems from the disrespect the barrel racers and their event receive from some of the other contestants. "Barrel racing doesn't get the same respect as roughstock events," notes one top-ranked barrel racer. "The guys don't think we are in as great a risk for injury as they are. The guys also look down on the women barrel racers because they chew up the arena."

Criticism expressed by other women connected with rodeo tends to focus on the barrel racers' perceived aloofness and attitudes. "Some of the women barrel racers get reputations for being real rough," notes one PRCA rodeo secretary. "Many are not too talkative. A lot of them have attitudes. The nickname for several of them is 'Barrel Bitches.'" A second rodeo secretary expressed a similar opinion. "Women in rodeo have more of a 'loner' type attitude compared to cowboys in general," she notes. "Women competitors seem to exclude themselves a lot."

Even some of the barrel racers view themselves as more solitary than the cowboys. "There doesn't appear to be the camaraderie among women barrel racers that there is among the men and their events," notes one top-ranked barrel racer. "I don't know why that is. Perhaps because we travel more by ourselves or with our families, and we don't get to know the other women as well." Another barrel racer sums up the differences this way: "Maybe it's because we're too competitive with each other."

CEREMONIAL AND SUPPORTIVE ROLES

Apart from competing in the arena, women perform several other important functions in professional rodeo. These can be loosely broken down into ceremonial and supportive roles.

One key ceremonial event is the grand entry, which involves both men and women. The men involved include the timed event contestants, rodeo clowns, the stock contractor, and selected rodeo committee members. The women involved in the grand entry include the rodeo queens, the flag bearers (who fly the banners of the sponsors of the rodeo), the female contract acts (such as precision equestrian drill teams or trick riders), and the barrel racers. Women participants in these ceremonies often outnumber the men. Often adorned in elaborate, colorful costumes, these women and their horses add flash and glamour, as well as precision riding, to the opening of each rodeo.

The Miss Rodeo America contest is not like other pageants, since horsemanship is an integral component, though class and appearance are also emphasized. Several clinics are held each year to help women prepare for the competition. In 1995, thirty-three women competed for the honor of being crowned Miss Rodeo America. What the sponsors look for—and what the rodeo fans, stock contractors, and cowboys are interested in—is someone who can be a competent spokesperson for the sport of rodeo. Being a spokesperson for rodeo presents challenges that no other beauty contest winners must contend with. Often under attack from animal rights activists as well as people who do not consider rodeo a real sport, the rodeo queen must be able to deal effectively with a variety of people and organizations.

"Sometimes rodeo doesn't get the recognition it always needs," according to Lisa Poese, former Miss Rodeo America. "The general public doesn't respect rodeo as a genuine sport. It's because the cowboys aren't promoted. There's not press releases and interviews like football or baseball. We just don't have the mass media like other sports. Miss Rodeo can help if she's intelligent, if she can work the press and stress the importance of rodeo, the sport and the history, and she can re-educate the public about why we still have rodeo."[10]

Women also perform a variety of "behind the scenes" tasks during each rodeo performance—as rodeo secretaries and timers, playing the taped music and songs that serve as background for the rodeo action, and pulling the flank straps during the roughstock events. Women also serve as rodeo photographers. One such woman, Leslie Buskirk of Los Angeles, California, looks back over her twenty-year career as a photographer: "The Pendleton Round-Up would not let women shoot pictures inside of the arena until 1985, for fear of their getting hurt. One of the rodeo committee members at Pendleton told me, in no uncertain terms, 'No woman's been behind the chutes for seventy-five years, and no woman's getting in!' But in 1985 I got in. They even announced it on the [loud]speaker. I got in because I had a [PRCA photographer's] card, and I told them, 'This card allows me behind the chutes.'"

Buskirk takes about 8,000 negatives a year, traveling on the road from rodeo to rodeo. Mostly permit holders purchase the pictures she sells out of her van, which she parks near the bucking chutes at each rodeo she attends. Although she now covers mainly the Sierra Circuit rodeos in California, Buskirk has traveled to the big national rodeos as well during her long career. "When I was starting out, the cowboys treated me as a groupie," notes Buskirk. "But once they'd see my work, they realized I was serious. I had more trouble with their girlfriends. They thought I was out to get their guys. So the barrel racers would not buy my pictures. But they've long since overcome their initial resistance."

Women not directly involved in rodeo themselves also play an important role. Girlfriends, wives, mothers, siblings, and friends provide much-needed supportive roles as well. Because there are no guaranteed checks in the rodeo business, it is often mandatory for rodeo wives to stay home to provide the family with a stable home life, and often a regular paycheck. And even the great cowboys have their down periods, when their draw is not great or they are sidelined by injury. The kids still have to eat and it is here where rodeo's unsung heroes take over. For most, the life of a rodeo wife (or girlfriend) is more about hard work than about the glamour of the road. "You have to be a bit crazy to marry a cowboy," according to Karen Cathey, wife of eight-time NFR qualifier in bull riding, Wacey Cathey.[11] "It's real fun and I wouldn't trade it for anything but it doesn't afford you very much. You spend all your money traveling."

"The divorce rate is very high among cowboys," according to Susan Ford, wife of five-time world champion bareback rider Bruce Ford.[12] "Most rodeo divorces come from women thinking they want the glamorous rodeo life. They don't have a clue what they're getting into. When you're a rodeo wife, you're a rodeo widow. If he's chasing a title, you're on the back burner. You have to know that going in or you're not going to make it."

Rodeo wives who are home raising children must "hold down the fort," playing the roles of mother, father, teacher, and ranch manager for weeks if not months on end while their husbands hit the trail. "It's a big misconception that every night the Marlboro man comes home to you," notes one such wife.

RODEO GROUPIES

And what about those cheatin' hearts? "There are plenty of buckle bunnies and rodeo fluff," says Cindy Burwash, wife of Canadian NFR-qualifier Robin Burwash. "But you've got to trust your husband or you would spend every day away from him wondering what he was doing."[13]

Baseball players call them "Annies." To riders on the rodeo circuit, they are known as buckle bunnies. But to most other athletes, they are just "the girls"—the readily available groupies who offer free and easy recreational sex to athletes. The idea of sexually available women hanging around rodeo competitors is nothing new. LeCompte, discussing the early years of cowgirls in rodeo, notes how some women allegedly joined rodeo to chase the cowboys. According to rodeo folklore, during the late 1920s and 1930s, these women—known as "chippies"—were viewed as having won their titles by bestowing sexual favors on the judges, even though there was no substantiation of these charges.[14]

Many experts believe the groupie subculture has flourished as professional sports became more lucrative. Most of the women seek money, attention, and the glamour of associating with sport celebrities. Groupie action appears to be heaviest in sports such as baseball, basketball, and rodeo, where the athletes have a long season on the road.[15]

Most buckle bunnies are younger females looking to meet the cowboys and out for a good time. And there can be humor in this situation. One year at the NFR, several contestants were riding down the elevator at the Thomas & Mack Arena when a middle-aged woman got on. Looking over the cowboys in the cramped enclosure, she commented with a grin, "When I come back in my next life, I want to be a rodeo groupie."

The cowboys are often criticized for being sexist and patronizing towards women in general. Commenting on the availability of "the girls," one rodeo secretary complained that their presence and behavior merely reinforces inappropriate behavior on the part of the men. "The groupies are numerous," stated one young rodeo secretary, upset that the cowboys were constantly "hitting" on her as well. "The cowboys get so egotistical and think that every girl is available," she commented. "They develop a real attitude towards women."

Another female photographer discussed the casual attitude towards sex that many cowboys share, even in this age of sexually transmitted diseases. "After my divorce, I started dating again," stated this woman. "I was astounded about the cowboy's philosophy in this time of AIDS. It's not macho for guys to use rubbers. The cowboys expect women to carry the rubbers or they use none at all. If AIDS were ever to enter into the rodeo athlete's group, they'd all be wiped out. The cowboys pass the girls around."

To its credit, professional rodeo has been spared the headlines linking groups of athletes to sex orgies, or to sex with minors or to charges of rape and sexual assault. Such incidents have occurred in other sports, at both the collegiate and professional levels, and those athletes have been charged with a variety of sex-related criminal offenses. On balance, the transgressions committed by rodeo athletes appear to be minor ones compared to those of athletes in other pro sports. But with rodeo's increasing popularity and cowboys' increasing fame will come greater temptations. So, too, will come criticism for sexist or inappropriate sexual behavior from time to time, as well as greater scrutiny by the press.

FAMILY CONCERNS

All family members worry about their cowboys getting hurt either on the road or riding. Sandra Semas, mother of Aaron Semas, three-time NFR-qualifier in bull riding, wrote:

I'm a very nervous mother when it comes to Aaron riding bulls, but I've tried not to inflict that on Aaron. It's due to my own insecurity about the danger of the sport, and it got to the point where I was putting something on Aaron that was unnecessary. But I realized about two years ago that I needed to be behind him 100 percent, and I worked at getting over that insecurity. I got over it when I started believing in his goals a little more. I decided that I was missing a very important event in his life; it is his joy. Then I realized that things can happen to a person no matter what he is doing. You have to let go of your kids at some point.[16]

No greater pain can be experienced by a parent than the loss of a child. In early December 1995, a year after her 25-year-old son, bull rider Brent Thurman, was killed in the final round of the NFR, Kay Thurman returned to Las Vegas. She was to receive a check for $10,000 to go toward the Brent Thurman Crisis Fund, which she set up after her son's death to benefit injured cowboys and handicapped children. Thanking the Las Vegas and rodeo community that so generously had embraced her the year before, she reflected on her son's life and his choice to be a bull rider:

"Brent got more joy, more satisfaction, than I will get out of my life if I live to be 100 because he did what he loved to do. As a mother, now, I would have killed for him to have loved golf. But the love wasn't there. The love was with the bulls. He loved his bulls more than I've ever loved anything in my life. Except for my children. It makes it terribly, terribly hard to lose him, but I am so thankful to have had him even as briefly as I [did]."[17]

"I don't have any regrets about my career. The fans, well, they've just been terrific to me over the years. Why have I been a fan favorite? Well, I think it's because I'm a fish out of water, the underdog. I come from the city, and people wonder how a person can come from that atmosphere and be successful in the rodeo world. Then they meet this guy, Charles Sampson, and they find out he's a pretty nice guy."

—Charles Sampson, the first African-American cowboy to win a world title, upon his retirement in March 1994[1]

11

THE MANY

FACES OF

RODEO

Besides North America, modern rodeo is practiced in Mexico, Brazil, New Zealand, and Australia, and rodeo producers have taken American cowboys and bucking stock to Europe, Asia, and the Middle East to put on exhibition rodeos. Cowboys from abroad also travel to North America to try their luck at the more lucrative rodeos. Furthermore, each year at the National Finals Rodeo a special night is set aside to honor the NFR qualifiers from Canada and the loyal Canadian flag-waving fans who attend the event. As one Canadian cowboy notes, "Today, there are no borders to cowboys."

North American–style rodeo has also served as a cultural event for foreign students and dignitaries who visit the United States. As part of their introduction into American culture, for instance, foreign exchange students to the United States routinely frequent rodeos, and on July 8, 1990, at the request of President George Bush, the chairman of the Houston Livestock Show and

Rodeo held an exhibition rodeo for foreign dignitaries and journalists who were attending an economic summit in the Houston, Texas, area. The special rodeo featured the three roughstock events and women's barrel racing.

VARIETIES OF AMERICAN RODEO

Over the years, several rodeo associations have formed that cater to specific ethnic and cultural groups. These groups were formed, in part, to preserve and promote their cultural heritage, offering rodeo events not held in professional rodeo. But they also wanted to participate in rodeo without facing the discrimination and prejudice that many had experienced over the years competing in rodeos of other associations. Others saw these amateur-level rodeos as an excellent opportunity for cowboys to provide important role modeling for youth from their respective communities.

MEXICAN-AMERICAN OR HISPANIC RODEO

The traditional Mexican-style rodeos known as *charreadas* continue to be popular in California and throughout the Southwest. Because the Mexican charros introduced many of the modern cowboy skills, equipment, and language to the early settlers in these regions, these rodeos help acknowledge and preserve that heritage.

Eighteen teams, which can range in size from as few as eight members to as many as fourteen men and boys, compete in the charreadas. As in other team sports, each player has a position (or specialty) in the nine men's rodeo events, and each charro wears an elaborate and expensive costume that includes leather chaps, starched shirt, stiff bow tie, and wide-brimmed hat.

The classic charreada includes ten standard events. It usually begins with the *cala de caballo*, which demonstrates the horse's training and the cowboy's ability to handle the animal. The charro must display a stop (a sliding stop is preferable), turns, and backing up. In the second event, the *piales*, riders have to heel a horse (bring it to a complete stop) running at full speed alongside the arena. They, too, are judged on style and control. Next is the *coleadero*, an event in which the charro on horseback runs alongside a steer and attempts to trip it by wrapping its tail around his leg and stirrup. The event is judged on style and the way the animal falls.

The *jaripeo de toros*, or bull riding, is similar to North American–style bull riding, although the cowboy may use a one- or two-handed leather surcingle. Whether he rides with one hand or two, the cowboy must ride the bull until it stops bucking. If the rider falls off, he is disqualified. Negative points may be assessed if he loses his composure or his form while on the bull. Extra points are given to him if he removes the flank strap before dismounting. The *terna en el ruedo* event is a form of team roping, but it is not judged on the basis of time. Most of the points are accumulated through the execution of the head catch and the heel. The most difficult maneuvers and rope twirling score the most points. This event in a typical charreada is followed by the *jinetes de yeguas,* or bronc riding, where once again the charro may hold onto the rigging with either one or two hands. He must demonstrate his ability to ride an unbroken horse until it stops bucking. The rider is disqualified if he falls off, and negative points may be given if he loses his composure or form.

In the *manganas a pie* and the *manganas a caballo,* a charro displays his rope-handling abilities. In the first event, he is on foot; in the second, on horseback. As a horse runs around the arena, he must catch its two front feet and trip it. The contestant is judged on twirling, execution, and catching. The only event for women is called the *ezcaramuza,* a form of side-saddle drill team riding. Women are judged on general appearance, timing, and their ability to handle their mounts. In the final event, *paso de la muerte* (the pass or leap of death) a charro mounted bareback on his horse attempts to cross over and mount an unbroken horse running at a full gallop.

In Southern California, the larger charreadas are held in specially built arenas, and some attract Sunday afternoon crowds of 4,000 or more. At one such rodeo held in Pico Rivera, California, each fan paid a hefty $25 to attend the three-and-a-half-hour rodeo. Both the announcements and program were in Spanish. The festive atmosphere was reminiscent of the shopping areas and street fairs common in town centers throughout Latin America. Various concession stands served traditional foods, and fans could purchase novelty items typically found in street bazaars throughout Central and South America.

Since the early 1980s, amateur Mexican-style rodeos have become increasingly popular in the western United States. In a recent five-year period, the number of registered teams (or associations) more than tripled in California (from eight to twenty-nine) and more than doubled in the Southwest (from thirty-two to eighty-three). According to Aleajandro Aguillar, president of the California Federation of Charros, "Each week a charreada takes place in Southern California, and the number of rings continues to grow."[2]

The charreada helps maintain cultural traditions and provides entertainment, but it also serves the Mexican-American community in other ways. Many Mexican-American families encourage their sons to get involved with the charreada as an alternative to neighborhood gangs and drugs. Fathers who competed as youngsters in the charreadas in Mexico now have the opportunity to teach their offspring to be charros. Family ties are strengthened, and youngsters are provided with opportunities to earn respect amongst their peers in constructive ways.[3]

Over the years, Cotton Rosser's Flying U Company has produced the Fiesta del Charro rodeos in various California communities where there are large Mexican and other Spanish-speaking rodeo aficionados. These Fiesta del Charro rodeos emphasize a spectacular opening ceremony, with the American flag presented side by side with the Mexican flag, and blend selected events from both North American and Mexican-style rodeos. Hispanic trick ropers and entertainers from Mexico perform between rodeo events.

Several Mexican-Americans have also performed well in North American–style professional rodeo. Kendra Santos, a long-time writer for the *Prorodeo Sports News*, documented the contributions of several Mexican-American rodeo cowboys. One standout has been Leo Camarillo, a PRCA world champion team roper and all-around cowboy. Camarillo has made his living with a rope since joining the professional ranks in the late 1960s. "The sport [of rodeo] is my life, and it's been my love," Camarillo told Santos. "A Hispanic athlete, whether it's me or my cousin who's a [football] quarterback, gives the community an identity. And I think Hispanics in our country are looking for an identity."[4]

Rudy Vela of Edinburg, Texas, the only Hispanic stock contractor in the PRCA, was also interviewed by Santos. The 59-year-old Vela provides rodeo livestock each year for some 350 performances in ten states and is noted for the Vela bulls he raises on his 5,000-acre ranch. Vela notes how prejudice had worked both against and for him in his long rodeo career: "Before the civil rights movement, it wasn't unusual to be turned away at a restaurant or hotel. There were people in Texas who wouldn't think of having a Mexican come in and put on their rodeo. You just shut your mouth, went about your business, and had to perform a little better than anybody else. Now, being Hispanic actually helps me get contracts."[5]

NATIVE AMERICAN RODEO

The All Indian Rodeo Cowboys Association (AIRCA) sponsors rodeos in ten different regions of Canada and the United States. Each year the top twenty cowboys in the seven standard rodeo events compete at the Indian National Finals. Specific PRCA-sanctioned rodeos also attract the Native American cowboy. The Seminole Tribe of Florida, for instance, hosts two rodeos: the annual Brighton Field Day Rodeo, first begun in 1949, in Brighton, Florida; and the annual Tribal Festival and Rodeo, first introduced in 1971, in Hollywood, Florida. Other Indian tribes across the country also produce their own rodeos, at both the amateur and professional level.

The Native American has long been part of the pageantry and evening shows at the big PRCA-sanctioned outdoor rodeos held in the summer. Ritual tribal dance performances as well as complete Indian villages are popular staples at the Calgary Stampede, Cheyenne Frontier Days, and Pendleton Round-Up. For many Native Americans, the chance to relive their past and the opportunity to preserve their culture and pass it on to their children are strong incentives to participate in these extravagant shows. Tourists flock to these events, as much for the chance to enjoy the Native American shows and culture as for the top quality rodeos.

Some rodeos even have specific events such as a relay race for Native Americans. Held around the oval race track that forms the circumference of the rodeo arena at large-scale rodeos such as Cheyenne Frontier Days, Indian contestants compete in teams much like relay teams in a track meet. The Indian cowboys ride in bareback fashion at break-neck speeds around the race track, dismounting at the start/finish line where a second member of the team then mounts the team's horse and continues the competition.

Cowboys of American Indian ancestry have been successful in the professional rodeo ranks. PRCA saddle bronc rider Bud Longbrake, who is one-quarter (Lakota) Sioux, was honored with the Indian name of Sung Wa Togla Hoksila by the Cherry Creek, South Dakota, Sioux Indians after qualifying for the 1990 NFR and winning the saddle bronc riding average. Longbrake, who was born on the Cheyenne Agency reservation in Eagle Butte, South Dakota, lives with his wife and children on the Cheyenne River Sioux Reservation. Upon his return from the finals, Longbrake received a hero's welcome. He was given a hand-woven Indian blanket, his Indian name, and an eagle feather. Visitors to Dupree, South Dakota, now are greeted with a Bud Longbrake billboard at the entrance of town, acknowledging his many rodeo accomplishments.[6]

Rodeo is also popular in Alaska where contestants of native heritage compete at both the amateur and professional level. In a recent PRCA-sanctioned rodeo held in Anchorage, several half-Eskimo women competed in the barrel racing event.

HAWAIIAN RODEO

Cattle ranching has a long and honorable history in Hawaii, one that commenced even before Texans began driving Longhorn cattle north to railheads and northern ranges. British sea captain George Vancouver reportedly brought the first cattle to the islands in 1793. They flourished, and within a generation Hawaii had a booming trade in cattle hides, meat, and tallow. By the mid-1800s, Spanish vaqueros from the California missions were brought to the islands to teach the natives how to handle cattle. The Hawaiians called them *paniolos*, their way of saying *espanol*. Eventually, paniolo came to mean any Hawaiian cowboy. The huge Parker Ranch was founded during this era, and it is now one of the largest ranches in the world.

Like their mainland counterparts, the Hawaiians participated in contests of skill. These early competitions focused mainly on roping—the pride of the paniolo. The first cowboy contest apparently took place at Honolulu in 1903, with the paniolos defeating their mainland counterparts.[7]

When a Wild West show was held in Honolulu in 1907, a paniolo cowboy named Ikua Purdy defeated the champion roper Angus McPhee of Wyoming. McPhee, a top competitor in his day, was reportedly stunned by the loss. The following year, several of the top Hawaiians competed at the famous Cheyenne Frontier Days Rodeo. Purdy made rodeo history when he won the single steer roping championship in Cheyenne. Two other paniolos, Archie Kaaua and Jack Low, finished third and sixth, respectively, in the steer roping event.

Rodeo in Hawaii ebbed and flowed, hitting its peak in the 1940s and 1950s when servicemen stationed on the islands competed in formal competitions. Occasionally, rodeo stars from the mainland, such as Jim Shoulders, Casey Tibbs, and Harry Tompkins, competed in exhibition rodeos that helped to revitalize the Hawaiians' interest in rodeo.

In the early 1980s, bull rider Donnie Gay flew to Hawaii at the invitation of Honolulu stock contractor Buddy Gibson to try the bull Rocky, who remained unridden after more than 200 attempts. When Gay arrived, some 15,000 fans packed the stands despite a rainstorm to see Gay successfully ride the bull. Perhaps Gay's ride inspired the island bull riders to improve their skills, and Gibson worked hard to give them better bucking stock. The payoff has been a generation of cowboys who can compete with mainlanders on their own terms.

The Hawaiian invasion began in 1988 at the National High School Rodeo Finals in Pueblo, Colorado. About a dozen Hawaiian cowboys and cowgirls got their first taste of mainland rodeo, competing admirably against a field of seasoned junior rodeo competitors. In 1991, Myron Duarte, a native of Maui, moved to eastern Oregon to rodeo full time, attending Eastern Oregon State College. In 1992, Duarte left college to travel with Cody Custer, the Wickenburg, Arizona, cowboy who went on to win the world title that year. Duarte said the transition from Hawaiian rodeo to PRCA competition demanded a lot of him at first. "A guy who comes here [from Hawaii] has to do lots of homework. The nice bulls that you won't place on here could go unridden there for years," he said. "When you get here and ride bulls day-in and day-out for a living, you either get better or get a day job."

Duarte has gotten better. He won the first major PRCA rodeo of the 1994 point year, the American Royal Rodeo in Kansas City. After that, he slumped through the winter and slipped down among the top thirty bull riders in the PRCA world standings. But in July, Duarte came alive at Cheyenne—the rodeo that was good to his countrymen eighty-six years ago. Duarte won the first two rounds at the daddy of 'em all, banking $9,700. Although he would finish a respectable eighteenth overall in 1994, he did not give up. The following year he qualified for the National Finals and proudly carried the Hawaiian flag in the grand entry ceremony for each performance.

Besides the standard PRCA events, local rodeos in Hawaii also have events that hark back to the early days. One such event, "double mugging," grew out of a time when there was a shortage of horses on Hawaiian ranches. Paniolos had to team up, with one cowboy mounted and one on foot, to catch and doctor cattle. In the rodeo timed event, a mugging team consists of a header, as in team roping, and a mugger, like a steer wrestler. As in regulation team roping, the header nods for his draw to be released from the timed event chute. Once he ropes the steer, the mugger runs in from the side of the arena to get a headlock on the animal while the header dismounts, rope in hand, to assist the mugger in throwing the steer. Ideally, the mugger holds the steer down while the header, in typical calf roping style, gathers up and ties three of the steer's legs.

BLACK AMERICAN RODEO

At least one in six cowboys on the great nineteenth-century cattle drives was of African descent. Many were former slaves who had mastered the skills of riding and roping. Cowboying was one of the few jobs where blacks were paid equal wages, and many became cowboys because there was not as much prejudice on the job. Cowboys had to use teamwork to control large herds of cattle, and they had to respect each other's ability. When the drives ended in the 1880s, many of these cowboys joined Wild West shows.

The most notable cowboy of that era was Bill Pickett, the only black member of the 101 Ranch Wild West Show and the man credited with the invention of bulldogging. In 1971, Bill Pickett became the first black cowboy admitted to the Cowboy Hall of Fame in Oklahoma City. One black-only rodeo association today is named Bill Pickett Rodeos in honor of this early cowboy's many accomplishments.

Although even casual rodeo followers know about Bill Pickett, very few are aware of other early black rodeo greats such as Jesse Stahl, a saddle bronc rider who was also inducted into the Cowboy Hall of Fame. Although exceptionally talented, Stahl seldom placed higher than third at the major rodeos. At one rodeo where he had clearly bested his competitors, Stahl was awarded second place. Perhaps to mock the judges, he rode a second bronc while facing backward.

In the 1950s, a top hand emerged from the ranks. Marvel Rogers, who had worked for stock contractor Lynn Beutler for many years, was known as a competent all-around cowboy. Cleo Hearn, producer of the Cowboys of Color rodeo series in Texas and Oklahoma, recalls that Rogers was an inspiration to black cowboys like himself. "Marvel was a great all-around cowboy, but his specialty was bronc riding," remembers Hearn. "He was known to ride with a cigar in his mouth, puffing out a cloud of blue smoke each time the bucking horse touched his feet to the ground."

Hearn also recalls how black rodeo athletes survived financially in that period. "In the days of segregated rodeo, they'd hold hat rides," states Hearn. "They'd put money in the hat to see him ride. And the cowboys used to say that those hat rides often paid more than first-place rides in the regular rodeo. Marvel Rogers was a close friend of legendary all-around champion Harry Tompkins, who was quoted as saying, 'Rogers was the most-robbed cowboy in rodeo.'"

Other black athletes also recall the difficulties of the early days in rodeo. Wayne Orme, a 45-year-old roper from Poway, California, remembered when a black cowboy's presence brought out an ugly streak in people: "Judges fixed competitions, fans and fellow riders hurled epithets and promoters refused to pay out prize money to winners."[8] Orme also recalled the time he swallowed his pride and successfully rode a rank bareback bronc named Nigger in the 1960s. "I never blamed that horse for his name," Orme remarked. "He was a champion horse. He didn't care if you were black or white or brown or purple. If you were on his back, he treated you exactly the same. He was just plain mean to everybody."

In the 1960s Wayne Orme brought the first all-black rodeo to large black audiences in the Watts area of Los Angeles, and in the 1970s he helped organize the American Black Cowboy's Association to further black participation. Today, he is a successful businessman and Hollywood stuntman, continuing to serve as a mentor to black athletes in the sport of rodeo. Orme is particularly concerned that today's black youth learn of their ancestors' contributions to the country's western heritage. For too long, he contends, blacks have been seen as outsiders to the rough and tumble sport of rodeo, whose very roots they helped develop. "For years, I was looked at as a freak," Orme remarked. "People came to point and laugh at the funny-looking cowboy with the black face. They didn't understand what blacks had meant to cowboying."[9]

Though the Rodeo Cowboys Association (now the PRCA) never officially excluded minority competitors, the lack of black cowboys among the pros, as well as an underlying racism, effectively kept most blacks from competing with whites until the 1950s. To combat that situation, black cowboys of the 1940s and 1950s formed the Southwestern Colored Cowboys Association, which served as a farm league for cowboys who aspired to become professionals. Many of those cowboys graduated to the professional level, and by the 1960s rodeo had become integrated enough for blacks to succeed in the professional ranks.

The most successful black cowboy of that era was Myrtis Dightman, a bullfighter turned bull rider from Houston. In 1966, Dightman became the first black cowboy to qualify for the National Finals Rodeo. The following year, Dightman finished third in the bull riding world standings, as close as he ever came to a world title. From 1966 to 1972, Dightman missed qualifying for the NFR only once. Amazingly, Dightman had not even picked up a bull rope until the age of twenty-five. Two decades later he was still climbing aboard bulls.

Dightman has been compared to Jackie Robinson, who achieved similar feats in professional baseball. Although he was not the first black to compete in the RCA, Dightman was the first serious contender for the world title. The cowboys backed him, but the fans were not always sure how to take him. Dightman took it all in good humor. In the dangerous world of professional rodeo, he worried more about Brahma bulls than he did about racial prejudice. Even so, he often slept in his car when he was on the road, rather than risk being turned away from hotels.

Dightman's career helped pave the way for an energetic black bull rider from Los Angeles—Charles Sampson. In 1982, his fourth year in the pro ranks, Sampson wrote his name in the PRCA history books as the first black cowboy to win a world championship. It was fitting that Myrtis Dightman, who had pulled Sampson's bull rope throughout the NFR, was the first to offer his hand in congratulation.

Sampson, an unabashed promoter of rodeo, was a high-profile role model for aspiring cowboys of all colors and races during his sixteen-year rodeo career. In 1996, two years after retirement, Sampson was inducted into the Pro Rodeo Hall of Fame. Sampson, well known for overcoming injuries, became one of the PRCA's most popular cowboys. Qualifying for the NFR ten times, he ended his PRCA career with $741,588 in earnings. In 1986, fans voted him the Coors Fans Favorite Cowboy.[10]

Leon Coffee, Dwayne Hargo, Ervin Williams, and several other younger black cowboys like Fred Whitfield and Chris Littlejohn are part of the current group of African-American professional rodeo athletes. Coffee and Hargo both rose to the top in the sport's most dangerous profession—bullfighting. Luke "Leon" Coffee was only a first-year professional bullfighter when he was selected for one of the two coveted bullfighter positions at the NFR back in 1979. He became the first black bullfighter ever to perform at the NFR and the second black ever to be a part of the NFR in any capacity.

Coffee is often billed as the "Boogie Man" because of a dance he does when he senses that a bull is willing to spar with him. The bull stands nearly mesmerized while Leon dances and drops into a full split, inching his way back up in beat to the music. How does he do it? "With great difficulty," he jokes. The truth is that Coffee has a brown belt in karate, and he uses the splits to stretch his muscles. He is also a former Texas All-State linebacker.

Leon Coffee was born in 1954 and raised around mules and horses in the heart of Texas. His grandfather raised and broke mule teams for road crews. "I grew up around it," says Leon, "and I always wanted to rodeo. The first event I worked was the bareback riding when I was nine." Coffee went on to compete in the Texas Youth Rodeo Association, Little Britches, and even qualify for the National High School Rodeo Finals before joining the army in 1973. After a three-year stint, Coffee returned to his rodeo roots and became a rodeo clown and bullfighter. In 1983, he was voted PRCA Clown of the Year by the top cowboys.

Another black bullfighter, Dwayne Hargo, was born in 1961 and grew up in San Bernardino, California, where he developed a love for horses and an admiration for cowboys. As a kid, he looked up to champion cowboys like Don Gay, since there were few black cowboys to serve as role models. But when he reached the pro ranks, Hargo found a support group. Sampson, along with legendary bullfighter Wick Peth and 1970 world champion bull rider Gary Leffew, signed his PRCA card. Those impressive signatures lent credibility and prestige to Hargo's résumé.

Leon Coffee often worked with Hargo to develop the younger man's skills as an entertainer. Hargo, dubbed by one reporter as the "Joe Montana of Bullfighters" (although he would rather be known as Ronnie Lott), was crowned the PRCA Wrangler world champion bullfighter in 1989.

Ervin Williams of Tulsa, Oklahoma, has carved out an impressive career as a bull rider, so far earning four trips to the National Finals. His highest mark has been a third place in the world standings in 1989. Although admittedly not much of an athlete in high school, bull riding was came naturally after growing up on his family's ranch. "I used to try calf roping, but I kept falling off the horse," said Williams. During the 1991 National Finals Rodeo, Ervin Williams was asked by a Las Vegas news reporter whether or not he had experienced prejudice. He replied that he had received some racial abuse from fans during the NFR but that he had learned to deal with it: "If I'm a winner, people are going to have to like me. And I'm a winner." [11]

Unlike the African-American cowboys who have made their mark at the roughstock end of the arena, Fred Whitfield of Cypress, Texas, has excelled as a calf roping specialist. He burst onto the scene in 1989, winning rookie of the year and calf roping rookie of the year awards. A year later, he became the first black cowboy to win the title of world champion calf roper, a title he would recapture in 1995. Whitfield hopes his success encourages other black ropers to compete on the national level. "There aren't many black athletes in rodeo. There are a lot of black athletes with the talent, but they're just not into rodeoing," Whitfield says. "There's a lot of good ropers around Houston. Most of them stay home because they lack confidence and finances to do this full time."

Thanks to the efforts of black rodeo promoters such as Hearn and Orme, and the successes of Sampson, Whitfield, and others, that situation may change. "To the black communities of my generation, the black cowboy was nonexistent," Hearn says. "Presently, of the 5,700 PRCA members, there are only about 130 black cowboys." Hearn's goal in rodeos of color is to give blacks, Indians, and Hispanics a place to hone their skills and prepare them for professional rodeo. "I want to graduate five or ten cowboys to the pro ranks every year," he said. These efforts of Hearn and others, along with the successes of today's generation of black cowboys, should make the future more promising.

GAY RODEO

Gay rodeo, in one form or another, has been produced since 1975, when Phil Ragsdale of Reno, Nevada, encouraged the local gay and lesbian community to raise money for the Muscular Dystrophy Association by staging a rodeo. At first, Ragsdale was unable to find any local ranchers willing to lease livestock for a gay rodeo, but eventually animals were obtained. The rodeo went on as planned and became an annual event.

Over the next few years, the Reno Gay Rodeo drew more and more contestants and spectators from across the country. By 1982, the National Reno Gay Rodeo included a mounted drill team and forty-three rodeo contestants. Comedienne Joan Rivers was the Grand Marshal that year, and there were over 10,000 spectators in the grandstands. The following year, in 1983, Denver became the second city in the United States to host a gay rodeo.

By 1985, with the new regional gay rodeo associations in Colorado, Texas, California, and Arizona producing their own rodeos, it became apparent that gay rodeo had become so large that it needed to get better organized. That year, the International Gay Rodeo Association (IGRA) was formed to standardize rules, guarantee greater uniformity to the regional rodeos, and set objectives for the regional associations. Plans called for the development of a gay rodeo circuit that would allow contestants to compete around the country on a more frequent and scheduled basis.

Over the past decade, the International Gay Rodeo Association has grown to a twenty-member association representing twenty-eight states, the District of Columbia, two Canadian provinces, and over 8,000 individual members. And during the same period, well over $1.5 million has been distributed back to the gay and lesbian community as charity contributions raised at IGRA rodeos, events, and activities.

The IGRA has firmed up major corporate sponsors for the regional rodeos (primarily beer, liquor, and cigarette companies, since they are less likely to be affected by church boycotts). It has also purses totaling $20,000 at certain of the regional competitions, and it draws thousands of spectators to its community celebrations held in major rodeo arenas across the country. Twenty-three regional rodeos were produced in 1995, along with the IGRA Finals Rodeo that was held in Denver, Colorado. Future plans call for expansion to Sydney, Australia, and Ontario, Canada.[12]

Even with these changes and growth, gay rodeo has maintained its initial focus which, according to Wayne Jakino, founding president of the IGRA, is to "let the competitors feel good about themselves and open closet doors." In fact, the stated goals of the International Gay Rodeo Association are "to promote and nurture, through fellowship, the sport of rodeo within the gay community; to foster a positive image of gay cowboys and cowgirls within all communities; to provide anyone with education and training in the production of, and participation in, rodeo; and to participate in the preservation of our western heritage."

"Gay rodeo really still is put on by gays for gays and no attempt is made for acceptance or recognition of any other group," says John King, one of the directors of the IGRA. "There are many of us who see gay rodeo as a forum for enhancing self-esteem," he continues, explaining why gay rodeo remains popular for both contestants and fans alike. "Many of the contestants are those that grew up in rural areas and have moved to cities for work or to find companionship. Typically, the small-town guy moves to the city and social-izes to the urban gay stereotype. For many of us from rural areas, we didn't fit in well with the city gay scene. We were forced to become someone we weren't. We ended up being the wallflower misfits."

According to King, "Gay rodeo shows that you don't have to change. For many of us growing up, one of the biggest weekends of the year was going to a rodeo. Now, we have gay rodeo for these people to celebrate. This is pri-marily gay rodeo's main function—to give these people a place to integrate their two identities, being gay and enjoying rodeo."

Some 750 contestants now compete on the IGRA circuit, with 200 to 300 entered at the two-day regional rodeos. The various rodeo events are divided into four categories: roughstock events (bull riding, wild steer riding, and bare-back bronc riding); roping events (breakaway calf roping, calf roping on foot, and team roping); horse events (barrel racing, flag racing, and pole bending); and "camp" events (the wild drag race, steer decorating, and goat dressing).

All rodeo events are open to both men and women. The rules require that the roughstock contestants sign forms indicating they have had prior riding experience in the roughstock events, though most riders have grown up on ranches or learned to ride at rodeo training schools or buck-outs. The level of roughstock ridden in competition is comparable to that used at other amateur-level rodeos.

Several of the regional gay rodeo associations have arranged for permanent practice facilities so that their members can train throughout the year. Many cowboys are dedicated to their sport. "I practice roping two or three times a week," said Greg Olsen, seven-time all-around IGRA champion from 1987 through 1993. "I live in Phoenix, and every Wednesday night we can use the rodeo grounds."

Greg Olsen has competed in nearly every event during his successful career. His two older brothers compete in non-gay rodeo associations and sup-port his endeavors. Olsen earns more than they do, averaging close to $2,000 per rodeo, and over $10,000 per year. "Here we are all amateurs," Olsen points out, "but we take our hobby seriously. I really feel out of place at straight rodeos. Here it's great. We're gay and together, and nothing else matters."

According to Gary Robinson, head of IGRA media relations, "Some gay cowboys perform in mainstream rodeos, too, and make a good bit of money, but they remain closeted among their colleagues in the conservative country western world of rodeos. That's why some of the winners [at our rodeos] have only their initials listed because it's not safe for them to feel openly gay yet." [13] Since no "open" gays or lesbians compete in the pro rodeo ranks, it is difficult to know how they might be treated by the other contestants. When asked about this issue, one PRCA saddle bronc rider said, "It probably wouldn't matter. So long as they are talented and treat you with respect, they'd be treated in the same way. It all comes down to what kind of person you are."

However, one gay cowboy interviewed for a Northern California newspaper did not share this view. Mike Biggs (an alias) was asked how the straight rodeo cowboys would react if they knew he was gay. "I would be dead," Biggs responded. "No question. They would kill me. Literally. Gay rodeo and straight rodeo do not get along. There are other gay cowboys that compete in the straight circuit, but most of them use aliases like me. It can be very lonely." [14]

The existence of homophobia in both men's and women's sports reflects persisting cultural ideas. Two sociologists, summarizing the findings of several scholarly studies, point out that sport remains a place for men, where stereotypical masculinity is highly valued: "Although sport is no longer a strictly male preserve in the United States and many other nations, women still find their presence unwelcome or unappreciated in many sports. Female athletes are often presumed to be lesbians, and actual and presumed lesbian and gay athletes both feel the sting of stigma and homophobic reactions." [15] These patterns hold true for the sport of rodeo.

CELEBRITY AND SPECIALIZED RODEOS

Hollywood celebrities often participate in fund-raising rodeos. The most notable of these are the Ben Johnson Pro/Celebrity Rodeos that have taken place in Los Angeles, Houston, Dallas–Fort Worth, and Colorado Springs. Johnson, an actor who earned an Academy Award for his performance in *The Last Picture Show*, has won the world title in team roping. He helped put together the contests that bear his name. Begun in 1988, these annual charity rodeos involve both Hollywood celebrities and professional rodeo cowboys.

In one recent Pro/Celebrity Rodeo at the Los Angeles Equestrian Center, more than 200 contestants participated in events that ranged from professional saddle bronc riding and bull riding to celebrity team roping, team penning, and women's barrel racing. Besides raising money through ticket sales, individuals were invited to pay $200 to pair up in the team penning with one of the celebrities.

Television actor Bruce Boxleitner, one of the cohosts of the Los Angeles event, has been involved with the Pro/Celebrity Rodeos since 1989. Boxleitner, who has performed in several westerns, has a ranch in the San Fernando Valley and team ropes as a hobby. "I'm a better cowboy than an actor," jokes Boxleitner. "It's a way for me to play out something I never did when I was young. It's a fantasy, a challenge. It's a good way to get away from show business."

Several charitable organizations raise money to support the efforts of equestrian and rodeo programs established for cowboys and cowgirls with special needs. Horseback-riding therapy (or hippotherapy) appears to improve a rider's muscle tone, balance, posture, coordination, motor development, and emotional and psychological well-being. For these reasons, it has proven effective in treating both the mentally and physically handicapped. As one specialist notes: "A horse is nonjudgmental. Its rhythmic movement shifts riders in ways similar to walking. The kids learn balance and coordination you can't create in a clinical setting."

Hearing-impaired cowboys and cowgirls, members of the American Rodeo Association of the Deaf, compete each year at the Summer Rodeo for the Deaf held at the Santa Fe, New Mexico, fairgrounds. Rodeo events include breakaway roping, calf roping, ribbon roping, team roping, bulldogging, goat tying, and barrel racing. Hearing contestants may also participate, provided that a hearing-impaired relative is entered in the rodeo.

PRISON RODEO

Horse and rodeo programs have also been effectively used in working with convicts and troubled juveniles. One program, Home on the Range, was inaugurated in 1950 to give juveniles a chance to do meaningful work that would help them develop self-esteem. Based on a 1,500-acre ranch near Sentinel Butte, North Dakota, the program typically houses fifty boys and twenty girls, aged eleven to eighteen. The juveniles—all formerly abused, disadvantaged, drug-dependent, and/or delinquent—learn ranch work and the responsibilities of taking care of farm animals. They also learn to ride and care for horses.

The youngsters serve as part of the work crew for the annual Champions Ride, held on the ranch, where many of the PRCA's top cowboys compete in a benefit rodeo that raises funds for this home for troubled kids. Six of the top Badlands Circuit and six of the top Montana Circuit cowboys go head to head in this unique intersectional rodeo.[16]

Several states have developed programs that give "hard-to-handle" juveniles either a wilderness or western experience. A program named Vision Quest takes teenagers between the ages of thirteen and eighteen on three-to-four-month covered wagon treks from Arizona to Montana and back. The youngsters are taught survival skills as well as how to ride and the proper care of horses.

Other innovative programs have attempted to reconstruct the western lifestyle, teaching youngsters outdoor skills and introducing them to rodeo competition. One PRCA bareback rider, Clay W. Kirkham of Lehi, Utah, works with emotionally disturbed and delinquent adolescents in such a program. "I teach 'life skills' at a unique vocational-style program," he says. "I have eighteen head of horses and ninety kids in the program. They range in level from kindergarten through twelfth grade. Some are short-term and some stay longer in the program. It's a full-time job, but it allows me to rodeo on the side. I buy kids' kind of horses. The horses are unpredictable, just like the kids. But the kids love the program because it challenges them. Some of the kids, once they've learned how to ride, and seeing what I do, want to try out rodeo."

Horse and rodeo programs can also be found in a number of our nation's prisons. Horses are used for farm labor in Dixon Correctional Institution, a medium-security prison for 1,900 inmates near Jackson, Louisiana, and a similar program in Canon City, Colorado, allows inmates to break and train wild burros and horses, which are later sold to the public. Penal institutions in Texas, Arizona, and New Mexico have programs that train inmates how to break wild horses. In some programs, the Bureau of Land Management captures the horses in the wild and delivers them to the prison for the inmates to break. The horses are then sold to the public. Several prisons are interested in adopting similar programs. Although these programs are not strictly rodeo-related, they are typically administered by people from rodeo backgrounds and include components of rodeo competition.[17]

The prison documentary movie *Doing Time: Ten Years Later*, on the Central New Mexico Correctional Facility, highlights one such program. Twenty inmates in the Wild Horse Breaking Program (dubbed "Mustang City" by the convicts) were interviewed. One inmate, who had recently been released, hoped to become a veterinarian, having gained an appreciation for animals while behind bars.

The most famous of the prison rodeo programs is the one in Huntsville,

Texas, where inmates trained and competed in the various rodeo events. That program has subsequently been dropped, owing to a change in administrative priorities, and currently the only all-inmate rodeo program in the United States is that of the Louisiana State Penitentiary at Angola. According to one *Time* magazine article, some 20,000 Louisianans paid $7 apiece in 1995 to attend the sold-out shows at the state's only maximum-security prison. One of the event winners was Terry Hawkins, a former butcher shop employee who had killed his supervisor with a hammer. He was quickest to remove a poker chip taped to the forehead of an angry bull in the "Guts and Glory" event. All-around champion cowboy honors went to Clifford Snow, one of the "gang of crazy convict cowboys," as the event's organizers touted them.[18]

Prison rodeo programs have also been dramatized in motion pictures. In fact, in the 1980 comedy *Stir Crazy*, starring Richard Pryor and Gene Wilder, a prison rodeo served as the distraction as several inmates attempted their escape. The Hunstville, Texas, facility was also featured in the 1980 film *Urban Cowboy*. More recently, a 1995 made-for-television movie, *Convict Cowboy*, focused on the warden of a Montana jailhouse (played by Ben Gazzara) who uses rodeo to rehabilitate prisoners, including an ex-rodeo star doing life (played by Jon Voight).

In Stockton, Kansas, inmates from one of the nearby minimum-security prisons assist with the upkeep of the county-owned rodeo grounds. Under supervision, over half of the ninety-four inmates, in groups of seven, are rotated into the work-release program. Besides preparing the fairgrounds and rodeo arena for the annual event, the inmates also clean up after each performance. To show the community's appreciation, the inmates are allowed to attend the rodeo under supervision, sitting in a specially designated section. Half of the inmates attend one night, the other half the second, of the two-performance rodeo. The local townspeople have shown their support because they know that the inmates have worked to ready the grounds. It has also been good public relations for the prison program, showing the public than these soon-to-be released inmates can do something constructive.

POLICE, FIREFIGHTER, AND MILITARY RODEOS

Police, firefighters, and military cowboys compete in their own rodeo associations. In California, for instance, close to 300 police officers—from undercover narcotics officers to highway patrol and border patrol officers—compete in one or more of the eight rodeos held each year. The rodeos are sponsored by the National Police Rodeo Association, whose membership includes thousands of contestants. Firefighters also compete in these rodeos but have their own organization as well, the National Firefighters Rodeo Association. The $2,000 to $3,000 raised in each of the police rodeos is donated to various local charities.

Most competitors in these rodeos ride in the roughstock events, particularly bull and bareback riding, and most learn and practice their events in buck-out sessions. "The military guys like the rough type events," notes one bull rider. Under the auspices of the Military Rodeo Cowboys Association (MRCA), military rodeos are held on or near military bases throughout the country and overseas. In California, many military cowboys compete in jackpot competitions and at other amateur-level rodeos as well.

The military rodeos were particularly hard hit during the Desert Storm military engagement in 1990 when, according to Sonny Borrelli, commissioner of the MRCA, 99 percent of the MRCA membership was deployed to the Persian Gulf. The military cowboys' absence was noticed in several of the PRCA-sanctioned rodeos as well. Since many of these cowboys work to fulfill their PRCA permit card while still in the service, the number of bull and bareback riders competing in some of the regional smaller rodeos on the West Coast also declined during the war.

Once their term of service is completed, and with more time to devote to rodeo, some talented military cowboys graduate to the ranks of pro rodeo. Jimbo Thibert, former runner-up national champion in bareback in the MRCA, has had an active career in the PRCA's Sierra Circuit. Likewise, Greg Richins, a former all-around cowboy titlist in the MRCA and competitor in all three roughstock events, now competes in bull riding in the PRCA. "I plan to work on a dairy farm and get to know the personality of animals and critters once again," Richins stated, shortly after completing three years in the military. "A guy rides better when he's been around animals."

Many military bases are well equipped for rodeo, with grazing fields and holding pens for livestock and permanent arenas for practice and competition. Military rodeos serve as good public relations ventures as well. In 1990, the marines at Camp Pendleton, California, sponsored a rodeo for 300 visiting Russian sailors on leave from their navy ship anchored in nearby San Diego. "When their ship docked, they [the military brass] figured the Russians would want to go to Disneyland," says a marine who competed in this special rodeo. "But, instead, they wanted to see cowboys." The Russians were treated to all of the standard rodeo events, and American Indians in traditional costume were part of the festivities as well. "The Russians were enthralled," the bull rider continues. "One traded his whole uniform for an old bull rider's glove. It was a dream come true [for them]. The Soviet sailors were young and seemed fascinated by the myth of the American West cowboy."

SENIOR RODEO

The National Senior Professional Rodeo Association sponsors some seventy regional rodeos a year for older cowboys. The National Senior Pro Rodeo Finals, featuring many of the sport's legendary competitors, is held each November at the Reno (Nevada) Livestock Events Center. There, approximately 400 contestants ranging from forty to over seventy years old compete for over $150,000 in prize money. These seniors—most of them former champions—compete in all of the regular rodeo events. Other highlights include jackpot roping, ribbon roping, and a western holiday gift show.

Some senior cowboys have never quit the sport of rodeo. Others dropped out and went on to careers in other fields, raised families, and then came back to rodeo. Some senior competitors are the cowboys who competed in the 1950s and initiated the National Finals Rodeo in 1959. "This is the generation that always led the way," says Terry Taillon, manager of the Senior Pro Rodeo Finals. "They broke ground for those who followed."[19]

Some of the PRCA-sanctioned rodeos, such as Cheyenne Frontier Days, offer select events such as steer roping for senior cowboys. One 59-year-old banker, Randy Moore of Omaha, Texas, who competed at Cheyenne recently, says: "The special competition gives you a reason to keep in shape. The [assembly of] older cowboys gives younger men a chance to meet some of the grand old men of the sport."[20]

Though many old timers never quit competing, most cowboys are content to finish their careers in their twenties and thirties. "You have to realize that rodeo cannot be your profession for the biggest portion of your life," maintains bull rider Denny Flynn, of Charleston, Arkansas, ten-time National Finals bull rider from the mid-seventies through the mid-eighties. "The thing about rodeo is it never completely leaves your blood. You've got to find some avenue where you can still be involved in the sport after you quit competing, but also find an alternative way to make a living."[21]

But for those veteran older cowboys who still are "addicted to eight," the Senior Pro Rodeo program has been a welcome addition. "Why put us out to pasture?" asks P. J. Ward, a bull rider throughout the sixties and early seventies. He was ranked one year as high as eighth in the standings before injuries dropped him out of the top fifteen and destroyed his chance to compete in the NFR. "These old-timers rodeos are a good idea for the seniors," Ward concludes. "I don't want to wind up an old bum, telling stories, getting a free beer. I still want to do something."

Other veteran cowboys are attracted to the Senior Pro Rodeo Tour because it reminds them of the professional rodeo of an earlier era. Billy Trimble of Fernley, Nevada, who first began competing in the timed events in 1966, comments on the shift in pro rodeo during the last several decades: "I don't like it as well today. When I did rodeos, it was more like a family thing. It was a big gathering. Every rodeo you went to, you'd see the same people. Now, it's more of a business. Now, if you want to be one of the best, you don't have time to have a good time. That's the reason why I moved on to the senior circuit. It's the way the [PRCA] tour was twenty years ago."[22]

"You see rodeo movies come out from time to time. But they're usually about the washed up old guy who makes a comeback. This will be a movie about a kid coming into an exciting new world, and I don't think that's ever been done before with a rodeo film."

—Michael Shamberg, producer of the movie *8 Seconds*[1]

12

RODEO

COWBOYS,

HOLLYWOOD

STYLE

Hollywood film makers have always shown something of an ambivalence towards the rodeo cowboy, whose battles mostly are fought in the arena rather than in the dusty streets of the Old West. And since a six-shooter and a rifle are not tools of the rodeo cowboys' trade, the opportunity for the exciting shoot-out does not often present itself in the portrayal of the rodeo cowboy. Furthermore, the rodeo cowboy competes in a sport that requires a certain amount of explanation to the viewing audience, a pesky detail in the plot development of a western film. For these reasons, perhaps, as well as a general lack of understanding among screen writers and directors of how the rodeo game is played, rodeo films make up only a small portion of western films. Still, Hollywood has had its share of rodeo films, and a few of them have made valuable contributions to the motion picture industry.

FILMS ABOUT RODEO

From the 1950s to the early 1970s, rodeo films focused on two types of cowboys: either the older cowboy making a comeback or the aging competitor whose talents were waning. As Kim Newman points out in his book *Wild West Movies*, "The overwhelming impression given by rodeo-set movies is of broken bones and hearts, and a dusty fall from grace."[2] In reviewing the films of that era, he notes that Budd Boetticher's *Bronco Buster* (1952), Nicolas Ray's *The Lusty Men* (1952), Richard Fleischer's *Arena* (1953), and four motion pictures all released in 1972—Steve Ihnat's *The Honkers*, Stuart Millar's *When the Legends Die*, Cliff Robertson's *J. W. Coop*, and Sam Peckinpaugh's *Junior Bonner*—seem cut from the same cloth.

In these movies, the rodeo cowboy is a metaphor for the West. His values and his actions are noble but out of sync with the society at large. Forces he tries desperately to control only seem to drive him down and make him, ultimately, a nostalgic and lonely figure. Though the rodeo cowboy may win in the end, the message is that his time is running out. The western ideals that he embodies are still treated as honorable, but the extreme difficulties he must endure to support them virtually require him to be superhuman.

Perhaps the quintessential examples of the classic rodeo character are the protagonists of the films *J. W. Coop* and *Junior Bonner*. In *J. W. Coop*, Cliff Robertson plays a recently released ex-con and former rodeo performer who goes back on the circuit. What he finds is a competitive environment far different than the one he left behind. For example, Coop stands by the roadside with his saddle, thumbing a ride to the next rodeo, where he encounters star cowboys who use personal planes to fly from one rodeo to the next. Coop must prove his valor without compromising his archaic values. In one scene, the cowboy rides despite having a plaster cast on his newly broken leg. Coop is a nostalgic and romanticized figure of a West in which people were physically tough and mentally strong. He stands in contrast to the modern rodeo athlete, who was portrayed in the film as just another sports prima donna.

Junior Bonner follows essentially the same theme. Steve McQueen's character, Junior Bonner, is a man who must contend with a rapidly changing rodeo society where money and influence are paramount. Again, the character makes a last stand in a desperate attempt to hold on to the values of the Old West.

Besides these two films, the early 1970s saw two less memorable Hollywood films that depicted rodeo cowboys and their world. In *When the Legends Die*, Richard Widmark stars as an aging and drunken rodeo promoter who assists a young Native American boy as he tries his luck on the rodeo circuit. It represented a slightly different twist—the older cowboy who seeks redemption and a new lease on life through the efforts of a young man. In *The Honkers*, directed by Steve Ihnat, James Coburn plays a self-centered, second-rate rodeo performer attracted to "honkers," a term referring to wild bulls and available women. A typical theme emerges here—that of the irresponsible rodeo cowboy who drinks, carouses, and generally lives in a state of suspended adolescence. Often, the rodeo cowboy is portrayed as a reckless man who forsakes a settled life and its responsibilities in favor of the footloose life of the traveling cowboy. One commentator notes that *The Honkers* was based on a "tried-and-true rodeo plot: the rodeo rider's conflict between spending time with his wife and spending time on the road."[3]

Such themes had already surfaced in the rodeo films of the 1950s, which used the gypsy-like life of the cowboy as a vehicle for critiquing the lifestyle of the social nonconformist. The 1952 movie *Bronco Buster*, directed by Budd Boetticher, depicts a rodeo veteran, played by Chill Wills, teaching the newcomer, played by John Lund, the "ropes of the trade." All-around world champion Casey Tibbs, featured on the cover of *Life* magazine the year before, also stars in the movie. In this film, the aging rodeo star is once again held up as the hero, while Lund, the representative of the younger generation, tries to take a shortcut to the top.

In another 1952 film, *The Lusty Men*, the plot turns on the competition between a weathered, down-and-out rodeo veteran, played by Robert Mitchum, who is challenged by a rising young rodeo star, played by Arthur Kennedy, who lets his success in the rodeo arena compromise his relationship with his wife. In the 1953 movie *Arena*, directed by Richard Fleischer, with Gig Young and Polly Bergen, Lee Van Cleef stars as a rodeo rider competing for prize money in a Tucson, Arizona, rodeo. Weak in plot, this film is notable only as an early attempt to include rodeo as subject matter.

These films almost invariably portray rodeo cowboys as bar-brawling, hard-drinking men hell-bent on imitating not only the virtues of the Old West but also its vices. They are not the clean-cut characters that were so popular in the B-grade westerns of the 1940s and the cowboy television shows that proliferated in the 1950s and early 1960s. In a sense, the rodeo cowboy was viewed as a pale substitute for the mythical cowboy of the open range, an impostor whose claims as the inheritor of the Old West were either a sham or a lost cause.

According to Kim Newman, implicit in this message is the idea that the mythological cowboy hero of television and motion picture fame was the true carrier of the cowboy tradition. The rodeo cowboy, who actually lived and worked in the cattle industry, was much closer to the reality of range life before the turn of the century than Hollywood's heroes. Yet he was portrayed as an individual who had somehow corrupted the purity of the cowboy myth. Perhaps because the rodeo cowboy was a real person, and real people seldom stack up to the ideals of the heroic cowboy of the American imagination, he was an easy target for Hollywood film makers to ridicule.

William W. Savage, Jr., in his 1979 book *The Cowboy Hero*, notes that the rodeo performer depicted in the films of this period "is one, and perhaps the foremost, of life's losers." Savage contends that the heroic status of the cowboy is not extended to rodeo performers, who are portrayed in fiction and film as being "puerile, petulant, shallow, egocentric, often violent, and almost always self-destructive men who are heroic for perhaps no more than fifteen seconds at a time and whose relationships with other human beings—especially female human beings—are generally defective."[4]

Though the film portrayals of the rodeo cowboy stripped away his heroism, there was a degree of realism in those early films—perhaps too much realism for the cowboys of that era. Bar fights, alcoholic reveries, and broken relationships were not a myth but a reality among cowboys competing in the 1940s, 1950s, and 1960s. In many ways, the cowboys of that age were as trapped in society's stereotypes as were the film makers.

Only a relatively small portion of the cowboys of this era viewed themselves as professional athletes. It was not until contestants like PRCA all-around cowboy Larry Mahan and bull rider Gary Leffew began conducting their careers as athletes and businessmen that a new pattern began to replace the hard-living, hard-drinking lifestyle that was so often depicted in film. Savage also notes that the rodeo character in the popular fiction of the period was portrayed in the same self-destructive mode (William Crawford's *The Bronc Rider* [1965] and Aaron Fletcher's *Cowboy* [1977]). Only on occasion was the rodeo performer depicted as a family man with middle-class values who experienced a successful rodeo career and emerged a hero (Herbert Harker's *Goldenrod* [1972]).[5]

Even in television, the rodeo cowboy was no match for the heroic Hollywood cowboy who personified the Old West. Westerns ruled the new medium of television throughout the 1950s and early 1960s. As one observer notes, the TV western's appeal grew out of a rebellion against the conformity of the period: "The more boring and dull the routine of men's work became, the more exciting and glamorous were their fantasies of escape. None were more glorious than those rhetorical returns to those thrilling days of yesteryear offered by the western."[6]

In the 1950s, over 10 percent of all fictional works published were westerns, and eight of the top ten television shows for the decade were "horse operas." A total of thirty prime-time TV western shows were produced in the 1950s, and fifty-four western feature films were made in 1958 alone.[7] (By contrast, in 1994, only nine big-studio western films were released, and of these, only one, *Maverick*, was a box office hit.) The 1958–1959 season was the most successful year for the television western; seven of the top ten shows were westerns, including the top four shows: *Gunsmoke*, *Wagon Train*, *Have Gun, Will Travel*, and *The Rifleman* (*Maverick* was number six, *Tales of Wells Fargo* number seven, and *Wyatt Earp* number ten).[8]

Throughout the decade of the 1970s, Hollywood was slow to recast the cowboy in the role of athlete, failing to reflect the changes that were going on inside the sport of rodeo itself. Instead, the film industry continued to perpetuate the stereotype of the reckless, drunken rodeo performer or the aging rodeo cowboy. *The Electric Horseman*, a 1979 film directed by Sydney Pollack and starring Robert Redford and Jane Fonda, was an example of this scenario. Redford plays Sonny Steele, a drunken ex–rodeo champ, whose career has deteriorated to the point where he finds himself endorsing breakfast cereal with the help of a prize-winning race horse. Sobering up, Steele eventually saves the horse from the greedy corporate sponsor.

In 1980, the movie *Urban Cowboy*, directed by James Bridges and starring John Travolta, Debra Winger, and Scott Glenn, introduced a new kind of rodeo cowboy: the urbanite with limited ranching background who, by learning to mimic the rodeo rides on a mechanical bull in a Texas honky-tonk bar, comes to vicariously experience and embrace the cowboy lifestyle. The enormous popularity of this movie affected the sport of rodeo in several ways. For one, it introduced a new generation of Americans to country music, country dancing, and the sport of rodeo. The popularity of the movie impacted the western apparel industry, suddenly making boots, tight jeans, bright shirts, and cowboy hats the height of fashion. About this fashion trend, the authentic rodeo cowboys would complain, as it shot the costs of their apparel sky high.

This new audience of urbanites was suddenly enchanted with a sport that had, until that time, been mainly the province of rural folk. Overall, the number of rodeos and the number of PRCA rodeo contestants increased in the aftermath of *Urban Cowboy* and the cowboy craze it helped to create. In a sense, the proliferation of things western can be attributed to the success of *Urban Cowboy* in reaching a broader mainstream audience. It appealed to a new generation coming of age in the early 1980s that was hungry for a new style to embrace. Its sudden popularity was, in part, a post-disco backlash, a fashion trend rather than a change in lifestyle. It was interesting and amusing to many that the *Urban Cowboy* craze and the disco era (captured in the 1977 movie *Saturday Night Fever*) were both launched with the help of Travolta, an actor raised in New Jersey and certainly an unlikely character to become inextricably linked to rodeo and the western lifestyle. Years later, the Professional Rodeo Cowboys Association and others affiliated with the sport would try to re-create the marketing boom inspired by *Urban Cowboy*. Later films such as *My Heroes Have Always Been Cowboys* (1991), *Harley Davidson and the Marlboro Man* (1991), and *8 Seconds* (1994) were all made with the help and cooperation of the PRCA.

Although western movies and television shows (including the immensely popular and critically acclaimed series *Lonesome Dove*) would continue to be made, it was not until the 1991 movie *My Heroes Have Always Been Cowboys* that the rodeo cowboy reappeared as a central theme in a major studio release. Starring Scott Glenn (a principal character in *Urban Cowboy*), the film was thematically similar to *Rocky*, Sylvester Stallone's 1976 Academy Award–winner. In *Heroes*, Glenn portrays an aging rodeo cowboy, H. D. Dalton, who returns after many years to his home in Oklahoma, only to find his family in shambles. His father, played by real-life rodeo world champ, Ben Johnson, has been committed to a retirement home by H. D.'s sister and brother-in-law, who want to sell off the family ranch. H. D. Dalton not only hopes to save the ranch and spring his father from retirement prison but also win back the heart of his old sweetheart, Jolie (played by Kate Capshaw). To accomplish this, Dalton must get his battered body in shape and overcome his low self-esteem in order to win a $100,000 prize paid to the winner of a bull riding event.

My Heroes Have Always Been Cowboys (the title and theme of a popular country western song) is a return to the tried-and-true formula of *The Karate Kid* (1984), *Rocky*, and other movies that feature an underdog who overcomes long odds to emerge triumphant. It is also a return to the formula used in so many early rodeo films.

Heroes was a disappointment to rodeo insiders, who expected more from a film that was independently produced by a notable rodeo figure, Ed Gaylord III. Gaylord—whose Lazy E Arena in Guthrie, Oklahoma, is featured extensively in the film's conclusion—had an opportunity to portray rodeo in a realistic light. Instead, he fell back on the Hollywood stereotypes that have depicted the cowboy as an aging, down-and-out character rather than an actual athlete. And technically, the cowboy's rise to the top is too abrupt—he goes from rodeo clown and former bull rider to a contender in an elite bull riding event without any qualifying competitions.

Success that comes too quickly is a common flaw in Hollywood films about rodeo. In the 1991 film *Harley Davidson and the Marlboro Man*, a mediocre movie starring a biker (Mickey O'Rourke) who has an unlikely friendship with a rodeo bull rider (Don Johnson), the cowboy character similarly emerges from retirement to compete in a national tournament. After saving a friend's bar from the schemes of an unscrupulous developer, Johnson is shown competing for a world championship at the National Finals Rodeo. Given that a cowboy must compete for an entire year to get to the NFR, the scenario is preposterous.

This inaccurate portrayal of rodeo competition disturbs many rodeo cowboys. They feel that they are misrepresented and marginalized by popular culture films that seldom deal with the sport as it actually is played. "It's the down-and-out cowboy and not the rodeo athlete in the sports section that gets all the media attention," notes saddle bronc rider Clayton Price. "No one who is educated, middle class, or from a good background is ever portrayed. Nor do these films emphasize the training and skill involved to any great extent."

This criticism of Hollywood's habitual portrayal of rodeo cowboys is, perhaps, a criticism that one could level at the entire genre of sports movies. By their very nature, movie plots must create tension. And a portrayal of an athlete's rise to the top must, for cinematic tension, involve overcoming insurmountable odds, and it must be condensed into ninety minutes. Movies like *Rocky* and other come-from-behind sports films focus on the positive, uplifting side of athletic competition. They educate an audience about the years of sacrifice, the dream of achieving one's goal, and the challenges of physical and mental preparation in becoming a top-level athlete.

The sport of rodeo and the lives of the rodeo athletes, however, have seldom been depicted in such a light. Rather, their portrayal in Hollywood films has more closely followed the other path that sports movies often take, showing the depressing, self-destructive side of athletic competition. Although these films can have great artistic merit (such as the 1980 film *Raging Bull*, in which Robert De Niro depicts prize fighter Jake La Motta), more often than not, their message seems to be that athletic competition leads to self-loathing and despair. These films (such as the 1988 baseball film *Bull Durham* and others) depict individuals who have lost faith in whatever dream they might have had. Struggling with a mid-life crisis and wallowing in self-pity, the protagonist in such films often attempts to reclaim his life by returning to a sport that had once given him some meaning or sense of purpose. Granted, such films, if done well, can promote higher values, but they often sensationalize the darker side of human nature and stereotype the sport being depicted.

Because of these concerns, many in the rodeo industry had great hope that the 1994 movie *8 Seconds*, on the life and times of world champion bull rider Lane Frost, would be a break-through film. Here would be a movie that would deemphasize the traditional Hollywood stereotypes of the rodeo cowboy—a movie that would dwell on the more positive treatment that has accompanied other sports.

A biographical movie on rodeo star Lane Frost seemed like the perfect model for a Hollywood film. Struck down at the peak of his career when he was gored on the final day of the 1989 Cheyenne Frontier Days Rodeo, Frost, age twenty-five, became an overnight folk hero in the rodeo world. The story of Frost's fantastic career and tragic death had the potential to make an important statement about the inherent risks and rewards of rodeo competition. With the support of the rodeo industry, several of whom (such as stock contractor John Growney) played themselves in the movie, and script approval given to Lane Frost's real-life traveling partners, bull riders Tuff Hedeman and Cody Lambert, the movie seemed to have everything going for it. Luke Perry, the actor of *Beverly Hills, 90210*, fame who portrayed Lane Frost in the film, was determined to learn to ride bulls so he could perform some of his own stunt work for the movie. "I want to make sure we get the absolute best, gnarliest, scariest action footage that we can," Perry said early in the making of the film. "And if that requires me getting my ass whipped a little, I'll do it."[9] Even former bull riding champ and rodeo guru Gary Leffew was impressed with Perry's skill and tenacity.

Unfortunately for all concerned, the movie *8 Seconds* lacked the dramatic tension and skillful plot development necessary to make it a success. Directed by John Avidson, who had won an Academy Award for directing *Rocky*, the movie received only lukewarm reviews and did only moderate business. For many, the only reason to see the movie was for the credits at the end of the film that showed several minutes of documentary footage of Lane Frost.

The mixed review in *Daily Variety* best sums up the film's ineffectual treatment of Frost's story and his sport. "*8 Seconds* takes a smooth, sappy ride through the life of a great bucking bull rider. Sweet, sentimental and rose-colored to a fault, this family-oriented biopic has none of the grit, dust and bruises that define the sport in question."[10] The review also criticizes the use of slow motion when filming the bull rides. "The elaborate preparation for a rider's quick trip in the arena are largely glossed over, and the vivid immediacy of the man-vs.-beast contests is softened by the gross extension of the rides," notes the review.[11]

By contrast, on the same page in *Daily Variety* as the review for *8 Sec-*

onds, there appeared a glowing review (written by the same film critic) for the basketball documentary, *Hoop Dreams*, released at the same time. "A prodigious achievement that conveys the fabric of modern American life, aspirations and incidentally, sports, in close-up and at length" begins that review.[12] *Hoop Dreams*, a documentary that went on to become one of the surprise box-office successes of the year, captured the dedication and desire, the sacrifices and perils that an athlete must face. Noted film critics Gene Siskel and Roger Ebert even selected *Hoop Dreams* as their favorite film for 1994.

RODEO FILM DOCUMENTARIES

The documentary, unlike the standard Hollywood movie, has depicted rodeo with great success. Documentaries have had an intrinsic advantage over fictionalized films, at least among western aficionados: realism. Realism is a constant in depictions of the western lifestyle. Artwork, novels, and other forms that portray the American West are scrutinized by western aficionados for their accuracy. It is not surprising that the paintings of Frederic Remington and Charles M. Russell are the standard references by which all other efforts are compared. Each of these artists was careful in the accuracy of his depictions and attention to the proper form of dress and speech of the cowboy. For the most part, conservative westerners feel most comfortable with realism. In rodeo, this means portraying the cowboy as he really is, and that tends to make the documentary a satisfying experience for people involved directly with the sport or who subscribe to a western lifestyle.

In 1974, *The Great American Cowboy*, directed by Keith Merrill and starring real rodeo cowboys and competitors Larry Mahan and Phil Lynne, was honored with the Academy Award for Best Documentary. Following the trials and tribulations of an entire rodeo season, the film captures the rivalry and tensions as well as camaraderie of these two seasoned all-around world champion cowboys as they spun their way to the National Finals.

Two recent films have lived up to the standard set by *The Great American Cowboy* of two decades ago. Both the 1991 Canadian film *Moon of the Desperados* and the 1994 American film *Colorado Cowboy: The Bruce Ford Story* successfully convey the real-life experiences of modern professional rodeo cowboys.

Desperados, a fifty-minute, low-budget documentary filmed over four years, was named Film of the Year at the 1991 Alberta Motion Picture Industry Awards. It also won top honors for best direction nondramatic, best writing nondramatic, and best documentary as well. *Desperados,* a team effort by Calgary film makers Jeth Weinrich and Jordie Thomson, focuses on rodeo arena action, interviews with cowboys, and the history of rodeo in Canada.

"Most of the films I'd seen about rodeo seemed to be made from an outsider's viewpoint. They seemed to inflict a viewpoint of their own," notes Weinrich, describing the appeal of his rodeo documentary. "I didn't want to get caught up in any stereotypical image of the cowboy. I wanted the cowboys who saw it to say, 'Yeah, this is our story.'"

Thomson is a former Canadian Professional Rodeo Association (CPRA) champion bull rider. He had competed in nine Canadian Finals and two PRCA National Finals Rodeos before he was forced to retire from rodeo when he broke his spine at the 1979 NFR. A cowboy poet, actor, writer, and horse trainer, Thomson helped Weinrich gain the perspective of the rodeo insider. Or as Thomson put it, "It was my job to make sure the film wasn't hokey."

Rather than taking the guts-and-glory vantage point of so many rodeo film directors, Weinrich focuses his camera on the very delicate movements involved in remaining balanced atop a spinning bull or a pitching bronc, using extreme close-ups to bring forth the minute movements of a rodeo roughstock rider. The effect is to dispel the myth that roughstock riding requires brute strength or ape-like tenacity. The film forces the uninitiated to appreciate the anticipation, timing, and balance that make a great ride possible. "I looked for ways to surprise people, to keep them interested," Weinrich said of his documentary style, which could be said to borrow more from MTV than from *National Geographic.* "I wanted something modern, more accessible to a younger audience."

In Thomson's mind, camaraderie and freedom bind modern rodeo cowboys to their sport's historical past. "For someone who knows nothing about rodeo, the film might explain why cowboys continue to do it," says Thomson. "If I were watching it for the first time, I'd be intrigued by the camaraderie and the freedom of the cowboy's life. We tried to show the rodeo cowboy as he really is, why he does what he does and wouldn't do anything else."

Colorado Cowboy uses a similar approach in trying to be truthful about the lifestyle of modern rodeo cowboys. Named Best Documentary in the 1994 Sundance Film Festival, the seventy-eight-minute film tells the story of five-time world bareback champion rider Bruce Ford from Kersey, Colorado. *Cowboy* was directed by internationally celebrated fashion photographer Arthur Elgort. Elgort had also been interested in creating a series of documentaries on American heroes, and wanted to feature a cowboy in one film.

In 1989, Elgort was at the Cheyenne Frontier Days Rodeo, on assignment to photograph model Cindy Crawford in a western setting. Drawn to Ford because of his quintessential cowboy features, Elgort was introduced to the cowboy by another rodeo photographer. Thus began an odyssey that lasted more than three years, covered thousands of highway miles, and produced hundreds of hours of film. In the end, what emerged was the documentary *Colorado Cowboy*, an emotionally stirring, accurate portrayal of one of pro rodeo's legendary figures.

Elgort, assistant director Ronit Avneri, and a crew of cameramen followed Ford from rodeo to rodeo. They visited the Fords at home and filmed him on the open road, carefully creating a portrait of the great bareback rider and his family. Although the rodeo action is powerful, it is the behind-the-scenes work that really gives audiences a feel for this unique and interesting man. In one quiet scene, for example, Ford is in his hotel room. He makes a phone call to his family, then sits down before a television, and finally, he lies down to sleep—a poignant reminder of the lonely separation a cowboy feels when he is on the road.

But most of the film shows Ford with his family, either at home or heading to a rodeo. The passing of rodeo traditions from one generation to the next is explored. Old films of Ford and his brother and their father, Jim, riding together establish the tradition. Later, the film shows Ford's son, Royce, and daughter, Courtney May, competing at Little Britches rodeos. "I felt the movie portrayed me the way I wanted to be portrayed," Ford says. "A man who loves his family, the Lord, and his friends. That's all I've wanted to portray in my life."

Both *Moon of the Desperados* and *Colorado Cowboy* have made important contributions in educating the general public about the world of professional rodeo. Both films have been heavily marketed in the western magazines, rodeo sports news, and western apparel stores and are available for rent at video outlet stores.

THE COWBOY AND RODEO CRAZE

> Well, it's bulls and blood
> It's dust and mud
> It's the roar of a Sunday crowd
> It's the white in his knuckles
> The gold in the buckle
> He'll win the next go 'round

It's boots and chaps
It's cowboy hats
It's spurs and latigo
It's the ropes and the reins
And the joy and the pain
And they call the thing Rodeo
Written by Larry Bastian [13]

The recent resurgence in popularity of the cowboy has generated an enormous cottage industry. The expression "everything old seems new again" is one that can be aptly applied to the world of rodeo and the American cowboy. It seems that the public can't get enough of cowboys.

It is now possible to purchase every conceivable item of apparel—hats, shirts, skirts, jeans, boots, earrings, bow ties, ties, underwear, and socks—in a cowboy motif. In fact, the consumer with an unlimited budget can outfit nearly every room in the house in a western theme. There are western-style furniture and lamps for the living room and bedrooms; matching bedspreads, pillows, curtains, and wallpaper; and rodeo-patterned china for the kitchen and dining room. Novelty items are available too, such as board games and cowboy trading cards—sets of ninety-five cards featuring past and present stars of the rodeo arena.

Rodeo aficionados can purchase videos of important rodeos, best rides and best wrecks, training tapes for every rodeo event, and profiles of top rodeo athletes. Sellers and consumers bump elbows at western trade fairs during big indoor rodeos and at the National Finals at Las Vegas. In fact, the "shop 'til you drop" Christmas buyers with a hunger for the Old West are attracted in droves to three competing western trade fairs held during the National Finals.

Many rodeo fans go to Las Vegas as much for the trade shows and country western entertainment as for the rodeo itself. In recent years, the world of country music has reinvented itself, appealing to a younger generation, and grown faster than any other category of music. Much of the crossover success is attributed to Garth Brooks, whose album "Ropin' the Wind" and song "Rodeo" topped the charts as soon as they were released in 1991. The boom in country radio stations, videos, and dance clubs have made superstars of such artists as Randy Travis, the Judds, and Reba McEntire. Country favorite McEntire has a long association with the pro rodeo circuit. She is the daughter of rodeo champion Clark McEntire and was once a competitive barrel racer herself. McEntire was discovered by record producer Red Steagall when she sang the national anthem at the 1974 NFR.[14]

At NFR time each December, the list of headliners at the casino show-rooms in Las Vegas reads like a Who's Who of country music artists, both old and new. Appearing in 1995, for instance, were Brooks and Dunn, Merle Haggard, Toby Keith, Randy Travis, and The Mavericks, to name but a few. Even comedians and entertainers such as Ricky and the Redstreaks and rodeo performers-turned-entertainers such as Chris LeDoux, Monte "Hawk-eye" Henson, Wayne Vold, and others who focus on rodeo and the cowboy lifestyle draw turn-away crowds.

Western poets chronicle the rodeo cowboys' travails and gather several times a year across the country for poetry readings. One of the most respected, Baxter Black, serves as a kind of poet laureate for the PRCA, frequently pro-viding commentary and witty observations about professional rodeo in much the same way that Will Rogers served as humorist for the nation in the early part of the twentieth century.

For several years now the Old West has become a force in popular culture as well as literary and intellectual life, perhaps in response to a general cul-tural malaise—what some commentators have called a national crisis of con-fidence and others have termed the post–Cold War end-of-the-millennium blahs. "Americans are rooting through the attic trunk of their history in search of a renewed sense of identity and purpose," notes one observer.[15]

Sociologists and historians argue that demographics have much to do with this new interest. Some note that as the population shifted westward, the west-ern states have become more important politically, economically, and cultur-ally. Others contend that the New Western historians' debunking of frontier myths has reshifted inquiry into the roles of American Indians, women, and Latinos and other ethnic minorities in the settling of the West. This move-ment has also "expanded the appetite for things Western, particularly on the part of groups long left out of the story. By including perspectives once ignored, films and books of the New West have broadened the appeal of a saga long seen as the domain of white men."[16]

B. Byron Price, executive director of the National Cowboy Hall of Fame and Western Heritage Center in Oklahoma City, offers a different explana-tion. Price views the West and, in particular, the cowboys, as the epitome of core American values to which society turns each time it begins to lose its equilibrium. "Every time that Americans get involved in things that take us away from our roots and create periods of uncertainty, we always come back to our core beliefs," according to Price. "We're now looking to value something. We're looking for an understanding of our problems in Western mythology."[17]

"Television audiences thrive on celebrity, and rodeos produce few celebrities. In rodeo, unlike in most professional sports, hobbyists compete alongside the most talented cowboys. That's a custom deeply rooted in tradition."

—Katherine Weisman, *Forbes*[1]

13

ECONOMIC

CONCERNS &

MARKETING

STRATEGIES

*I*n a far-ranging interview published in the *Prorodeo Sports News* in 1991, then-chairman of the PRCA board of directors, Bob Thain, commented on the greatest problems facing rodeo: "There isn't enough money coming into the system. We need more, and I'm not sure where it's going to come from. The money the cowboys want, and are justified in asking for, cannot continue to come from the committees and our current sponsors. The cowboys are not making as much as they should be for what they put out. And neither is anyone else."[2]

Thain's solution to this problem of bringing more money into the sport is twofold: increase television coverage of the sport and increase corporate sponsorship. More television coverage would highlight and promote the rodeo stars, and increased sponsorship would expand the overall prize money available at every level of the rodeo operation. But if rodeo is to follow the success pathway established by other sports, it must reach a threshold of public acceptance sufficient to entice television networks to pay for the right to tele-vise the sport. At present, it is the PRCA and its sponsors who must come up with the money to take the sport to a broader audience.

TELEVISION AND RODEO

Howard L. Nixon II and James H. Frey, in their 1996 book, A *Sociology of Sport*, devote an entire chapter to the business side of professional sports. Noting the proliferation of professional sports leagues and teams in recent decades, Nixon and Frey see a parallel with the accompanying growth in the range of viewing opportunities for spectators. The number of franchises, for instance, of the four major North American sports leagues alone (the National Basketball Association, the National Football League, Major League Base-ball, and the Major Hockey League) expanded from 61 in 1967 to 102 in the early 1990s. "The expansion of these and many other sports has happened in large part because of the financial investment and coverage by television, with cable networks and super stations such as TBS and WGN joining the major networks as prominent actors," conclude Nixon and Frey.[3]

But television coverage of professional rodeo differs from that of big-league professional sports, at least in terms of the contracts established between ESPN and the PRCA. Since 1990, ESPN, in an exclusive contract with the Professional Rodeo Cowboys Association, has covered roughly ten selected PRCA-sanctioned rodeos annually. ESPN also broadcasts the National Finals Rodeo. In 1994 it increased its coverage to all ten performances (with ESPN2 broadcasting the first seven nights of the ten-go competition and ESPN show-ing the final three performances).

Even before ESPN, the Mesquite Championship Rodeo had hit the air-ways. Although initially airing in 1980, it was not until 1986 that TNN, largely a country music network, bought the shows from Reid/Land Sports and then sold advertising to pay for them. For the past decade, some 3 million rodeo fans have been able to tune in on a weekly basis to the Mesquite; as of 1995, they could watch the Bull Riders Only competition as well. "We've never rated less than fourth on TNN, and we've been No. 1 many times," said eight-time world champion bull rider Don Gay, one of four owners of Mesquite Arena and color commentator for the show, when interviewed in 1990. "We can't get through all our fan mail. Viewers count on it. It's regular and it has a schedule. It's fun to watch and listen to."[4]

The arrangement between ESPN and the PRCA differs from that between TNN and the Mesquite Championship Rodeo. From the beginning, rather than ESPN paying the PRCA for broadcast privileges, it has been the other way around. The PRCA buys network time to have the rodeo programs it produces broadcast over the network. The PRCA faces the question that other fringe sports in America face: how can it generate a television audience large enough to create new revenue-producing opportunities. Other sports, such as snowboarding, surfing, beach volleyball, and mountain biking, have also had to pay for television exposure. What differentiates these sports from rodeo, however, is that these are all relatively new sports with rapidly expanding participation bases. Rodeo, on the other hand, is a well-established sport with a fairly static pool of participants. Whereas many of the sports vying for audiences are participation-oriented, the sport of rodeo is, for most people, a spectator sport.

In marked contrast are the big-league sports, whose phenomenal growth over the past three decades can be directly attributed to the fortunes of the television industry. Television and cable networks compete against each other for the privilege of broadcasting collegiate and professional sports. This competition reached a high point in 1994, when the FOX television network astutely outbid two of the noncable networks for the rights to broadcast the National Football League games. Stiff bidding wars between the networks also take place over rights to broadcast Olympic events, various professional league championships, and special athletic competitions.

Back in the 1950s, the Rodeo Cowboys Association was offered the chance to televise its major rodeos, and the networks even offered to pay the RCA for the right to broadcast. According to Buster Ivory, then the group's secretary, the association's board turned down the offer. Its directors believed that if rodeo fans could stay at home and watch rodeo on TV, they would have no reason to buy tickets at the contests themselves. This may have been the greatest marketing miscalculation in professional sports history. Since that time, rodeo has struggled to get in front of the public eye via the airwaves. But instead of the networks coming to rodeo, rodeo has had to go to the networks. Obviously, a major increase in revenue to the PRCA would occur if the pattern were reversed.

In North America, people can watch over 7,500 hours of sports programs in a year if they have access to cable stations.[5] Television networks and cable companies respond to the viewers' appetite for sport by broadcasting many hours and different types of sports. In recent years, rodeo has benefited from this growth industry as television network executives and producers have quickly discovered that the viewing public will tune in to exciting televised rodeo action.

According to a pamphlet published by the Denver-based rodeo management company, ProRodeo Sports Inc., an estimated 19 million people watch rodeo on television. In a 1991 survey conducted on behalf of the PRCA, 92.7 percent of those rodeo viewers said that they would like to see more rodeo coverage. This considerable audience may eventually help move rodeo from the position of paying for television time to bargaining for network payments for television rights.

Other trends in televised sports, however, may make television a more likely revenue source for rodeo. One such trend is the increasing number of outlets for sports spectacles. The twenty-four-hour cable networks, such as ESPN, Prime Ticket, and Prime Sports Network, and the newer television networks such as FOX, which broadcast selected sporting events, find themselves in stiff competition with the traditional networks. CBS, NBC, and ABC all continue their weekend coverage of all major league sports throughout the year. All these franchises, cable and noncable alike, find it increasingly difficult to find enough sports events to fill their schedules. This situation has the potential for improving the revenues of second-tier sports like rodeo. By offering its events at affordable market rates, rodeo may be able to exploit the programming vacuum.

A recent move in this direction has already occurred with the proliferation of the breakaway rodeo competitions such as the Bull Riders Only and the Professional Bull Riders Association. Both the BRO and the PBR have been able to survive because of the lucrative contracts signed with cable networks. In 1995, for instance, over $330,000 in prize money was awarded to the cowboys during the PBR Finals alone. This impressive purse came from both ticket sales for the event, held in the Las Vegas MGM Grand indoor sports arena, and from television revenue.

Furthermore, the cowboys selected to compete in each of these bull riders' tours—recruited from the top PRCA standings—pay no entry fees. Lodging and, in many instances, transportation costs are also picked up by the event promoters—substantial incentive for the bull riders to choose these competitions instead of paying their own way to a sanctioned PRCA contest. In Professional Bull Riders events, the cowboys even own shares in the company and receive additional money for supporting its events.

PRCA cowboys can compete in these specialty associations such as PBR and BRO without penalty, like ropers who compete in jackpots, although the

PRCA and affected rodeo committees are not pleased when bull riding competitions are scheduled against top PRCA-sanctioned rodeos. They are also unhappy when injuries in nonsanctioned competitions force a bull rider out of his place in the top fifteen.

In the years since Bob Thain's comments about how increased TV coverage and corporate sponsorship could benefit rodeo, the PRCA *has* been able to point to improvements in its financial picture. Commissioner Lewis Cryer, in remarks at the year-end PRCA convention in 1994, claimed that the present year "had been the best year ever for professional rodeo." Not only had the association increased its sponsorship revenue by $5.6 million during the preceding five-year period, but television coverage of rodeo had continued to grow as well. With pride he pointed to how even the world champion's banquet was to be televised for the first time on ESPN2. "USA *Today* has published over two million copies of the 8-page supplement for its Friday, December 2 issue at a cost of $400,000 for the entire budget," Cryer noted.

RODEO STARS

"Being wild, being free, being crazy is *critical* to rodeo. It needs some jazz," states Bernie Smyth, an Australian all-around cowboy who immigrated to Canada in 1990 to compete in North American rodeos. Many would agree with Smyth.

Professional sports are star-driven. The fans come to watch a particular athlete play or perform. In professional rodeo, however, rodeo committees have had to market their rodeos as western spectacles and not as showcases for professional athletes. The reason, in part, is that the athletes are not in town for long, nor are there many star athletes with media appeal who currently compete on the pro circuit. Furthermore, localities where rodeos are held seldom send sports writers to cover the event. Instead, the rodeo is depicted by the media as recreational family entertainment—if it is covered at all.

The cowboys themselves offer other explanations for the lack of stars in rodeo. "Rodeo has tried to please the cowboy. We need to please the spectator," Bernie Smyth says. "We need to analyze what spectators want, not what they like. They want a western hero they can look up to. A John Wayne or someone like that they can be like and live it for one day. They want to be able to identify and think they are part of us."

Smyth is also critical of his fellow contestants, who tend to remain aloof from their fans: "Cowboys isolate themselves from the public, and this is bad.

Cowboys need to be out more with the public. The people need to find cowboys they can idolize." Smyth contends that this has not happened in recent years because the modern top rodeo cowboy has become "cloned with the rest of the businessmen." Without personalities, the media does not seem to pay attention to the sport.

Other cowboys have expressed opinions about the changes needed to make the rodeo experience more enjoyable to a viewing audience. One top timed event contestant suggests team competitions: "People like teams. The normal, average North American likes to root for a team. So just showing the individual cowboys in their events is not dressy or classy enough."

Others feel that the complexity of the rodeo events and judging confuses a viewer new to the sport. "People don't know what is going on when they watch the [rodeo] events on TV," notes a timed event contestant. "They don't understand the judging or the scoring. When the people they think should be winning don't win, they get frustrated." This point is well taken. In most other sports like football, baseball, or basketball, the vast majority of people have played the sport or have an intuitive understanding of it. By contrast, few people have any direct experience with rodeo.

Many cowboys agree that rodeo must promote star athletes—the ones with charisma and media appeal. But at the same time, the cowboy culture is critical of those within its ranks who draw too much attention to themselves. "The cowboys do keep each other down," agrees one bareback rider. "But the good thing about that is that as a group, we stand united and are strong."

The issue of promoting rodeo personalities, then, butts up against the cowboy norm, or sense of decorum. As one saddle bronc rider observed, "A cowboy's image or demeanor is one which maintains a humble aspect. He is the cowboy who walks through the crowd unnoticed, not drawing attention to himself." His is an image, in other words, that is not always conducive to star appeal, at least as defined by television and the broader popular culture.

Some star rodeo athletes *have* been successful in relating to the outside world without triggering criticism from within their ranks. "[Australian] Dave Appleton became an all-around world champion [in 1988] just at the time that American popular culture was interested in things Australian," notes one cowboy. "In part, this interest was fueled by the enormous popularity of Paul Hogan during the *Crocodile Dundee* movie era. Dave Appleton was able to walk that tightrope. He was individualistic and talented without being offensive to the cowboy's scheme of things."

This top cowboy also spoke about the censoring that takes place if a cowboy becomes too flamboyant. "Sometimes if a cowboy gets too out of line, peer pressure will bring him into conformity. [Bull rider] Glen McIlvain, for instance, was flamboyant, wore wild shirts, and was pressured to conform. But others like Charlie Sampson, Hawkeye Henson, and Ted Nuce each have their own style. Each, in the eyes of the cowboy, only go so far, and so it doesn't get too offensive. When they get too far out, peer pressure is applied."

Far from being too flamboyant, however, many of the top cowboys are rather shy and ill at ease when they are interviewed by the press or appear before television cameras. In recent years, the PRCA has helped the newly crowned world champions feel more comfortable interacting with the media through workshops and special tapes. Even so, rodeo committees have learned that they can not depend upon, nor base their rodeo promotion on, the cowboys. Since there are few top rodeo personalities and no guarantee that the top cowboys, even when entered, will show up for the contest, the majority of committees resort to other strategies to market their event.

Obviously, the strategies employed vary. But to help committees focus their marketing efforts, the professional sport has encouraged them to take a hard look at the product they are promoting, the nature of the audience they must appeal to, and some of the new approaches in rodeo marketing.

RODEO FANS

As part of this information gathering, both the national office and selected rodeos have occasionally solicited the fans' opinions. In recent years, rodeo fans have been surveyed at several of the big rodeos, such as Reno, Dodge City, and the NFR.

Until these surveys, little was known about the fans' perspective on rodeo. What do they like or dislike about a particular rodeo? How far did they travel to get to the rodeo? What are their demographic characteristics — their educational and socio-economic levels, ages, and occupations? Some surveys also focused on the consumption patterns of the typical rodeo fan — their use of western attire, their musical tastes, and the like. Some of the findings were surprising and have helped shape the marketing strategies used by several rodeo committees. And even though the rodeo marketplace is as diverse as the United States, some common patterns have emerged.

National research results from the Professional Rodeo Cowboys Association show that rodeo fans are loyal, affluent, and active consumers. Rodeo fans attend an average of seventeen rodeos per year, while 68 percent regularly follow professional rodeo standings and news. Slightly more women (51 percent) than men make up a typical rodeo audience. While some rodeo fans could be described as affluent (9 percent earn between $75,000 and $99,999; another 9 percent earn more than $100,000), the majority would comfortably be described as middle class, with household incomes between $35,000 and $75,000 a year.[6] They are also an educated group. According to the national survey, 48 percent had attended college or completed a college degree, and an additional 13 percent had attended graduate school or completed a graduate degree. In total, 61 percent of rodeo spectators had some post-secondary education. And more than 85 percent own their own homes.

In the PRCA survey, respondents were classified into those living on ranches or farms (28 percent), in small towns (24 percent), cities (26 percent), and metropolitan areas (22 percent). Nearly half of rodeo fans, then, reside in cities or metropolitan areas rather than on ranches or in small towns as one might expect. They are, by and large, middle aged or older. Twenty-one percent were thirty to thirty-nine years old, and 19 percent were twenty-nine or younger. The remainder, three-fifths of those surveyed, were at least forty years old.

In summary, the typical spectator attending PRCA rodeos is solidly middle-class, well-educated, and middle-aged. Further, that rodeo fan is as likely to be female as male, and as likely to live in an urban or metropolitan area as a rural setting.

In addition to the casual rodeo fans, a core group of *rodeo aficionados* follow the sport with the same devotion others might feel toward a favorite college or professional football team. Sandy Jones, a 32-year-old auto parts manager from Vacaville, California, is just such a fan. Over the course of a year, Jones has traveled to "about forty rodeos," often driving "thousands of miles with a few buddies to take in a remote show." Although he loves the action, Jones says that rodeo is a difficult sport to follow because the events are spread out all across the country and it's hard to find out much information beyond the dates and the locations. It's also difficult, he says, to order tickets and arrange for accommodations. Typical rodeo aficionados travel to Las Vegas each year to attend the NFR, provided they can get tickets, and plan summer vacations around the big traditional rodeos: the Calgary Stampede, Cheyenne Frontier Days, the California Rodeo (Salinas), and Pendleton Round-Up.

Bill Prouty, sixty-five, from West Covina, California, is another type of rodeo fan. Recently retired from a sales job that required much traveling, Prouty has, in his words, "taken up rodeo as a hobby." His interest stems from having met a cowboy competing on the national circuit through his job. With nothing else to do, and with his own wife still employed and not able to join him in his travels, Prouty drove to several of the big summer rodeos in 1995, following the career of the cowboy he knew. "Get this out of your system," teased his wife, Rene, about Prouty's new hobby. "Because when I retire, I don't want to go on the road."

In 1995 Maupintour, a national tour operator, noting the widening audience for specialized tours to the big summer rodeos, developed a package of tours, "Rodeos of the Wild West." Five seven-to-ten-day guided tours incorporate favorite summer rodeos and tourist destinations. These packaged tours, though pricey, were a success.

Most rodeo fans, however, are home-based, traveling to a few nearby rodeos and attending their own local event. They are not likely to follow the national circuit, except for those rodeos they watch on television. Many fans, like Bill Prouty, do develop affiliations with particular cowboys and follow their careers as time and opportunities warrant. But unlike other professional or collegiate sports, rodeo offers no chartered planes and buses to take loyal fans to the "away games" on a regular basis.

Interviews conducted with fans at various rodeos have found them to be fairly content with their experience. Seminars held during the annual PRCA convention examine the areas of dissatisfaction so that rodeo committees can take into consideration the criticisms of their paying customers.

Steve Gander, speaking before a recent PRCA convention on the topic of "Rodeo Marketing in the 90s," urged the attendees to take a critical look at the rodeo "product" they were producing in their communities. "It is possible that the people—announcer, clown—we think are good for the rodeo are not what the customers like or want," Gander pointed out. "Our competition is not other rodeos but other sporting events. A mother who wears a new clean pair of pants or slacks and sits in dusty bleachers is not going to be very happy. The customer wants 'creature comforts' and rodeos often do not provide this."

In interviews with spectators, their most frequently mentioned complaints are rude spectators, the inconvenience of sitting in uncomfortable grandstands, and being pestered by concessionaires hawking their wares during the performance. Some fans also complain about loud or grating sound systems, the nonstop talking of some rodeo announcers, and the traffic congestion in arena parking lots.

Fans sometimes criticize the lack of publicity for the rodeo, the difficulty in finding the event, and over-selling the rodeo—forcing paying customers to stand rather than sit during the show and denying admission to spectators who have traveled sizable distances only to discover the event to be sold out.

But most of these complaints are not unique to rodeo, and most rodeo fans seem to enjoy the rodeos they attend.

The contestants and their spouses also suggested improvements for rodeo committees to consider. At the big rodeos, where the cowboys and their families stay for several days, the wives desire special services. "What would be nice would be a list of possible baby-sitters so that we could get away one night with our husbands and watch the entertainment show," notes one wife. "Maybe local 4-H kids or the Girl Scouts would be interested in helping with this. Also, the Boy Scouts could provide an escort service to assist mothers with babies in strollers." Other contestants' family members ask for better bathroom facilities, so that mothers do not have to change their children's diapers on cold, damp floors, and a hospitality room with laundry facilities.

Several cowboys want sign-up sheets for lodging at major rodeos. Since the contestants must compete with the out-of-town spectators for scarce motel accommodations, many cowboys find that there is no lodging available when they roll into town. "You can't believe the number of times we've had to sleep in our trucks because we can't find any place to stay," notes one saddle bronc rider on the national circuit. "Sometimes at night, after we've pulled into town, we'll stop at a motel—maybe it's one where cowboys have stayed at before—and drive around the parking lot to see if any cowboy trucks are there. If we find any, we'll get out and bang on doors until we find cowboys we know and pile into their rooms, sleeping on the floor."

Rod Lyman, eight-time NFR-qualifier in steer wrestling, spoke to a recent PRCA convention about the "hot button" issues that upset the contestants. "At the long-term rodeos, you need to provide the timed event contestants with stalls for their horses and electrical outlets to plug in their trailers," Lyman suggested. Lyman, like others, noted the importance of a friendly gate man. "When the contestants are treated well or warmly greeted by the gate man, it starts the rodeo out on the right foot," said Lyman.

Cowboys appreciate committees that work hard to make their arena surfaces favorable for competition. Each year the top thirty cowboys in each event are asked to choose their favorite rodeo, and the winners in several categories—including best indoor, small outdoor, and large outdoor rodeo committee—are honored at the PRCA convention. The winners are often those committees that have taken the cowboys and their families' special needs into consideration.

Unlike other professional sports, which use similar stadium facilities from one end of the country to the other, rodeo locales vary, as does the atmosphere surrounding the event. There is no consistency from rodeo to rodeo. At one rodeo fans may be able to meet the cowboys during the contest or afterward, at an autograph signing. At others, the only time the fan sees the cowboy is when he is riding. From the stands, one rodeo may afford clear and close views of the action; at another rodeo, fans may be so far from the arena they cannot distinguish one cowboy from the next. Some rodeos now have outdoor instant replay screens and electronic scoreboards, while other contests fail to provide fans with even a contestant roster and never post the contestants' scores. Fans sometimes leave the rodeo without knowing who won a particular event, let alone remembering who won last year's rodeo.

Rodeo must strive to find a way to let the typical fan "in on the action." For many, rodeo is a closed community, too remote for the average observer. If the sport is to grow and improve its financial footing, it must broaden its traditional base of fans. The spectator not schooled in rodeo still does not know what to look for, how to process what a win means in a particular rodeo, and how this win fits into the overall scheme. However, informed rodeo announcers help in setting the stage for the viewer, and the increasing television coverage of rodeo events is a step in the right direction.

NEW MARKETING STRATEGIES

With few top rodeo stars, and with no assurance that those stars will show up at a particular rodeo, rodeo committees in less traditional urban markets have increasingly relied on new marketing strategies. Since in the urban marketplace they must compete with other recreational and sporting events, these rodeos have learned to repackage their product and still keep their traditional base of fans.

In the early 1990s the Grand National faced just such a dilemma. According to Mark Furrer, who was in charge of promotions, a decision was made to shift the marketing strategy to draw in a larger crowd. "The thing was being sold on tradition and it was difficult to market in this area," Furrer explained. "We developed marketing spots which read, 'Rougher than hockey, tougher than football. More traditional than baseball. America's first sport is back—rodeo!'"

The Grand National was the first rodeo to use a giant video screen, placing cameramen near the bucking chutes to record the contestants as they settled down on their mounts. "The jumbo screen let us show the faces of the cowboy," noted Furrer. "People could now identify with the cowboy. The big screen also gave us a chance to put people inside the chute."

Other fresh marketing strategies used by the Cow Palace included focusing on the bull riding event in all the print media ads and, in effect, making stars of the rodeo animals. "No one understands rodeo. But they do know bull riding," remarked Furrer. "We needed to create a sense of urgency. ESPN shows car wrecks. We decided to advertise the bull. That's why they come anyway to rodeo—to see the bull wrecks. This year the bull and danger are our main focus."

Other rodeo committees have jumped on the bandwagon with innovative approaches to keep their rodeos appealing. Some use catchy phrases to advertise their event, such as "Most fun you can have with your boots on!" Others use telemarketing, keeping extensive lists of past attendees and mailing out brochures or using the phone to get people to purchase tickets with credit cards. "Telephone solicitation is the only thing that saves us," notes one rodeo committee chairman. "We 'boiler room' the event, getting as much of the rodeo presold as possible." Many committees strive to presell at least one-third of their rodeo tickets—a practice that is particularly important when foul weather on the day of the performance decreases the "walk-in" audience. Few rodeos are ever canceled because of weather conditions, but stormy days do affect attendance.

Other novel marketing approaches include having local sponsors insert rodeo fliers in bills mailed to customers a month or so before the event. The Reno Rodeo committee, in conjunction with their local Coca-Cola distributor (Coca-Cola is a national corporate sponsor of pro rodeo), has arranged for soft drinks to be sold in cans carrying the logo of the Reno Rodeo, its dates, as well as a toll-free number for ticket orders. The specially designed cans are available two months before the rodeo. Some committees get their local supermarkets to use shopping bags or milk cartons that advertise the upcoming rodeo. Others encourage local disc jockeys or sportscasters to promote the rodeo, even arranging for them to compete against each other in a special novelty event during one of the performances. Fans of these local celebrities, who may or may not be interested in rodeo, flock to the event to cheer for their favorite radio or television personality. At the Cow Palace one recent year, a few of the radio disc jockeys spent several weeks before the rodeo learning how to ride tame bulls in order to compete in the novelty event. The winning jockey rode his bull out of the chutes to thunderous applause and made the eight-second whistle. But he added a unique twist to his ride—he sat atop the bull facing backwards.

Many committees sell their rodeo tickets with detachable discount coupons. After the rodeo, when the fans turn in the stubs for the items advertised, the local sponsors can measure how effective their involvement with the rodeo has been. A similar marketing ploy is used with certain advertisements inside the extensive rodeo programs as well—discount coupons that can be redeemed later.

Some rodeo committees offer discounts for tickets purchased before the day of the performance or special family tickets that entitle the family to parking, admission, and discounts on concessions. Others presell only their box seats or VIP sections, creating a sense of urgency in those who wish to purchase the better but more expensive seats while they're still available.

Not all of these ideas work as planned, however. "We introduced a Carload Ticket concept last year," commented one rodeo committee member during a roundtable session at a recent PRCA convention. "We priced the ticket at $20. Unfortunately, people tried to take advantage of this by stuffing as many people into the car or van as they could. The record was one van that had four adults and fifteen children. We had to let the entire group in for the advertised $20."

The price of tickets typically ranges from $8 to $12 for the smaller outdoor events, but there is much debate about whether or not the price is too low among rodeo committee members and producers. "Since we are a professional sport, we need to price ourselves up," says Cotton Rosser. "Most rodeos sell their tickets too cheap." Others express a similar concern. "By discounting everything, we are giving rodeo away and cheapening the event," says one rodeo committee member. "This is why most people equate rodeo with a truck pull. We've priced ourselves into that same class."

But others disagree, arguing that rodeo's core audiences are families, and so admission prices must be in line with what typical families can afford. Some fans drawn to rodeo as a "family event" are offended when the rodeo committee, at the same time, heavily promotes beer sales and tolerates rowdy behavior. When such issues arise, the committees try to separate the beer and booze drinkers into designated areas. Some rodeo committees have even built Old West–style saloons on their permanent rodeo grounds to accommodate the party crowd.

Still other rodeo producers see rodeo's task as appealing to an upscale clientele. They urge that ticket prices be increased, advertising the event as quality entertainment and showcasing the star rodeo athletes and bucking stock. "Rodeo has to be sold as a professional sport in order to draw in a more affluent rodeo fan," notes one such producer.

Recently produced new rodeos in Southern California and elsewhere seem to be marketing their rodeos in this fashion. "The new fans to rodeo are definitely money people," notes a committee member affiliated with the Rancho Santa Margarita rodeo. "They want an excuse to go out and buy a new wardrobe. They want to be 'Western chic' and fit in to the new craze. These are the markets rodeo should be going after."

In order to attract this type of audience, several committees have added team penning competition as a special event to their rodeos. Team penning is a timed equestrian event involving three riders who single out three calves from a small herd inside the arena. Each of the calves has a large number taped to its sides. At the beginning of the event, the team is given a number and must separate the three calves with that particular number and drive them to the opposite end of the arena and pen them within a specific time.

During the past two decades, more and more affluent Americans have purchased five-to-twenty-acre parcels and moved to newly developed country-style communities. Tired of living in urban or suburban environments, affluent young and middle-aged adults have "gone country," buying up ranchettes and taking up equestrian activities. Purchasing horses for themselves and or their children, many are entirely new to country-style living, and new to rodeo.

Team penning and equestrian events allow these people to compete without having to be good riders or even dismount from their horses. It is a relatively risk-free sport. To attract these people to rodeo, several committees have astutely added team penning as an extra event to their rodeo. By emphasizing that their rodeo is a quality sporting event as well, these committees have been successful in appealing to a crossover audience.

Some rodeo committees coordinate their publicity, distributing colorful, collector-type rodeo posters that portray that year's distinctive rodeo theme. This theme or image is carried through to the rodeo brochures, programs, postcards, collector pins, and other promotional items. Many of these posters and marketing items become an important part of the rodeo committee's revenue. Rodeo-related publicity and artwork increase in value over the years as well. Many rodeos encourage western artists to display their wares in booths inside the rodeo grounds or at local art stores and fairs, all of which serve to keep the image of a particular rodeo in the public's eye.

Some rodeos have their own distinctive logo (usually of a cowboy on horseback or on a bull), which is used from year to year. These committees market their own promotional or gift items such as key-chains, drinking cups, T-shirts, sweatshirts, jackets, calendars, hats, scarves, shot glasses, mugs, money clips, tie-tacks, and the like. Profits from the sales of these items are an important part of a rodeo committee's revenue.

Similar items that carry the PRCA logo (or a particular stock contractor's logo), are available for purchase at various booths on the rodeo grounds at most of the big rodeos. Rodeo America, a small company located in the Bay Area, handles the official licensed products of the PRCA, including the specially designed items commemorating each year's National Finals Rodeo.

Besides the use of large TV screens and scoreboards during the actual rodeo performance, attention is now being paid to elaborate sound systems. Several of the big-time rodeos hire sound technicians to provide popular country western music and sound effects to accompany the action inside the rodeo arena. Others add pyrotechnics and staged entertainment effects to the shows. One of the attractions of the Bull Riders Only competitions is a sound system blaring high-intensity music, hyping the rodeo fans for the action to come, a practice familiar to anyone who has attended pro basketball or hockey games.

Other committees have hired photographers to focus on new and unique action shots to use in their extensive rodeo programs and print media, looking for a focus that would set their rodeo apart from other rodeos. "What you need to focus on is the 'casual' rodeo fan," commented a marketing consultant, addressing the PRCA convention in 1994. "Get him off his Barcalounger. Get him hooked so that he thinks rodeo is something special."

Other rodeo committees have worked with their local media—print, radio, and television—to come up with new strategies to push their rodeos. Although the PRCA provides rodeo committees with commercials to use in marketing their rodeos, some committees have developed their own commercials, highlighting unusual rides or special features from their own event. Some distribute postcards at the end of each performance listing the dates and times for the next year's rodeo.

Committees have used "fan hot-lines" with an 800 number to call to get a recorded message about forthcoming events. The message provides information about the rodeo as well as local contact numbers to call if one gets lost or needs assistance with lodging, baby-sitters, or medical attention.

Some have suggested that rodeo committees boost regional and fan loyalty by chartering "rodeo buses" to take their members to nearby rodeos, thus supporting other rodeo committees and their endeavors. Rodeo buses have also been used to bring groups of people to and from rodeos, such as residents in senior citizen centers or military personnel.

Friendly competition between rodeo committees, as well as linking selective rodeos together in six-pack series (whereby cowboys enter a specially designated group of rodeos and compete for additional prize money) have also worked. Some have even talked about selling season tickets to these specially linked rodeos.

Some committees would like to see local beer, soft drink, or pizza distributors put together rodeo posters, wallet-size cards, and restaurant and tavern table displays listing the rodeos in certain regions, thus alerting fans to the other rodeos located not far from where they reside. Like those used in other professional sports, the displays would include the times and dates, as well as a map indicating the locations of each rodeo arena in the area.

Some rodeo committees work diligently with local and regional press, hosting a media event several days before the rodeo so that reporters can interview those associated with the celebration. Some assign a committee person to be a full-time liaison with the media, arranging for chute tours, interviews with contestants, and providing them with packets of sports, news, and feature stories that have been written about other rodeos.

Some committees encourage top cowboys to write special columns for the local press. The Reno Rodeo has done this for several years, encouraging selected cowboys to share their experiences at the rodeo from the contestant's point of view. Many rodeos bring out tables into the center of the arena or to a designated area during intermission so that the fans can get their rodeo programs or posters signed by the cowboys. The kids love to run around the arena, peer into the empty bucking chutes, get autographs, and see the cowboys up close. And many youngsters are accompanied by excited parents, who also enjoy the more personal vantage point. As one rodeo committee member notes, watching eager parents push their kids to the front of the line, "This is the best thing to happen to the sport. Where else, and in what other sport, would the fan in the stand get to see this many competitors up close, and get to shake their hands."

Most rodeos, however, are too quick-paced for this sort of autograph signing, and many in the audience do not know who the contestants are to ask for their autographs. And frequently, contestants up early in the competition change out of their riding clothes and dress like others in the stands. Thus, the fans often cannot tell the rodeo cowboys from the spectators dressed in western attire.

Some committees encourage faculty at local colleges to assign students to collect news clippings of past community rodeos and develop historical archives. College classes have been assigned to cover rodeos as well, and committee members might link up with local teachers or faculty to encourage classroom assignments as a way to bring together "town and gown." Analyzing the financial impact of the rodeo on the local community or conducting oral histories with veteran rodeo and committee members are useful projects for students to undertake. Even local junior high and high school teachers may be interested in getting their classes involved.

Some rodeo committees keep arena records, urging the announcers to highlight the top scores and times in each event. Perpetual trophies and plaques are kept with the cowboys' names on them and displayed for the spectators as they enter the rodeo grounds in much the same way that local high schools and colleges keep such athletic records and display the names and achievements of the winners. Other committees use freeway billboards to promote their event or take out advertisements in the travel brochures that are given free to tourists in their hotels and motels.

Rodeo committees also advertise their event in nearby college and university school newspapers, urging students to attend the event, even introducing local youth rodeo clubs and programs. Some committees offer rodeo scholarships for committed students or sponsor local rodeo athletes to training schools where, once they have perfected their skills, they return to the community that sponsored them to assist with promoting the rodeo. Other committees hire students trained in college rodeo management programs to assist with the marketing.

Some committees provide information to the rodeo fans about the status of cowboys who might have been injured in their rodeo. Many fans leave a performance worried about the medical condition of a particular cowboy, and thus have a way to find out about his or her health status.

Inside the media headquarters at the Grand National Rodeo is a wall filled with clippings of stories from the local press, which gives other reporters ideas about how to cover the event. One recent year world champion Ty Murray was hired to be in town a week before the Cow Palace rodeo so that he could be available for the local press. Several of the posted articles in the press room focused on Murray's amazing feats, adding to his legend.

But one clipping, written by Jane Gottesman for the San Francisco Chronicle, *began with a discussion of the Grand National in terms that the cosmopolitan and style-conscious San Franciscan could best understand: "Chaps isn't a scent. Ranch is neither a salad dressing or suburban architecture style. Hogs are swine, not impolite eaters, and broncos have four hoofs rather than four-wheel drive."[7]*

And Gottesman's spin on stock contractor Cotton Rosser focused on Rosser's role of getting the "meanest damn animals" he could find for the rodeo: "I need rank animals. People are sadistic as hell. They want to be entertained by dan-

ger. *It's been going on since Roman times when they fed people to lions. If you didn't have rank animals at rodeo, it would be like going to a boxing match and having both fighters dance around the ring without punching.*"[8]

In his own unique way, Cotton Rosser was restating the marketing strategy employed by the Grand National that year: hype the bulls, hype the danger. It is a strategy that rodeo is likely to pursue in the future in order to draw the urban audiences less attuned to the myths surrounding cowboys and the Old West.

14

PROFESSIONAL

RODEO AT THE

CROSSROADS

Chance Henderson sits tall and straight in the saddle as the band at the Pikes Peak or Bust Rodeo in Colorado Springs strikes up "The Star-Spangled Banner." His head bowed, Henderson is still as a statue as the flag is paraded by. There's obvious pride in his military bearing.

A cadet at the Air Force Academy in Colorado Springs, Henderson is an unusual rodeo cowboy—equal parts scholar, military man, and athlete. As a high school student in Paris, Texas, Henderson distinguished himself on the football field and was recruited by several Texas universities. He was among the students honored in a Who's Who book of high school scholars and an All-American in football and scholastics. Henderson also excelled in rodeo. He was champion high school calf roper in the Four States High School Rodeo Association and the Oklahoma Youth Rodeo Association.

Henderson played football for the Air Force Academy in 1990, and was expected to start at fullback when he dropped out of the academy to pursue other interests. Jack Braley, a strength coach for the Air Force football team who has worked with many athletes over the years, remembers Henderson well: "Chance was well-gifted. He had strength—he could bench press more than 355 pounds—and speed—he ran the 40 in 4.52 seconds. You can still see that strength and speed in the way he throws a calf and runs down the rope. He had all the ingredients to be a great football player and a great calf roper."

Henderson left the academy at the end of his sophomore year to attend Texas A & M. After he graduated (with a 3.97 grade-point average), Henderson was accepted into medical school. But his desire to graduate from the Air Force Academy as well eventually lured him back to Colorado.

"I really wanted to graduate from the Academy, and they have been very open in letting me pursue rodeo," says Henderson, who is ranked one of the top five cadets at the Academy. Although cadets never got to cheer Henderson as a starter on the varsity football team, they did get their chance to cheer him in August 1995 at the Pikes Peak or Bust Rodeo. More than 1,000 cadets looked on as Henderson competed. But to his disappointment, his rope snagged on the calf's tail and he finished out of the money. Nevertheless, he received a standing ovation from the cadets to the accompaniment of the Air Force Fight Song.

"It felt good to rope in front of those guys," said Henderson. "Many of them are my friends. And I think, like tonight, people are tickled to see someone competing who also represents their country."

Henderson joined the Professional Rodeo Cowboys Association in 1992 but didn't compete in 1993–1994. The next season, though, the cowboy impressed many calf roping fans. His roping has earned the praise of champions such as Joe Beaver and Roy Cooper. In July, the busiest time of year for rodeo cowboys, Henderson won a rodeo in Monte Vista, Colorado, placed second at a rodeo in Gunnison, Colorado, took fourth place at Cody, Wyoming, and qualified for the finals at the famous Cheyenne Frontier Days Rodeo.

Now Henderson is faced with the dilemma of what to do next. "I have to choose between rodeo, flying, or going to med school," he says. "I'm twenty-four and hoping to get my run at the National Finals Rodeo. Roy Cooper [the eight-time world champion] has said, 'Come along anytime. I'll pull for you.'"

With all of these options and career choices, why does Chance Henderson even consider professional rodeo? What draws young men and women with skills like his to a profession that offers no long-term financial security and little acclaim? What is it about rodeo that continues to appeal to each new generation?

Granted, not all cowboys and cowgirls have the array of choices of a Chance Henderson. But increasingly, rodeo athletes are college educated and have more options than previous generations. Many are also multisport athletes like Henderson, who could conceivably dedicate their efforts to success in other sports.

Rodeo's appeal is, in part, its traditions and the chance it offers competitors to pursue a western lifestyle. But many athletes have faith in the sport itself and believe that professional rodeo offers them something no other endeavor can provide. Certainly, winning a gold buckle and being the champion are the dreams of most rodeo athletes. Likewise, the excitement of competing in a dangerous sport and the fun of hitting the road and seeing the country make rodeo attractive.

But if cowboys cannot earn a decent living, these dreams will fade. For rodeo to continue to prosper, it must at least remain as strong and healthy as it is today. And for it to expand its talent pool, it must become even more successful.

Professional rodeo is at a crossroads. Will it continue to grow as a professional sport, improving the livelihood and financial well-being of its top athletes? Or will it continue to be a community celebration, the means for young and old alike to celebrate their western heritage and relive the past? Will rodeo be a professional sport or a hobby sport? Can rodeo be both? And Chance Henderson is only one of many young rodeo athletes whose decisions may depend on the actions of rodeo's leaders as he weighs his short-term and long-term goals and dreams.

Pressures from contestants, stock contractors, rodeo committees, and others have pulled the PRCA from one side to the other in a giant tug-of-war. The conflict is not new—it began when the sport took its first steps toward organization. But the problems today seem more acute. Competition in the entertainment industry has never been keener. Major league sports siphon off talent the minute a child picks up a football or basketball rather than a rope and saddle. And an increasingly urban population has little contact with horses and cattle, the elements that give rodeo its context and meaning.

If rodeo is to thrive, it must reconsider its cultural importance, its financial appeal, its socialization process, and its marketing strategies with the goal of attracting spectators and contestants. To take the sport into the next century, rodeo's leadership must make many choices. The futures of athletes like Chance Henderson stand in the balance.

HOW RODEO'S PAST HAS SHAPED ITS PRESENT

In 1996, the PRCA celebrated its sixty-year anniversary. The issues that helped to create the association are still major concerns among its members. Chief among the complaints of the athletes who compete on a full-time basis is the amount of money they can hope to earn during their competitive years. In most cases, the top cowboys feel that they are not making enough money for the risks they take and the costs they must bear, particularly in light of the benefit their activities generate in ticket sales and rodeo concessions for rodeo committees and local communities.

As Katherine Weisman points out in a *Forbes* article, "Don't Let Your Babies Grow Up to Be Cowboys," the sport is caught on the horns of a dilemma.[1] On the one hand, much of the prize money at rodeos and the dues paid to keep the PRCA in business come from the hobbyists (or traditionalists and weekend warriors, as we have referred to them in this book), whose skills are not at the same level as those of the elite cowboys. But the competitors themselves cannot fund rodeo adequately. Other sources must be found. In order for rodeo to match the financial rewards and largesse of other top professional sports—a level it has not come close to approaching—rodeo must become a more marketable commodity.

To do so, rodeo must generate stars and personalities and recapture its "Golden Age," the 1950s. Then, there were media-savvy rodeo cowboys like Casey Tibbs and media writers who were astute in promoting them. But the 1950s were a simpler age. Postwar prosperity was widespread and interest in the West was at an all-time high. People were traveling again, after a long period of war-imposed restrictions, and many of them headed west for the first time. Television sets were just becoming household appliances, and much of the programming revolved around cowboy-inspired programs and performers. The cowboy and his sport benefited from the increased interest in a way that would be impossible to reproduce today, when many more interests compete for the spotlight and the cowboy is just one of many cultural symbols. And yet, rodeo must stir up a greater level of public interest than it currently enjoys if it hopes to compete for entertainment dollars and advertising revenues—the only way to increase the overall prosperity of the sport.

To improve the product and promote rodeo's stars, the sport will have to be fundamentally restructured—a change that may require pushing the hobbyists' interests aside. In lieu of bringing back the cowboy hero as a cultural icon—a nearly impossible task—rodeo must promote itself as a professional sport. How can this be accomplished in an organization that requires the support of its full membership, an organization hide-bound by more than sixty years of tradition?

The problem has few concrete solutions. But virtually everyone connected with professional rodeo has an opinion on this matter, from the bull rider in the chute to the local rodeo committee members to the commissioner in his office at PRCA headquarters. Commissioner Lewis Cryer acknowledges that the sport remains on the fringes of public recognition and its athletes are unknown to the general public. "Should rodeo start striving for quality instead of quantity?" he asked a group of college students who were studying the sport. "It's always been the philosophy that if you pay your entry fee, you have the right to compete." But if everyone is allowed to compete on an equal basis, how can the sport feature its top stars? Cryer agrees that the dilemma is a difficult one. Focusing on the stars is "a tough philosophy to sell to this organization. Since everyone can enter in the sport as it is [and has been historically], if we can't overcome this, then what we have is a rodeo club."

DIVISIONAL RODEO

One solution, says Cryer, is separating the top contestants from the general membership and letting only these top winning riders compete in the top 100 or so rodeos. This move would result in better competition, according to Cryer, because only elite riders would compete, and the rodeo stock contractors could also supply better livestock. And with fewer contestants at the top shows, competitors would compete on more stock and, thus, would stay in town longer. Fans would have an opportunity to meet the athletes and interact with them. "But the rank-and-file contestants balk at this proposal because they want to wear the number or say, 'I've been in such-and-such a rodeo,'" Cryer noted.

The concept Cryer discussed is divisional competition—the tiered system common to most professional sports. In order for athletes to compete at the highest level, they must first prove their ability at a lower level of competition. Although many people have proposed organizational schemes for divisional rodeo, the suggestion that has probably received the most serious consideration is a three-tiered system of professional rodeo.

Division One Rodeos would be open to the top thirty cowboys in each event. They would compete in about thirty rodeos—those selected in open bidding to host the top cowboys. The current top-paying rodeos on the national circuit would have the highest chance of being selected as division one events. The amount of money earned in these rodeos would determine a cowboy's national standings. If rankings were based on only these select, high-paying rodeos, competitors' expenses would be reduced and, at the same time, they would make more money, since additional prize money and corporate sponsorship would be guaranteed. Even more prize money would be generated by television broadcasting of these select rodeos.

Spots in these top-paying division one rodeos would be open to cowboys from the two lower divisions. Although most of the rodeo competition would occur within a division, a mid-year adjustment of divisions would allow cowboys to move into higher divisions when vacancies were created by injuries or dropouts.

Cowboys selected into division one rodeos would sign contracts with the host rodeos guaranteeing that they would attend those rodeos and be available for promotional work—"appearance agreements." Each of these rodeos would consist of several performances, so a cowboy would be committed to be in a particular area for a specific period of time. In turn, the selected rodeo committees would agree to provide special services to the cowboys and their families.

According to Bryan McDonald of Eaton, Colorado, a long-time bull rider's representative on the PRCA board of directors, current and potential sponsors support the concept of divisional rodeo. "The corporate sponsors are the strong advocates of divisional rodeo," notes McDonald. "They've said they'd give up their exclusive rights for division two rodeos so that related products could enter rodeo."

As the corporate arrangement currently stands, a particular corporate sponsor often has *exclusive* rights to all PRCA-sanctioned rodeo events or, at least, first right of refusal. Thus, a rodeo committee that plans to sell beer at its rodeo must give the local Coors distributor first opportunity to be involved, since Coors is a national corporate sponsor of pro rodeo. With added sponsors, more revenues would flow into pro rodeo at all three divisional levels.

Division Two Rodeos would include the next 100 rodeos, based on added monies and purse. *Division Three Rodeos* would be grouped into six geographic regions, structured by different marketing contingencies and needs.

The rodeo committees that have expressed reservations about such proposals are those of the more traditional, large-scale rodeos such as Cheyenne Frontier Days and the Calgary Stampede. In part, their objections stem from the fact several hundred cowboys now enter each event in these rodeos. With performances held over a ten-day period, they question how they can run their rodeos if only thirty contestants per event can enter. In this case, proponents of the divisional system propose that two divisions compete in the rodeo. Early in the week, the rodeos will be division two, and the second half of the week would be devoted to division one. There could also be opportunities for cross-competition between the two groups at a particular rodeo.

Over the past several years, a variety of voices have spoken about the merits of this or another form of divisional rodeo. Dan Gattis, one of two rodeo committee directors on the PRCA board of directors, discussed the possibility of putting more professionalism into the sport: "I'd like us to classify rodeos. It would involve a scheme where some rodeos would be Class A. Other smaller, support rodeos, would serve as a minor-league system. That way, the big cowboys, the world champion–caliber guys, would have to do less traveling and could make more money."[2] Gattis also noted that in this system, beginners would not have to compete against the more seasoned veterans: "It would give starting cowboys a chance to improve their skills against equal competition, and the big names would make more money against big-league competition."

Rodeo cowboys have also expressed support for the concept. "My vision is to someday take the bigger rodeos and develop qualification limits so that the contestants that did get in could have a chance to get on more good livestock in one location," said former PRCA board member Bruce Ford, five-time world champion bareback rider. "It would take care of the turn out problem, because if you had a chance to get on more than one head of good stock at one place, and to ride for big money, no one would turn out."[3] Likewise, the divisional concept has appealed to stock contractors. "Rodeo needs to be classified," notes Cotton Rosser. "Cowboys are spending $3 to get $2. Rodeo, as it is now, is really just a hobby."

Bob Thain, past chairman of the board of directors for the PRCA, also expresses support for the divisional rodeo concept. "Nobody wants to make a change," notes Thain. "We have to decide ultimately if the rodeo business is going to be geared to all members or just those who do it for a living. Should a guy who enters ten rodeos a year get the same benefits of membership as Ty Murray? As it is now, he does."[4]

Although the professional sport has not officially endorsed a multitiered concept, in reality, the top cowboys have already begun to sort themselves out. "Rodeo has tiered itself because of the money involved," according to Cryer. "The top fifteen or twenty cowboys are not going to the out-of-the-way rodeos. We just don't label it as such."

In recent years, in fact, the full-time professional rodeo cowboy has selected fewer rodeos to enter. According to figures compiled by the PRCA for 1993, only 272 (out of 7,500) cowboys competed at seventy-five rodeos or more, down from the figure of 321 for 1991. For 1993, the top five bareback riders averaged seventy rodeos, the top five bull riders averaged seventy-eight, and the top five saddle bronc riders averaged eighty-eight. Furthermore, the top fifty cowboys per event averaged $40,000 in year-end earnings, although this figure was affected by the high earnings of those at the very top. The top fifty in each event (350 cowboys in the seven standard events) earned 58 percent of the total prize money awarded in 1993. The average earnings of the top fifteen NFR-qualifiers in each event rose as well. In 1989 this select group had earned an average of $62,000. By 1993 that amount rose to $80,500 — 35 percent of the total earnings for the year. In summary, the top fifty cowboys per event earned roughly three-fifths of the year's prize money for 1993, with the top fifteen cowboys per event earning roughly one-third of the total prize money distributed.

According to figures compiled by the PRCA, changes have occurred that have sweetened the pot for the cowboys. In 1994, for instance, $22 million in prize money was up for grabs during the regular season. During the year as well, over 395 rodeo committees, accounting for over half of the PRCA-sanctioned rodeo committees, had added $1,000 more to their pay-offs. From 1989 to 1994, there was also an increase of $5.6 million in sponsorship. But even with these gains, cowboys are not earning large sums, once their expenses are subtracted. In five of the standard rodeo events, for example (bareback and saddle bronc, bull riding, calf roping, and steer wrestling), the cowboy ranked twenty-fifth in each event averaged $24,390 in arena earnings during the 1993 season — less than the cost of travel, entry fees, and other expenses. In short, unless a cowboy can qualify for the National Finals, it is doubtful that he can support himself or his family on PRCA rodeo earnings alone.

In 1995, the last qualifier in each event for the NFR — the cowboy holding down the fifteenth spot — had earned between $44,000 and $49,000 in five of the seven standard PRCA events. For the fifteenth-ranked team ropers and barrel racer, pre-NFR earnings were between $30,500 and $36,000.

Because of the shortfalls of arena earnings for rodeo cowboys, an entrepreneurial class of cowboy has arisen to take advantage of new opportunities in the competitive marketplace. In addition to the stand-alone bull riding contests, other competitive events now compete with traditional rodeo contests. There is also serious talk that the top cowboys in the roughstock events become unionized in order to guarantee higher wages and better working conditions.

ProRodeo Sports Inc., a Colorado-based promotion company, has begun to organize its clients into riding teams, each sponsored by a corporation. Each team of roughstock riders—a bareback bronc rider, a saddle bronc rider, and a bull rider—compete in an abbreviated roughstock rodeo. As in the Professional Bull Riders company, the roughstock riding concern will eventually include contestant shareholders who will reap proceeds from their partial ownership of the company.

Opportunities for timed event competitors are less obvious and organized but nonetheless available and attractive. Stand-alone team roping events have gained immense popularity in the past five years. In these contests, which often stretch over several days and involve thousands of competitors, prize purses may exceed those of traditional rodeos. Virtually all of the prize money is paid by contestants, although many "bonus" awards, such as trailers, trophy saddles, trophy buckles, and similar awards, are provided by sponsors.

Perhaps the most unusual example of these special roping events is the United States Team Roping Championships (USTRC). At these local, regional, and national events, competitors are handicapped in much the same way as golfers. An amateur roper may team with another amateur to compete in the novice events or with an experienced roper to compete in a mid-level event; and top-ranked professionals (those who, perhaps, have already made trips to the NFR) may team up to compete in the professional level contests. By segregating the ropers by ability, these events give contestants something that the PRCA does not offer: the chance to compete against teams of similar skill levels. And because the purse money is distributed fairly evenly at all levels, even novice ropers have the chance to compete for large purses. In many cases, placing well in a class can result in a pay-off of several thousand dollars. Before the USTRC introduced this competition format, only the top-ranked ropers had a realistic chance to win such lucrative pay-offs.

Team ropers are enthusiastic about this classification system and pay-off scheme, and the USTRC today includes in excess of 20,000 registered team ropers. The rapid growth of this organization seems to indicate that cowboys will accept a divisional form of competition, as long as the rewards and opportunities are not strictly limited to only the top-ranked competitors.

The proliferation of these breakaway rodeos has ramifications for the PRCA. In the bull riding events, in particular, several top-name rodeo cowboys—including world champion bull riders Ty Murray, Cody Custer, and Tuff Hedeman—have been hurt in what the PRCA refers to as "non-sanctioned events," and their injuries took them out of the PRCA season competition. In Ty Murray's case, it meant that he could not qualify for a seventh consecutive all-around world title in 1995.

Granted, these cowboys could get hurt in any rodeo. But the quality of the bucking stock in the bull-riding-only competitions is high, and contestants who make the final money rounds often must turn around after one ride, grab their bull rope, and ride another bull, which hurries them in ways that some are not accustomed to. Getting on several top-ranked bulls tests the skills of even the best bull riders. But with live television beckoning, the riders are often more like 100-yard-dash men, sprinting to get to their next bull and cross the finish line for the big pay-offs. Aaron Semas, three-time NFR qualifier in bull riding, complained to a fellow cowboy about the pace of the Bull Riders Only competition: "The damn thing goes so fast, I didn't even have time to take a piss."

CONCLUDING THOUGHTS

Clearly, much of the focus of this chapter, and indeed of this book, is on the economic situation of the rodeo athlete and the sport of rodeo. No other single factor has as much impact upon the sport.

Today's rodeo cowboys can enjoy a reasonable income if they can rise to the top of their sport. World champions and NFR-qualifiers who can string together several successful seasons have been able to amass arena incomes in excess of $1 million. All told, more than a dozen rodeo athletes have topped $1 million in career earnings. New forms of rodeo-related competitions, such as bull ridings, team roping events, barrel racing futurity events, and roughstock competitions, also provide the contestants the opportunity to add considerable outside income to their coffers. Individual sponsorship arrangements, too, have helped defray expenses for cowboys and barrel racers with the business savvy and name marketability to exploit corporate opportunities.

In a society that equates success with earnings, attention accrues to the sports that pay the most money to their competitors. Rodeo has come a long way toward providing a better standard of living for its competitors, but it has yet to climb to the highest rung of the sports ladder. To maintain viability of the sport, the following steps must be taken.

TAKE FULL ADVANTAGE OF CULTURAL TRENDS AND FASHIONS TO MARKET RODEO

Rodeo's viability will depend on the continued public interest in the American cowboy and the western lifestyle. This interest is largely cyclical and depends on forces outside of the control of the sport itself, such as current fashion in the movie industry, television, popular reading, music, and other cultural forms. Although rodeo cannot control these trends, it can, and must, capitalize on the cyclical return of the cowboy brought on by these larger social forces. The rodeo community must make a concerted effort to market the sport of rodeo if it hopes to continue building its spectator base and contestant pool. Rodeo's longevity should not be taken for granted. Public tastes change, and rodeo must both protect itself during the lulls and take advantage of the peaks.

FIND NEW AVENUES TO DRAW YOUTH INTO THE SPORT

Paramount to the continued success of the sport is the recruitment of athletes—no easy task for rodeo considering the trend toward urbanization. Since the beginning of this century, America has become increasingly urban. With the depopulation of rural areas and the expansion of urban sprawl beyond suburbia into the countryside comes a diminishment of the rural and western lifestyles, the training grounds for rodeo athletes. In the next century, rodeo must find a way of attracting urban athletes and providing them with facilities and the opportunity to participate in the sport.

As our study has shown, these urban athletes are already becoming cowboys. More and more rodeo cowboys are being drawn to the sport from non-ranching backgrounds and from urban areas. This trend will undoubtedly continue, and special recruitment and training programs must be in place to transform these "city slickers" into rodeo stars. At the same time, rural athletes must not be forgotten. They are, after all, the backbone of the sport, the carriers of the traditional western way of life. Rodeo must continue to encourage rural youth to take part in the sport—their heritage. They must be encouraged to feel proud of being cowboys.

New and different programs must be implemented to assure this socialization. Scholarship opportunities need to be cultivated to send young people to those junior-, high school-, and college-level programs that promote high educational standards and instill solid rodeo skills. Rodeo committees, for instance, should step in and offer scholarships to motivated and talented youngsters from their communities. By sponsoring and sending the future rodeo athlete to a bona fide training school, the committee plays an important role in continuing the sport. Professional rodeo associations of all types must also remain involved in helping young athletes prepare to enter competition.

PERPETUATE THE COWBOY AS A SYMBOL

The portion of the public that supports rodeo and the cowboy lifestyle must become more vocal. Rodeo cowboys, their family members, and their fans should actively insist on more realistic portrayals of rodeo cowgirls and cowboys in film and other print media. To assure longevity in the sport of rodeo, they must help draw new viewers to the rodeos that are televised. They should also urge local newspapers and television stations to cover rodeo as a sporting event instead of relegating what little coverage there is to controversial issues or bland community event–style coverage. Professional rodeo is a sport. Fan, supporters, and athletes must make sure it is treated as such by the opinion molders in small and large communities alike.

The younger generation should be taught the positive ideals of the cowboy. Increasingly, modern urban youth are exposed only to negative peer pressure that pulls them into self-destructive behavior. Positive alternatives must be promoted. Organizations that help youth get involved in activities connected with animals and the sport of rodeo should be supported.

Continued coverage of the cowboys' lifestyle by new, trendy magazines such as *American Cowboy, Cowboys & Indians, Cowboys & Country*, and *Cowboy Magazine* are welcome. More educational tools, perhaps, a monthly or quarterly magazine directed towards the younger segment of the population, might open up new avenues for youngsters to pursue. As one rodeo athlete remarked, "What we need is an entire movement that supports the concept of Cowboy America. We need a well-coordinated campaign which puts this image across to the public."

EXPAND RODEO'S BASE AND IMPROVE ITS FINANCIAL STATUS

Finally, rodeo must become more inclusive and reach out to broader segments of the community. Rodeo needs to be brought to diverse communities —affluent and less-affluent alike—in order to expand its base. The PRCA has already begun this process by helping its membership with innovative marketing strategies and rodeo promotion at its annual conventions. The PRCA must also be willing to provide opportunities for restructuring and find ways to improve the financial well-being of rodeo athletes.

Rodeo has endured for more than a century, adjusting to changes and growth. It has gone from an unorganized frontier pastime to a full-blown professional sport complete with formalized rules of competition and a cadre of top-notch, committed athletes. In the next century, its success as a professional sport is far from assured, yet rodeo is likely to endure in some fashion.

People the world over have been enchanted with the American cowboy, and that fascination seems to derive from an association with the self-confident man on horseback who values his freedom and is willing to take his chances in order to gain a deserved reward. This has always been the image that Americans wish to project to the world, even if it is not in the nature of every individual to take the risks that the cowboys willingly accept. Although rodeo is a sport, it is also a symbol of the American character. As we move forward toward a new century, we hope that Americans will continue to view rodeo as the keeper of an American tradition that, though it spanned only a brief period in history, remains forever a part of this country's core values and its soul.

ℋotes

CHAPTER 1. INTRODUCTION AND BRIEF HISTORY OF RODEO

1. Michael S. Kimmel, "The Cult of Masculinity: American Social Character and the Legacy of the Cowboy," in *Beyond Patriarchy: Essays by Men on Pleasure, Power, and Change*, ed. M. Kaufman (Toronto: Oxford University Press, 1987).

2. Elizabeth Atwood Lawrence, *Rodeo: An Anthropologist Looks at the Wild and the Tame* (Chicago: University of Chicago Press, 1982).

3. Dirk Johnson, *Biting the Dust: The Wild Ride and Dark Romance of the Rodeo Cowboy and the American West* (New York: Simon and Schuster, 1994).

4. Clifford P. Westermeier, *Man, Beast, Dust: The Story of Rodeo* (Denver, Colo.: World Press, 1947).

5. Bob Jordan, *Rodeo History and Legends* (Privately printed, n.d.), p. 11.

6. Johnie Fain and Learah Cooper Morgan, "The Cowboy and the Rodeo," *Arizona Highways* 36:2 (February 1960): 30.

7. Jordan, *Rodeo History and Legends*, p. 11.

8. William H. Forbis, *The Cowboys* (New York: Time-Life Books, 1973), p. 220.

9. Milt Riske, *Cheyenne Frontier Days: A History of the "Daddy of 'Em All"* (Cheyenne, Wyo.: Frontier Printing, 1984).

10. Virgil Rupp, *Let'er Buck! A History of the Pendleton Round-Up* (Pendleton, Ore.: Pendleton Round-Up Association, 1985).

11. Ibid.

12. James H. Gray, *A Brand of Its Own: The 100 Year History of the Calgary Exhibition and Stampede* (Saskatoon: Western Producer Prairie Books, 1985).

13. Ibid.

14. Mary Lou LeCompte, *Cowgirls of the Rodeo: Pioneer Professional Athletes* (Chicago: University of Illinois Press, 1993), pp. 40–41.

15. Rupp, *Let'er Buck!* p. 18.

16. LeCompte, *Cowgirls of the Rodeo*, p. 96.

17. Kristine Fredriksson, *American Rodeo: From Buffalo Bill to Big Business* (College Station: Texas A & M University Press, 1985), pp. 36–40.

CHAPTER 2. RODEO EVENTS & JUDGING

1. Mike Quesenberry, "Watching Rodeo Broncs: Scoring Bareback Bronc Riders," *Rodeo News* (August 1995): 30.

2. "Fairness in Judging," *Calgary Sun*, 8 July 1991, p. B-1.

CHAPTER 3. GROWING UP COWBOY

1. David Haldane, "Teens Today Examining the Species," *Riverside Press-Enterprise*, 8 July 1983, p. F-1.

2. See the Appendix for a discussion of the research methodology used in conducting the survey as well as a copy of the questionnaire and the complete findings.

3. Roy Cooper et al., *Why We Win* (Amarillo, Tex.: Corriente Press, 1981), p. 3.

4. Ibid., p. 5.

5. "College Was No Party for Murray," *Las Vegas Review-Journal*, 3 December 1992, p. D-18.

CHAPTER 4. GOING DOWN THE ROAD

1. "Clint Corey's Advice to Cowboys About to Join the PRCA," *Prorodeo Sports News*, 5 April 1995, p. 12.

2. "The Rookie Season," *Prorodeo Sports News*, 10 February 1993, p. 18.

3. Robert Etbauer, "Only Family Outranks Rodeo in This World Champ's Book," *Prorodeo Sports News*, 16 October 1991, pp. 8–9.

4. Ibid.

CHAPTER 5. RODEO COWBOYS OR PROFESSIONAL ATHLETES?

1. Roy Cooper, et al., *Why We Win* (Amarillo, Tex.: Corriente Press, 1981), p. 6.

CHAPTER 6. SUPPORT PROGRAMS & HEALTH ISSUES

1. Brett Hoffman, "Patchwork," *Fort Worth Star-Telegram*, 27 January 1991, p. I-1.

2. Katherine Weisman, "Don't Let Your Babies Grow Up to Be Cowboys," *Forbes*, 29 April 1991, p. 123.

3. J. C. Casey, "Safety Zone: Braces and Protective Vests Have Come to the Forefront of the Rodeo Industry," *Rodeo News* (April 1995): 8.

4. "Directors Ponder Ethics of Beer and Tobacco," *Ramona Sentinel*, 16 May 1991, p. A-12.

5. Tony Perry, "Brawley Group Wants to Add Last Call to Cattle Call," *Los Angeles Times*, 24 May 1994, p. A-3.

6. Kendra Santos, "RAWHIDE Helps Keep Kids Drug-free," *Prorodeo Sports News*, 15 June 1994, p. 20.

7. "Rodeo Blasts from Chute," *Monterey County Herald*, 17 July 1992, p. B-1.

8. "Study Reveals Smokeless Tobacco Risk," *San Francisco Chronicle*, 29 March 1994, p. A-5.

9. Bethann Cinelli et al., "Implications of Smokeless Tobacco Use in Sports," *Athletic Training* (Fall 1990): 264–267.

10. "Helping Hands: Justin Crisis Fund Comes to Cowboys' Aid," *Prorodeo Sports News*, 7 October 1994, p. 26.

11. "Prayers and the Pros: An Expanding Link," *Los Angeles Times*, 25 January 1992, p. F-17.

12. Ibid.

13. Dave Appleton, "Injury Forces Appleton to Learn About Life After Rodeo," *Prorodeo Sports News*, 10 March 1993, p. 7.

CHAPTER 7. STOCK CONTRACTORS & ANIMAL WELFARE

1. Baron L. Miller, "Intimidation and Rodeos," *MGW*, 15 June 1995, p. 2.
2. Jane Stern and Michael Stern, "Raging Bulls," *New Yorker*, 14 September 1992, p. 98.
3. Wayne Hipsley, comments in "Event Guidelines for Handling Animal Activists" portion of the "Animal Welfare Issues" session of the 1992 Professional Rodeo Cowboys Association's annual convention, Las Vegas, Nevada.
4. "Humane Facts" (Colorado Springs: Professional Rodeo Cowboys Association, 1992), p. 7.
5. Bob Ragsdale, "Ragsdale Outlines New Group," *Prorodeo Sports News*, 10 February 1993, p. 10.
6. "A Question of Culture or Cruelty?" *Los Angeles Times*, 16 December 1994, p. A-1.

CHAPTER 8. CONTRACT PERSONNEL, CLOWNS, & BULLFIGHTERS

1. Bob Tallman, "Every Day Brings a Thrill for the Voice of Rodeo," *Reno Gazette-Journal*, 25 June 1991, p. D-3.
2. Mildred Farris, "There's More to Being a Rodeo Secretary Than Writing Paychecks," *Prorodeo Sports News*, 15 January 1992, p. 10.
3. Marty Burleson, "Rodeo 'Pick-up Men' Steer Cowboys in Right Direction," *Californian*, 19 July 1991, p. C-3.
4. James Drew, "Cowboy Lifeguards: Pickup Men Credit Their Horses, but Cowboys Praise Pickup Men," *Prorodeo Sports News*, 26 August 1992, pp. 20–21.
5. Ibid., p. 20.
6. "Tony Lama Mobile Video Replay Screens Premiere at Reno Rodeo," 1992 press release, Tony Lama Company, El Paso, Texas.
7. Butch Lehmkuhler, "Two-Time PRCA Clown of the Year Lehmkuhler Takes His Job Seriously," *Prorodeo Sports News*, 30 October 1991, p. 8.
8. Eve Britton, "Senator a Real Clown, but Loves Every Minute," *Monterey County Herald*, 18 September 1992, p. B-1.
9. James Drew, "Rodeo's Daredevils," *Prorodeo Sports News*, 18 May 1994, pp. 24–25.
10. Oscar Guerra, "A Rodeo with a Twist," *Press Enterprise*, 31 May 1993, p. B-1.
11. Drew, "Rodeo's Daredevils," p. 25.

CHAPTER 9. RODEO COMMITTEES & SPECIAL PROGRAMS

1. Gene Sheley, "Smokey, PRCA Team Up for Third Year," *Prorodeo Sports News*, 10 March 1991, p. 25.
2. Paul Asay, "Program Realizes Kids' 'Western Wishes,'" *Prorodeo Sports News*, 22 March 1995, p. 14.
3. Dora DePaoli, "Celebration Means Bug Bucks for Valley Economy," *Brawley Times*, 3 November 1991, p. 19.
4. "Rodeo Proves a Good Ride for Local Economy," *Californian*, 11 July 1991, p. 24.

5. Greg Hernandez, "Riders in the Sky: Broncs Kick Up Their Heels at Rancho Santa Margarita Rodeo," *Los Angeles Times*, 19 May 1991, p. B-6.

6. Richard J. Ossenberg, "Social Class and Bar Behaviour During the Calgary Stampede," *Human Organization* 28:1 (Spring 1969): 29–34.

7. Frederick Errington, "The Rock Creek Rodeo: Excess and Constraint in Men's Lives," *American Ethnologist* 17 (November 1990): 628–645.

8. Kendra Santos, "July's Jam," *Prorodeo Sports News*, 7 August 1991, pp. 20–21.

9. Bill Austen, "Dodge City Round-Up's Secret to Winning," *Prorodeo Sports News*, 12 February 1992, p. 14.

10. Melissa Metzler, "Care for the Cowboys Is Dodge City Committee's Secret to Success," *Prorodeo Sports News*, 5 September 1990, p. 34.

CHAPTER 10. WOMEN AND RODEO

1. Howard L. Nixon II and James H. Frey, *A Sociology of Sport* (Belmont, Calif.: Wadsworth Publishing Company, 1996), p. 257.

2. Bil Gilbert and Nancy Williamson, "Three-Part Series on Women in Sport," *Sports Illustrated*, 23 and 30 June, 7 July 1973.

3. Mary Lou LeCompte, *Cowgirls of the Rodeo: Pioneer Professional Athletes* (Chicago: University of Illinois Press, 1993).

4. Ibid., pp. 16–19.

5. Ibid., p. 137.

6. Jeff Coplon, *Gold Buckle: The Grand Obsession of Rodeo Bull Riders* (New York: HarperCollins, 1995), p. 166.

7. Ibid., p. 164.

8. Jeannie McCabe, "Charmayne Rodman: Winner and Still Champion," *Western Horseman* (June 1985): 34–38.

9. Coplon, *Gold Buckle*, p. 167.

10. Brock Mullins, "Miss Rodeo America Crowned," *Las Vegas Review-Journal*, 2 December 1990, p. D-16.

11. Ardith Finnegan, "Rodeo Wives Share Pain, Glory," *Calgary Herald*, 17 July 1991, p. F-5.

12. "Life for Cowboy's Wife Not Always Glamorous," *Las Vegas Review-Journal*, 2 December 1993, p. C-22.

13. Finnegan, "Rodeo Wives Share Pain, Glory," p. F-5.

14. Mary Lou LeCompte, *Cowgirls of the Rodeo: Pioneer Professional Athletes* (Chicago: University of Illinois Press, 1993), p. 13.

15. John Elson, "The Dangerous World of Wannabes," *Time*, 25 November 1991, p. 77.

16. Sandra Semas, "Being a Cowboy's Mom Isn't as Easy as It Looks," *Prorodeo Sports News*, 20 May 1992, p. 10.

17. John L. Smith, "A Year After Bull Rider's Death, a Mother Looks Back with Pride," *Las Vegas Review-Journal*, 3 December 1995, p. B-1.

1. Charles Sampson, "Sampson Finally Throws in the Towel," *Prorodeo Sports News*, 9 March 1994, p. 10.

2. Susan Paterno, "Riding for Respect: A Father Teaches His Son the Art of the Mexican Rodeo in Hopes of Keeping Him in the Ring and off the Streets," *Los Angeles Times*, 29 October 1991, p. E-1.

3. Ibid.

4. Kendra Santos, "Ride'em, Vaquero! The All-American Rodeo Has Echoes of Spain," *Vista* magazine, *Los Angeles Times*, 29 April 1990, pp. 6–8.

5. Ibid., p. 6.

6. Kendra Santos, "Bud Longbrake: Native-American Cowboy," *Prorodeo Sports News*, 20 March 1991, p. 8.

7. Virginia Cowan-Smith and Bonnie Domrose Stone, *Aloha Cowboy* (Honolulu: University of Hawaii Press, 1988), p. 32.

8. John M. Glionna, "Horseman Lassos Recognition for Black Riders," *Los Angeles Times*, 18 August 1992, p. A-3.

9. Ibid.

10. "Hall of Fame Opens Doors to 1996 Inductees," *Prorodeo Sports News*, 13 March 1996, p. 21.

11. Greg Bortolin, "Blacks Win NFR Events," *Las Vegas Review-Journal*, 12 December 1991, p. E-1.

12. Michael Szymanski, "Renaissance Cowboy: The IGRA's President Is Also a Rodeo Judge and Forester," *Roundup: The Gay and Lesbian Western Magazine* (August 1995): 23–27.

13. Gary Robinson, "The 1995 IGRA Annual Convention," *Roundup: The Gay and Lesbian Western Magazine* (October 1995): 12.

14. Michael R. Gorman, "Confessions of a Real Rodeo Cowboy," *Issue* (December 1993): 8.

15. Howard L. Nixon II and James H. Frey, *A Sociology of Sport* (Belmont, Calif.: Wadsworth Publishing Company, 1996), p. 272.

16. Kendra Santos, "Bronc Ride Benefits Home for Troubled Kids," *Prorodeo Sports News*, 7 August 1991, p. 36.

17. Jane Menard, "Horses in Prison," *Western Horseman* (May 1992): 74–76.

18. Adam Cohen, "Cowpokes in Chains," *Time*, 20 November 1995, p. 46.

19. Randy Witte, "National Senior Pro Rodeo Finals: The Once-Young Lions Are Graying, but They Still Have the Fire," *Western Horseman* (February 1992): 136.

20. Pat McGraw, "Old Cowpokes Don't Always Fade Away," *Denver Post*, 29 July 1990, p. B-4.

21. James Drew, "Real Life After Rodeo," *Prorodeo Sports News*, 1 July 1992, pp. 20–21.

22. Dixie Reid, "The Not-So-Young Riders," *Sacramento Bee*, 16 December 1990, p. E-1.

1. James Drew, "Lane Frost Story Due in Theaters Next Year," *Prorodeo Sports News*, 5 April 1993, p. 37.

2. Kim Newman, *Wild West Movies: How the West Was Found, Won, Lost, Lied About, Filmed, and Forgotten* (London: Bloomsbury Publishing, 1990), pp. 174–175.

3. Richard W. Slatta, *The Cowboy Encyclopedia* (Santa Barbara: ABC-CLIO, 1994).

4. William W. Savage, Jr., *The Cowboy Hero: His Image in American History and Culture* (Norman: University of Oklahoma Press, 1979), p. 130.

5. Ibid., p. 131.

6. Michael Kimmel, *Manhood in America: A Cultural History* (New York: Free Press, 1996), p. 252.

7. Ibid.

8. Beginning with the 1957–1958 season, TV westerns would hold on to the top-rated spot until dethroned by *The Beverly Hillbillies* in the 1962–1963 season. According to the A. C. Nielsen Company ratings, *Gunsmoke* was the longest-running of the TV westerns (1956–1963) to hold down one of the annual top ten spots. Although not always in the top ten, other westerns would also have great longevity on television, including the "oaters" *Rawhide* (1959–1965) and *Bonanza* (1959–1973). By the 1963–1964 season, only *Bonanza* remained on the top ten list, as TV shows such as *Candid Camera*, *The Red Skeleton Show*, *The Lucy Show*, and *The Andy Griffith Show* became more popular with viewers.

Of the TV westerns, only two focused on the world of the rodeo cowboy—*Stoney Burke* (ABC) and, to a lesser degree, *The Wide Country* (NBC). Both series appeared in 1962, late in the run of TV westerns, as America's viewing habits were changing. *Stoney Burke*, starring Jack Lord (of later *Hawaii Five-O* fame), focused on weekly changes of locale as it followed rodeo cowboys from rodeo to rodeo. Though the show was popular with those who followed the sport, *Stoney Burke* (and *The Wide Country* as well) were canceled after a single season.

Stock contractor Cotton Rosser contends that *Stoney Burke* brought in as many new people to the sport of rodeo in the early 1960s as did the movie *Urban Cowboy* when it reignited the western craze nearly two decades later. (According to one observer, not all cowboys of the period appreciated Stoney's rodeo exploits. They would often refer to the TV fantasy character as "Phony Stoney.")

9. Craig Thomashoff, "Ride'em Luke," *People*, 19 July 1993, p. 37.

10. Todd McCarthy, "8 Seconds," *Variety*, 14 February 1994, p. 2.

11. Ibid., p. 12.

12. Ibid.

13. *RODEO*, words and music by Larry B. Bastian © 1983 Rio Bravo Music, Inc. (BMI). All rights reserved, used by permission, Warner Bros. Publications U.S. Inc., Miami, FL 33014.

14. Kristine McKenzie, "Horsin' Around at the National Finals Rodeo," *What's On*, 4 December 1995, p. 92.

15. Janny Scott, "We're Wild About the West Again," *Los Angeles Times*, 5 May 1993, p. A-1.

16. Ibid., p. A-18.

17. Ibid.

CHAPTER 13. ECONOMIC CONCERNS & MARKETING STRATEGIES

1. Katherine Weisman, "Don't Let Your Babies Grow Up to Be Cowboys," *Forbes*, 29 April 1991, p. 123.

2. "An interview with Chairman Bob Thain," *Prorodeo Sports News*, 3 April 1991, p. 14.

3. Howard L. Nixon II and James H. Frey, *A Sociology of Sport* (Belmont, Calif.: Wadsworth Publishing Company, 1996), p. 168.

4. Kendra Santos, "Three Million Fans Tune in Mesquite on TNN," *Prorodeo Sports News*, 13 June 1990, p. 8.

5. Jay J. Coakley, *Sport in Society: Issues and Controversies* (St. Louis, Mo.: Mosby, 1994), p. 338.

6. "Demographics of Rodeo Fans" (Denver: ProRodeo Sports, Inc., 1994).

7. Jane Gottesman, "Big-Time Rodeo to the Cow Palace," *San Francisco Chronicle*, 25 October 1991, p. D-1.

8. Ibid.

CHAPTER 14. PROFESSIONAL RODEO AT THE CROSSROADS

1. Katherine Weisman, "Don't Let Your Babies Grow Up to Be Cowboys," *Forbes*, 29 April 1991, p. 124.

2. "Houston Livestock Show and Rodeo's Don Gattis: Rodeo Committee Director," *Prorodeo Sports News*, 30 October 1991, p. 9.

3. "The Cowboy Doesn't Mince His Words," *Prorodeo Sports News*, 1 May 1991, p. 10.

4. An Interview with Chairman Bob Thain," *Prorodeo Sports News*, 3 April 1991, p. 14.

Appendix

PROFILE OF PRCA COWBOYS

To date, no one has examined in any great detail the attitudes and identity of the modern rodeo professional cowboy. In order to better understand these athletes, the principal investigator of this book undertook a survey of PRCA rodeo cowboys. The goal was to gain information on cowboys' training techniques, backgrounds, levels of education, annual expenses, attitudes towards sponsors, and opinions about the increasing professionalism of the sport.

Research Methodology

A 35-item questionnaire was field tested in May 1990, at the Casey Tibbs Memorial Rodeo held in Ramona, California. After some slight modification, it was sent to Steve Fleming, director of communications for the PRCA, to see if any additional questions should be included. In fact, before the questionnaire was even field tested, prior approval from the PRCA had been received, as a study of this sort necessitated the full cooperation of the governing body of the sport.

In the year and a half that it took to administer the questionnaire (July 1990 through December 1991), a variety of research techniques were used to gain a representative sampling of the professional cowboys competing on the rodeo circuit. Six hundred eleven males completed two-page questionnaires, which were then analyzed. (The results of the pilot study of 32 barrel racers is discussed in the chapter on women and rodeo.)

Although it is difficult to know precisely the total number of cowboys who compete in professional rodeo, at least two-thirds of the full-time competitors during that period—mid-1990 to 1991—completed the survey. This claim is based on the following data. In 1992, 5,700 cowboys renewed their PRCA card. Not all of these cowboys compete, however. Of this group of 5,700, roughly 1,000 cowboys tried to make a living by rodeoing, though only 300 contestants earned $10,000 or more in prize money in 1991. The 611 males who completed the questionnaire appear to be representative of the cowboys competing on the professional circuit. In fact, 40 percent of those surveyed (202 out of 611) reported they had won prize money in excess of $10,000 during the preceding year. This number reflected two-thirds (202 of 300) of *all* cowboys earning that amount of money during the preceding year.

A variety of research techniques were employed to gain a representative sample of the pro cowboys.

(1) As many of the contestants at the 1990 Cheyenne Frontier Days Rodeo as possible were surveyed. In total, 19 percent of the contestants entered at that rodeo completed the questionnaire. Further, only a couple of the cowboys who were asked to complete the survey refused to do so. Those that participated were also proportionately representative of the male contestants entered in the different standard rodeo events at Cheyenne.

(2) Under the auspices of the PRCA, the questionnaire, with a cover letter, was

mailed to the top 30 cowboys in each event with instructions to complete the survey and return it to the principal investigator who had provided a stamped, self-addressed envelope.

(3) Questionnaires were also distributed to cowboys at thirty other rodeos, including such big rodeos as the Dodge City Days Round-Up Rodeo and the Grand National Rodeo, as well as many of the Sierra Circuit regional California-based rodeos.

(4) Copies of the questionnaire were mailed to all 119 collegiate rodeo programs across the country with the request that students who had their PRCA card and were competing on the pro circuit complete the questionnaire and return it to the principal investigator.

(5) The questionnaire was distributed to those PRCA cowboys who participated in one of Gary Leffew's bull riding schools.

General Patterns

An analysis of the 611 completed surveys provided several general patterns or characteristics common to pro rodeo cowboys.

Age breakdown: Two-thirds (65 percent) of the contestants were between 19 and 29 years of age; one-fourth (26 percent) were in their thirties; several were in their forties (7 percent); and a few (2 percent) were age 50 or over. The sport of pro rodeo is a young person's activity.

Nearly all of those surveyed (91 percent) were Caucasian, reflective of the racial and ethnic breakdown of the pro rodeo cowboy. Only three black cowboys, for instance, competed in the National Finals Rodeo in 1990 and only two competed in 1991. Black cowboys comprised 3 percent of those surveyed, American Indians comprised 3 percent, Hispanics comprised 2 percent, and 1 percent reported "other" when asked for their race or ethnicity.

Two-thirds of the rodeo contestants (67 percent) cited some religious affiliation, although one-third listed "none" or left the open-ended question blank. For those who listed a religion, most defined themselves as Protestant (34 percent), followed by Christian (17 percent) and Catholic (16 percent).

Three-fourths of the cowboys sampled (75 percent) indicated they had attended college. In fact, half of those surveyed noted they had completed some college (usually attending a two-year junior college), and one-fourth reported having received a four-year college degree. The most common majors in college were animal sciences and ag business, followed by physical education and health.

Half of those surveyed were single (52 percent) while the others reported either being married (39 percent) or separated or divorced (9 percent). The high percentage of single men competing in rodeo is due to the younger age of the typical rodeo contestant. Older cowboys were more likely to report being married or divorced.

Apart from rodeoing, the cowboys were asked to list their occupation, if they had one. For those that reported an occupation, over one-third indicated ranching (36 percent), followed by construction-related jobs (16 percent), being a full-time student (13 percent), or professional, managerial, or business-related occupations (10 percent).

The majority of cowboys surveyed (57 percent) had competed in the pro rodeo circuit for over five years. In fact, one-fourth of the contestants (26 percent) had competed between five and nine years; 17 percent had competed between ten and fourteen years; and 14 percent had competed in pro rodeo for over fifteen years. By contrast, 43 percent of the cowboys were new to professional rodeo, having competed for less than five years.

Forty percent of the sample had participated in over fifty PRCA-sanctioned rodeos during the preceding year. In fact, 26 percent competed in 50 to 100 rodeos, and 14 percent competed in over 100 rodeos. Another question asked about the percentage of rodeos entered in which they had won prize money. Of those sampled, 28 percent reported having won prize money in over half of the rodeos they had entered; half won money between 20 and 50 percent of the time; others won money less than 20 percent of the time (16 percent); while some indicated they had not won any prize money during the preceding year (6 percent).

The cowboys sampled were evenly divided between those who competed in the roughstock events and those who competed in the timed events. More roughstock contestants were sampled since they were more easily accessible behind the chutes. By contrast, the timed event contestants were frequently tending to their horses away from the rodeo arena, or were on horseback where it was more difficult to request their participation with the survey. Special efforts were made to sample timed event contestants during slack competition or when they were paying their entry fees.

In terms of specific events, the sample was distributed as follows: bareback riding (14 percent), saddle bronc riding (14 percent), bull riding (22 percent), calf roping (16 percent), steer wrestling (16 percent), and team roping (18 percent). The oversampling of bull riders was due, in part, to their being more accessible behind the chutes since bull riding was often the last rodeo event.

The cowboys were asked to list all of the rodeo events in which they competed. Most listed only one event (69 percent). However, some listed two rodeo events (21 percent), and several listed three or more events (10 percent). If multiple events were listed, a cowboy typically competed in either all roughstock or all timed events, although several did indicate that they competed in events at both ends of the arena. Several older timed event competitors mentioned they had competed in the roughstock events when younger.

Several questions pertained to the expenses involved in competing in rodeo. Cowboys were asked about the most prize money they had won in one rodeo. Nearly one-fourth (23 percent) indicated that they had won over $5,000 in one rodeo. Twenty percent had won between $2,500 and $4,999, 26 percent had won between $1,000 and $2,499, and 31 percent reported they had won less than $1,000 in one rodeo.

In terms of expenses, a few cowboys (5 percent) indicated they had spent more than $50,000 competing on the national circuit during the preceding year. Several others (4 percent) noted that they had spent between $35,000 and $49,999, while others (14 percent) reported having spent between $20,000 and $34,999. Most of the cowboys, however, indicated they had spent either between $5,000 and $19,999 (40 percent) or under $5,000 (37 percent).

As previously mentioned, 40 percent indicated they had won over $10,000 in prize money during the preceding year. Of that group, 19 percent won between $10,000 and $24,999, 11 percent won between $25,000 and $49,999, an additional 5 percent won between $50,000 and $74,999, and 5 percent won over $75,000 in prize money during the preceding year. With respect to the 60 percent who earned less than $10,000 during the preceding year, 18 percent won between $5,000 and $9,999, 27 percent won between $1,000 and $4,999, and 15 percent won under $1,000.

Several questions examined the training methods used to prepare for competition. Four-fifths of the contestants (80 percent) indicated that they trained for their sport while others reported no specific training outside of competing in rodeo itself. The roughstock contestants were more varied in their responses. Weight training was most frequently listed (12 percent), followed by running (10 percent), stretching and aerobics (9 percent), and visualization or cybernetics (6 percent).

Another area examined was their family rodeo and ranch background. Over half (56 percent) reported they first learned to rodeo at home on the family ranch. The others reported they had learned their sport either at school (14 percent), or in some other fashion such as from friends, attending rodeo training programs or in the military (30 percent).

Most cowboys reported they had come from ranching backgrounds (77 percent) although one-fourth had not grown up in a ranching environment. The bull riders were least likely to have had prior ranching experience. Two-thirds of those sampled (67 percent) reported that other family members had competed in rodeo, with 41 percent stating their parents had competed, and 44 percent indicating another family member (siblings, uncles, or grandparents) had competed.

One-third indicated they had participated in three or all four programs such as Little Britches or Junior Rodeo, high school-age rodeo, collegiate rodeo, or a rodeo training school. Most indicated they had competed in a high school-age rodeo program (78 percent); three-fifths (61 percent) had competed in one (or more) collegiate rodeo program; one-third (35 percent) had been part of Little Britches or Junior Rodeo; while one-fourth (26 percent) had enrolled in a training school.

The following table, "Attitudes Toward Rodeo," summarizes the opinions expressed by the cowboys on a variety of topics related to the sport of professional rodeo. To these 13 statements, a cowboy could either agree (A), indicate they were not sure of their response (NS), or disagree with the statement (D).

ATTITUDES TOWARD RODEO

A	NS	D	
91%	7%	2%	I have always wanted to be a cowboy.
19	8	73	For me, being a cowboy and competing in rodeos is only a weekend hobby.
40	0	60	I place in most rodeos that I enter.
50	27	23	I consider myself to be an athlete rather than a cowboy.
90	6	4	It takes a lot of money in order to compete as a cowboy on the rodeo circuit.
20	0	80	I have made it to the National Finals Rodeo on at least one occasion.
13	17	70	Rodeos have become too much a big business and too professional in operation.
22	7	71	I only compete in my regional circuit and do not compete in many rodeos outside of this region.
24	21	55	One must have a sponsor in order to compete successfully in today's rodeo.

66	23	11	I would encourage my children to become cowboys.
69	19	12	I wish that rodeos could be grouped together and scheduled in such a way that it would cut down on my traveling expenses.
70	18	12	One can make a living as a rodeo contestant.
63	20	17	I train as much for the sport of rodeo as do other professional athletes train for their sport.

Analysis of the Responses

The first statement read, "I have always wanted to be a cowboy." Nearly all of the respondents (91 percent) agreed with this statement. Being a cowboy was something that they had long identified with. Likewise, most (73 percent) disagreed with the statement, "For me, being a cowboy and competing in rodeos is only a weekend hobby."

As predicted, most were split between identifying as a rodeo athlete or as a rodeo cowboy. Exactly half of those sampled agreed with the statement, "I consider myself to be an athlete rather than a cowboy," while the others either indicated they were not sure (27 percent) or disagreed with the statement (23 percent). (Several contestants wrote in "both" to this question. For analysis purposes, their responses were grouped in the not sure category.)

Nearly all of the cowboys (90 percent) agreed with the statement, "It takes a lot of money in order to compete as a cowboy on the rodeo circuit." Most (70 percent) disagreed with the statement, "Rodeos have become too much a big business and too professional in operation," indicating they thought pro rodeo should become even more professional and even more of a big business. They saw greater professionalism as being beneficial to the sport of rodeo, and potentially more lucrative to themselves.

Most of the cowboys surveyed (71 percent) indicated they competed in rodeos other than just those in their own regional circuit. One-fifth of those sampled had competed at the National Finals Rodeo.

Most cowboys were split on the statement, "One must have a sponsor in order to compete successfully in today's rodeo." Over half (55 percent) disagreed with the statement, although one-fourth (24 percent) agreed with the view, while the others were not sure (21 percent). This disparity can be explained, in part, by the fact that the Patch Program (the individual sponsorship program) was just being introduced the year the survey was conducted. At that time, the idea of individual sponsorship was too new for there to be a consensus on whether or not it was a good program.

Two-thirds of the cowboys surveyed (66 percent) agreed with the statement, "I would encourage my children to become cowboys." However, some (11 percent) disagreed, implying they would not encourage their children to follow in their footsteps; while others indicated they were not sure (23 percent).

Most of the cowboys (69 percent) agreed with the statement, "I wish that rodeos could be grouped together and scheduled in such a way that it could cut down on my traveling expenses." Even with the financial difficulties faced, most cowboys (70 percent) agreed with the statement, "One can make a living as a rodeo contestant." And, finally, most respondents (63 percent) concurred with the statement, "I train as much for the sport of rodeo as do other professional athletes train for their sport."

Roughstock Versus Timed Event Contestants
The data were also analyzed comparing the roughstock to the timed event contestants. Several significant differences were noted. Roughstock contestants were younger, more likely to be single, more often list working class occupations such as construction as their jobs apart from rodeoing (which was particularly true for the bull riders), and less likely to have graduated from college.

Compared to the timed event cowboys, the roughstock riders indicated they had competed in more rodeos and regional circuits, reported earning more money in a higher percentage of rodeos entered, but winning less money overall during the preceding year. Roughstock riders also indicated they competed in fewer events, and had learned the sport of rodeo apart from the family ranch—either at high school age or college rodeo, or at rodeo training schools. They were less likely to report having other family members compete in rodeo.

Roughstock riders were less likely to agree with the following two statements: "For me, being a cowboy and competing in rodeos is only a weekend hobby" and "Rodeos have become too much a big business and too professional in operation." Compared to timed event cowboys, roughstock riders were less likely to want the rodeos grouped together to cut down on traveling expenses, and less likely to agree they trained as much for their sport as other pro athletes trained for their sport.

Finally, the roughstock cowboys were significantly more likely to agree with the statement, "One can make a living as a rodeo contestant." This was one of the more significant differences between the two groups (sig.= <.0001). Whereas 83 percent of the roughstock cowboys agreed that one could make a living in rodeo, fewer timed event cowboys (57 percent) felt that way. Further, only 2 percent of the roughstock riders disagreed with the statement, implying that they could *not* make a living, whereas one-fifth of the timed event contestants (21 percent) disagreed. It should be pointed out once again that the roughstock cowboys were generally younger and single, and so perhaps their living expenses were comparatively reduced in contrast to the older timed event competitor who often had a family and a ranch operation to support.

1. Age _____
2. Sex _____ male
   _____ female
3. Ethnicity _____
4. Religious affiliation _____
5. Level of education _____ some high school
   _____ high school graduate
   _____ some college
   _____ college graduate
   Which college? _____
   What was your major? _____
6. Marital status _____ single, never married
   _____ married, remarried
   _____ separated, divorced
7. At what age did you begin to rodeo professionally? _____
8. How many years have you been involved with rodeos? _____
9. What is your occupation apart from rodeoing? _____
10. How many rodeos did you enter last year? _____
11. In how many of these rodeos did you win money? _____
12. On the average, how many rodeos do you compete in per year? _____
    Which circuit? _____
13. What is your rodeo event(s)? _____
14. What has been your highest score (or lowest time) you have ever received in this event? _____
15. What has been the most prize money you have ever received in one rodeo?
    _____
16. Approximately how much money did you spend last year in order to compete on the rodeo circuit? _____
17. How much total prize money did you earn last year? _____
18. What type of special training do you do to prepare for competing on the rodeo circuit? _____
19. Where did you first learn to rodeo? _____
20. What kind of farming/ranching background did you have before becoming a professional cowboy? _____
21. Has anyone else in your family competed on the rodeo circuit? _____
    If so, whom? _____
    In what event(s)? _____
22. In which of these did you compete (check all that apply)?
    _____ Little Britches   _____ High School rodeo
    _____ Collegiate Rodeo   _____ Training school

Please respond to the following statements in this way:
(A = Agree; NS = Not Sure; D = Disagree)

A	NS	D	
1	2	3	23. I have always wanted to be a cowboy.
1	2	3	24. For me, being a cowboy and competing in rodeos is only a weekend hobby.
1	2	3	25. I place in most rodeos that I enter.
1	2	3	26. I consider myself to be an athlete rather than a cowboy.
1	2	3	27. It takes a lot of money in order to compete as a cowboy on the rodeo circuit.
1	2	3	28. I have made it to the National Finals Rodeo on at least one occasion.
1	2	3	29. Rodeos have become too much a big business and too professional in operation.
1	2	3	30. I only compete in my regional circuit and do not compete in many rodeos outside of this region.
1	2	3	31. One must have a sponsor in order to compete successfully in today's rodeos.
1	2	3	32. I would encourage my children to become cowboys.
1	2	3	33. I wish that rodeos could be grouped together and scheduled in such a way that it would cut down on my traveling expenses.
1	2	3	34. One can make a living as a rodeo contestant.
1	2	3	35. I train as much for the sport of rodeo as do other professional athletes train for their sport.

Thank you for your cooperation. Please feel free to add any other comments on your involvement with being a cowboy and with rodeos.

Index

Academy Award, 229
Adair, Julie, 39
Agrarian life, 4
Aguillar, Aleajandro, 203
AIDS (acquired immune deficiency syndrome), 199
AIRCA. *See* All Indian Rodeo Cowboys Association
Alaska, 205
Alberta Motion Picture Industry Film of the Year, 229
Alexander, Joe, 28
Allen, Guy, 21
All Indian Rodeo Cowboys Association (AIRCA), 204
Allred, Casey, 27
All Women's Rodeo (Durango, Colo.), 186, 187
Alpine (Tex.), 10, 41
Alsbaugh, Walt, 157
Altizer, Jim Bob, 114
Altizer, Mark, 114, 115
American Black Cowboy's Association, 208
American Cowboy (magazine), 263
American Junior Rodeo Association
American Professional Bullfighters Association (APBA), 169
American Quarter horse, 19, 41
American Quarter Horse Association, 189
American Rodeo Association of the Deaf, 215
American Royal Rodeo (Kansas City), 207
Anchorage (Alaska) rodeo, 205
Andrews, Don, 93
Andrews, Gene, 94
Angel (horse), 13
Animal names, 114, 115, 119
Animal rights activist groups, 5, 6, 32, 126–127, 128, 129, 130–132, 133–134

Animal trainers, 112
"Animal Welfare Issues" *(Prorodeo Sports News)*, 133
APBA. *See* American Professional Bullfighters Association
Appleton, Dave, 64, 88, 107, 239
ARC. *See* Association of Rodeo Committees
Arena (film), 222, 223
Association of Rodeo Committees (ARC), 181
Austen, Bill, 184
Australian rodeo, 201
Autry, Gene, 112, 188–189
Avidson, John, 228
Avneri, Ronit, 231
Award Design Metals (company), 189

Bad Company Rodeo, 114
Badlands Circuit, 216
Baldy (horse), 116
Bank robbery (Joseph, Ore.), 172–173
Bareback riders, 37, 42, 43, 44–45, 54, 55, 59, 60, 64, 67, 68–69, 73, 89, 91–92, 98, 145(photo), 208, 216
champion, 28, 33, 38, 60, 63, 85, 197
injuries, 40, 59, 140(photo)
rookie of the year, 43
Bareback riding, 14, 17, 18, 42, 190
description, 23, 28–29, 121
equipment, 18, 58–59
Mexican, 203
scoring, 28–29, 31
Barrelmen, 164, 165, 166, 168–169
barrels, 168–169
Barrel racers, 190, 192, 232
champion, 148(captions), 177, 190–194
Eskimo, 205
prize money, 194
in survey, 194–196
Barrel racing, 6, 17, 39, 42, 49,

Barrel racing (*cont'd*)
     148(photos), 189, 190
  description, 20
  equipment, 58
Baumgartner, Joe, 146(photo)
B Bar J Rodeo Company (Tex.), 117
Be Aggressive (horse), 69
Beard, Pat, 102
Beaver, Joe, 56, 147(photo), 253
Bedouins, 7
Bergen, Polly, 223
Berry, Ote, 4, 70
Beutler, Benny, 111
Beutler, Lynn, 208
Biggs, Mike, 214
Billboard (magazine), 13, 14
Bill Shows. *See* Wild West shows
*Biting the Dust: The Wild Ride and
     Dark Romance of the Rodeo
     Cowboy and the American West*
     (Johnson), 6
Black, Baxter, 233
Bloopers, 122
Bobby Joe Skoal (horse), 118–119
Boetticher, Budd, 222
Bogue, Richard, 179
"Boogie Man," 210
Bordertown (horse), 28
Borrelli, Sonny, 218
Boxleitner, Bruce, 215
Boyd, Bill, 67
Bradley, Rick, 37
Brainard, John, 192
Braley, Jack, 252
*Brand of Its Own, A: The 100 Year
     History of the Calgary Exhibition
     and Stampede* (Gray), 181
Brawley Cattle Call Rodeo (Calif.), 36,
     100, 179
  Mini for Special Kids, 176
Brazilian rodeo, 2, 210
Bridges, James, 225
Brighton Field Day Rodeo (Fla.), 204
BRO. *See* Bull Riders Only
Bronco Buster (film), 222, 223

Bronco busters, 22
Bronco peelers, 22
Bronc rein, 57
Bronc Rider, The (Crawford), 224
Bronc (saddle) riders, 12, 13, 28, 44,
     45 53, 55, 75, 88, 89, 139(photo),
     141(photo), 143–144(photos), 162,
     165, 205, 208
  champion, 27–28, 42, 53, 67,
     144(photo)
  death, 188
  injuries, 94, 95
  women, 14, 188, 190
Bronc (saddle) riding, 10, 12, 14, 17, 18,
     28, 42
  description, 22, 121
  equipment, 45, 57, 58, 132
  first contest, 9
  injuries, 40
  scoring, 28, 31
Brooks, Garth, 232, 233
Bucher, Richard, 53
Buckaroo, 8
Bucking Bull of the Year Award, 116
Bucking stock, 116–118. *See also* Bulls;
     Horses, bucking
Buckle bunnies. *See* Rodeo, groupies
Buffalo Bill's Wild West and Congress of
     Rough Riders, 11
Bull dogging, 11, 207. *See also* Steer
     wrestling
Bull fighters, 45–46, 59, 146(photo),
     164, 168, 169–171, 210
  champion, 96, 170, 171, 211
  equipment, 95–96
  injuries, 94
Bull riders, 1, 2, 5, 26–27, 36, 40, 44,
     55, 86, 89, 92, 93, 101, 108–109,
     140(photo), 142(photo), 145–
     146(photos), 184, 194, 197, 209,
     219
  champion, 4, 27, 38, 43, 96, 98, 209,
     230
  deaths, 119
  injuries, 40, 94, 95, 261

school, 40
shirt, 137(photo)
women, 186, 190
Bull Riders Only (BRO), 160, 237, 261
Bull riding, 7, 17, 18, 42, 45, 46, 48,
    123–124, 169
    description, 22–23
    entry fees, 65
    equipment, 18, 58, 59, 95, 96
    Mexican, 202–203
    scoring, 29
    stand-alone competitions, 88
Bull rope, 23, 57, 59
Bulls
    bucking, 2, 27, 116, 117, 119–121,
        123–124, 125
    fighting, 118, 124, 170
    injuries, 132
    mechanical, 46
    Mexican, 170
Bureau of Land Management, 216
Burns, Pete, 120
Burton, Jo, 186–187
Burwash, Cindy, 198
Burwash, Robin, 59, 67, 198
Bush, George, 201
Buskirk, Leslie, 197

Caldwell, Lee, 12
Calf ropers, 32, 44, 59, 68, 184
    champion, 38, 56, 114, 211, 252
    injuries, 94
    women, 42, 190
Calf roping, 17, 18, 32, 131
    breakaway, 190
    description, 19
    tie down, 190
    youth, 177
Calgary Stampede (Canada), 12, 13–14,
    87, 126, 180, 182, 183, 188, 205
California, 21, 32, 104, 132–133
California Federation of Charros, 203
California Polytechnic State University
    (San Luis Obispo), 44, 104
California Rodeo, 129, 179, 182, 183

Camarillo, Leo, 204
Camp Pendleton (Calif.) rodeo, 218–219
Canada, 13, 39, 40, 42, 67, 201, 230
Canadian Pacific Railway, 14
Canadian Professional Rodeo Asso-
    ciation (CPRA), 19, 20, 50, 79, 230
Canon City (Colo.) prison program, 216
Canutt, Yakima, 13
Capshaw, Kate, 226
Carrillo, Adam, 145(photo)
Carrillo, Gilbert, 145(caption)
Casey, J. D., 97
Cathey, Karen, 197
Cathey, Wacey, 197
Cattle
    dogs, 157, 158
    in Hawaii, 206
    in New World, 8–9
    roping, 116, 122
    See also Steer roping; Steer wrestling
Central New Mexico Correctional
    Facility, 216
Cervi, Mike, 111, 193
Cervi, Mike, Jr., 193
Champions Ride, 215
Chaps, 58
Chariot races, 7
Charreada. See Mexican rodeos
Cheyenne Frontier Days: A History
    of the "Daddy of 'Em All" (Riske),
    181
Cheyenne Frontier Days Rodeo, 12, 14,
    27, 56, 116, 119, 120, 182, 183, 205,
    206, 207
    parade, 135(photo)
Chief Joseph (Nez Perce), 13
Chief Joseph Days Rodeo (Ore.), 108,
    173
Chiropractors, 94–95
Cholach, Darryl, 67
Chuckwagon races, 7
Chute boss, 162
Chute laborers, 161–162
Cities in Schools program, 177
Clabaugh, Kenny, 162

Clark, Derek, 88, 182

Clowns, 4–5, 60, 113, 150(photo), 164–168, 169, 210
awards, 165
injuries, 94
women, 165

CNFR. *See* College National Finals Rodeo

Coburn, James, 223

Coca-Cola (company), 66, 190, 245

Cody, William F. ("Buffalo Bill"), 10–11

Coffee, Luke "Leon," 165, 210

Coliseum sports, 7

College National Finals Rodeo (CNFR), 41
first (1949), 44

College rodeo, 38, 41–44, 50, 102
champion, 43
first (1948), 41
women in, 41, 42

Colorado, 113

Colorado Cowboy: The Bruce Ford Story (film), 229, 230–231

Columbia River Circuit Finals Rodeo, 27

Combs, Benny, 70

Combs, Willard, 70

Convict Cowboy (film), 217

Cooper, Kent, 27

Cooper, Roy, 38, 39, 47, 56, 68, 253

Coors Brewing Company, 66, 99, 189–190, 257

Coors Fans Favorite Cowboy, 210

Copenhagen Skoal Pro Rodeo, 120
scoreboard, 163

Copenhagen Skoal tobacco, 99, 103, 104

Corey, Clint, 60, 64, 93

Corey, Mike, 162

Corley, Ed, 94

Corley, Randy, 174

"Cory Corriente" (doll steer), 176

Cossack Drag (trick riding), 159

Cossacks, 7

Country western music, 36, 232–233

Cowbells, 18

Cowboy (Fletcher), 224

Cowboy Assistance Foundation, 105–106

Cowboy Church, 106

Cowboy Hero, The: His Image in American History and Culture (Savage), 270

Cowboy Magazine, 263

Cowboys
African American, 177, 207–211
assistance to, 85, 105, 106–107 (*see also* Justin Boot Company, Cowboy Crisis Fund; Rodeo, corporate sponsors; Rodeo, sports medicine programs)
association, 16
as athletes, 72, 73, 77–83, 97
backgrounds, 34–39
buddy system, 52, 66–69
car pooling, 63
Christian, 106–107
code, 4–5
and corporate advertising, 84, 86
deaf, 215
and divisional rodeo proposal, 257–261
earnings, 6, 33, 37, 52, 60, 72, 78–79, 254, 259–260, 261–262
education, 41, 61
as elite athletes, 72, 73, 75, 79–83, 259
equipment, 57–59, 95–97
family, 6, 34–38, 197–198
Hawaiian, 108–109, 205–206
health care, 1, 6
Mexican American, 204
myth/mystique, 4, 5, 6–7, 36, 72, 73, 219, 223–224, 262
origins, 8–9
poets, 233
pranks, 52–53
as professional athletes, 72, 73, 77–79
publicity, 64, 87, 239–240, 255
rookie, 52–53, 55, 56–57, 58
socializing influences, 35–38
song, 231–232

strike (1936), 16
substance abuse, 99–105
traditionalists, 72–73, 255
types, 72
as weekend warriors, 72, 74–77, 114, 255
in Wild West shows, 11
and women, attitude towards, 188–189, 195, 198–199
world champion all-around, 3, 33, 147(photo)
See also Rodeo; Westerns
Cowboys & Country (magazine), 263
Cowboys & Indians (magazine), 263
Cowboys of Color rodeo series, 208
Cowboys' Turtle Association (1936), 16, 25, 188
Cowboy tournaments, 10
Cowgirls. *See* Rodeo, women in
Cowgirls of the Rodeo: Pioneer Professional Athletes (LeCompte), 188
Cow Palace (San Francisco), 41. *See also* Grand National Rodeo
Cowtown Coliseum (Fort Worth), 190
CPRA. *See* Canadian Professional Rodeo Association
Crawford, William, 224
Crown Royal (company), 90–91
Cryer, Lewis A., 31, 64, 75, 82, 83, 91, 110–111, 178, 238, 256
"Cult of Masculinity, The: American Social Character and the Legacy of the Cowboy" (Kimmel), 5–6
Custer, Cody, 96, 206, 261

Dally ribbon roping, 39
Dally roping, 18, 19
Danish (horse), 192, 193
Davis, Jerome, 194
Day, A. D., 13–14
Daylighted, 19
Deer Trail (Colo.), 9
Delvecchio, Bobby, 36

Denver
gay rodeo, 212
rodeo, 10 (*see also* National Western Stock Show)
Desert Storm (horse), 91
Diaz, Gerardo "Jerry," 149(photo)
Dightman, Myrtis, 209
Disaster victim aid, 4–5
Discount coupons, 245–246
Dixon Correctional Institution (La.), 216
DNCFR. *See* Dodge National Circuit Finals Rodeo
Dodge City Days Round-Up Rodeo (Kansas), 183, 184–185
Dodge National Circuit Finals Rodeo (DNCFR), 77
Dodge Trucks (company), 66, 89, 162, 189
Rodeo, 89
Dogs, 167
Doing Time: Ten Years Later (film), 216
"Don't Let Your Babies Grow Up to Be Cowboys" (Weisman), 87, 255
Douglas, Jennifer, 152(photo)
Dowdy, Gene, 176
Duarte, Myron, 206–207
Dunn, Bill, 113
Dunn, Troy, 91–92
Duvall, Roy, 70–71
Duvall, Sam, 70, 71

8 Seconds (film), 36, 153(photo), 226, 228–229
Electric Horseman, The (film), 225
Electric prods, 129, 130
Electronic timers, 20
Elgort, Arthur, 230–231
English equitation, 46
Errington, Frederick, 180
ESPN (cable network), 235, 236
Wrangler World of Rodeo, 86
Etbauer, Billy, 53, 67, 95, 103, 153(photo)
Etbauer, Dan, 54, 67, 153(photo), 184
Etbauer, Lyle, 153(photo)

Etbauer, Robert, 67, 144(photo), 153(photo)
Evans, J. Pat, 93
Exceptional Rodeo (PRCA), 175–176

Fancy roping, 11, 113, 149(photo), 159
Farris, Mildred, 160
Federal Communications Commission, 90
Fellowship of Christian Athletes (FCA), 106
Fiesta del Charro (Calif.), 204
Fiestas, 10
Filipek, Clint, 46
Firefighter rodeo, 217–218
Flag bearers, 196
Flagman, 29
Flag racing, 39, 176
Flank man, 68–69, 161
Flank strap/strip, 57, 127, 129–130, 161, 203
Fleischer, Richard, 222
Fletcher, Aaron, 224
Florida Indian rodeo, 205
Flying U Rodeo Company (Calif.), 112, 113–114, 128, 182, 204
Flynn, Denny, 27, 219
Fonda, Jane, 225
Forbes magazine, 255
Ford, Bruce, 38, 47, 197, 229, 258
Ford, Susan, 197
Fort Carson (Colorado military base), 174
Fort Worth Star Telegram, 85
Four States High School Rodeo Association, 252
Fox, Todd, 183
Freeman, Danny, 181
Frey, James H., 187, 235
Friends of Rodeo, 134
Frontier spirit, 6
Frost, Lane, 27, 52, 119. See also 8 Seconds
Furrer, Mark, 244, 245

Gander, Steve, 242
Garrett, Mark, 54, 183

Garrett, Marvin, 60
Gattis, Dan, 258
Gay, Don, 27, 38, 48, 92, 206, 210, 235
Gay, Neal, 111
Gaylord, Ed, III, 226
Gay rodeo, 211–214
Gear bags, 52–53, 57, 59
George Michael Sports Medicine (television program), 86
Gibbs, George, 30
Gibson, Buddy, 206
Gilbert, Bil, 187
Ginger (horse), 192
Girls Rodeo Association (GRA), 189. See also Women's Professional Rodeo Association
Glenn, Scott, 225, 226
Gloves, 58–59, 92, 156(photo)
Goat relay, 175
Goat riding, 36–37
Goat tying competition, girls', 39, 42
Gold buckle, 49
Goldenrod (Harker), 224
Golf, 98
Gonzales, Conrad, 98
Gottesman, Jane, 250
GRA. See Girls Rodeo Association
Gradenshire, Emilnie, 9
Grand National Rodeo (San Francisco), 53 67, 116, 130, 184, 245, 250
Grant, Gogi, 163
Grasshopper (bull), 116
Gray, James H., 181
Great American Cowboy (film), 229
Greeley (Colo.) potato celebration, 12
Greeley Independence Stampede, 183
Greenough, Deb, 63
Growney, John, 26, 27, 56, 108–109, 116, 119–120, 121, 124, 125, 127
Gunnison (Colo.) rodeo, 253
Gunsmoke (television show), 225, 270(n8)

Hale, Billy, 70
Hang'em High (horse), 28
Hargo, Dwayne, 96, 170, 171, 210–211

Harker, Herbert, 224
Harley Davidson and the Marlboro Man (film), 226, 227
Hartnell College (Calif.), 42
Have Gun, Will Travel (television show), 225
Hawaiian rodeo, 205–207
Hawk (horse), 192, 193
Hawkins, Terry, 217
Hayes, Lindsay, 193
Hazer, 20
Header, 19, 20
Hearn, Cleo, 208, 211
Hedeman, Tuff, 52, 95, 177, 261
Heeler, 19, 20
Helmets, 97
Henderson, Chance, 252–254
Henderson, Prairie Rose, 14
Henson, Monte "Hawkeye," 233, 240
Herefords, 9
Herman, Wayne, 44–45, 85–86
High School Finals Rodeo, 39–40
High school rodeo, 38, 39–41, 192, 252
Hippodrome Stand (trick riding), 159
Hitchcock, Ryer, 110
Holm, Ben, 26–37
Home on the Range program, 215
Honeycutt, Jerry, 115
Honeycutt, Roy, 115
Honeycutt, Scott, 115
Honeycutt, Virginia, 115
Honeycutt & Sons Rodeo Company (Colo.), 115–116
Honkers, The (film), 222, 223
Horse meat, 117
Horses, 13, 27–28, 69, 91
    bareback, 118 (*see also* Bareback riding)
    breaking, 216
    bucking, 116–119, 121, 123, 125, 127, 129, 132, 192
    genetics, 118
    halter-broken, 113, 121
    and mud, 124
    saddle broncs, 118–119, 121 (*see also* Bronc (saddle) riding)

as therapy, 215
tripping of, 132, 133, 203
wild, 18, 117, 118, 216
See also Barrel racers
Houston Livestock Show and Rodeo, 56, 96, 116, 173, 183, 201–202
Huffman, Coy, 106, 162
Humane facts pamphlet (PRCA), 128
Humane Society of the United States, 132
Hurley, Marv, 68–69, 92

IGRA. *See* International Gay Rodeo Association
Ihnat, Steve, 222
Indian National Finals, 204
Industry Hills Charity Pro Rodeo (Calif.), 91–92, 174–175
International Gay Rodeo Association (IGRA), 212–214
International Professional Rodeo Association (IPRA) (Oklahoma City), 4, 19, 50–51, 79
International Rodeo Association, 16, 20
IPRA. *See* International Professional Rodeo Association
Ivory, Buster, 236
I Witness Video (television show), 132

Jakino, Wayne, 212
James-Rodman, Charmayne. *See* Rodman, Charmayne (James)
Jet Royal Speed. *See* Hawk
Johnson, Ben, 214
Johnson, Dirk, 6
Johnson, William T., 15–16
Jonckowski, Jonnie, 190
Jones, John W., Jr., 183
Jones, Sandy, 241
Junior Bonner (film), 222
Junior Rodeo, 38, 39
Junior rodeos, 38–39, 192, 210
Justin Boot Company, 89, 164
    Cowboy Crisis Fund, 5, 105
    Sports Medicine Program, 90, 93–94
J. W. Coop (film), 222

Kaaua, Archie, 206
Kapernick, Bertha Blancett, 14
Keipe, Dave, 161
Keith, Tommy, 30
Kelly, Tammy, 186
Kemple, C. R., 123
Kennedy, Arthur, 223
Ketchum, Lloyd, 146(photo)
Kevlar fiber, 168
Kids Day Rodeo (Industry Hills Charity Pro Rodeo), 174
Kimmel, Michael S., 5–6
King, John, 213
Kirkham, Clay W., 216
Kish, Don, 119, 120
Knights, 7
Korkow, Jim, 45, 46
Korkow Ranch training school (Pierre, S.D.), 44–46

La Fiesta De Los Vaqueros Rodeo (Tucson), 131
Lambert, Cody, 52, 97
Landis, Donnie, 164, 167
Latham, Craig, 67
Latin American culture, 3
Lawrence, Elizabeth Atwood, 6
Lazy E Arena (Okla.), 21, 190, 226
"Leaping Llama" act, 167
Lecasse, Roger, 140(photo)
LeCompte, Mary Lou, 187, 188, 189, 198
Ledbetter, Jody, 177–178
LeDoux, Chris, 233
Leffew, Gary, 40, 46, 47–48, 97, 171, 210, 224
Lehmkuhler, Butch, 165
Leivas, Juan, 9
Leslie, Wade, 26, 27, 119
Let 'er Buck! A History of the Pendleton Round-Up (Rapp), 181
Lewis, Raymond, 26
Linderman, Bill, 43
Linderman Award (PRCA), 43
Little Britches Rodeo, 38–39, 210
Littlejohn, Chris, 210

Logue, Bob, 54, 97–98
Lonesome Dove (television show), 36, 226
Longbrake, Bud, 205
Longhorns, 8, 9, 112
Los Angeles Times, 107, 133
Louisiana State Penitentiary all-inmate rodeo, 217
Low, Jack, 206
Lucas, Joe, 184
Lund, John, 223
Lund, Wendi, 152(photo)
Lusty Men, The (film), 222, 223
Lyman, Rod, 243
Lynne, Phil, 229

McCarroll, Bonny, 14, 188
McDonald, Bryan, 123, 257
McDonald's franchises, 85
McEntire, Clark, 232
McEntire, Reba, 232
McMullen, H. C., 14
McPhee, Angus, 206
McQueen, Steve, 222
McRoberts, Sean, 40
MADD. See Mothers Against Drunk Drivers
Madison Square Garden Rodeo, 11, 112, 184
Magic (horse), 194
Mahan, Larry, 224, 229
Major Reno (horse), 192
Mangana. See Horses, tripping of
Mark-out rule, 28
Marlboro (horse), 28
Masculine dominance, 5–6
Maupintour (company), 242
Maverick (television show), 225
Mayer, Tony, 180
Maynard, Ted, 103
Mechanical bucking bulls, 46
Medicine Man (bull), 187
Mental conditioning, 47–48, 138(photo)
Merrill, Keith, 229
Mesquite Championship Rodeo, 235

Mexican charros, 112–113, 133,
149(photo), 202
Mexican rodeos, 112–113, 132, 133,
149(photo), 201, 202–204
Meyers, Butch, 36
Military rodeo, 218
Military Rodeo Cowboys Association,
218
Milking, 18, 19
Millar, Stuart, 222
Miller, Tom, 45
Mills, Daryl, 98–99
Minoans, 7
Minton, Casey, 43
Miss Rodeo America, 189, 196
Mr. T (bull), 120
Mitchum, Robert, 223
Moiso, Anthony R., 180
Monkeys, 167
Montana Circuit, 216
Montana State University (Bozeman), 41
Monte Vista (Colo.) rodeo, 253
Montrose (Colo.) rodeo, 10
Moon of the Desperados (film), 229–230,
231
Moore, Randy, 219
Moraes, Adriano, 2–3
Moreno, Cindy, 182
Moreno, Julio, 113
Mothers Against Drunk Drivers
(MADD), 101
Mugging team, 207
Mulhall, Lucille, 14
Murray, Joy, 105
Murray, Ty, 3, 28, 33–34, 35–36, 39, 43,
55–56, 82–83, 84–85, 96, 98, 105,
136(photo), 139(photo), 177, 195,
250, 261
Mutton bustin', 38
*"My Heroes Have Always Been
Cowboys"* (song/film), 1, 36, 46,
77, 226

Nashville Network (television), 86
National Cancer Institute, 104

National Cowboy Hall of Fame and
Western Heritage Center (Okla.),
207, 208, 233
National Finals Rodeo (NFR)
(December) (Las Vegas), 1–2, 21,
35, 93, 193
bucking stock sale, 116
championships, 49, 56, 147(caption)
event director, 123
expenses, 86
fatality, 93, 146(photo)
grand entry, 135(photo)
injuries, 95
judges, 26
pen rankings, 123–124
prize money, 79
qualified competitors, 49, 56, 67, 70,
79–80, 81, 201, 210
qualified rides, 2, 189
qualified stock, 122, 123–125
queens, 152(photo)
televised, 86
National Finals Steer Roping (NFSR),
21
National Firefighters Rodeo Association
218
National High School Rodeo
Association (NHSRA), 39–41
Finals, 206, 210
National Intercollegiate Rodeo
Association (NIRA), 41–42, 43
Rodeo Athletes on Wellness Helping
Individualize Drug and Alcohol
Education (RAWHIDE), 102
and women, 42
National Little Britches Rodeo, 38–39,
210
National Little Britches Rodeo
Association (NLBRA), 38–39
National Police Rodeo Association, 217
National Reno Gay Rodeo, 212
National Senior Professional Rodeo
Association, 219
National Senior Pro Rodeo Finals
(Reno), 219, 220
National Western Stock Show (Denver),

National Western Stock Show (*cont'd*)
56, 116, 149(photo), 183
Native Americans, 7, 12, 13,
149(photo), 173
Newman, Kim, 222, 223
New Mexico, 21, 113
New Mexico Junior Rodeo Association,
39
New Mexico State Fair Rodeo, 184
New West, 233
New Zealand rodeo, 201
Nez Perce, 13
NFR. *See* National Finals Rodeo
NFSR. *See* National Finals Steer
Roping
NHSRA. *See* National High School
Rodeo Association
Nigger (horse), 208
NIRA. *See* National Intercollegiate
Rodeo Association
Nixon, Howard L., II, 187, 235
NLBRA. *See* National Little Britches
Rodeo Association
North Platte (Nebr.), 11
Nuce, Ted, 95, 177, 178, 240

Oakland and Berkeley (Calif.) fires
(1991)
victims' aid, 4–5
OCPA. *See* Orange County People for
Animals
Odessa College (Tex.), 43
Oklahoma, 21, 101
Oklahoma City, 51, 87
bombing victims' aid, 4
Oklahoma Youth Rodeo Association, 252
Olsen, Greg, 213
Olson, Allen, 45
Olson, Jerry Wayne, 166
One-Armed Bandit and Company, 158
101 Ranch Wild West Show, 11, 13, 207
Orange County People for Animals
(OCPA), 131
Oregon, 21, 26

Original Coors Chute-Out Pro Rodeo
Series, 66
Orme, Wayne, 208–209, 211
Oscar (bull), 26, 27, 119
Ossenberg, Richard J., 180
Outlaw (bull), 120

Pacific Bell (bull), 116, 120
Paniolo. *See* Cowboys, Hawaiian
Park, Ava, 131
Parker Ranch (Hawaii), 206
Pawnee Bill's Wild West Show, 11
"Payday" (hand-rocked bareback horse),
175
Payne, John, 157–158
PBR. *See* Professional Bull Riders
Association)
Peckinpaugh, Sam, 222
Pecos (Tex.), 10
Pendleton Round-Up Rodeo (Ore.),
12–13, 182, 184, 188, 205
and women photographers, 197
People for the Ethical Treatment of
Animals (PETA), 127
Perry, Luke, 153(photo)
Peterson, Kristie, 191, 193, 194
Peth, Wick, 210
Pickett, Bill, 11, 207–208
Rodeos, 208
Pickup men, 58, 59, 115, 162
Pierce College (Los Angeles), 42
Pigging string, 19
Pikes Peak or Bust Rodeo (Colorado
Springs), 60, 110, 145(photo), 252,
253
charity, 174
Pittsburgh rodeo (Pa.), 132
Plaugher, Wilbur, 166
Poese, Lisa, 196
Pole bending, 42
Police rodeo, 217
Pollack, Sydney, 225
Posting, 23
Potter, Mel, 191–192
Potter, Wendy, 191–192

Potter-Cervi, Sherry, 148(caption), 191, 192–194
PRCA. *See* Professional Rodeo Cowboys Association
Precision equestrian drill teams, 196
Prescott Frontier Days Rodeo (Ariz.), 10, 181, 182
firsts, 9
Price, B. Byron, 233
Price, Clayton, 42, 47, 73, 78, 227
Prime ticket cable network, 86
Prince (horse), 118
Prison rodeo, 215–217
Pro/Celebrity Rodeo, 214–215
PROCOM (Pro Rodeo Communications, computerized entry system), 31, 62, 63, 64, 115
Professional Bull Riders Association (PBR), 237, 238
Professional Bull Riders Tour, 86
Professional Rodeo Cowboys Association (PRCA) (Colorado Springs)
alcohol risk management seminar, 101
and animal care, 128–134
annual convention, 181, 263
antecedents, 16
awards, 43, 178, 184, 211
board of directors, 234, 258
and breakaway groups, 88–89, 237, 261
championship record, 50
Clown of the Year, 165, 210
commissioner (*see* Cryer, Lewis A.)
competition system, 15, 17, 18, 19, 21, 51, 65, 76–77, 263–264 (*see also* National Finals Rodeo)
competitors, 49, 50, 71, 205, 207, 209
competitors' dress code, 155–156(photos)
and contestant income, 255, 259–260
contestant survey (1991), 34, 41, 80, 81, 106, 194–196
contestant survey methodology, analysis, and questionnaire, 273–280

and corporate sponsors, 88–91, 162
Crisis Fund, Cowboy (*see under* Justin Boot Company; Thurman, Brent)
Exceptional Rodeo, 175–176
fans survey, 240–244
and films, 226
humane officer, 128
information form, 113
judges, 29, 30, 31
and medical personnel, 94
members, 10, 36, 51
membership dues, 75
patch program, 85
permit system, 51
Pro Officials Program, 25
publications (*see* Humane facts pamphlet; *Prorodeo Sports News*)
ranking points, 64–65
-Resistol overall, 43
Rodeo Secretary of the Year, 160
rules, 24, 32, 155(caption)
sanctioned rodeos, 42–43, 51, 61–62, 68
speciality acts, 158, 166, 167
standardized events, 19, 20
television arrangement, 235–236
and women, 190
Professional Women's Rodeo Association (PWRA), 186, 190
Finals, 190
Pro Rodeo Canada Media Guide, 98
Pro Rodeo Hall of Fame, 9, 87, 210
bulls in, 26, 119
horse in, 191
Pro Rodeo Ministries program, 116
ProRodeo Sports Inc., 237, 260
Prorodeo Sports News (PRCA), 62, 66, 107, 133, 165, 183, 204, 234
Pro Rodeo Tour, 87, 88
Prouty, Bill, 241–242
Pueblo State Fair, 184
Purdy, Ikua, 206
Purina Mills (company), 189

PWRA. *See* Professional Women's
    Rodeo Association

"Question of Culture or Cruelty, A?"
    (*Los Angeles Times*), 133
Quintana, Donnalyn, 177
Quirt, 22

RAA. *See* Rodeo Association of America
Ragsdale, Bob, 79, 132
Ragsdale, Phil, 211–212
Railroads, 8, 9
Ram Tough (bull), 109
Rancho Santa Margarita Fiesta Rodeo
    (Calif.), 179–180
Rapp, Virgil, 181
RAWHIDE. *See* National Intercollegiate
    Rodeo Association, Rodeo Athletes
    on Wellness Helping Individualize
    Drug and Alcohol Education
Rawhide handle, 23
Ray, Nicolas, 222
RCA. *See* Rodeo Cowboys Association
REACh. *See* Rodeo Education and
    Children
Red Bluff Round-Up (Calif.), 96
Redford, Robert, 225
Red Lightning (bull), 27
Red Rock (bull), 26–27, 119–120
Red Top Ranch (Colo.), 119
Red Wolf (bull), 2
Relay racing, 14, 18, 188, 205
Remington, Frederic, 229
Reno Gay Rodeo, 212
Reno Gazette-Journal, 160
Reno Rodeo, 54, 177, 183, 245, 249
Resistol Hats (company), 43, 66, 84, 89,
    90, 189
Reynolds, Benny, 147(caption)
Reynolds, R. J., Tobacco Company, 88
Reynolds, Robin, 130
Reynolds, Rooster, 147(photo)
Richins, Greg, 218
Rifleman, The (television show), 225
Riske, Milt, 180

Rivers, Joan, 212
Roberts, Ken, 173
Robertson, Cliff, 222
Robinson, Clay, 44
Robinson, Gary, 214
Robinson, Jade, 31
"Robo Bull" routine, 167
"Rock Creek Rodeo, The: Excess
    and Constraint in Men's Lives"
    (Errington), 180
Rocky (bull), 116
Roddy, Jack, 130
Rodear, 10
Rodeo
    accidents, 2, 5, 14–15
    advertising and promotion, 245,
        263–264
    advertising signs, 90
    alcohol sales, 100
    all-women event (*see* Barrel racing)
    amateur, 133
    American Indians in, 12, 13, 173,
        204–205
    and animal cruelty, 5–6, 22, 32,
        125–126, 127–134
    animals, 63, 64 (*see also* Stock
        contractors)
    announcers, 159–160, 167, 174
    ban proposal (1926), 126
    celebrity, 214–215, 245
    championship determination, 15
    change proposals, 238, 251, 254–255,
        256–261, 262
    and charity, 173–178, 214, 215
    circuit system, 51, 76–77, 216
    committees, 65–66, 101, 109, 110,
        159, 176, 178–182, 184–185, 243,
        248–249
    contract acts, 158–159, 164–168, 196
    corporate sponsors, 66, 84–85, 87–91,
        99, 104, 189, 212, 245, 257
    culture, 3–4, 5, 6, 56, 256
    cutbacks, 112–113
    divisional, 256–261
    early, 9–16, 17–18, 25
    as educational, 174–175, 176–177

entry fees, 12, 15, 62, 65, 75, 82, 160–161
films, 36, 217, 221–231
films, documentary, 229–231
fines, 31–32
firefighters, 218
first, 9–10
future of, 165–166, 234, 254, 256, 261–264
gay, 211–214
gift items, 247–248
grand entry, 11, 115, 135(photo), 196
groupies, 198–199
historians, 180–181, 249–250
information form (PRCA), 113
injuries, 40, 46, 50, 80, 85, 92–93
judges, 15, 24–26, 29–32
judges, women, 29, 30
as lifestyle, 7, 60–64, 87, 254, 263
and local economy, 179
lodging, 243
logos, 247, 248
marketing strategies, 244–251
media coverage, 86–87
Mexican, 132, 133, 202–204
military, 218–219
Native American, 204–205
nonappearance at (see Turning out)
as not-for-profit sport, 4, 173
organizers and promoters, 12, 15–16
parade, 135(photo), 173
performance tape, 98
photographers, 162–163, 197, 248
police, 217
pre-performance routines, 55–56, 97–98, 138–141(photos)
prize purses, 10, 11, 15, 16, 33, 51, 62, 65–66, 75, 82–83, 182, 185, 255, 259–260, 261
queens, 189, 196
ranking of by contestants, 182–185
roughstock events, 17, 21–22, 41, 61–62, 63, 80, 260 (see also Bareback riding; Bronc (saddle) riding; Bull riding)
rules of competition, standardized, 15

scholarships, 41–42, 192
scoring, 28–30 (see also Timers)
season, 183–184
secretaries, 160–161
senior, 219–220
spectators, 10, 12, 238 (see also Rodeo fans)
spirit of, 3, 4–5, 37
as sport, 4, 86–87, 256
sports medicine programs, 85, 90, 93–95
television coverage, 36, 85, 86, 234–238, 255
ticket prices, 226
timed events, 17, 41, 62, 80, 260 (see also Barrel racing; Calf roping; Steer wrestling; Team roping)
traditions, 3, 5, 7–8, 180–181, 188, 214, 254
training programs, 35, 38–44, 97, 98
training schools, 34, 35, 44–48
varieties, 202–220
vendors, 151(photo), 155(photo)
veterinarians, 128–129
violence and danger, 3, 4, 5, 37, 146(photo), 250–251
volunteers, 173, 174, 178
women in, 6, 14–15, 20, 39, 186–200
word origin, 9, 10
youth, 38–44, 262–263
youth programs, 174–178
See also Cowboys
Rodeo: An Anthropologist Looks at the Wild and the Tame (Lawrence), 7
"Rodeo" (song), 231–232
Rodeo America (company), 248
Rodeo Association of America (RAA), 15, 16, 188
Rodeo Corral program, 177
Rodeo Cowboys Association (RCA), 16, 79, 236
Rodeo Education and Children (REACh), 176–177
Rodeo fans, 86, 88, 89, 99, 150(photo), 210, 232
survey, 240–244

Rodeo News, 97
Rodeos, Inc., 192
"Rodeos of the Wild West" tour
    package, 242
"Rodeo steak," 60
Rodman, Charmayne (James),
    148(caption), 177, 190–191, 194
Rogers, Marvel, 208
Rogers, Will, 13
Romans, 7
Roping, 154(photo). *See also* Calf
    roping; Dally roping; Steer roping;
    Team roping; Trick roping
Ross, Kenny, 134
Rosser, Cotton, 44, 87, 111–112, 113, 114,
    115, 128, 204, 250–251, 258, 270(n8)
Roughstock riding
  and women, 190, 195, 213
  See also Rodeo, roughstock events
Roughstock Team Rodeo, 88–89
Round-ups, 10
Russell, Charles M., 229
Russell, Dan, Jr., 116, 120
Russell, Dan, Sr., 116
Russell, Linda, 120
Russo, Louis, 90

Saddles, 57–58, 59
Sampson, Charles, 4, 86, 201(epigraph),
    209–210, 211, 240
San Antonio Livestock Exposition
    Rodeo, 183
San Francisco, 41
  Bay area earthquake victims' aid, 4–5
  See also Grand National Rodeo
San Francisco Chronicle, 250
Santa Maria Elks Rodeo (Calif.), 163
Santos, Kendra, 204
Savage, William W., Jr., 224
Scamper (horse), 191
Scarrot, John, 45–46
Schomp, Judd, 45
Scivetti, Frank, 164
Score (rope), 113
Scoreboards, 163–164

Seagram, House of. *See* Crown Royal
Semas, Aaron, 140(photo), 199, 261
Semas, Sandra, 199
Seminole Tribe (Fla.), 204–205
Senior rodeo, 219–220
Sharp, Jim, 43, 52
Shea, Johnny, 101
Shearer, Jeff, 53, 113
Sheep riding, 38
Sherod, David, 64
Shoshone, 12
Shoulders, Jim, 3, 47, 50, 85, 119, 206
Sierra Circuit, 76, 197, 218
Simi Valley Days Elks Rodeo, 75
Simonson, Chuck, 5
Sir Double Delight. *See* Troubles
Slack, E. A., 12
Slack performances, 62, 174
Slone, Tod, 59
Small, Butch, 185
Smets, Rob, 171
Smith, Phil, 73
Smokey Bear and the American
    Cowboy fire prevention program
    (U.S. Forest Service), 176
Smyth, Bernie, 238–239
Snow, Clifford, 217
Snow, John, 192
Snowflake (horse), 118
"Social Class and Bar Behavior During
    the Calgary Stampede"
    (Ossenberg), 180
Society for the Prevention of Cruelty to
    Animals (SPCA), 132
Sociology of Sport, A (Nixon and Frey),
    235
Sound systems, 163
Southwestern Colored Cowboys
    Association, 209
Southwestern Exposition and Livestock
    Show and Rodeo (Fort Worth), 183
Spaniards in New World, 7, 8
Sparks, Ronny, 170
SPCA. *See* Society for the Prevention of
    Cruelty to Animals

Sports films, 226, 227, 229
Sports Illustrated, 187
Sportsmanship, 5
Sports marketing, 84–85
Sports psychology, 47
Spur board, 98
Spurs/spurring, 22, 23, 28, 29, 31, 58,
    129, 130, 142(photo)
Stahl, Jesse, 208
Stampedes, 10
Staneart, Marty, 120
Steagall, Rocky, 98
Steer riding, 169 (*see also* Bull riding)
Steer ropers
    champion, 21, 38, 206
    women, 14, 188
Steer roping, 9, 10, 14, 18, 126, 207
    champion, 21
    description, 21
    as illegal, 21
Steer wrestlers, 11, 98, 147(photo), 243
    ban (1923), 126
    champion, 4, 36, 70, 147(caption),
        183
    injuries, 94
Steer wrestling, 14, 17, 18, 80
    description, 20–21, 71
    stock, 122
Stir Crazy (film), 217
Stirrup leathers, 58
Stock contractors, 44, 63, 87, 109, 111,
    114–116, 118, 120, 157, 191–192, 206
    and animal care, 127–128
    and animal evaluation, 111–112,
        121–122
    animal names, 114, 115, 119
    and animal numbers, 115
    animals, 116–125
    chute tours, 134
    classes of, 110–111
    responsibilities, 110, 113–114
    of the year, 118
Stockton (Kans.) prisoners, 117
Stoney Burke (film), 270(n8)
Stopwatches, 20, 160

Strickland, Mabel, 14
Suicide wrap, 59
Sul Ross State University (Alpine, Tex.),
    41
Summer Rodeo for the Deaf (Santa Fe),
    215
Sundance Film Festival Best
    Documentary, 230
Sundown, Jackson, 13
Superstition, 53–54
Surcingles, 18
Swearington, Dennis, 75–76

Taillon, Terry, 219
Tales of Wells Fargo (television show),
    225
Tallman, Bob, 160
Team penning, 247
Team ropers
    champion, 204
    injuries, 94
    women, 190
Team roping, 17, 18, 42, 260–261
    description, 19–20
    Mexican, 203
Tea Trader (horse), 192
Telemarketing, 245
Texas "cow burbs," 82
Texas Youth Rodeo Association, 210
Thain, Bob, 234, 258
Thibert, Jimbo, 68–69, 218
Thomson, Jordie, 230
Thurman, Brent, 1–2, 3, 93,
    146(caption), 199–200
    Crisis Fund, 199
Thurman, Kay, 199
Tibbs, Casey, 99, 206, 223, 255
Timers, 115, 160
Timex watches, 86
TNN (television network), 235
Toad (horse), 192
Tomac, Steve, 169
Tompkins, Harry, 206, 208
Tony Llama Boot Company, 164
Tooke, Ernest, 118

Tornado (bull), 119
Trail drives, 22
Trail riding course, 39
Transport (horse), 27
Travolta, John, 225, 226
Tribal Festival and Rodeo (Fla.), 205
Trick riders, 196
Trick riding, 11, 18, 112, 159, 188
Trick ropers, women, 14, 188
Trick roping, 14, 18, 159. *See also* Fancy
    roping
Trimble, Billy, 220
Troubles (horse), 191, 192, 193
Tucker, Dave, 173
Turning out, 63–64
20/20 (television show), 132

Union Pacific Railway, 12
United States Forest Service program,
    176
United States Team Roping
    Championships (USTRC), 260
Urban Cowboy (film), 36, 46, 217,
    225–226, 270(n8)
USA Today, 238
U.S. Tobacco Company, 42, 66, 103
USTRC. *See* United States Team
    Roping Championships
Utah, 113

Van Cleef, Lee, 223
Vancouver, George, 206
Vann, Jimmy, 96
Vant, Shawn, 67
Vaqueros, 8
Vela, Rudy, 204
Vests, 95–97
Veterans of Foreign Wars, 174
Veterinarians, 128–129
Video screens, 163, 164, 244
Vision Quest program, 216
Vold, Doug, 27
Vold, Harry, 110, 111, 118–119, 125, 128
Vold, Wayne, 233
Vollin, Casey, 42, 99

Wagon Train (television show), 225
Waldhauser, Chad, 59
Walker, David, 177
Walter, T. J., 61
Walton, Scott, 119
War bags. *See* Gear bags
Ward, P. J., 219–220
Ward, "Wild" Wes, 54
Ware, Charlie, 179
Wares, Sandy, 163
Washington State Humane Society, 126
Watson, Art, 184
Weadick, Guy, 13–14
Weinrich, Jeth, 230
Weisman, Katherine, 87, 255
West, Charlie "Too Tall," 150(photo)
Western Horseman (magazine), 79
Western lifestyle, 36, 174, 216, 262
Western Rodeos (Calif.), 116
Westerns
    films, 223
    television, 224–225, 226, 270(n8)
Western trade fairs, 232
Western Wishes program, 177–178
West Hills College (Calif.), 43
West of the Pecos Rodeo, 10
When Legends Die (film), 222
Whitfield, Fred, 68, 210, 211
Why We Win (Cooper), 38
Wide Country, The (television show),
    270(n8)
Widmark, Richard, 222
Wild burros, 216
Wild cow milking, 18, 19
Wild Horse Breaking Program, 216
Wild Rogue Rodeo (Ore.), 26
*Wild West Movies: How the West Was
    Found, Lost, Lied About, Filmed,
    and Forgotten* (Newman), 222
Wild West shows, 10–12, 18, 188, 206,
    207
Williams, Ervin, 210, 211
Williamson, Nancy, 187
Wills, Chill, 123
Wilson, Kara, 177

"Wimpy" (hand-rocked bull), 175
Winger, Debra, 225
Wise, Wayne, 103, 159–160
Witte, Randy, 79
Wolfman Skoal (bull), 26, 27, 119, 120, 178
Women's Professional Rodeo Association (WPRA) (Colorado Springs), 20, 49, 189, 190
off-shoot (*see* Professional Women's Rodeo Association)
Woodard, Dale, 166

World's Oldest Rodeo (Freeman), 181
WPRA. *See* Women's Professional Rodeo Association
Wrangler Jeans (company), 26, 66, 84, 85, 89, 90, 189
Bullfight Finals, 170
Bullfight Tour, 169
Sports Chiropractic Program, 94–95
Wyatt Earp (television show), 225
Wyoming, 21, 113

Young, Gig, 223